The OXFAM POVERTY REPORT

Kevin Watkins

Oxfam
UK & Ireland

A catalogue record for this book is available from the British Library.

ISBN 0 85598 318 3

Available in Ireland from Oxfam in Ireland, 19 Clanwilliam Terrace, Dublin 2.
Tel: 01 661 8544.

Published by Oxfam (UK and Ireland), 274 Banbury Road, Oxford OX2 7DZ, UK.
in association with Oxfam America, Oxfam Canada, and Oxfam New Zealand (for contact addresses, see p.250).
Designed by Oxfam Design Department OX1834/PK/95
Printed by Oxfam Print Unit
Oxfam is a registered charity no. 202918.

Introduction

Figures and tables

Acknowledgements

This report is a co-operative effort which has drawn heavily upon contributions from Oxfam's staff and partners. Chapter 5 was written by Caroline Lequesne. A number of case studies were prepared by Siddo Deva, who also contributed to Chapter 1. Chapter 2 draws on the work of Ed Cairns and Guy Vassall-Adams. Substantial parts of Chapter 6 were written by Tricia Feeney and Chris Roche. Dianna Melrose contributed to the writing of sections of the report, and was responsible for overall co-ordination of the project.

We are especially grateful to Rosemary Thorp of St Antony's College, Oxford, and Queen Elizabeth House, Oxford, for acting as chairperson for a small group of Oxfam trustees who made an important contribution to the development of the report. The other members of this group were Chaloka Beyani of Wolfson College, Oxford, Bruce Coles QC, and Jeremy Swift of the Institute for Development Studies, Sussex, whose comments were particularly challenging and thoughtful.

Several other external readers made time to comment on various drafts. Michael Holman of the *Financial Times* and Professor Sir Hans Singer of the Institute for Development Studies, offered constructive criticism and perceptive observation throughout, despite being presented with virtually impossible deadlines. Gavin Williams of St Peter's College, Oxford, provided particularly helpful comments on Chapter 3. Guy Mhone of the Southern African Regional Institute for Policy Studies, and Niki Jazdowska of the Training and Research Support Centre (TARSC) offered valuable insights and criticisms of various parts of the report. We hope they will feel that their combined efforts have brought about improvements in our analysis, although any errors remain the responsibility of Oxfam alone.

There is insufficient space to acknowledge all of the Oxfam staff who have contributed directly or indirectly to the report. However, special thanks are due to Michael Bailey, Cowan Coventry, Justin Forsyth, Pushpanath Krishnamurthy, Ruth Mayne, Lucy Muyoyeta, Ben Rogaly, Mogha Smith, Simon Ticehurst, Helen Walsh, and Ian Woodmansey, for their input; and also to Paul Kendall, for designing the graphics.

Kevin Watkins, Oxfam Policy Department
Oxford, May 1995

Introduction

The battle for peace has to be fought on two fronts. The first is the security front, where victory spells freedom from fear. The second is the economic and social front, where victory spells freedom from want.

US Secretary of State, Cordell Hull, 1945

Our common humanity transcends the oceans and all national boundaries ... Let it never be asked of any of us — what did we do when we knew another was oppressed?

Nelson Mandela, President of South Africa, 1992

Were all humanity a single nation-state, the present North–South divide would make it an unviable, semi-feudal entity, split by internal conflicts ... a world so divided should be regarded as inherently unstable.

The South Commission, 1992

The vision that faded

Half-a-century ago, the United Nations emerged as a beacon of hope out of the darkness of the Second World War and the years of economic depression, social dislocation, and international tension which preceded it. The institutions of global governance which emerged alongside the UN in the post-war period were partly a response to the failures of the 1930s, and partly the product of an inspired vision for the future. The resolve which under-pinned that vision was rooted in the two simple words 'never again'. Never again should violence and conflict be allowed to destroy the lives of the world's people. Never again should poverty and mass unemployment be tolerated. And never again should governments relinquish responsibility for protecting the most basic social and economic rights of their citizens.

The UN Charter and the Universal Declaration of Human Rights provided the moral framework for a new system of rights and obligations upon which the new order was to be built. Far from being empty rhetorical flourishes, these documents were statements of intent. As President Roosevelt wrote: 'this is no vision of a distant millenium. It is a definite basis for a world attainable in our own time and generation.'[1]

The five decades which have elapsed since the UN was founded have witnessed some remarkable changes. Global economic wealth has increased sevenfold and average incomes have tripled. The record of advancement in human welfare, measured by increased life expectancy, falling infant mortality, improved nutrition, and increased educational attainment, has been unprecedented. Yet in the midst of this progress, the basic rights enshrined in the UN Charter are being violated on a massive scale. For the millions of women, men, and children whose lives are being destroyed by armed conflict, the Charter's pledge to 'save succeeding generations from the scourge of war' offers a cruel parody of reality. As we near the beginning of the twenty-first century, genocide, systematic attacks upon civilian populations, and mass rape, are claiming unprecedented numbers of victims.

But no combination of war or natural disaster inflicts suffering or destroys human potential on the scale of the 'silent emergency' of poverty. Today, one-in-four of the world's people live in a state of absolute want, unable to meet their basic needs. Millions more live close to this perilous condition on the very margins of survival. In a world where technological frontiers are being pushed back at a breathtaking rate, 35,000 children die *every day* from diseases which could be prevented through access to adequate nutrition and the most basic health provision.[2] Meanwhile, one half of the world's population is systematically discriminated against and denied opportunity, for the 'crime' of having a female chromosome.

Even stated in cold figures, the scale of global deprivation retains the power to shock. But facts and words alone can never capture the suffering inflicted by poverty. They cannot, for example, convey the tragedy of the one-in-six African children who will not live to see their fifth birthday; or of the half-a-million women who die each year from causes related to pregnancy and inadequate health care. Nor can they hope to capture the vast wastage of potential represented by the 130 million children who do not attend primary school.

Through its international programme, Oxfam witnesses on a daily basis the destructive power of poverty in the poorest villages and slums of the developing world. It also witnesses the quiet heroism of ordinary women and men seeking to protect their communities and rebuild their lives

in the face of forces over which they have little control. Few of these people have heard of the UN Charter, yet through their actions they are striving to achieve a world which reflects its principles. In the slums of Peru and Zambia, Oxfam's partners are working with communities who are attempting to maintain the most basic levels of health, education, and nutrition despite devastating economic pressures. In the free-trade zones of Mexico and the Dominican Republic, they are supporting the efforts of female workers to establish basic employment rights, non-discriminatory labour practices, and a living wage. In ecologically degraded drought-prone areas in southern Africa, vulnerable communities are developing water conservation and cropping systems aimed at enhancing their security. And in Brazil and Colombia, local groups are working with Indian communities and black farmers to protect the land rights upon which their survival depends from encroachment by commercial interests.

Working together for change

Local initiatives of this type provide a powerful force for change. So, too, do the growing number of community groups and non-governmental organisations (NGOs) which have emerged in response to the deepening development crisis. New alliances for change are emerging. In Brazil, a mass campaign against hunger has brought together churches, trade unions, NGOs, the private sector, and local government, involving millions of people in practical local-level action to raise awareness of the causes of extreme poverty. This is a powerful example of co-operation between different layers of civil society in response to an erosion of social and economic rights.

Alliances are also emerging on the international stage. Many of Oxfam's partners were among the thousands of NGOs which lobbied the Earth Summit in 1992 and the World Summit for Social Development in 1995. The communiqués agreed at those Summits bear the imprint of their influence. Some NGOs are now working to encourage the public pressure for change which will be needed to translate the agreed principles into practice. Others are working together in regional and international networks to address human development problems associated with conflict, trade, and finance, in an attempt to force the interests of the poor on to the agendas of the world's governments.

The new global alliances which are emerging reflect a growing recognition of the challenges created by the globalisation of the world economy. Foreign investment and international trade flows are creating a world of increasingly porous borders, in which governments are being superseded by formidably powerful transnational companies (TNCs). The deregulation of markets and the growing power of international financial institutions have contributed to this trend. Yet there have been no countervailing measures to protect global citizenship rights in the manner envisaged by the UN. In a small way, the international alliances of citzens' groups which are now emerging are starting to fill this gap, building bridges between local action and international policy debates. Once again, this is a positive contribution towards the creation of the type of world envisaged by the United Nations

Rich and poor: the widening gap

But while local communities and citizens' groups have emerged as a powerful force for positive change, the same cannot be said for governments. If poverty were an infectious disease, which could be caught by the rich as well as the poor, it would have been eradicated long ago. Political will and financial resources would have been found in abundance, just as they were to develop instruments of mass destruction during the Cold War. Yet governments, North and South, have been willing to tolerate and acquiesce in the steady marginalisation of the poor.

Fifty years ago, the post-war settlement sought to establish a framework for shared prosperity. Markets were to play a central role in expanding that prosperity. But the extremes of poverty, inequality, and instability associated with uncontrolled markets were to be avoided through state regulation, in the public interest, at both national and global level. Today, however, most governments and the international financial institutions created at Bretton Woods to oversee the new order, place far too much faith in *laissez-faire* economic policies. Poverty redution is supposed to emerge principally as a by-product of market deregulation, with the benefits of growth gradually trickling down to the lowest stratas of societies. In reality, the divergence in living standards between rich and poor is assuming ever more signigicant proportions.

Economic growth is imperative if poverty is to be reduced. But the distribution of wealth is as important as its creation. At an international level there is a gross maldistribution, with the structures of world trade and finance supporting an increasing concentration of wealth in the industrialised world. In 1960, the richest fifth of the world's population living in the industrially advanced countries, had average incomes 30 times greater than the poorest fifth, living in the developing world. By 1990, they were receiving 60 times more.[3] Calculating real purchasing power differences, as the International Monetary Fund now does, reduces the disparity — but it is still greater than 50:1.[4] While it is true that the Third World is not a homogeneous bloc, and that some countries, notably in East Asia, have increased their share of world income, the poorest countries are falling further behind. The poorest 50 countries, mostly in Africa, have seen their incomes decline to the point where they now account for less than 2 per cent of global income.[5] These countries are home to one-fifth of the world's people.

The persistence of poverty

Developments within countries have mirrored the trends in the international economy, with the poorest sections of society becoming increasingly marginalised. In most developing

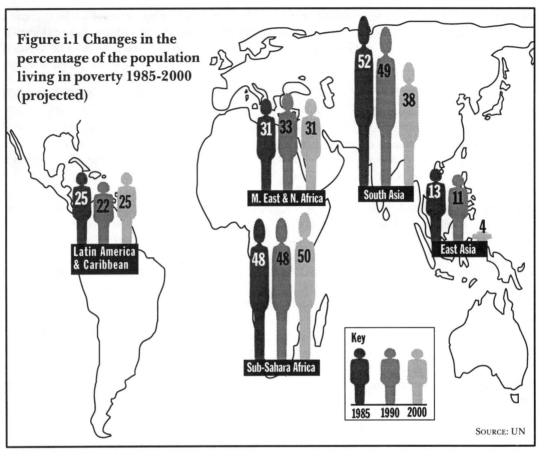

Figure i.1 Changes in the percentage of the population living in poverty 1985-2000 (projected)

Latin America & Caribbean: 25, 22, 25

M. East & N. Africa: 31, 33, 31

South Asia: 52, 49, 38

East Asia: 13, 11, 4

Sub-Sahara Africa: 48, 48, 50

Key: 1985, 1990, 2000

SOURCE: UN

countries, the poorest fifth of the population share between them, on average, little more than 5 per cent of national income, while the wealthiest fifth claim over half.

Nowhere in the developing world are the contrasts between poverty and national wealth more striking than in Latin America and the Caribbean. While average incomes are six times those in Africa, some 200 million people live in poverty. Inequalities are widening across the region. Despite its financial crisis, Mexico has achieved one economic distinction: it has the world's fastest growing number of billionaires, with 13 in 1994.[6] The combined wealth of these individuals is more than double the combined wealth of the poorest 17 million Mexicans, whose share of national income is falling. More generally, while the middle and upper classes of the region enjoy living standards comparable to

those of the industrial world, millions of families — from the Altiplano of Bolivia to the slums of Peru and Brazil — are no better off than sub-Saharan Africans. Almost one million children in the region die each year from causes which are largely preventible, and another seven million are malnourished.[7]

Left unchecked, poverty will continue to claim victims on a growing scale. On present trends, the number of people living in poverty could rise to 1.5 billion by 2025. In South Asia, home to the world's largest population of poor people, the proportion of people living below the poverty line is falling, but the absolute number is rising. Sub-Saharan Africa is a special source of concern because poverty is increasing not only in terms of the total numbers affected but also as a proportion of the population. By the end of the decade, the ranks of the 218 million Africans living in poverty will have swelled to 300 million, with the downward spiral in human welfare indicators likely to continue into the next century. Sub-Saharan Africa is now the only part of the developing world in which infant mortality rates are rising and literacy levels falling. For Latin America, growth patterns imposed on the region's grossly unequal social structures offer a future of increased marginalisation for the poor.

The tendency towards increased poverty and inequality is not confined to developing countries. In the United States an additional four million children fell into poverty during the 1980s, even though the wealth generated by the country's economy expanded by one-fifth.[8] By 1992, child poverty affected 22 per cent of all children, and infant mortality rates for black children were more than double those for white children.[9] In the European Union, the number of people living in poverty grew from 38 million to 52 million between 1975 and 1988. Several countries experienced a dramatic increase in poverty and inequality.[10] For example, until the mid-1970s, income inequality in the UK was in steady decline as economic growth increased general prosperity. However, over the period 1979-1992, the poorest quarter of the population failed to benefit from economic growth. As a result, the proportion of the population with less than half the average income has trebled since 1977. Today, 12 million people live on less than half the average income, more than double the number in 1979; and the number of individuals living below the poverty line has increased from 5 million to almost 14 million.[11]

The 'culture of contentment'

Of course, poverty in the industrialised world is not in the same category as poverty in the developing world, being measured in terms of relative deprivation rather than absolute want. However, the willingness of governments in the world's richest countries to tolerate the exclusion of so many people from an acceptable way of life at home, speaks volumes about a wider indifference to poverty.

Writing about his own society, the American economist JK Galbraith has described a 'culture of contentment', in which governments representing a prosperous majority are willing to maintain an economic system which disenfranchises a large 'underclass'.[12] The enjoyment of prosperity for the contented majority is disturbed only by a continuing threat of 'underclass' social disorder, crime, and conflict. The role of the state, in Galbraith's account, is becoming similar to that of a security firm, containing social tensions within urban ghettos at minimal cost. The alternative of raising taxes to address the underlying causes of social marginalisation, is ruled out on the grounds that it would alienate the prosperous majority upon whom re-election depends. Yet it is in this tension between security and the suppression of the 'underclass' that Galbraith identifies a force for change. He writes: 'The age of contentment will come to an end only when and if the adverse developments that it fosters challenge the sense of comfortable well-being.'[13]

Most people in the industrial world will find a resonance between Galbraith's sobering description of US political life and their own experience. While the majority of people in most industrial countries have attained levels of affluence which would have been unthinkable even 20 years ago, insecurity has also reached record levels. Drug dealing, inner-city crime, family disintegration, mass unemployment, are now all aspects of everday experience. The most immediate costs are borne by the poor, but there is a deep and pervasive sense of society breaking down in a manner which threatens everybody. There is also a deepening sense of unease at the social and moral implications of allowing poverty, homelessness, and widening inequality to destroy the lives of vast numbers of people, and at the waste of human potential caused by poverty. The ethos of the 1980s, when the pursuit of individual advancement was presented as a form of inadvertent altruism, is now questioned both on grounds of self-interest and out of moral concern. The new ethos of enlightened self-interest was reflected in one recent report on inequality in Britain, which concluded:

Failure to reintegrate (the) excluded minority into the mainstream of society will leave the well-to-do majority with a heavy price to pay in terms of increased public spending, wasted economic resources and social dislocation.[14]

The challenge is to extend this enlightened self-interest and moral concern to the international stage and to developing countries. There, too, a culture of contentment is much in evidence. Northern governments, which control the governance of the world economy, are content to tolerate and maintain trade and financial structures which concentrate wealth in the industrialised world, while excluding the poorest countries and people from a share in global prosperity.

For their part, most Third World governments have their own culture of contentment. They maintain systems of income and land distribution which exclude poor people; they concentrate public investment in areas where it maximises returns to the wealthy and minimises returns to the poor; and all too often they waste vast sums on armaments, creating military machines which are as impressive as their country's human welfare indicators are depressing. One aim of Oxfam's campaign is to build a bridge between citizens in the North and the South who are working to challenge the forces which deprive people of their rights at local, national, and international levels.

Shutting out the problems

Underpinning the global culture of contentment is a presumption on the part of Northern governments that the social problems associated with international deprivation can be 'ring-fenced', or contained within discrete boundaries; but this is not possible. Deepening poverty is one of the main driving forces behind the civil conflicts which are creating unprece-

dented numbers of refugees and displaced people. It is also causing the growth of sprawling urban slums, which have become focal points for social tension, and political disaffection. Migration to these slums is being enforced by environmental degradation, linking town and country in a vicious circle of social decline.

The consequences of such trends cannot, as Northern governments appear to imagine, be contained by border controls. Social collapse and the disintegration of states has been accompanied by the mass migration of refugees, the increase in international drug trafficking and organised crime, the spread of regional tensions, and recourse to violence. Just as crime and social breakdown in the industrial world will not respect the boundaries of affluent middle-class suburbs, so the forces unleashed by conflict and global poverty will not respect national borders, however well-defended they may be; and however restrictive the immigration policies of the states which control them.

The architects of the UN system, with the experience of the Great Depression a vivid memory, recognised that real security could never be built upon poverty. That was the overwhelming lesson of the 1930s which they took with them into the San Francisco conference which established the UN. Without peace, the UN Charter recognised, there could be no lasting social progress; but without social progress there could be no lasting peace. Thus 'freedom from want' and 'freedom from fear' became the rallying calls for a new order to be built upon the foundations of international co-operation and shared prosperity. Fifty years on, there is a new crisis in human security every bit as threatening as that which gave rise to the UN.

People are desperate for alternatives which offer hope, instead of a world scarred by deepening poverty, inequality, and insecurity. Yet the institutions created 50 years ago to win the peace are failing, with governments, to offer alternatives. In large measure, this can be traced to a vacuum in political leadership. Indeed, at no stage in post-war history have the challenges facing humanity been so great and the political vision of world leaders so myopic.

The need for a renewed vision

The anniversary of the UN provides an opportunity for governments and citizens' groups to provide a new vision for human security and poverty eradication into the next century. In the past, moments of crisis in the twentieth century have brought forward acts of great political courage and imagination. The New Deal of the 1930s and the Beveridge Report which founded the British welfare state are two examples. Writing in the 1940s, William Beveridge defended his declaration of war against the 'five great evils' of ignorance, disease, squalor, idleness, and unemployment, by emphasing the scale of the challenge to be confronted. 'A revolutionary moment in world history,' he wrote, 'is a time for revolutions, not for patching.' A similar sense of purpose underpinned the UN Charter, which established in embryonic form an international charter of citizenship rights. The challenge today is both to develop and to implement new social compacts at the national and international level through which these rights can be realised. This will require institutional change as well as reforms in economic policy. Weak institutions which are loosely connected to civil society cannot oversee the effective implementation of strategies for achieving social and economic rights, however well-intentioned governments may be. That is why transparent and accountable government, popular participation in decision-making, and investment in institutional reform are essential to genuine development.

Much of the overall framework for translating social and economic rights from principle into practice already exists. The International Covenant on Economic, Social and Cultural Rights, which came into force in 1976, enshrines most of the social and economic rights contained in the UN Charter and the Universal Declaration, including the rights to adequate nutrition, basic education and health care,

shelter, and non-discrimination. Most of the world's governments have signed this Covenant. Unfortunately, they have done so without any serious intention of implementing it. This reflects a wider debasement of the currency of social and economic rights.

In 1993, the world's governments adopted a communiqué at the Vienna Conference on Human Rights confirming that all rights, social and economic as well as civil and political, were 'indivisible, inter-dependent and universal'.[15] Yet they continue to tolerate violations of social and economic rights which, if repeated in the sphere of civil and political rights, would provoke international outrage. One of the underlying reasons for this discrepancy is a view, widespread among governments, that the extension of human rights provisions into the social and economic sphere is misplaced. In particular, many governments claim that full social and economic rights are unattainable, especially in the poorest countries, because of inadequate financial resources. This is at once partially true and totally irrelevant.

It goes without saying that not all countries can immediately provide universal health care, education, and secure employment for their citizens from their own resources. But the purpose of the UN's social and economic rights provisions is to secure the *progressive* achievement of rights through international co-operation. That is why the International Covenant on Economic, Social and Cultural Rights does not demand that states immediately provide for all citizenship rights. Rather, it calls on them to:

take steps, individually and through international assistance and cooperation, especially economic and technical, to the maximum of available resources, with a view to achieving progressively the full realisation of rights recognised in the present Covenant.[16]

In other words, there is a collective obligation on governments to adopt policies aimed at enhancing, within the limits of the resources available, the most basic rights of the world's citizens. Regardless of whether or not the full citizenship rights envisaged by the Covenant are ever realised, the moral entitlements it establishes must remain a guide to action. Writing over 60 years ago in an appeal for greater social equality, RH Tawney faced criticism similar to those levelled at the International Covenant. He responded in the following terms:

The important thing, however, is not that it (i.e. equality) should be completely attained, but that it should be sincerely sought. What matters to the health of society is the objective towards which its face is set, and to suggest that it is immaterial in which direction it moves, because, whatever the direction, the goal must always elude, is not scientific, but irrational. It is like using the impossibility of absolute cleanliness as a pretext for rolling in a manure heap.[17]

An end to poverty

What is vital for the health of our global society today is that governments and citizens set their faces towards global poverty eradication. Inevitably, there are limits to what governments can do for people. But there are no limits to what people can do for themselves when they are given the opportunity to realise their potential. Providing that opportunity within the broad framework of human rights principles established by the UN should be a shared objective for governments, citizens' groups and individuals worldwide.

This is not an argument for the recitation of yet more vacuous statements at the UN, more 'high-level' conferences, or new layers of UN bureaucracy to monitor and oversee the non-performance of governments in protecting the social and economic rights of their citizens. Indeed, the focus should be firmly upon making existing UN machinery for monitoring social and economic rights work more effectively (an issue which we address in our recommendations). For example, the various bodies which monitor compliance with UN human rights conventions should have a strengthened role in monitoring and reporting on the performance of government and international

financial institutions in relation to their obligations under the Covenant on Cultural, Economic and Social Rights. Similarly, the Economic and Social Council of the UN, which is becoming increasingly marginal, should be responsible for public debates on the impact of macro-economic trends and policies on social and economic rights.

What is required to translate UN principles into action is the adoption by governments of tangible targets for creating opportunities and, through international co-operation, for them to embark on the task of poverty eradication 'to the maximum of available resources'. There have already been steps taken in the right direction. One of the most encouraging developments in recent years has been the preparation of national programmes of action to achieve the targets set by the 1990 World Summit for Children. These targets include a reduction by one-third in child mortality; a reduction by half in maternal mortality; the provision of universal primary education; and the provision of safe drinking water for all. One advantage of such targets is that they serve as a benchmark against which government policies can be measured. Another is that they expose the fallacy behind the argument that poverty eradication is not affordable. For example, can we really talk about the non-affordability of social and economic rights when:

- Governments can find $800bn a year in military expenditure to finance the acquisition of the means of destruction, but claim to be unable to find the $5bn a year which would provide basic education to all children, helping to release their creative potential for the benefit of all.
- African governments spend more in repaying debts than they do on the health and education of their citizens.
- The costs of meeting the health and education targets agreed at the World Summit for Children represent around 16 per cent of what developing countries currently spend on weapons.

Creating an enabling environment

In this report, we outline some of the wider policy and institutional reforms needed to create an enabling environment for poverty reduction. The starting point, as we stress throughout, must be that of involving men and women in the design of policies which affect their lives. When it comes to understanding poverty, the real experts are the poor themselves. Popular participation, improved accountability, and transparency must be central to any project for poverty reduction which is to have a chance of success.

At a national level, as we argue in Chapter 1, governments in developing countries could do far more to give the poor a stake in society if they were to abandon their preference for defending vested interests. Land redistribution and wider agrarian reform, including the protection of common property resources, is long overdue in Latin America, parts of Africa, and much of Asia. There is also scope for wider redistributive measures, especially in Latin America. According to the World Bank, raising all the poor in that continent above the poverty line would cost the equivalent of only 0.7 per cent of GDP — the approximate equivalent of a 2 per cent income tax increase on the wealthiest fifth of the population.[18]

Public spending priorities are in urgent need of reform in much of the developing world. At present, social sector spending is concentrated in areas which maximise the benefits to the wealthy, while bypassing the poor. The focus should be firmly upon providing primary health care and basic education. Resources for investment in these areas could be released by a reduction in military spending and more effective regulation of state finances to prevent large-scale corruption. Contrary to the claim that there is a trade-off between economic growth and redistribution, the high-performing economies of South-East Asia have built their high growth rates upon redistributive land and income policies, and the provision of universal primary health care and basic education.

Armed conflict, which we discuss in Chapter 2, is a major source of vulnerability and poverty in many of the countries in which Oxfam works. Increasingly, the victims of these conflicts, whether in Bosnia, Rwanda, or Afghanistan, are civilians. The picture is this area is not entirely bleak. If the peace settlement in Angola holds, southern Africa will be free from war for the first time since the 1960s. Long-running conflicts in Central America have been brought to an end. The durability of peace in these regions will depend critically upon international support for post-conflict reconstruction. In the case of Central America, it will also depend upon the willingness of governments to address the long-standing social inequalities which gave rise to armed conflict in the first place.

But while there are opportunities for peace which must be grasped, the spread of conflict is a source of mounting concern. Deep-rooted ethnic tensions, separatist ambitions, widening social divisions, social disintegration, and environmental degradation are all fuelling armed conflicts. It is increasingly clear that conflict prevention must start, as the UN Charter envisaged, with investment in human development and poverty eradication. More immediately, governments should establish restrictions on arms transfers and a comprehensive ban on the production, storage and sale of a weapon which has come to symbolise the gruesome reality of modern conflict: the land mine.

As we suggest in this report, the UN has suffered from a surfeit of expectation and a deficit in financial reources and leadership. However, more effective forms of UN intervention must be developed to resolve conflict before large-scale violence breaks out, and to provide more responses to the inter-related tasks of peace-making, peace-keeping and delivering humanitarian relief.

The Bretton Woods institutions — the IMF and the World Bank — were created to provide the framework for post-war global economic governance. Their aim was to facilitate full employment and shared prosperity. Today, both institutions publicly proclaim povety reduction as their central priority. As we argue in Chapter 3, however, their policies have evolved in a manner at variance with that objective. Instead of promoting full employment and the regulation of markets in the interests of social welfare, both agencies place their faith in the type of *laissez-faire* prescriptions and deregulated labour markets which their founders saw as directly responsible for the crisis of the 1930s. Moreover, while advocating universal primary health care and basic education, the Bretton Woods agencies have encouraged governments to introduce user-fees for social welfare provision. The result of this incursion of 'market principles' has been to deny vulnerable communities access to health and education.

To make matters worse, the economic policies associated with the structural adjustment programmes of the World Bank and the IMF have comprehensively failed to bring economic recovery to many of the world's poorest countries. Even where growth has been achieved, it has been built upon the increased marginalisation and exclusion of the poor. New forms of adjustment are needed to translate any commitment to poverty reduction into practice. Nobody today questions the case for economic reforms aimed at reducing destabilising budget deficits, establishing realistic currency alignments, and restoring balance-of-payment viability. The challenge is to reach these objectives in a manner which protects the vulnerable, is socially inclusive rather than exclusive, and which establishes a foundation for sustainable economic growth.

International trade is one of the main threads of global interdependence. However, as we show in Chapter 4, the benefits of international trade have been disproportionately concentrated in the industrialised countries and a relatively small group of developing countries. The Uruguay Round agreement will do little to change this balance. Nor will it address two deeper problems which have emerged with the accelerating movement towards a globalised economy. First, it is now clear that the relentless expansion of trade has placed an unbearable strain on the natural resource base of many countries, undermining environmental sustainability. Reconciling global commerce with the higher claims of sustainable resource management must occupy a central place on the international trade agenda of the twenty-first century.

Second, globalisation has been accompanied by a formidable increase in the power of TNCs. Increasingly, these companies are able to exploit national differences in social and environmental standards by locating their investment in the sites of maximum profitability. The GATT Uruguay Round will further strengthen their position by limiting the right of governments to regulate foreign investment. The danger which this creates is that of a downward spiral in standards towards the lowest common denominator. Reversing that spiral will require a social clause in international trade rules to enforce compliance with minimum standards.

As we suggest in Chapter 5, the Earth Summit increased public awareness of the formidable threats posed by over-consumption and pollution in the industrial world. While the world's poorest countries account for the bulk of world population, their citizens walk more lightly on the planet and leave a smaller ecological footprint. The average American citizen has an environmental impact on the planet some 140 times greater than the average Bangladeshi, and 250 times greater than the average African. These differences are rooted in the galloping consumerism upon which Northern prosperity has been built. That consumerism imposes a huge strain on the world's resources. With 16 per cent of the world's population, the industrialised countries generate two-thirds of its industrial waste, over one-third of the greenhouse gases responsible for global warming, and they consume over one half of its fossil fuels. Were the developing world to follow the same path to economic growth as the industrial world it would destroy our planet's biosphere, with unthinkable consequences.

Governments and citizens in the industrial world have a responsibility to adopt life-styles and energy-conservation measures more compatible with a sustainable future for the planet. That means regulating markets in a manner which ensures that prices reflect more accurately the environmental costs of production. And it means investing in technologies which will lower the pollution associated with production. Such technologies must also be transferred to developing countries on affordable terms.

In Chapter 6, we argue for a major overhaul of financial relations between the industrial and developing world. Debt repayments continue to impose a crushing burden on the world's poorest countries. Moroever, a growing proportion of that debt is owed to multilateral creditors, which steadfastly refuse to countenance large-scale debt reduction. There is an urgent case for a comprehensive write-off of official debt and for new initiatives to reduce the burden of multilateral debt. In Latin America, the surge in private capital flows since the late 1980s has ended the outflow of financial resources from that region. Despite this, the region still suffers from acute debt problems. For the world's poorest countries, excluded from private capital markets, international development assistance will remain the major source of external finance. However, the bulk of international aid flows are of questionable relevance to the poor, since donors continue to attach a higher priority to the promotion of com-mercial self-interest than to poverty reduction.

This report outlines our views on some of the policy changes which are needed to eradicate poverty. As a non-governmental organisation working in over 70 developing countries, Oxfam is acutely aware that there are no easy answers when it comes to development. Much of what we say in this report is highly critical of governments and international financial institutions. But NGOs, Oxfam included, make their share of policy mistakes. Our perspective is informed by what we have learned from our involvement with grassroots communities and popular organisations. In the pages which follow, we set out an analysis which reflects that perspective, and which we hope will be a contribution to a wider debate. Ultimately, however, real progress towards poverty reduction will depend upon local communities coming together to act as a catalyst for change; and on governments, NGOs, and international financial institutions alike listening and learning from them.

1 Poverty and livelihoods

Dorothy Chiredze's story

Masvingo province in the semi-arid southern part of Zimbabwe is a hostile environment. Rainfall is low and erratic, and drought a regular occurrence. Tree cover is almost non-existent. The scrubland is largely bare except for occasional colonies of Mopane trees, known locally as 'the camels' because of their ability to survive with little water. During the long dry season the fragile top soil, unprotected from the sun, bakes into a solid concrete-like crust. When the rains come, that crust disintegrates and is transported through the deep gullies which scar the land, into fast-flowing river tributaries. These in turn feed into once mighty rivers, like the Tokwe and Runde, which carried Victorian explorers into the interior. Now little more than streams for most of the year, during the rainy season they are briefly transformed into torrents which carry the soil from Masvingo down to the Indian Ocean.

Dorothy Chiredze lives in the village of Katule, which is typical of many in Masvingo. She farms just over one hectare of land, ploughing the soil with a hoe. In April, just before harvest, her widely-spaced, thin stalks of maize wilt in the sun. They are nourished by water carried before dawn from a spring two hours' walk away. If it is a good harvest, Dorothy will grow three sacks of maize. After she has sold one to pay for school fees, seeds for next year's harvest, oil, and other basic items, she will have enough left for herself, her two daughters and one son to last until January. Then she will have to work clearing land for wealthier neighbours, or on some larger commercial farms about ten kilometres away. Dorothy also grows small amounts of millet, which she brews into beer for cash, and some green vegetables.

The poorest families in Katule, most of them headed by women like Dorothy Chiredze, typically have less than two hectares of land, and no irrigation. What sets them apart from the wealthier people in the village, most of them say, is that they do not have cattle for draught power. This restricts the area of land they are able to plough, and the amount of crops they can produce. Most cannot afford fertiliser, which explains why their maize stalks are smaller and paler than those of richer farmers. Few have savings or other assets, except a few goats, which they can sell to get through times of stress. In a good year, the poorest families will grow enough maize to feed their families for three or four months.

But many years are not good. In 1992, Masvingo experienced the worst drought of the century. Almost the entire maize crop was destroyed, and the majority of oxen died. This is how Dorothy Chiredze recounted her story to Oxfam staff one year after the drought:

Last year, the rains did not come. It was the worst we had ever seen. Our maize was destroyed. We were left only with a little millet. Even those with much land lost their crops, so there was no work for us. There was emergency food, but it came so late … There was much hunger in our villages, some children died from dysentery. My husband used to send money from Harare. He worked in a factory. But he came home because there was no more work. Our children ate only one meal each day. For many weeks we just had sadza (boiled maize meal) with no meat or vegetables. Our daughter became sick. The children were too weak to walk to school. Even if they were strong we did not have enough money to send them because the school was charging higher fees. The school said they had no choice because the government was giving them less... This year we will have a small harvest. We could not buy seed or fertiliser, and we have planted less. There was no money to hire any oxen, so I ploughed the land by hand. If the rains are good, maybe we will grow two bags of maize; in a good year we used to grow three. I will have to work on the farms of others for food maybe as early as December. If the rains are bad again, I don't know if we will survive. We pray for rain... but life is hard. We struggle to stay alive, but life is so hard.

As Dorothy Chiredze's story suggests, deprivation has many dimensions. 'Absolute poverty,' wrote Robert McNamara, President of the World Bank, in 1978, is 'a condition of life so limited by malnutrition, illiteracy, disease, squalid surroundings, high infant mortality, and low life expectancy as to be beneath any reasonable definition of human decency.'[1] That remains a powerful description of the reality experienced by a large segment of the world's population.

But the deprivation experienced by Dorothy and millions of people like her is not a static condition. Nor is it rooted solely in inadequate income or the state of perpetual and absolute want suggested by Robert McNamara's definition. What defines the situation of the world's poorest people is their insecurity and vulnerability.[2] When the rains failed, Dorothy's wealthier neighbours were able to maintain their food supply and send their children to school by drawing on their savings, or selling off their assets. Others perhaps had relatives in government service who were able to support them through hard times. But Dorothy's husband, an unskilled labourer, was highly vulnerable to the rising unemployment caused by the economic recession which accompanied the drought and

the introduction of a structural adjustment programme. Typically, the poorest families lack the capacity to cope with stress, and suffer acute difficulties, such as sickness, physical weakness, and economic impoverishment. Such disadvantages become self-perpetuating; inadequate nutrition and ill health reduce the productivity of the poor, and lower productivity means less income and less food. Vulnerability leads to a downward spiral, as events that suddenly make people poorer also reduce their assets. In Dorothy Chiredze's case, the next year's harvest will be smaller because she was unable to plough her land with oxen, and she lacked the income to buy seed and fertiliser. As a result, she will have to spend more time working on the farms of her wealthier neighbours, and less on her own farm. This forced transfer of labour in turn undermines family production. Meanwhile, Dorothy's children have been denied schooling, diminishing their prospects of a more secure future; which illustrates the mechanisms through which poverty is transmitted through generations.

The poverty trap

Dorothy Chiredze's story reveals how natural disasters and economic crises claim their victims from among the most vulnerable sections of society. In every society, the poor live shorter, less healthy lives than those who are better off. The insecurity and vulnerability behind this grim reality has many causes. War and civil conflict are destroying the livelihoods of unprecedented numbers of people, creating vast flows of refugees. Employment is increasingly insecure in many countries and wages have fallen. State provision of health care, education, clean water, and sanitation is restricted, exposing poor people to health risks, reducing their productivity and opportunities. Geographical isolation cuts people off from social welfare provision, markets, and sources of information. More people are living in ecologically fragile areas, where they are exposed to risks of flooding and soil erosion. Structures of social 'inferiority' related to caste, race, and ethnicity, coupled with lack of control over resources, increase the vulnerability of the poor.[3] In rural Punjab, for instance, child mortality among the landless is one-third higher than among landowning classes. Underlying all these disadvantages is the denial of rights suffered by women, who experience systematic social and economic discrimination from the cradle to the grave.

In the world of the poor, these various structures of disadvantage interlock with one another to create an all-encompassing poverty trap. Where poor people are forced by their poverty to over-farm steep hillsides, they become the unwilling agents of a vicious cycle of environmental degradation and increased insecurity. About half of the world's poorest people live on marginal or fragile lands. The cycle of poverty and environmental degradation in which they are trapped underlies the struggle for scarce resources which is at the root of many conflicts. Conflict, in turn exacerbates poverty, as communities are displaced, crops destroyed, and livelihoods undermined. Economic crisis is another destroyer of livelihoods and a potent source of conflict. Women bear a disproportionate part of the costs of economic recession, since it is they who assume responsibility for family survival strategies by working longer hours inside and outside of the home, caring for the sick, and raising children. When women have to devote more and more time to obtaining fuel and water, they have less time to devote to food production, to pursue their education, and to care for their children. These growing burdens can have adverse social and economic consequences for themselves and their families.

Just as poverty is not solely a matter of lack of income or perpetual want, it follows that its eradication must be achieved through strategies which enhance the ability of local communities to adapt to stress, to overcome emergencies, and to improve long-term productivity. As we suggest below, such strategies must be built upon an understanding of the complex livelihood structures of poor people. These typically encompass food production, the harvesting of common resources, and diverse forms of employment. In the sections which follow, we look at how some of Oxfam's partners are working with communities to identify and enhance opportunities for more sustainable livelihoods.

The poverty trap which destroys the lives of so many people operates at many levels, from the village economy to the international market-place. In later chapters we explain how international forces, of which the poor are only dimly aware, undermine their livelihoods. Ruinously low commodity prices, crushing external debt burdens, anarchic capital markets, failure to prevent conflicts, and misallocated aid, all restrict the prospects for poverty reduction. Future threats also loom large. Global environmental problems such as climate change, rooted in the consumption patterns of the rich world, pose an acute threat to the livelihoods of vulnerable communities in the developing world. This means that local initiatives aimed at promoting sustainable livelihoods in areas such as the Ganges Delta will count for little if sea-levels rise and the frequency and intensity of flooding increase. More directly, the consumption patterns of the industrial world are undermining livelihoods by imposing an unacceptable burden on the natural resource base of developing countries — an issue we address in Chapter 5.

At the local level, which we examine in this chapter, elements of the poverty trap include unequal rights to land and other productive resources, inadequate provision of health care and education, and the inability of the poorest to influence decisions affecting their lives. Corrupt and unaccountable governments, misplaced public-spending priorities, and development policies which marginalise poor people in the name of economic progress, are all part of the picture. Once again, the various elements interact with one another. External debt repayments and low commodity prices deprive countries and communities of the resources they need to invest in production and social welfare provision, increasing their exposure to economic crisis and poverty. This lethal interaction of global forces with local structures of poverty is the basis of the poverty trap.

A strategy for ending poverty

Throughout its international programme, Oxfam witnesses how local communities are attempting to force open the poverty trap at a local level, often in the face of overwhelming odds. Some of their initiatives are described in this chapter. But turning the potential created by local action into a wider movement towards poverty eradication requires the creation of an enabling environment at a national and international level. There is no simple development blueprint for achieving this objective. Indeed, the poor have long been the victims of development blueprints designed for their benefit, though typically without their consultation, by national governments, international agencies, and non-governmental organisations (NGOs). If there is one lesson which Oxfam has learnt from its international experience, it is that listening to poor women and men, working in support of their participation and empowerment, are pre-conditions for success in reducing vulnerability. When it comes to understanding poverty, the real experts are to be found among the poor themselves. More broadly, however, there are five building blocks upon which any successful poverty eradication strategy should be built. These are:

- **Increased equity:** Apart from being socially unjust, high levels of inequality and widespread poverty are a source of economic inefficiency since they waste human potential. Wider distribution of productive assets; secure and equitable forms of employment; and an end to discriminatory measures which benefit a small, wealthy elite but consign large numbers of people to poverty, excluding them from a share in the prosperity they have

helped to create, are all important elements of a strategy to end poverty.
- **Enhanced opportunity:** poverty eradication demands that poor people have the productive assets they need to maintain sustainable livelihoods. But they also need the opportunity to develop greater autonomy through education, health care, and the provision of clean water and sanitation, and control over the common resources on which their survival often depends.
- **Peace and security:** without development there can be no lasting human security; but without peace and security, genuine human development will remain an elusive goal. Even in the absence of armed conflict, many of the poorest are prey to harassment and physical intimidation. Women are particularly vulnerable in this respect.
- **Participation:** genuine development demands that local communities have a say in shaping critical decisions affecting their lives, through open and accountable political structures from the village council up to the international level. Genuine development is concerned with enhancing people's capacity to be active participants in the process of social change.
- **A sustainable future:** to reduce the vulnerability of poor people and bring about lasting improvements in their lives, they need to have secure livelihoods. This in turn depends on making more sustainable and equitable use of finite resources, from the local to the global level.

We will now look in more detail at the structures of political and economic power which deny people productive assets and opportunities, in rural and urban contexts. In rural areas, productive assets include land, credit, and, crucially, common resources such as forests and waterways. In urban areas, the single most important asset of the poor is their labour. In both rural and urban areas, the opportunities for poor people are constrained to a considerable degree by the existence of oppressive power structures; and by the inadequate provision of services, such as education and health care, and public utilities.

Rural poverty

In rural areas, the most crucial asset is land. Gross inequality in land ownership is a major obstacle in many countries to improved human security and to agricultural progress. The concentration of land in the hands of a few also reduces productivity and leads to an inefficient use of resources. When modernisation of agriculture takes place in this situation, it frequently results in the further marginalisation of poor people, who become landless labourers, or smallholders with insufficient land to meet family needs for food and income.

Concentration of land ownership is most marked in Latin America, where feeble efforts at land reform have left the agrarian structures inherited from Spanish and Portuguese colonialism largely intact in many countries. Ownership of land in Brazil is among the most concentrated in the world. Nearly eleven million Brazilians who work the land are either landless, or have holdings which are too small to support a family. The poorest one-third of rural families own less than 1 per cent of arable land.[4] At the other end of the scale are the giant *latifundia*. With an average size in excess of 1000 hectares, these estates control over 50 per cent of the country's farmland. The 18 largest landowners in Brazil own, between them, a land area equivalent to that of the Netherlands, Portugal, and Switzerland combined.[5] These big estates account for the bulk of the soya, fruit, and vegetable exports which make Brazil the world's fourth-largest agricultural exporter, and one of the main suppliers of high-protein feedstuffs for the European beef farmers. In 1990, soya products destined for markets in Europe were Brazil's third-largest source of foreign-exchange earnings.[6]

The hidden side of this economic success story is to be found in the social costs of the country's agrarian structure. Smallholder farmers have been forced off their land in the south of the country to make way for giant soya estates. Resettled in the north, these producers have joined millions of other smallholders and landless labourers, squeezed on to tiny plots or forced to work for meagre wages. The resulting poverty has forced people to migrate to already overcrowded cities or work in environmentally damaging gold-mining. It has also left Brazil with some of the world's worst social indicators. If the north-east of Brazil, where rural poverty is most concentrated, were a separate country it would rank as number 111 on the UNDP's Human Development Index (Brazil as a whole is number 63).[7] Infant mortality is twice as high in the north-east as in the south, with rates comparable to those in sub-Saharan Africa, and life-expectancy seven years less. What such human welfare indicators suggest is that the social structure of rural Brazil is better equipped to feed Northern consumers and European cattle than to provide for Brazilians.

Agriculture in Zimbabwe

In sub-Saharan Africa, land ownership patterns are typically less concentrated, in part because traditional systems of land tenure have curtailed private ownership; and in part because it is labour rather than land which is in short supply in most countries. There are, however, important exceptions. Three hours' drive to the north of Masvingo, the province in which Dorothy Chiredze lives, is the other side of Zimbabwean agriculture. Here, in the commercial farmlands around Harare, vast estates produce wheat and maize for the domestic market, and *mange tout* peas and flowers for retailing chains in Europe. With their aerial spraying, computerised sprinkler systems, and highly developed marketing infrastructure, a greater contrast with the tiny, eroded plots on which people like Dorothy Chiredze eke out a living is difficult to imagine. Indeed, Zimbabwe's commercial farms would not look out of place alongside the 'grain baron' estates of East Anglia and the Paris Basin.

The two faces of Zimbabwean agriculture may appear to be worlds apart, but they are intimately connected through the legacy of Zimbabwe's colonial history. In the late 1920s, the country's farmland was effectively partitioned along racial lines, with white settlers being given the most fertile land in areas with the most rainfall.[8] A vast production and marketing infrastructure was built up around this privileged community, providing them with irrigation subsidies and price support. For their part, black farmers were forced on to environmentally fragile 'native reserves', or communal areas, located in low-rainfall areas; and they were prevented from competing with white farmers through discriminatory marketing laws.[9] While these laws have now gone, the structural inequalities inherited from the colonial era, and enshrined in independent Zimbabwe's constitution, remain firmly in place.

There are some 4,500 commercial farms in Zimbabwe, still overwhelmingly owned by white farmers, although a few black farmers have joined their ranks. The average size of these farms is about 2,400 hectares, or 800 times the average size of holdings in communal areas.[10] The commercial farms also account for about 80 per cent of all irrigated land.[11] Meanwhile, more than six million black farmers continue to work the land in severely-degraded, overcrowded communal areas. Even within this sector there is a stark differentiation between producers. About 20 per cent of communal farms are located in more favourable climatic zones. Although these farms occupy less than 10 per cent of the total communal farm area, they produce more than 80 per cent of the maize sold through official channels.[12] The rest of the communal farming population is located in the parts of the country with the most inhospitable climate. The vast majority of these farmers are unable to grow sufficient food to meet their household needs, forcing men to migrate to towns.

Zimbabwe's grossly unequal agrarian structure helps to explain what has been called the 'food security paradox': the co-existence of widespread malnutrition in the midst of a food system which produces a surplus of food for export.[13] Almost one-third of children have low height-for-age, indicating chronic malnutrition.[14] The groups most affected are households on large-scale commercial farms, where stunting affects over 40 per cent of children.[15] Low wages, insecurity and the seasonality of employment in the midst of vast agricultural wealth are the main causes of poverty. Amenities such as health facilities and schools are rare in commercial farm areas. Households in semi-arid communal areas are the second most poverty-prone group. In 1990, a government nutrition survey conceded that 'the prevalence of stunting does not appear to have decreased appreciably since 1980.'[16] Like that of Brazil, Zimbabwe's agrarian structure is ill-designed to enable poor people to realise their potential.[17] While this type of structure remains the exception rather than the rule for Africa, landlessness and increasing marginalisation are a source of mounting concern in countries such as Malawi, Kenya, and South Africa.

Insecurity and isolation

Land ownership patterns are less concentrated in Asia than in Latin America, but here too population growth, inheritance laws which encourage sub-division of land, and a shrinkage of cultivable area in some regions, make landlessness a growing problem. In India, the number of holdings smaller than two hectares grew from 47 million in the early 1970s to 63 million in the 1980s. As the number of small and marginal holding have increased, so has the number of households dependent on wage labour. Women account for a rising proportion of that labour, which is becoming increasingly casual and insecure. According to one study, the proportion of casual labourers in the agricultural work force increased from 22 per cent in the early 1970s to 29 per cent in the mid-1980s, which is significant in view of the fact that over half of casual workers live below the poverty line.[18] In Bangladesh, 80 per cent of rural families are either landless or near landless, while 10 per cent of rural households own 50 per cent of the cultivable land area.

Geographical isolation, low income, and lack of productive assets often reinforce the effects of unequal land ownership. In Zambia, approximately 22 per cent of rural households live more than one kilometre from the nearest water source, and this is likely to be polluted.[19] During the dry season, women can spend up to five hours each day fetching water. The time and energy spent in this task imposes an enormous burden on women, and diverts their labour from household production and child-care, increasing household vulnerability.

There is a close correlation between distance from markets and poverty. Around one-third of the poorest families in Zambia live over 20km away from the nearest food market, and cannot afford transport to these markets. Inability to obtain credit is another major problem for poor farmers, preventing them adopting new technologies. It has been estimated that as few as 5 per cent of farmers in Africa and between 15-20 per cent in Asia are able to benefit from formal credit.[20] The remainder are excluded from credit markets or forced to borrow at excessively high interest rates. This applies especially to women heads-of-households, who often do not have the land rights which could provide collateral for borrowing.[21]

Poor rural households are trapped in a vicious spiral of insecurity. With insufficient land, often of poor quality, unable to buy seeds or fertiliser or to use draught power, their productivity is low. Unable to produce or purchase sufficient food, they are malnourished and so more likely to fall sick. Children from poor households are more likely to work, primarily as unpaid family labourers, debarring them from opportunities for education, which may in any case be unaffordable for the poor, creating an inter-generational poverty trap.

The power of rural elites

Grossly unequal agrarian structures are invariably maintained through equally gross inequalities in political power. In Latin America, states have often deployed their coercive apparatus on behalf of landlords to drive small farmers off their land, to make way for big commercial estates.[22] In the north-east of Brazil, landowners control the administration of rural areas, often running them as personal fiefdoms. Local communities have united in an effort to protect themselves and claim their land rights. For instance, the Landless People's Movement works in the state of Paraiba with people driven from their land by sugar estates and cattle farming. Under state laws, they are allowed to squat on land which has ben left idle and, after cultivating it for a number of years, to claim title to it.[23] Despite facing intimidation and threats from state authorities and landlords, they have achieved some notable successes in terms of establishing land rights.

Inequalities in political power are also significant for indigenous Indian communities. Under Brazilian law, all Amazonian Indian lands were to have been demarcated, and protected from encroachments by settlers, commercial logging operators, and gold miners, by 1993. In practice, only half of that land has been demarcated, and even this remains under threat.[24] The National Indian Foundation, the state agency responsible for enforcing Indian claims, known by its Portuguese acronym, FUNAI, is understaffed and under-funded, reflecting the low priority attached to its work. Indian peoples such as the Yanomani, Macuxi, Kaxinawa, and Wanana, are co-operating to resist encroachments by loggers, goldminers, and ranchers, but are often faced with extreme violence. Despite this, Indian organisations, supported by Brazilian NGOs and the Catholic Church, continue to assert their legal claims, in a daily struggle for justice and survival. Euclides Perreira, a Macuxi Indian and Coordinator of the Roraima Indigenous Council, summarises the lessons learned in these terms:

The movement has grown and strengthened because we have realised that only we ourselves can solve our problems, not the government. Nowadays, FUNAI does practically nothing for the communities because it has no money. Today, the indigenous movement is much stronger than FUNAI.

Efforts to establish land rights in Bangladesh have encountered similarly violent reactions from vested interests. In 1984, a government land reform ordinance provided for the distribution of state land, known as *khas*, to landless and marginal producers. However, much of this land has been acquired by larger farmers, often through corruption and political influence; and sometimes through violent intimidation preventing landless people from asserting their rights.[25] Several of Oxfam's project partners in the country are working with the landless, supporting their efforts to gain ownership of *khas* land. Their accounts provide testimony to the violence which often results when local communities try to claim the rights provided for in government legislation. The Association for Land Reform and Development[26] recorded the consequences of one attempt by landless labourers to assert their rights to *khas* land:

For Abdul Hanif, aged 14, life has ceased to hold meaning. During an attack on his village, the land-lords caught the young boy and chopped off his right wrist. They also stabbed him...Hanif did not know anything about the dispute. His only fault was that he was the son of a landless farmer.

Where local communities lack land rights they are often forced into highly exploitative forms of employment. In the Pakistan Province of Sindh, Oxfam's partners work with minority groups such as the Kholis and Bhils, employed as share-croppers for landlords. They often transfer as much as three-quarters of their total harvest under this arrangement. In theory, they are entitled by law to claim tenancy rights to the plots they farm after a number of years of permanent cultivation. In practice, landlords circumvent these rights through the simple expedient of moving share-croppers from plot to plot, or transferring them between one another. Arrangements such as these increase the vulnerability of the poor by transferring a disproportionate share of the benefits of their labour to others, reinforcing their dependency in the process.[27]

Agricultural modernisation

Where agricultural 'modernisation' is super-imposed on highly inequitable systems, it often serves to reinforce those systems. The Green Revolution seeds and technologies, introduced in the 1960s in various parts of the world, are an example. Large farmers were able to take advantage of the new technologics, oftcn by consolidating their holdings, displacing small producers, and contributing to an overall decline in the demand for rural labour. The most marginal farmers were excluded from the benefits of the Green Revolution, or suffered increased marginalisation.[28] There are impor-tant exceptions to this picture, especially in South India. There, the introduction of high-yielding rice and mechanised irrigation pumps increased demand for labour and, in many areas, small farmers were able to benefit from the new technology.[29] At the same time, extra demand for labour at harvest time before the monsoon increased rural wages.

Common property resources

To a far greater extent than the wealthy, poor people depend for their survival on the use of common resources. They fish, hunt, produce goods for sale from leaves and fibres, make medicine from forest products, and gather nuts and berries for food.[30] During the drought which swept southern Africa in 1992-1993, Oxfam staff witnessed how villagers in Zambia and Zimbabwe drew upon local knowledge of roots, leaves, and other forest products, to survive chronic food shortages. Without that knowledge, which has been passed down over centuries from generation to generation, the human costs of the drought would have been much higher. In the dryland regions of India, it has been estimated that landless labourers derive up to one-fifth of their income, along with a significant proportion of their food, medicines, and building materials, by harvesting natural resources from common areas.[31] Women play a critical role in managing and conserving such areas, and in harvesting them in a sustainable manner.

Rights of usage of common resources are enshrined in customary law. Indigenous communities, such as tribals in India, and Indians in Latin America, are able to trace these rights back through many generations. Today, however, such rights are under threat in many countries.[32] Appropriation by the state, the intrusion of commercial interests, and the privatisation of land in the interests of the privileged, have become potent threats to the welfare of the poor.

Forests

The Dandakaranya forest, in the Gadchiroli district of Maharashtra, is home to a large tribal population, 80 per cent of whom are estimated to live below the poverty line. Tribal communities in Gadchiroli have depended on the Dandakaranya forest for their survival for centuries. They grew crops using traditional slash and burn agriculture, in which parts of the forest were felled and burned to provide natural fertiliser, and then allowed to replenish after one growing season. They also hunted birds and wildlife, and collected edible fruits, leaves, flowers, and roots, for food and medicine, and to sell. Since the mid-1970s, however, the state government has allowed increasingly intensive commercial timber operations in the forest, to meet the demands of industry. This has brought lucrative profits for commercial companies and state authorities, who gain revenue by selling concessions. Less than 5 per cent of that revenue has been ploughed back into the district. The clash between commercial interests and customary rights has left tribal communities in the forest facing the destruction of their livelihood systems, as the fragile ecosystem of the forest is destroyed by logging operations.

Fisheries

Fish from coastal and inland waters are vital to the livelihoods of poor communities throughout the developing world. Yet it is here that the clash between commercial interest and customary right is at its most intense. In the Indian state of Kerala, for example, legislation is likely to be introduced which will nullify the customary rights of fishworkers to coastal waters, rivers, and lakes, with potentially disastrous consequences for the livelihoods of local communities. Mechanised trawling has already severely depleted fish stocks and reduced the catches, and hence the food supply and income, of these communities.[33]

In the Philippines, a country consisting of 7000 islands, more than one million people are directly employed in fisheries. Widespread poverty has resulted in more and more people, from coastal and urban communities, turning to fishing for their livelihood, competing for the same shrinking natural resource base. Over the past 15 years, however, unregulated and unsustainable commercial fishing, notably by Japanese trawlers and powerful local entrepreneurs, has drastically reduced fish stocks and set in train a vicious spiral of poverty and environmental degradation.[34] Local fisher-folk have resorted, out of desperation, to using dynamite and other harmful fishing methods to maintain catches in the short term, but coral reefs, where fish breed, are destroyed in the process. Poverty has also forced people into cutting mangrove trees for firewood, destroying other fish breeding sites. At the same time, the government has encouraged commercial interests to drain mangrove swamps in order to develop commercial fish farms.[35] The overall effect has been to reinforce the pressures which cause unsustainable resource use.

Local communities are co-operating in political action to reverse this spiral and defend their customary rights. In 1990 several Oxfam partners were involved in the creation of a national fishing confederation, which took the lead in organising defensive action against commercial encroachment. Fisher-folk leaders lobbied local and national authorities for a legislative framework which would protect the traditional rights of coastal fishing communities, and actively involve them in sustainable resource management. Meanwhile, local communities were encouraged to monitor the activities of commercial trawlers, and to sail out to sea in an effort to persuade them to leave the fishing grounds, and, in some cases, to confiscate their catch. Ingenious new techniques have been developed to regenerate reefs, with car tyres being submerged and acting as a base for the growth of corals. Mangroves are being replanted to provide the shelter and spawning grounds needed to restore fish stocks, and these are being protected through no-fishing agreements.

Urban poverty

The global poverty profile is slowing changing and taking on a more urban face. In many countries, rapid population growth, agricultural modernisation, and inequalities in land ownership are resulting in an increase in landlessness among the rural poor, and an accelerating drift to urban centres. As urban populations increase, so does the extent of urban poverty.

Most of the urban poor live in unplanned squatter settlements on the periphery of urban centres, where their lack of legal status and inadequate service provision make them extremely vulnerable.[36] That vulnerability is made worse by insecure, low-wage employment. The vast majority of the urban poor work in the informal sector in a variety of activities, including petty-trading and casual labour.

During the 'lost decade' of the 1980s, it was the urban poor who bore the brunt of the crisis associated with debt, deteriorating terms of trade, and the economic policy failures of governments. Rising food prices, unemployment, and a steep decline in real wages, wrought havoc in the lives of urban communities across the developing world. In some countries wages have fallen so dramatically that families can only survive through a massive increase in labour time, much of it on the part of women. For example, in 1991, average wages in Zambia were a quarter of their level in the mid-1970s, in real terms. Employment in the formal sector

declined from 25 per cent of total employment in 1970 to less than 10 per cent in 1990.[37] Behind these cold statistics lies a human tragedy of enormous proportions, which is reflected most powerfully in an increase in the mortality rate for children under the age of five from 152 to 191 per 1000 live births between 1977/81 and 1991.[38] In a little more than a decade, the human welfare achievements of the post-independence period, which by 1970 were on a par even with many middle-income countries, had been reversed.

Through its programme in Zambia, Oxfam has witnessed the efforts of local communities to survive in the face of continued economic decline. One example is to be found in the Kawama compound, a slum area on the country's Copperbelt, which went into steep decline as a consequence of economic mismanagement and falling world copper prices in the 1980s. Health, education, and other services collapsed as state revenues fell, and mass unemployment devastated household incomes. The Kawama Development Committee responded to the crisis by developing 'self-help' alternatives. Members of the Committee built primary health care and school facilities, and then successfully lobbied the government to staff them. They built their own roads and maintained their own water and sanitation services. More recently, they have taken to market gardening, to improve their nutrition and income. However, such initiatives can provide little more than isolated islands of hope in a wider sea of social and economic despair.

Falling wages

In Latin America, minimum wages fell on average by 33 per cent during the 1980s. As millions sought desperately to supplement their incomes, the informal sector doubled in size, while incomes in that sector fell by around 40 per cent. The resulting rise in poverty was particularly dramatic in countries such as Chile, Guatemala, and Peru.[39] At the centre of the process of impoverishment was the labour market. In Peru, private sector wages in 1992 were only 25 per cent of their value in the early 1970s. At the same time, there was a transformation in the labour market away from permanent contracts towards more precarious forms of casual employment. By 1993, over 50 per cent of all employment in the private sector was casual, compared to 11 per cent in 1985.[40] For some countries, the 'lost decade' is extending into the 1990s. Real urban wages in Zimbabwe have fallen dramatically over the past three years, giving rise to an increasing incidence of child malnutrition.[41] Here, too, employment has become increasingly insecure, with the dilution of labour protection laws.

Changes in the structure of employment have had important implications for urban poverty. At the start of the 1980s, poverty was closely correlated with unemployment. There is still a correlation; but as wages have fallen and employment has become less secure, the proportion of employed families living in poverty has increased. In Chile, for example, inadequate wage levels are now the single most important cause of poverty; official estimates for 1992 suggest that one-third of the labour force live in conditions of poverty.[42] Oxfam's partners work with some of the victims of the 'new poverty' in the Patronato district of northern Santiago, the centre of the country's textile industry. An estimated 6000 small workshops do out-work for large manufacturers, and provide employment to over 12,000 mainly female workers. Very few of these workshops meet even the minimum specifications of Chile's weak health and safety law, and accidents are regular occur-rences. Most women do not have contracts, so can be made redundant without compensation. Piecework payments are so low that most women have to work shifts in excess of twelve hours, including night work. Even the most basic trade union rights are denied. Despite this, women employed in the sweatshops are organising to improve their working conditions. In early 1994, a trade union support group for women workers rented a small building for use as a canteen for textile workers in Patronato. Since then, the canteen has grown into an education centre, where the women can discuss their problems and attend courses on employment law and labour rights. Because their employment is so insecure, it is difficult for them to exert pressure for change. But there is a growing recognition among the women that collective action has the potential to improve their lives.

The economic crisis affecting so many countries has forced women and children to work longer and longer hours to generate income. The resulting costs are not reflected in national income accounts, but by other indicators, such as the psychological and physical stress experienced by women, the opportunities lost by children withdrawn from school to supplement family incomes, and the breakdown of families.

The failure of service provision

Like their rural counterparts, urban communities are involved in struggles to gain rights to security of tenure and to basic amenities. In Recife, Brazil's fifth-largest city, Oxfam's partners work with some of the 680,000 people who inhabit the *favelas*, sprawling shanty-towns dotted across the city. During the 1950s, Recife earned the sobriquet 'the Venice of the North' because of its canals and rivers. Today, most of the city's canals are open sewers which run through the *favelas*, where shacks made of corrugated tin, plastic, and wood serve as overcrowded homes. Unofficial estimates put the housing shortage at 400,000 homes.

The rapid growth of the *favela* community in Recife is replicated elsewhere in Brazil, and more widely throughout Latin America, Asia, and Africa. Driven to the city by rural hunger, landlessness, drought, and unemployment, the slum dwellers of Recife live on rubbish dumps, swamps, and derelict sites; victims of a social and economic order which regards them as surplus to requirements. Denied clean water, electricity, and paved roads, they are also subject to frequent displacement by police and local authorities to make way for road schemes and other amenities intended to improve life for the wealthy, enfranchised part of the population. But the underclass in Recife and other Brazilian cities are organising to claim their basic rights, and to resist forced displacement, provide their own services, and demand support from municipal authorities. Ivanete Tavares is president of one residents' association in Recife. Her home is a shelter made of black plastic, with an earth floor. She has no electricity or running water. These are her hopes:

My dream for here is to have water, light, public phones, a bus route, tarmac roads, and a secondary school. And we want a block factory; not cement blocks but mud blocks which people can afford to make their homes. We want our community to exist officially. Not like now, when it's not on the map, or in the computers of the city council. We are treated like an illegitimate child, we are not recognised or registered.

Work with the Zabaleen

Work with urban communities figures increasingly prominently in Oxfam's international programme. But as with rural projects, supporting the livelihoods of the poor is less easy to achieve in practice than is often assumed. Interventions intended to benefit the poor often fail when the communities of which they form a part, are treated as a homogenous group. For example, in 1981, Oxfam supported a recycling plant to generate income among the Zabaleen, a community living in slums on the outskirts of Cairo, which survives by collecting the city's waste and recycling it.[43] The aim was to enable the Zabaleen to bypass middlemen and maximise the income staying in Zabaleen hands. In 1985, a credit scheme was set up, with loans tied to the establishment of local carpentry and processing workshops. The intention was to expand the number of products which could be recycled for sale. The failure of both interventions, revealed by later evaluations, was that most of the benefits went to the wealthier sections of the community — and almost none to women, who had not participated in discussions about the design of the project. In 1988 the credit scheme was revised. Ceilings were placed on the amount which could be borrowed, and loans were provided to groups of three to five women. The original condition that loans should be used for recycling work and sales, activities controlled by men, was waived, allowing women to use the credit in support of their own livelihood strategies. Many have used their loans to raise goats, for milk for family consumption and to sell.

Social welfare provision

Investment in the health and education of poor people can reduce their vulnerability and expand their opportunities. Good health, mental and physical, is an important determinant of employment, productivity, and income. Conversely, poor health and poverty are closely correlated in all countries. There is a wealth of evidence linking educational attainment with virtually all significant human development indicators. While improvements in human health and education are important for their own sake, they can also play a critical role in facilitating the broad-based, equitable economic environment which is vital to poverty eradication.

Investment in health care

The linkages between health and human welfare are obvious and fundamental. Most people know from their own experience that treatment of ill health is vital to their welfare. For poor people, health care is particularly important, partly because they are ill more often, and partly because their income depends critically upon physical labour. Ill health is a potential disaster for low-income families, since it can wipe out their assets as ruthlessly as a drought, and expose children to acute risks.

Sickness is part of a vicious circle. Because people are poor, they are more exposed to risk from unhealthy conditions, including inadequate water supply and sanitation. They are also likely to suffer chronic health problems as the legacy of past illness and malnutrition. Without adequate health care, they are more likely to fall ill and to be slower in recovering, compounding the disadvantages they face.

For many people in the developing world, primary health care services are inadequate or non-existent. In sub-Saharan Africa, basic health-care provision is lacking for over 50 per cent of people. In Zambia, 30 per cent of the rural population live ten kilometres or more from the nearest health facility. Most poor people would be unable to reach a clinic this far away if they were sick. Even if they successfully negotiated the journey, few would be able to afford the treatment when they arrived. Moreover it is unlikely that the facility would have either the drugs or the trained staff needed for effective care. This situation, which is not untypical throughout sub-Saharan Africa, helps to explain the region's appalling health indicators.

Inadequate public investment in basic health exposes poor people to high risks. In Uganda, health spending per capita is less than half the level required to provide a basic primary health service.[44] As a result, preventable diseases like diarrhoea, pneumonia, measles, and meningitis account for over half of reported hospital deaths. But the problem is not merely one of inadequate investment. Most developing countries spend considerably more on high-cost curative treatment, which benefits mainly higher-income and urban populations, than low-cost preventive treatment. In Uganda's case, ten times as much is spent on curative as on preventive treatment. In Peru, health expenditure is concentrated in Lima and almost half of the budget dedicated to the curative sector, although poverty levels are far more severe in inland rural areas. Across the developing world, it is not untypical for one or two teaching hospitals to absorb more than a quarter of the entire health budget. Quite apart from the questionable social priorities this points to, the economic logic of such an allocation of resources leaves much to be desired. According to the UNDP, it costs between $100 and $600 to save a life through preventive care, while the corresponding figure for curative care is between $500 and $5000.[45]

There is a similarly skewed distribution of public investment in water and sanitation, which is one of the most critical forms of preventive investment. Of the $15bn spent on this area in sub-Saharan Africa during the 1980s, four-fifths was on high-cost technology, primarily for the improvement of services to people who were already supplied.[46] Such spending patterns entail a high price for the poor. For example, in Lima, Peru, poor people pay as much as $3 for a cubic metre of contaminated water from a private vendor, while the middle-class pay $0.5 for an equivalent amount of tap water.[47]

The advantages to individuals and society of investment in health are readily apparent. Healthier people lose fewer days to sickness, live longer, are more productive, and have more opportunities for employment. Health and nutritional status also have an important bearing on educational attainment. Healthier children are better at learning and will thus make a greater economic contribution to society. For women, effective public health systems are of particular significance. The social and cultural forces which condemn women to lower nutritional status and heavier workloads than men in many societies, also increase the risk of their contracting disease. Women and girl children also assume responsibility for looking after sick relatives, adding to their already heavy workloads.[48] Half of all women in Africa and South Asia, and two-thirds of all pregnant women in both regions, are anaemic. Primary health care systems are vital for the delivery of reproductive health care, including family planning services which enable women to control their fertility, and for providing care throughout high-risk periods such as during and after pregnancy.

Investment in education

Investment in education, especially primary education, is also one of the most important determinants of human welfare, opportunity, and economic growth. The linkages in each of these areas are now so well established as to be beyond serious dispute.[49] The low earnings of poor people are partly a consequence of their low levels of skill and literacy. Studies for agriculture and industry have shown that better-educated people adapt more easily to new technologies, and have higher rates of productivity.[50] This increases their earning capability and employment prospects, while bringing wider benefits for society. In an era of rapid technological change, the skill-base of the work force is becoming increasingly important to national competitiveness.

Investment in education is one of the best uses of its resources a country can make, as witnessed by the South-East Asian 'miracle' countries. According to the World Bank, investment in primary education has been the single largest contributor to the differences in growth between these countries and the rest of the developing world. When comparing South-East Asia with Latin America, one-third of the difference in growth rate can be attributed to higher investment in primary education.[51] Because economic growth is crucial to improvement in human welfare, such investment should be regarded as central to any strategy for poverty reduction. But investment in education also enhances the *quality* of growth by improving equity. One study of 49 countries concluded that about one-fifth of income inequality could be explained by educational inequality.[52]

Level of education, particularly in the case of women, plays a critical role in relation to health. Girls tend to receive less schooling than boys. Regarded as more important to household subsistence than their brothers, girls are often kept at home to perform domestic work or to care for younger siblings; and they are likely to be the first to be withdrawn from school if the family faces a crisis. Such practices have kept women trapped in cycles of poverty and illiteracy which are transmitted across generations.

Rising levels of maternal education reduce levels of infant mortality by about 8 per cent for each of the first ten years of schooling.[53] In Peru, seven or more years of maternal schooling reduce infant mortality rates by 75 per cent. Education for women is also closely associated with later marriage and smaller family size, and enhanced maternal health.

Allocating scarce resources

The strategy of broad-based investment in primary education pursued by the South-East Asian countries drew on lessons learnt from Western Europe and, more immediately, post-war Japan. The success-story of those countries confirm that well-targeted public investment can rapidly raise the skills-base of an economy, reduce poverty and inequality, and promote growth. Despite this, many developing country governments choose to allocate resources inappropriately. For example:

- Governments in sub-Saharan Africa spend a higher proportion (4.7 per cent) of the region's national income on education than East Asia (3.4 per cent), but a much smaller proportion goes on primary education.
- The share of public funds allocated to higher education in South-East Asia has averaged around 15 per cent for the past three decades, whereas in Latin America and sub-Saharan Africa it has averaged 24 per cent.
- While Bolivia spends 40 per cent of its education budget on primary education and has achieved commensurately low enrolment rates, Indonesia spends 90 per cent and is moving towards universal enrolment.

There are two factors which make statistics such as these a particular cause of concern. The first is that, 40 years after the Universal Declaration of Human Rights asserted that 'everyone has a right to basic education', there are 130 million children of primary-school age not enrolled in school. Unless policies change, the absolute number of children not attending school is likely to reach 162 million in the year 2015.[54] In Africa, where 50 per cent of primary-school age children are not attending school, enrolment rates are decreasing on average,

Figure 1.1 Children aged 6-11 out-of-school, 1980-2015 (total millions/percentage)

Region	1980	1990	*2000*	*2015*
Developing countries	158 (31%)	129 (24%)	145 (22%)	162 (23%)
Sub-Saharan Africa	26 (43%)	41 (50%)	59 (51%)	83 (51%)
Latin America and the Caribbean	9 (17%)	8 (13%)	7 (11%)	7 (11%)
East Asia	55 (25%)	26 (14%)	27 (13%)	21 (12%)
South Asia	59 (40%)	48 (27%)	47 (23%)	46 (20%)

SOURCE: WORLD BANK

leading to deepening poverty. On the surface the figures are more encouraging for Latin America, where only 8 per cent of children are not enrolled. However, only one-third of the countries in the region have completion rates above 80 per cent, so that the proportion of children reaching grade five is roughly the same as in Africa.[55]

The second source of concern is that policies appear to be moving in the wrong direction. As economic pressures have mounted since the early 1980s, public spending per child in primary education has fallen, while the share of education spending going to higher education has increased.[56] Some indication of the priorities of governments in developing countries is provided by the fact that spending on defence has been increasing on average at more than twice the rate of national income growth, with overall defence expenditure now equivalent to health and education spending combined.

Inequity between men and women

Women are subject to multiple forms of deprivation from the cradle to the grave. Throughout the world, women play a key role in household livelihood systems in a productive and reproductive capacity. As producers, they provide most of the food consumed by poor households, performing more than three-quarters of agricultural labour in many countries. In addition, they manage common resources, and are responsible for collecting water and firewood. Female labour also accounts for a growing proportion of employment in commercial agriculture and industry.[57]

Despite this contribution, women face a bewildering array of social, economic, cultural, and religious barriers to their equal participation in society. The consequences of these barriers in terms of lost opportunities and increased vulnerability and suffering are immeasurable. But some indication of their destructive effect can be summarised in a few revealing statistics. For example:

• Out of the 130 million children not attending primary school, some 70 per cent are female. In India, boys are twice as likely to attend secondary school as girls.

• Out of the 960 million illiterate adults in the world, two-thirds are women

• In many countries, especially in Asia, malnutrition rates are higher among girls than boys. In Bangladesh, they are three times higher. Mortality rates in early childhood are higher for women in India, Bangladesh, Pakistan, and Nepal.

Life expectancy is also shorter in much of Asia. Perhaps the single most telling indicator of the discrimination and neglect suffered by women is to be found in the fact that there are some 100 million fewer women in Asia than there would be if the region had the same male-to-female mortality rates as Africa.[58]

Most female labour goes undocumented and unpaid, even though it is vital to family survival and national economies, and in most cultures women have less opportunity than men to develop their capabilities. Although most food is produced by women, and female-headed households account for the majority of rural households in many countries, women lack ownership or effective control over land, water, and other resources. In Bangladesh, daughters inherit land at half their brothers' entitlement.[59] In some cases, traditional communal systems that once gave women rights of use of land, water, and trees have been replaced by private property systems which do not. In others, social and cultural barriers prevent women from realising their legal rights.

In much of Africa, women have no rights to resources such as trees or the land they cultivate.[60] Partly because of their restricted land rights, women in most developing countries find it impossible to obtain credit or banking services. It has been estimated that women receive less than 10 per cent of all rural credit.[61] This restricts their ability to purchase inputs which would reduce demands on their labour and raise their income. While women are forming an increasingly large proportion of the labour force in most countries, labour laws seldom give them adequate protection against discrimination, or protect their rights to employment and social security during illness and pregnancy.

The most invidious form of discrimination against women is violence in the home. One survey covering 35 countries found that an average of between one-fifth and one-half of women had suffered domestic violence at the hands of a male partner, on average three times a year.[62] In Egypt and Zambia, injuries resulting from domestic assaults are the most common reason for female visits to casualty units. The attitude of authorities to this violation of

women's most basic rights is captured in this chilling account given by a Zambian woman:

My husband followed me and got me in the house and said 'what are you doing?' He did not wait for me to finish. He kicked me and kicked me. The children ran back to the party and told my friends 'what are you doing standing here, daddy is killing mummy'. So they came and found me covered in blood. This time they took me to the police. When I got there I explained what happened. They said, 'Ah kaili iviniva munyumba' ['another domestic problem'].

In Latin America, domestic and sexual violence against women claim more victims than political violence. In response, an active move-ment, spearheaded by women's groups, is campaigning for domestic violence against women to be recognised as a fundamental issue of human rights and public responsibility. Oxfam is supporting some of these women's groups in their campaign and in providing help to victims of domestic violence.

Investing in women

Throughout the developing world, Oxfam's partners are working with women in an effort to remove deep-rooted structures of gender discrimination. In Bangladesh, Saptagram, one of Oxfam's project partners, is attempting to break the cycle of deprivation, in terms of nutrition, health, literacy, and poverty, faced by women by helping them to empower themselves. Through its network of 22,000 members spread across 900 villages, Saptagram supports local groups by providing literacy training, revolving credit funds, support for clean water and sanitation programmes, and education to enable women to challenge harmful cultural practices, such as child marriage and domestic violence.[63] At the heart of Saptagram's work is a commitment to enabling women to effect change. Collective action to protest against male violence, dowry extortion, and the violation of land rights, has become widespread among the groups; each victory brings another leap of confidence.

Investment in credit is an important element in wider strategies to remove the barriers facing women, as Oxfam's work in Zambia has underlined. In the Petauke, Chipata, and Nyimba districts of Eastern province, and in the Mumbwa district of Central Province, Oxfam works with women's farming co-operatives. These women are representative of the most poverty-prone groups in the country. Yet they are excluded from official credit schemes because they do not own titles to the land they cultivate. Oxfam has provided seed and cash, which is repaid after the next harvest, to establish a revolving credit fund, which should enable these farmers to develop more secure livelihoods. One co-operative, for example, has used its loan to hire oxen for ploughing a new field which is farmed co-operatively.

Contrary to claims that poor women farmers are bad credit risks, Oxfam's credit schemes in Zambia have repayment rates of over 90 per cent. This is more than double the repayment rates of state credit-agencies' lending to more 'commercially viable' farms. However, viewed from a gender empowerment perspective, credit provision is not without its risks. One of the best known credit schemes is the Grameen Bank in Bangladesh, which provides loans to around half-a-million members, of whom over 80 per cent are women. Once again, repayment rates are exceptionally high. But recent research has found that a significant proportion of the loans provided to women are controlled and invested by male relatives, with women bearing the liability for repayment, though not necessarily benefiting from the loan. Thus, while credit provision for women can offer valuable opportunities, without wider measures to ensure that women can control investments, it can reinforce unequal power structures within households.

Population and reproductive rights

In a similar way, unequal power relations and inadequate provision of reproductive health services are depriving women of the right to control their own fertility. Pregnancy itself is a health risk for poor women, as is unsafe abortion. In 1991, the WHO recommended action 'to encourage governments to do everything possible to prevent and eliminate the severe health consequences of unsafe abortion.' [64] According to UNFPA, the death toll associated with abortion-related complications is 200,000 per year;[65] and many more women suffer ill health and injury related to unsafe abortions. Those affected are overwhelmingly poor women and their familieas in developing countries. This underlines the need for women to receive much beetter reproductive health care, including information and choice over family-planning methods. Yet too often, the emphasis of official birth-control schemes has been on population control, motivated by a desire to curb population growth, rather than enhance women's reproductive rights and quality of life.

World population growth has vastly accelerated over the last century. During the 1980s, the number of people on earth grew by almost one billion, with 90 per cent of the increase in the developing world. This trend is set to continue. While fertility rates are in decline in Latin America and Asia, they remain highest in the world's poorest countries. Over the next 40 years, the population of sub-Saharan Africa is projected to treble to over 1.6 billion. In the same period, the population of Asia will rise from around 3 billion to over 5 billion. This prospect has prompted some to warn of a Malthusian crisis, with a growing population in the poorest countries placing increasingly unsustainable demands on economic and environmental resources. Catastrophic images of a population 'time-bomb' about to explode have made a significant impact on public attitudes in the North.[66] But while there are indeed reasons to worry about the effects of rapid population growth on the environment (although there is no simple correlation between population growth and environmental degradation), there are also strong reasons for concern about the adverse effects of high birth-rates on the quality of life, especially for women.[67] The emergency mentality generated by warnings of imminent cataclysm is not helpful. Rapid population growth is both a cause and consequence of poverty; and as the demographic history of today's developed countries underlines, creating opportunities for education, particularly for women, and improving provision of reproductive health-care, can both improve human welfare and lead to declining birth rates within a relatively short space of time.

Reproductive practices are influenced by a complex interaction of social, economic, cultural, religious, and other forces, which vary from society to society. However, the persistence of poverty and deprivation are pervasive causes of high birth-rates throughout the developing world. One of the primary reasons for having large numbers of children in many countries is economic: offspring provide labour for the survival of families lacking capital and technology, as well as insurance in old age. Children in poor households in poor countries assume responsibilities for fetching water, minding animals and collecting fuelwood, in addition to caring for their parents when they reach adulthood.[68] In societies where infant mortality rates are high, this creates a powerful rationale for high birth-rates. For example, in many sub-Saharan African countries poor rural women often lose one-third of their children by the end of their reproductive years.[69] In such a setting, lowering infant mortality is a precondition for reducing birth-rates.

Reliable and high-quality reproductive health services, including family planning, are vital if this objective is to be realised. Yet reproductive health services are available to only half of the female population in South Asia and only one-in-ten women in sub-Saharan Africa.[70] This denies women the opportunity to control their fertility, and diminishes the health and survival prospects of children. Inadequate maternal education has a similar effect.[71] The demographic history of almost all countries shows that as female literacy rises, fertility rates decline, child and maternal mortality rates fall, and nutrition levels improve. According to the World Bank, fertility rates fall on average by 10

per cent for every year of schooling a women receives, with educated women more likely to marry later, to have smaller families and to space pregnancies in a manner which minimises risk to their health and that of their children.[72]

The apocalyptic interpretation of the population problem expounded by some commentators, has helped to mould an emergency mentality which focuses on narrowly-defined birth-control measures. In China and some Indian states, outright coercion and economic incentives have been used to spearhead strategies for achieving population 'targets'. Aid donors are increasingly orientating their budgets towards family planning services in a bid to reduce population growth rates. In so far as this contributes to providing the safe and reliable services women need to control their fertility, it can play an important role in enhancing their opportunities and reducing birth rates. Ultimately, however, addressing population growth requires a comprehensive strategy of poverty reduction, provision of adequate health services, education (particularly for women), improving economic security, and the enhanced participation of women in employment, and decision-making. Above all, human rights must be respected. This broad approach was endorsed at the International Conference on Population and Development held in 1994.

Most commentators now accept the linkage between social welfare provision and reduced birth rates. However, many insist that the resolution of the population problem cannot await the economic growth which will improve access to health and education sufficiently to effect a demographic transformation. Yet the Indian state of Kerala has shown that poverty need not be an insuperable obstacle to enhanced social welfare provision. Despite being one of the poorer states, Kerala has a birth rate which is half the Indian average and lower than China's. This is the result not of coercion, but of investment in health and education, and of more equitable social relations. Infant mortality rates are one-quarter of the average for India and one half of that for China.[73] As a result of greater gender equity, women have not suffered from higher mortality rates than men, as they have in the rest of India and China. Nor have they been subject to entrenched discrimination in education. While in India as a whole, one in two girl children drops out of primary school, in Kerala completion is almost universal. Thus despite its economic backwardness. Kerala's social development has been remarkable, and it has played a central role in reducing fertility rates to levels comparable with those in industrialised countries.

In South Korea, a combination of high economic growth (in contrast to Kerala), and the creation of universal access to primary health care, education, and employment opportunities, resulted in a dramatic decline in poverty and inequality. It also contributed to a demographic transformation which saw the population growth rate more than halved in a little over three decades, despite an increase in life-expectancy from 53 to 72: a demographic transformation which it took the industrialised world one-and-a-half centuries from the industrial revolution to complete.

Poverty, population, and environmental degradation

The concentration of poverty in ecologically fragile regions where land is least productive and in urban areas where employment opportunities are most limited, results in a downward spiral of environmental degradation, increased poverty and population growth in many countries.[74] Yet it would be simplistic and misleading to draw global correlations between population densities on the one side and environmental degradation on the other. Were such correlations to exist, Holland would be considerably more environmentally degraded than the Sudan. Recent studies have drawn attention to the crucial importance of the policy environment in which population growth occurs. For instance, the Machakos district in Kenya was regarded before the Second World war as an environmental disaster-zone by colonial administrators monitoring rates of deforestation and soil erosion. Population density was seen as the main contributory factor. Today, the district has a far larger population, but local initiatives to conserve soils, plant trees, and develop appropriate farming systems, coupled with improved access to markets and education, have transformed the environment and repaired the damage evident 50 years ago. Similarly in Yemen, problems of soil erosion on fragile hillsides have been caused not by excessive population pressure, but by labour migration. This has resulted in the breakdown of the terracing systems previously maintained by highly labour-intensive practices. Elsewhere, exclusion from land and unequal control over resources, rather than rapid population growth, has been the major factor behind the environmental degradation. In Honduras, for example, the displacement of peasant small-holders by vast ranching estates was the catalyst for widespread environmental destruction in that country.[75] There are, of course, many counter examples. For example, in countries such as Sudan, population pressure has been one of the factors forcing women to travel longer and longer distances to collect firewood.[76] The crucial point, however, is that population growth is not an independent variable in determining poverty, but part of a broader set of social and economic pressures operating upon the poor.

Local action for sustainable livelihoods

The links between poverty and environmental degradation are related to poor people's rights to use and control natural resources. Often poor men and women are forced to exploit scarce natural resources or pollute their environment because they are struggling for survival. Their immediate environment is their resource base and source of livelihood, and they have no alternatives. These problems have to be tackled at many levels, starting with the local level, through the active involvement of the communities affected.

Bringing back the trees

The people of Kesharpur village, situated in the hills of Orissa state in India, provide an example of how grassroots initiatives are creating sustainable livelihoods.[77] Twenty years ago, the once densely-wooded hills around the village were being rapidly denuded of tree cover by a combination of population pressure, fuelwood gathering, goat grazing, and commercial logging. The hills directly above the village had become so denuded of tree cover that springs had dried up, depriving the villages of water supplies. Deep gullies, caused by the rapid run-off of water during the monsoon, scarred the slopes; fertile top-soil was rapidly disappearing to expose outcrops of rocks. As the villagers grew increasingly short of fuelwood, fodder, and water, with women having to walk further and further to fetch and carry, it seemed that an unstoppable spiral of poverty and environmental degradation had been set in motion.

Without co-operative action by the villagers to reverse that spiral, it would have been unstoppable. Acknowledging that they were partly responsible for the problem, they banned goats from the most degraded areas. Then, in the early 1980s, representatives from 22 villages came together and, with the help of a local NGO, established a tree nursery and a re-planting programme. The success of that programme is reflected in the dense tree cover which today cloaks the hills around the villages. These trees provide an important source of food, in the form of edible nuts and berries, and wildlife is returning. The springs have been re-charged, and carefully-managed grazing, and the gathering of fuelwood and fodder has been resumed. Meanwhile, the villages have succeeded, through a combination of protest and lobbying, in persuading local authorities to restrict commercial logging activities. Perhaps most important of all has been the success of creating a movement of people, called 'Friends of trees and living beings', which is now active in over 320 villages in the area in promoting environmental awareness and rehabilitation.

Kesharpur is a living testament to the power of local initiative, and to the ability of local communities to achieve change. Much of Oxfam's international programme is directed towards facilitating local solutions to local problems, building upon such community initiatives.

Restoring soil fertility

In southern Zimbabwe, as the story of Dorothy Chiredze recounted at the beginning of this chapter suggests, poor households face chronic problems of insecurity resulting from low rainfall, drought, and soil erosion. Masvingo province suffers some of the worst soil erosion in Zimbabwe, with losses estimated at over 50 tons per hectare every year, and double that in hilly areas. For outside 'experts', the problem is one of over-population in relation to the carrying capacity of the land. For their part, local communities see the problem as one of improving water conservation and land management, and of diversifying their livelihood system.

In 1987, Oxfam began supporting the work of the Zvishavane Water Resources Development project. This began when local farmers in the Midlands district got together to consider co-operative responses to their common problems, pooling local knowledge and expertise. The main objective was to find more effective ways of conserving water. Gullies were blocked with stones, and new systems of 'contour ridging' were developed, cutting across land gradients to slow water run-off. Labour, most of it female, was pooled to build small dams to capture rainwater. Initially, many of these failed as a result of siltation, but a solution was found in stone sandtraps planted across streams. By 1994, 87 wells, 28 small dams, and seven concrete water tanks had been built.

More effective water conservation has created new livelihood opportunities. Within 100m of a dry river bank, and beyond a massive gully parting the soil, women from the village of Chamba are to be found tending flourishing vegetables and relishes grown on neat mounds cutting across the slope of the field, and surrounded by a high ridge. They are members of a small scheme started with a loan from the Rural Unity Organisation for Development (RUDO), which works with 19,000 households spanning six districts. Over 70 per cent of its members are women.

One of them is Rose Mugwira. Like other women, she has four strips of garden land, each about six metres long. Each strip plays a crucial role in reducing family vulnerability. One is used to grow relish for home consumption, providing an important source of vitamins. Another two are used to grow vegetables for the local market, which enables her to buy seeds for next year and pay for school fees, clothes, and household items. The fourth is used to grow food which is sold by the co-operative to generate the funds needed to maintain the small borewell pump and water tank, and hire implements. Water conservation is maximised through the system of ridge cultivation, and through an ingenious system of clay pipes which run under the ridges. Irrigation water is poured into these pipes, instead of on to the soil surface, where it would swiftly evaporate, and is slowly released directly beside the roots of the vegetables.

Market gardening both provides for basic household needs and creates a more diverse income base. Women work on their garden plots most intensely from June to October, when many would previously have been walking long distances to work on commercial farms. It would be wrong, however, to suggest that such community initiatives distribute benefits equitably, or that they are free of problems. Male farmers have played a dominant role in many of the groups developing new conservation measures, but labour demands, for example, in plugging gullies, have fallen most heavily on women. Women also bear the brunt of the new workload imposed by market gardening. Moreover, even where women are involved in designing and implementing projects, poor women often carry less weight in decision-making and have more difficulty in

obtaining loans. Despite this, the women themselves have seen important gains in terms both of household nutrition and opportunities to earn extra income.

Supporting the pastoralist way of life

Throughout the developing world, local communities have suffered from the advice of development 'experts', local and foreign, who see problems in technical terms, and propose technical solutions, to be applied regardless of culture, country, or local context. Such approaches to development seek to impose uniformity upon diversity, often under the guise of narrowly-defined objectives of 'economic efficiency'.

Pastoral farmers have suffered more than most from 'experts'. Their agricultural systems, which involve migration across large areas of land to graze animals, are adapted to the high levels of uncertainty associated with climate in arid and semi-arid areas. Yet planners and aid agencies have spent millions of dollars in imposing ranching schemes and sedentary agriculture upon pastoralists, with socially and environmentally disastrous effects.[78]

Oxfam's own work with pastoralists has evolved over many years, and mistakes have been made. Some of these mistakes were rooted in a failure to build sufficiently upon local knowledge in designing project interventions. Others were a consequence of paying inadequate attention to gender issues. Today, learning about pastoralism from local communities is an integral element of Oxfam's approach, in order to avoid the mistakes of the past. In the North Tokar area of Red Sea State in Sudan, Oxfam has come to understand more about sustainable livelihoods by supporting the survival strategies of Beja pastoralists.[79] Successive droughts in 1980, 1984, and 1990, reduced herd sizes by more than half. At the same time, the adverse effects of drought were compounded as central government and private interests bought up land previously used for grazing, restricting the movement of herds.

Faced with a reduction in rangeland, herd loss, and increasingly regular droughts, many Beja have opted for an agro-pastoral existence, developing sedentary agriculture while some villagers graze smaller herds for part of the year. Thus goats are replacing camels in the hierarchy of tangible assets; cultivation of land and the use of forest resources have taken on a greater significance; and wage labour in nearby Port Sudan has expanded dramatically, as has production of charcoal to generate income.

Oxfam staff have gained an insight into community priorities through participatory learning exercises, and work with the Beja now reflects the diversity of the Beja's own livelihood security strategies and includes programmes which meet the needs of women as well as men, in the following areas:

- group and family gardens; co-operative horticultural farms; seed distribution; agricultural extension; and date-palm cultivation;
- the construction of small wells, water harvesting, and irrigated horticulture
- rangeland rehabilitation, green fodder production, and small-scale restocking, including the purchase of cattle from surplus areas with grain
- veterinary services and training; poultry raising; and predator control
- natural forest management; production of charcoal and higher-value-added wood products for sale in local markets
- income-generating activities such as handicrafts and tailoring; adult education, including literacy classes, and skills training.

Taken together these activities are designed to increase the resilience of Beja groups in coping with a rapidly changing and risk-prone environment. Through diversification into agriculture, and through spreading investment more widely, the Beja should be able to reduce the length of the recovery period following droughts and to develop a wider range of survival strategies. The programme has therefore also concentrated on strengthening village institutions to help the Beja to obtain support for their initiatives from other organisations, government authorities, and technical services. Integral to this approach has been Oxfam's desire to see women guaranteed a greater role in village committees.

Creating an enabling environment

In essence, development is a process of enlarging the range of people's choices by expanding their opportunities and realising their potential. Creating productive employment and income, improving education and health care, establishing the conditions for participation and political freedom, and managing resources in an environmentally sustainable manner, are all elements in the process of human development. Local communities, as the examples cited in this chapter illustrate, are working to make genuine development possible. Supporting their initiatives and drawing upon their ingenuity, energy, and commitment, must be the starting point for international efforts directed towards poverty eradication. This applies to governments, international agencies, and NGOs alike.

But while community mobilisation is a *necessary* condition for development, it is not a *sufficient* condition. Local efforts to protect employment, improve services, and maintain security are unlikely to succeed in the face of economic crisis and the general collapse of social welfare provision. And they cannot compensate for the effects of highly unequal social systems, which exclude vast number of poor people from a reasonable share in the wealth of their society. Community initiatives can help people to cope with crisis and to survive; but it is up to governments to create the enabling environment through which such initiatives can transform societies.

In theory, Northern and Southern governments, international agencies, and international financial institutions, are all in favour of 'human development'. That is one of the reasons why the concept has become a pious hope rather than a force for change; a slogan for recitation at UN conferences rather than an agenda for action. What local communities and Oxfam's partners want to see is principles translated into practice. Their aspirations find an echo in the industrialised countries, where people increasingly want to see a sustained assault on global poverty to create a more secure future for the world.

One widespread misconception is that the starting point for the creation of an enabling environment should be a narrow focus on the redistribution of wealth, rather than its creation. Nothing could be further from the truth. For the world's poorest countries economic growth is an imperative, not an optional extra. For them, a future without growth will be a future of deepening poverty and human misery; witness the current plight of sub-Saharan Africa. But growth alone is not necessarily a prescription for poverty reduction, and does not guarantee that there will be real improvements in people's lives. The issue, then, is not how *much* growth, but *what kind* of growth is likely to eradicate poverty. In other words, development must be concerned both with the creation of wealth and its use to maximise human capabilities.

Seen from the perspective of Oxfam's international programme, existing policies at the national and the international level create a disabling, rather than an enabling, environment for the poor. Poor people are the first to suffer during periods of economic recession, and the last to benefit from economic recovery. In some cases, economic growth actively contributes to the further marginalisation of the poor. Conversely, the rich are usually the last to suffer from economic downturn and the first to reap the benefits of national income growth. When public health systems collapse because of falling state spending, the poor pay the price in the form of increasing sickness and higher death rates; the wealthy simply attend private clinics. When adjustment policies seek to restructure economies, the poor typically lose jobs and receive lower wages; the rich make windfall gains from investing in newly-privatised com-

panies. How can this pattern be changed to ensure that poor people both contribute to and benefit from the production of wealth?

Above all, by giving them a stake in society. Patterns of gross inequality which leave large numbers of people landless, subjected to exploitative tenancy arrangements, in insecure employment or on incomes incapable of maintaining an adequate living standard, can never provide a foundation for development. Similarly, poor levels of health care, inadequate education, and restricted provision of services, prevent poor people from fully participating in the process of economic and social development. In both areas, the priority must be to develop people's capabilities and to enable them to use those capabilities productively.

It must be stressed that this is not simply a matter of social justice and ethical responsibility, powerful as these claims for action may be. It is also a matter of economic efficiency. No society can achieve its economic potential, let alone its human potential, where large numbers of people are consigned to poverty, or where inequalities inhibit their contribution. While there are always powerful vested interests prepared to defend the existing order, it is in society's interest to overcome the obstacle to change which they represent. What is essential to achieve this change is the empowerment and democratic participation of poor men and women, who, because of their poverty or because they belong to a minority group, have no means of influencing the critical decisions affecting their lives. This enfranchisement depends on the transformation of closed, autocratic, or repressive political systems, respect for the due processes of law, a free press, freedom of speech and association, and all the other elements vital for an active civil society. Stated differently, democracy is a central part of the development process, and vital to the realisation of human potential.

A strategy for change

In later chapters, we discuss the reforms needed to create an international enabling environment. As we move towards a genuinely global economy, international factors beyond the control of Third World governments, ranging from debt burdens to adverse terms of trade and changes in global economic conditions, have an increasingly important influence on poverty and human welfare. However, governments themselves can do a great deal to enhance the opportunities for the poor and promote equitable growth, as we outline below.

Changing the structure of agricultural production

Many governments have seen peasant producers as a source of 'surplus extraction', through manipulation of the agricultural terms of trade, forced sales of farm products at low prices to the state, and excessive agricultural taxation. Imports of cheap food have been systematically encouraged, even though these destroy markets for local producers and create an unhealthy dependence on imported foodstuffs. Such policies reflect ill-conceived development models, in which the value of peasant farmers is measured by the volume of resources they transfer to industry. The consequent stagnation in the rural economy has deepened rural poverty and impeded economic growth, in part by destroying the domestic market upon which industries depend. A policy framework that offers farmers adequate incentives to increase production is vital for a vibrant agricultural sector, rural employment, and increased self-reliance in food, all of which are necessary to reduce poverty.

Important as the macro-economic framework for agriculture may be, it will count for little as a mechanism for poverty reduction if it is not accompanied by agrarian reform and wider redistributive measures. It is frequently argued that equitable patterns of land ownership are bad for efficiency, on the grounds that bigger farms enjoy economics of scale which enable them to invest and produce more efficiently, especially for export. Such arguments are often based on questionable economic theories or are a defence of vested interests. In reality, large-scale agriculture is less effective than is often assumed, for at least three reasons.[80]

Firstly, the costs of large-scale agriculture are considerable. Some of these costs, such as irrigation subsidies, public investment in commercial farm infrastructure, and subsidised credit and fertiliser, are obvious. Other costs, such as those associated with the use of scarce foreign exchange to buy imported equipment, are less visible. The environmental costs of using that equipment, including tractors and land-clearing machinery, on thin soils such as those in Africa, are considerable.

Second, the large-scale commercial agricultural sector is typically only weakly connected to the rest of the economy. It not only over-uses resources, such as capital and foreign exchange, which are in short supply, and under-uses local labour; but it often transfers out of the country a large proportion of the profits generated. Over half of the profit generated by foreign-owned vegetable exporters in Chile is remitted to the US; and a large share of the income generated by exporting flowers and vegetables from Africa to Europe ends up in the accounts of European transnational companies, rather than in the exporting country.

Thirdly, and most importantly, smallholder production is considerably more efficient than is often assumed. Smallholder producers in Zimbabwe, Ghana, Kenya, and Tanzania have increased production of food and export crops dramatically when they have had the opportunity. So have the smallholder producers of coffee with whom Oxfam works in Central America. Where smallholders have been less successful, it is because of the type of misplaced policy priorities discussed above, or because they are excluded from taking advantage of market opportunities by inadequate infrastructure, lack of inputs, or outright discrimi-nation.[81] Many governments spend consider-ably more on building a marketing infra-structure around large-scale commercial farms than they invest in assisting smallholder pro-ducers to market their produce. This is a grave mistake. Smallholder producers produce more per acre than commercial producers, and they use land more efficiently. In Zimbabwe, around 40 per cent of the country's commercially-owned farmland, its prime agricultural asset, is not utilised. The land which is used absorbs vast amounts of public subsidies and is, in many cases, managed in an environmentally ruinous manner, being over-irrigated or over-grazed.[82] Here, as in other countries, there are sound ecological reasons for favouring smallholder producers. Labour-intensive production, the sustainable management of water and common resources, and cropping systems geared towards the long-term maintenance of soil fertility, all of which are characteristic of smallholder produc-tion, bring important social, economic, and environmental benefits.

Land reform

Agrarian reforms leading to more equitable patterns of ownership and more efficient use of resources are indispensable to poverty reduc-tion and broad-based agricultural growth. The experiences of many developing countries bear ample testimony to this. As the post-war histories of Japan, South Korea, and Taiwan have shown, land redistribution can produce increased incomes which are equitably distrib-uted, and can thus be consistent with the objectives of economic growth and of poverty reduction. There are, however, distinct region-al and country-specific requirements. In most of Latin America, where land ownership patterns defy in equal measure the principles of economic efficiency and social justice, there is a clear case for redistribution. However, govern-ments remain loath to move in this direction because of the entrenched power of vested interests. In sub-Saharan Africa, land redistrib-ution is vital in Zimbabwe and a small number

of other countries. Elsewhere, the aim must be to prevent the privatisation of land rights from leading to an unacceptable concentration of land ownership.

In South Asia, effective legislation to strength-en tenure laws, protect landless labourers and enhance the position of share-croppers is vital. The Indian state of West Bengal has shown what is possible in this area, introducing tenancy legislation which recognises the rights of 1.4 million tenant farmers, and redistri-buting land to 2.5 million farmers following the introduction of land-ceiling legislation.[83] Sub-stantial social benefits have resulted without any loss of production, underlining again the linkages between equity and efficiency. What is most distinctive about West Bengal's exper-ience, however, is the critical role which village-level mobilisation has played in achieving the implementation of agrarian reforms, under-lining the fact that community empowerment is central to any strategy for poverty reduction.[84] Though other states have adopted land reform measures of similar design, in most cases a combination of vested interest and inadequate community participation has rendered them ineffective.

To make land reform effective, a wide range of supportive mechanisms are required. The promotion and enforcement of women's land rights, increased public investment in marketing infrastructure in marginal areas, improved availability of inputs and new technologies, and investment in storage to counteract post-harvest crop-losses, are all necessary. So is support for local production systems. Too often, agricultural extension is seen as a matter of providing improved varieties of seed, and fertiliser and pesticides, rather than of listening to small-holders and supporting their efforts to develop local seed varieties and environmentally sustain-able inter-cropping patterns. In southern Africa, many of the poorest farmers grow cow-peas between their maize to fix nitrogen in the soil. Yet agricultural extension agencies provide them with little suport in the production and marketing of this crop, preferring to promote packages of hybrid seeds and imported nitrogen fertiliser. There is also a clear need to expand the availability of credit at affordable rates. Change in each of these areas will require the adoption of new priorities. But it will also require institutional reform. The decentralisation of extension services, more participative structures, and investment in staff training are necessary in many countries.

Changing the structure of employment

Like their rural counterparts, poor urban populations need a viable macro-economic framework to give them a share in national prosperity. The focus should be on the creation of secure employment at wage levels compatible with the maintenance of reasonable living standards. In the past, permanent and indiscriminate protection of capital-intensive industries has failed to achieve this objective. Today, the deregulation of imports and the parallel deregulation of labour markets, whether undertaken by governments under their own volition or prompted by conditions attached to loans, is increasing insecurity and reducing wage levels.

Once again, there are no simple prescriptions. However, the selective and temporary protection of potentially competitive labour-intensive industries is vital. So, too, is the promotion of a manufacturing base capable both of competing with imports and expanding exports. One of the most significant factors in South-East Asia's economic success was the provision of targeted credit to export industries, coupled with an active policy of carefully regulated protection, control over foreign investment, and the promotion of indigenous industries producing high-tech goods.

In many countries, labour market deregulation has been carried to excess. Starvation-level wages are not only socially unjust, they are inherently inefficient, for the simple reason that malnourished workers are not productive. The establishment of minimum wage levels, regulations to protect health and ensure safety, and equal pay for men and women doing equal work, should be the touchstones of modern employment policy. Instead, most governments and international financial institutions are promoting labour-employer relations in which the scales are heavily weighted against the weak in favour of the strong.

The effective alleviation of urban poverty will also require action at several other levels. Recognition of the rights of urban settlements to improved housing and public utilities is vital. So, too, is the withdrawal of unfair restrictions on the informal sector, including zoning regulations designed to prevent petty-trading. In many cases these regulations, which in Africa's case were drawn up during the colonial period, have been designed to protect the interests of established large-scale traders. Measures to provide credit and other forms of marketing support to the informal sector are also necessary, to expand employment opportunities.

Changing spending priorities for social welfare

For reasons which we have outlined in this chapter, social welfare provision is central to poverty reduction and economic growth. Healthy and educated people can, through productive employment, contribute effectively to economic growth. They can also benefit more from that growth. It is often argued that developing countries lack the resources substantially to improve the health care, education, and nutrition of poor people. But what is actually lacking in most cases is the political will to make these resources available and to invest them in an equitable manner.

Collectively, developing countries spend around 10 per cent of their government budgets on social priority areas. Doubling this to 20 per cent, as the UNDP and UNICEF have proposed, would generate approximately $30bn: a sum which would be sufficient to meet the minimum targets set for improving human welfare at the World Summit for Children.[85] This target could be met through a combination of raising increased revenue, transferring expenditure from non-priority to priority areas, and greater financial accountability. As we argue in Chapter 6, debt relief and well-targeted development assistance also have a significant role to play.

Changing taxation structures

The scope for increased revenue generation is particularly extensive in Latin America, which currently has the world's most inequitable income distribution and least progressive taxation system. Taxation in the region generates the equivalent of just under 4 per cent of GDP, which is 2 per cent lower than the average for developing countries as a group. Personal income tax is less than half the developing country average, while the proportion of tax revenue generated by sales duties (which have a regressive effect) is rising.[86] Bringing Latin American taxation levels up to the average for developing countries would generate more than enough resources to achieve universal provision of basic health care, primary education, and clean water and sanitation.

Clearly, any prescription for raising taxes must consider the wider economic implications, especially for investment and employment. In most countries, however, there is scope for additional revenue creation. For example, the taxation of commercial farm land would both provide a progressive source of tax revenue, and discourage large-scale landlords from leaving it unused. In Brazil, where an estimated 30 per cent of the land owned by cattle ranchers is not utilised, such a tax could provide a significant source of revenue for investment in social priority areas.

An example of what can be achieved has been provided by Peru. In 1990, tax revenue in that country had fallen to its lowest-ever proportion of GDP, representing less than 5 per cent of national income. Three years later, it had doubled to more than 10 per cent. This transformation was achieved partly through radical institutional reforms, which established the tax authority as a credible and independent body, and gave it wide-ranging powers of collection.[87]

During the 1980s, Burkina Faso, one of the world's poorest countries, protected social-sector expenditure during a protracted economic crisis in part by almost doubling its tax revenue.[88] Duties on commercial property, urban rental income, and imported luxury goods all contributed.

Such examples suggest that it is possible for governments to address simultaneously the task of reducing budget-deficits and protecting social welfare by expanding revenue. However, under structural adjustment policies negotiated with the World Bank, there has been an impetus towards the lowering of tax rates on corporations, foreign investors, and higher-income groups. This approach has been driven by a perception, informed by economic theories popular in Europe and North America during the early 1980s, that high taxation has been a major deterrent to investment. In many cases, however, taxation has been a minor deterrent to investment in comparison with infra-structural collapse and low skills-levels, which require public spending for their correction. Where structural adjustment policies result in massive gains for upper-income groups, they should be subject to a new windfall-gains tax. Examples would include the high rates of return generated for large-scale commercial agricultural exporters from currency devaluation and increased rights to hold foreign currency; the profits generated by privatisation and short-term speculative capital flows; and trading profits associated with the opening up of markets for imported luxury goods.

Reducing military spending

Military spending represents a massive diversion of resources from investment in human capacity, throughout the developing world. Over the past two decades, that spending has risen twice as fast as national incomes, and represents around $120bn.[89] Even more disturbing than this overall figure, is the proportion of national resources diverted to the military in some of the world's poorest countries. Sub-Saharan Africa, for example, devotes on average 3 per cent of its regional income to military expenditure. However, in the case of individual countries, the picture is even worse. For example, in Sudan, the Government allocates 16 per cent of its budget to the military, most of which goes towards financing a war against its own people in the southern part of the country. The health budget, by contrast, accounts for 0.3 per cent of expenditure. This is in a country where life expectancy in the southern region is 36 years: one of the lowest in the world.[90] In 1991, the Nigerian government purchased from Britain 80 battle tanks[91] at a cost which would have enabled them to immunise all of the two million un-immunised children in the country, and provide universal primary education in its poorest state.

While military spending has fallen by 20 per cent in the industrialised world since 1989, it has declined by less than ten per cent in the poorest countries. Citizens in the developing world suffer in a dual sense from the preoccupation of their governments with military hardware. First, they may become the victims of its deployment, since governments in the developing world are far more likely to use the military machines against their own citizens than against other nations. Second, military expenditure entails reduced provision of welfare services which are vital to poverty reduction. Governments may stress the need for defending the 'security' of their countries by military means. But whose security are they talking about? Citizens in the developing world are 33 times more likely to die because they lack a supply of clean water and sanitation, than as a result of conflict. When they do die during conflict, it is relatively rare for their deaths to be caused by external aggressors.

Overall, African governments were able to find $8bn for military spending in 1991, despite the pressing social needs of their peoples. To put this figure in context, it was equivalent to roughly three-quarters of the aid received by the region; or slightly less than the sum needed to meet the minimum targets for improving nutrition, basic health, education, water and sanitation, and improved health care for women agreed at the World Summit for Children. African governments are not alone in their addiction to costly military hardware. Between them, India and Pakistan account for just under half the total number of people in poverty. They also account for just under one-fifth of world arms imports. During the 1980s, Pakistan spent six times as much of its budget on the military as on health, education and agriculture *combined*. As a consequence, the country has some of the world's most impressive fighter jets, tanks and anti-aircraft systems, and some of its most depressing social indicators. These include infant mortality rates which are 9 per cent higher than the average for low-income countries, and primary school enrolment rates which are 25 per cent lower. Out of 177 countries on the UNDP's Human Development Index, Pakistan rated 132. For its part, India in 1992 spent more purchasing 20 MIG aircraft from Russia than it would have cost to provide primary education to the fifteen million girls who get none.

Reducing military expenditure in developing countries by 25 per cent would release extra resources which could double special priority spending. As we argue in Chapter 2, impressive human welfare gains could result from lowering military spending, although the vested interests involved in this sector are politically powerful. Northern governments could assist in the task of reducing military budgets both by providing financial support for demilitarisation, and by curtailing their arms exports. In Oxfam's view debt relief and development assistance should be linked to targets for reducing military expenditure. The peace dividend thus released should be used to finance the attainment of targets for improvements in social welfare agreed under the

National Plans for Action drawn up after the World Summit for Children. It might be suggested by some that this amounts to a violation of sovereignty. However, excessive military spending represents an obstacle to the attainment of the fundamental human rights enshrined in the UN Charter, which all governments have a responsibility to uphold.

Redirecting government spending

Almost all Third World governments need to undertake a fundamental review of their social spending allocations. Currently, most concentrate expenditure in areas where the returns to society are lowest, and the returns to the wealthy are highest. In Latin America, over half of government spending on education is directed towards the children of families who come from the wealthiest fifth of the population. In sub-Saharan Africa, university

Figure 1.2 Comparative spending on primary and secondary education

SOURCE: WORLD BANK

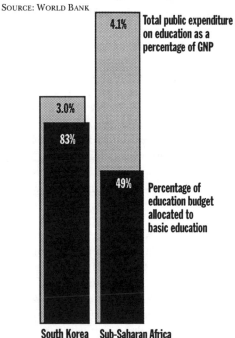

4.1% **Total public expenditure on education as a percentage of GNP**

3.0%

83%

49% **Percentage of education budget allocated to basic education**

South Korea   Sub-Saharan Africa

students receive levels of investment which are 60 times higher per student than for primary school children. Such expenditure patterns, repeated in the health sector, again protect the vested interests of the powerful, but represent a wasteful use of scarce resources in terms of the needs of society as a whole.

In many developing countries, misuse of public resources for extravagant or corrupt purposes is widespread. An impressive monument to excess is to be found in Côte d'Ivoire, where the late President, Houphouet Boigny, built a vast Catholic basilica, modelled on St Peter's in Rome, in his home village. Finished in Italian marble and trimmed with stained French glass, the church cost the equivalent of twice the combined budgets for health and education. This is in a country where seven million people have no basic health services and where an estimated one million children are malnourished.

In some cases, Third World governments have treated their country's wealth as a personal treasury, to be plundered and transferred to foreign bank accounts. In Kenya, financial fraud involving the falsification of export and import invoices in connection with structural adjustment loans, cost the country an estimated $430m between 1991 and 1993; more than the combined health and education budgets.

Successive Nigerian governments have enriched elites, and failed to account for large amounts of public funds. During the Gulf War a special government account was created to hold the windfall gains resulting from the rise in prices for the country's oil exports. These reached an estimated $12.4bn. In 1994, however, a Central Bank panel investigating the account revealed that $12.2bn had been spent without authorisation.[92] Some of that money was doubtless directed towards legitimate items of public expenditure, but much of it was directed towards foreign bank accounts. The head of the Central Bank panel summarised the economic costs of this misuse of public funds in stark terms:

Had these resources, or even only a significant proportion of them been paid into the external reserves, the impact on the exchange rate, on the attitude of our external creditors, on the credibility of Nigeria and on the environment for foreign investors would have been incalculable.[93]

The benefits of directing even a small part of the funds into priority social investment would have been similarly incalculable. Around 7.5 million Nigerian children under the age of five are malnourished, and the social welfare indicators in large parts of the country are appalling; if the state of Bendel were a country, it would rank bottom of the UNDP's human development index.

Changing political structures

Whereas authoritarian regimes have been replaced by formal democracies in much of Africa and Latin America, this is not sufficient to guarantee respect for basic rights. The resulting political structures of the 1990s are fragile, often corrupt, and impunity is still enjoyed by the powerful, including the military. Lack of an independent judiciary capable of implementing the rule of law heightens the need for information and education about rights. The newness of 'democracies' makes education for citizenship important to encourage active participation in processes of development and democratisation. For example, in Latin America many of the organisations Oxfam supports are working to encourage participation, community action, new moral values of responsibility and solidarity, and a new relationship with the state. The policy reforms needed to make genuine development a possibility will not be sustained without transparency and accountability on the part of governments, and genuine democratisation. Democratic institutions and popular participation in decision-making are therefore essential. If a government is to mobilise a country's resources in the interests of poverty eradication, it needs to interact with the people it represents. Once again, there are no ready-made

models. Multi-party elections can play an important role in improving accountability, but they are not synonymous with democracy. Nor are periodic elections, however free and fair, sufficient to secure genuine participation. Political systems need to be shaped by local needs and circumstances and democratically accountable local, regional and national institutions. People should have the freedom to determine in broad terms who forms the government, what the government does, and to influence the decisions it takes on their behalf. The vital preconditions for democracy are to be found not in unthinking transplantation of Western models, but in respect for human rights, the rule of law, and democratic principles.

All too often governments violate these principles, citing the supposedly 'special characteristics' of their people, or the imperative need to suppress political freedom in the interests of achieving higher rates of economic growth. Such arguments, popular with governments in South-East Asia, are usually a smokescreen for autocracy and vested interest, and they offer a lame rationale for political systems which suppress public participation in the interests of powerful elites. As Wangari Mathai, founder of the Kenyan Green Belt Movement, and herself a victim of political autocracy has put it:

Dictators will continue to argue that democracy is a Western value which cannot work in Africa. But at the same time they deny citizens the right to have constitutional conventions to decide for themselves what type of democracy they want...The truth is that Africans, like all other human beings, want justice, equity, transparency and accountability...They want to create a strong civil society which can hold its leaders accountable and responsible.[94]

Wangari Mathai's words have a global relevance, underlining the importance of strengthening civil and political rights in order to tackle effectively the underlying causes of poverty and injustice and create a more sustainable future for all.

2 A world at war

The nations and people of the United Nations are fortunate in a way that those of the League of Nations were not. We have been given a second chance to create the world of our Charter that they were denied. With the Cold War ended, we have drawn back from the brink of confrontation that threatened the world and, too often, paralysed our organisation.

BOUTROS-BOUTROS GHALI, SECRETARY-GENERAL OF THE UNITED NATIONS

The world has suddenly become unusually complex and far less intelligible. The old order has collapsed, but no one has yet created a new one

VACLAV HAVEL, PRESIDENT OF THE CZECH REPUBLIC

We women do not make war ... we are the ones who have to leave, the ones who have to fight for the survival of our children. We are tired of running, tired of not knowing what the future will bring, tired of not being able to plant. Why don't these people sit together and talk, why are the international organisations not helping the poor?

ELISABETH ALEK, DINKA WOMAN FROM SOUTHERN SUDAN

Introduction

The UN system was, in essence, a product of the bloodletting which made the first half of the twentieth century the most murderous in human history. The failure of the League of Nations to avert a recurrence of global hostilities became a symbol of the wider political failure of the inter-war years. The founders of the UN saw conflict prevention as the ultimate criterion against which the post-war order would be judged. Thus the UN Charter pledged to 'save succeeding generations from the scourge of war', its first Article committing governments to 'maintain international peace and security, and to that end to take effective collective measures for the prevention and removal of threats

to the peace, and for the suppression of acts of aggression or other breaches of the peace'.[1]

Fifty years after the Charter was adopted, the world's citizens are in greater need of a collective security system than ever. Throughout the world, the level of human rights violations resulting from current conflicts and rising violence is unprecedented. The costs are to be measured in deaths, broken lives, the destruction of livelihoods, loss of homes, and increased vulnerability. Yet as the human suffering mounts, the international community's response to conflict appears ever more inadequate.

Among the victims of conflict, the poor are disproportionately represented. Forced to become refugees or displaced within their own countries, millions of the world's poorest people have been pushed, by conflict, to the very margins of survival. At the same time, resources for development are being diverted from efforts to tackle the underlying causes of poverty and injustice, to conflict-related emergency response. Oxfam's international programme is a microcosm of this trend, with spending on emergency responses to conflict rising faster than spending on long-term development work.

People in the industrial world are increasingly aware of the human consequences of conflict. The public has responded to scenes of horror and suffering in countries such as Bosnia and Rwanda with an outpouring of compassion and support for the communities affected. There is less awareness of how such conflicts can cause an accelerating cycle of deepening poverty, insecurity, and violence which ultimately threatens us all.

The nature of current conflicts

In 1911, the *Encyclopedia Britannica* offered its readers a definition of 'civilised' warfare. Such activity, it suggested, was 'confined, as far as possible, to disablement of the armed forces of the enemy; otherwise war would continue until one of the parties was exterminated'.[2] Three years later, Europe hosted its last great 'civilised war', as millions of young men marched off to die. Civilian casualties accounted for fewer than 5 per cent of fatalities.

Contemporary conflicts are, on the *Encyclopedia Britannica*'s definition, distinctly uncivilised. Today, four out of every five casualties are civilians, most of them women and children. According to UNICEF, warfare claimed the lives of 1.5 million children between 1982 and 1992, and left another 4.5 million disabled.[3] Civilians are not, it must be stressed, 'accidental' victims caught in the cross-fire. In many recent conflicts, the systematic killing and terrorisation of civilians, and the destruction of their livelihoods, has been a central element in the strategies of government forces and paramilitary groups. Warfare, as we approach the twenty-first century, is waged primarily against non-combatants.

It is not only in the profile of their victims that modern conflicts differ from those of the past. The UN system was designed to defend the territorial integrity of its members from outside intervention. This reflected its origins in the security perceptions of Western states, themselves shaped by the rival territorial claims of princes, emperors, and empires. Today, however, violent conflict is predominantly an intra-state affair. Of the 82 major armed conflicts which took place between 1989 and 1992, all but three occurred *within* states. These conflicts, often between 'non-traditional' forces under dubious political control, have left more than 40 million people as refugees or internally displaced in their own countries — double the number of a decade ago.[4] Unless the conflicts which have caused these refugee flows are resolved, the number of refugees could rise to 100 million by the year 2000.[5]

Causes of conflict

The causes of conflict are diverse, and every conflict arises from a different combination of circumstances. Ethnic tension, denial of political rights, poverty, and competition over scarce resources can all fuel conflict, and weaken the fabric of nation states, many of which were built on fragile and artificial foundations in the colonial period.

For example, in Rwanda, the occupation classifications drawn up by the Belgian colonial authorities, which divided the population on the basis of asset ownership, provided the grounds for a Tutsi supremacist ideology, and a Hutu backlash. The genocide in 1994 was instigated by members of the Hutu political elite, who feared losing power, and were able to exploit ethnic tensions and fear with terrifying effect.[6] Underlying social and economic pressures increased their ability to manipulate the thousands of young Hutus who carried out the

Figure 2.1 Global refugee statistics 1988 and 1993

SOURCE: UNHCR

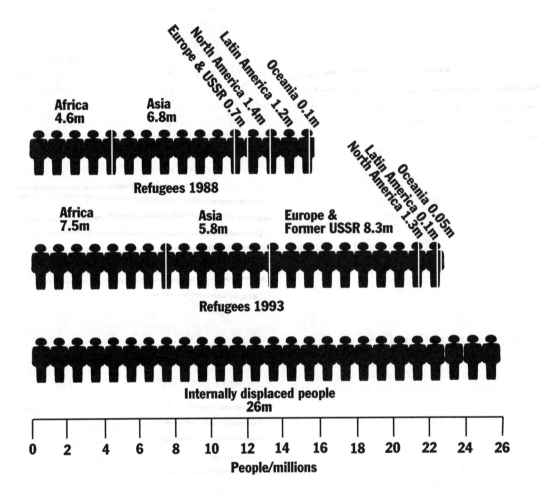

Refugees 1988
Africa 4.6m · Asia 6.8m · Europe & USSR 0.7m · North America 1.4m · Latin America 1.2m · Oceania 0.1m

Refugees 1993
Africa 7.5m · Asia 5.8m · Europe & Former USSR 8.3m · North America 1.3m · Latin America 0.1m · Oceania 0.05m

Internally displaced people 26m

People/millions

massacres. Rapid population growth in Rwanda had contributed to chronic land shortage. Rural poverty was further accentuated by the sharp fall in international coffee prices in the late 1980s and the subsequent collapse in employment and social services. These economic pressures created a fertile ground for the growth of genocidal violence.

Elsewhere, it is the breakdown of systems of political control that has led to the emergence of conflict. The demise of the former Soviet Union, while it marked an end to the Cold War, resulted in an intense struggle for control over resources, often under the banner of competing 'nationalisms' or 'ethnicities'. For example, in the Transcaucasus region, nationalist movements have sprung up and war has ravaged the economic foundations of Georgia, Armenia, and Azerbaijan. Group identity has become an increasingly important — and violent — focal point for dissent and political aspirations.

One hundred years ago, war in the Balkans heralded the collapse of empires, the birth of nations, and, ultimately, the First World War. Now the region is again the setting for conflict associated with the disintegration of states and the rise of nationalism. The breakdown of the system of federal checks and balances maintained by Tito unleashed ethnic tensions and competing claims over land and property. Notions of a 'Greater Serbia' and 'Greater Croatia', supposedly rooted in the mists of Balkan history, have been used to justify territorial expansionism and 'ethnic cleansing'.[7]

'Ethnic cleansing': Rwanda and Bosnia

The horror of modern conflict was presented in its most extreme form by the genocide which swept Rwanda in 1994, when around a million Tutsi were killed by gangs of militia, acting on the orders of the government, armed with machetes, nailed clubs, and fragmentation grenades. One report has compared the scale of the genocide to that of the Nazi death camps; and this in a country lacking the infrastructure and technology of mass extermination.[8] Words can never describe the suffering experienced by the people of Rwanda. An Oxfam staff member witnessed one *Interahamwe* massacre:

> *They sought out and killed seven members of the Tutsi nurse's family... Those killed included a three-year-old boy, his skull split open with a machete blow, and a pregnant woman whose body was split open and the unborn baby exposed... we all witnessed the elderly mission cook being beaten to death.*[9]

Media images of the slaughter in Rwanda briefly diverted public attention from Bosnia, where the term 'ethnic cleansing' was introduced into the vocabulary of modern warfare. Almost a quarter-of-a-million people have been killed and 2.5 million displaced. Civilian populations have been subjected to bombardment, torture, mass rape, and killing designed to achieve the expansionist designs of nationalist Serbs and Croats. The Bosnian conflict has given rise to the re-emergence on European soil of vast ghettos, deliberately fashioned so that the communities trapped within them can be terrorised, starved, and demoralised, and their will to resist destroyed.[10]

Though no side has entirely refrained from committing atrocities, the Bosnian Muslims have suffered most. The Muslim districts of towns such as Mostar, Gorazde, Sarajevo, and Kosevo, and towns such as Bihac, for example, have been the targets of relentless bombardment and sniping, often under the gaze of UN troops designated to protect 'safe areas'. Food, water, and electricity supplies have been cut and hospitals destroyed. Humanitarian relief to these ghettos has been systematically disrupted. In December 1993, for example, Oxfam was involved in delivering food and clothing to the citizens of Tuzla. However, staff reported that less than 14 per cent of the minimum food requirements were allowed through Serbian militia lines.

Women and war

Women have been the targets of particularly sadistic forms of violence, intended to degrade and terrorise them.[11] In 1993, the UN Economic and Social Council, which sent a delegation to Bosnia to investigate that violence, concluded: 'rape has been used as an instrument of ethnic cleansing...In this context, rape has been used not only as an attack on the individual, but is intended to humiliate, shame and terrify the entire ethnic group.'[12] Estimates of the number of women raped in former Yugoslavia range from 50,000 to 80,000.

In Rwanda, too, women have suffered terrible ordeals. The extent of rape by militiamen may never be fully known because of the stigma that disclosure brings. But it is clear that thousands of women were raped. Today many face the trauma of bearing the offspring of men who killed their families, and of being infected with HIV/AIDS.

The role of the media

We live in a world of global communications, and our perceptions of that world are increasingly shaped by news reports and television images. News coverage of the genocide and subsequent refugee crisis in Rwanda played a vital role in influencing public opinion. The images of refugees dying in the town of Goma elicited an overwhelming public response, which generated record levels of donations to agencies such as Oxfam, and demands for international action.

Amidst the carnage in Bosnia, it was a single act of destruction which brought the reality of the civil war to the attention of the Western public. The slaughter perpetrated by Bosnian Serbs who fired a single mortar shell into a Sarajevo bread queue in February, 1994, was not, by their grotesque standards, an exceptional act. But its capture on film generated an unprecedented wave of revulsion. It also prompted a threat of military action by NATO to defend civilian populations.[13]

The media have become powerful vehicles for change. Yet the media's preoccupation with 'news' stories with a novel interest for Western audiences has contributed to a perception of conflict as a passing phenomenon, which ceases to be of relevance once past its news 'sell-by date'.

Forgotten wars

Many conflicts barely register on the scale of international concern, either because they are considered unimportant to the West, or because they are regarded as yesterday's news. From Mali to Peru to the Transcaucasus, conflicts continue hidden from the glare of international attention. Yet these conflicts are destroying lives, displacing populations, and ruining livelihoods on a vast scale. In the Peruvian cities of Lima and Ayacucho, Oxfam works with local NGOs which are responding to the needs of over half-a-million people driven from the countryside by government forces and the Sendero Luminoso guerilla movement. In Burundi, where inter-ethnic violence again threatens to engulf the country, Oxfam responded to the conflict in 1993 which left over 200,000 people dead and many more displaced. In Angola, approximately 500,000 people were killed in the two years of war following the

breakdown of the accord between the Government and rebel UNITA forces. Angolan cities, such as Huambo, Cuito, and Luenga, are scenes of destruction reminiscent of Stalingrad.[14] Such conflicts cause immense human suffering, yet they have gone largely unreported in the industrial world.

The public concern generated by media coverage in Rwanda, Bosnia, and Somalia also contrasts strongly with apparent indifference towards other countries, such as Afghanistan. Five years after the departure of Soviet troops, that country remains trapped in a vicious civil war between the various Islamic groups which overthrew the previous regime. Backed by a variety of regional powers, including Pakistan, Iran, and Saudi Arabia, these groups conduct their struggle for control of Kabul, mainly by firing unguided missiles into the civilian populations living in areas controlled by their opponents. Oxfam works with some of the two million people who have fled Kabul, supporting their efforts to survive. Each has a harrowing tale to tell. Many have seen relatives killed, some 20,000 civilians having died in the past two years. Among the displaced survivors are families who have had to endure winters of sub-zero temperatures living in tents.

The media has a vital role to play in raising awareness of suffering, and in generating the public pressure needed to influence governments. But the absence of Western cameras should not be allowed to consign the victims of many of the world's most brutal conflicts to the margins of international concern. The media-driven public perception of conflict as a brief emergency, to be followed by rehabilitation and the return of normality, is far from the truth. In many of the countries in which Oxfam works, conflict is now a permanent reality to which communities adapt through elaborate survival strategies.[15]

Permanent conflicts

One such conflict is taking place in southern Sudan. It is a conflict which has rarely figured on the Security Council agenda, perhaps because it has not attracted the attention of CNN. Yet for the past 12 years, communities in this region have been trapped in the midst of one of the world's most brutal and least reported civil wars, which ranges different groupings in the south against the Government in Khartoum. At least a million people have died, and another 1.5 million have been driven from their homes either into camps, across borders or into the bush. Behind these statistics are the stories of people like Amer Kuay, a young Dinka woman from the Upper Nile District. This was her testimony to an Oxfam staff member:

We were attacked by cattle raiders working for the government. They took all of our cattle. They burned our houses. They took all our belongings...We were left with no tools and hardly any seed, so we harvested very little. By February we started to starve. There were still attacks by Nuer raiders. So we decided to cross the Nile to Yirol District where it was safer. We had to wait in the marshes for some time to get a fishing boat to take us across. We had no money to pay, so I had to give my daughters' clothes to the fisherman. Some of the people in our group were dying of hunger even as we started to walk from our village. Young children and old people died. I lost my youngest girl. She was just two years old.

Both government and separatist forces in Sudan have shown themselves willing and able to violate the most basic rights of people in pursuit of their military goals. In the Lakes Province of Bahr el Ghazal, where Oxfam is involved in supporting relief and rehabilitation work, civilians have been subjected to attack and aerial bombardment. All factions in the conflict have been responsible for burning villages, stealing or destroying crops and live-stock, and raping women. Long-standing tribal rivalries and disputes over cattle and grazing rights, previously contained by traditional conflict-resolution mechanisms, are being int-egrated into a wider conflict; and they are being settled by automatic weapons. The Nuer tribe which attacked Amer Kuay's village were both cattle raiding and exacting reprisals. Such

atrocities are not new. What is new is the destructive capacity of all sides in the conflict, and their willingness to use that capacity ruthlessly.

Conflict and the destruction of livelihoods

The conflict in Sudan illustrates how tribal and ethnic tensions can underlie strategies designed to disrupt food systems, destroy social life, and rob people of their means of survival. These strategies have left some 7.5 million people vulnerable to the effects of conflict and drought — among them people like Amer Kuay. Like many other women in southern Sudan, she has been displaced many times over and has not seen her husband for several years.

Nobody is immune to the effects of large-scale violence, especially in poor communities. The destruction of assets, crops, and food marketing systems makes communities intensely vulner-able. For the pastoral communities with which Oxfam works in southern Sudan, northern Uganda, and Kenya, conflict is the most per-vasive threat to day-to-day survival. Grazing ranges have become inaccessible, people have lost animals, and are therefore less able to with-stand adverse conditions such as drought. At the same time, the constant uprooting of com-munities hampers efforts to develop health care and education, and improve production, to strengthen survival strategies.

Within this broad picture, women suffer dis-proportionately from the effects of conflict. The loss of male labour forces women to take on more tasks in addition to those of household manager and care provider, often in traumatic situations with little support. Over 80 per cent of refugees are women and their children, and refugee women are especially vulnerable since the traditional support and kinship structures which offered them some protection at home have often broken down. According to one study carried out on behalf of the UN High Commissioner for Refugees (UNHCR), 200 cases of rape were recorded in the refugee camps of north-eastern Kenya during the first half of 1993 alone. (The study concluded that the real rate was probably ten times higher.)[16] Women also bear the wider costs of maintaining family welfare when men leave their villages to join the ranks of combatants, or are killed. In many countries, women face cultural and legal barriers in asserting their rights to resources. In southern Sudan, for example, where over half the households are female-headed, widows often face competing claims for ownership of livestock from the husband's family.[17]

Anti-personnel mines and livelihoods

Anti-personnel mines have come to symbolise the all-pervasive nature of modern conflict. They were invented as a defensive, tactical battlefield weapon designed to delay and demoralise advancing armies. But today, mines are used as indiscriminate weapons of terror to render fields uncultivable and roads and paths unusable.[18] They disrupt supplies and destroy food systems — and they kill and maim people. Afghanistan is the most heavily mined country in the world, followed by Angola. In Cambodia, where there are two mines for every child, one person in every 236 is an amputee, and mines claim over 500 victims a month.[19]

Unlike armed forces, mines do not respect peace settlements. Even after peace returns, civilians continue to be killed and maimed by anti-personnel mines as they try to reclaim their lands. In Mozambique, the South-African-backed rebel movement, Renamo, and government forces, systematically laid mines to disrupt food production in territories under their rival's control.[20] Mines were a major hinderance to the development of Oxfam's programme in Zambezia Province, prior to an extensive demining programme carried out by the Halo Trust. In Afghanistan, there are estemated to be 10 million mines in the fields, and irrigation channels, making it impossible to resume normal life or restart production. The tragedy of one family of returned refugees, interviewed by Oxfam staff in 1993, illustrates the plight of many: within hours of returning, after more then a decade in exile, their daughter was killed when she stepped on a mine. According to British deminers in Afghanistan, it can take six weeks to clear an area the size of a football pitch; at present rates of progress, it will take thousands of years to demine the country.

Structural violence and livelihoods: the Occupied Palestinian Territories

One effect of the television images of current conflicts is that people in the North think of conflict in terms of violent death and destruction. That is the reality in some countries. In others, however, conflict has less visible effects, destroying livelihoods and causing human suffering through forms of structural violence which are no less real, but which lend themselves less readily to sensational news coverage. One powerful example of such violence is to be found in the Occupied Palestinian Territories, where Palestinian livelihoods have been systematically undermined by the policies of the Israeli authorities.

Land is one of the issues at the heart of the conflict between Palestinians and Israelis. Since 1967, Israeli authorities and settlers have confiscated over two-thirds of the land area in the West Bank and 40 per cent of the land in the Gaza strip, which is home to a Palestinian population of 750,000 people.[21] This loss of control over land has been accompanied by a loss of control over the most vital and scarce resource for agricultural production: water. Less than 85 per cent of the aquifer system under the West Bank is used by Palestinians. The rest is diverted through a system of aquifers and deep wells to Israel, which derives a quarter of its water from the West Bank, and Israeli settlements on the West Bank, where water consumption per head is eight times higher than among the Palestinian community. Over half of Palestinian villages have no piped water supply, leaving them dependent on rainfed springs and increasing their vulnerability to water shortages.

The loss of Palestinian control over land and water has been reinforced by Israeli control over markets. Exports of Palestinian fruit and vegetables to Europe have been tightly controlled in the interests of protecting markets for Israeli producers. At the same time, Palestinian exports to Israel have been limited by import controls, whereas Israeli agricultural exports to the OPTs have not been subject to restriction. The destructive effects of this unbalanced trade regime on Palestinian rural livelihoods have been compounded by the Israeli government's policy of agricultural subsidisation. Cheap credit, minimum price support, investment in marketing infrastructure, and massive irrigation subsidies have meant that Israeli farmers on average receive subsidies equivalent to one-third of the value of their output.[22] Inevitably, these policies have resulted in a decline in agricultural output and employment, and a loss of autonomy for communities in the OPTs.

As agricultural production has declined, Palestinians have become increasingly dependent on employment in Israel. In the mid-1980s around 120,000 people from Gaza crossed into Israel every day to work in factories, fields, and on construction sites. However, as the *intifada* rebellion against Israeli control spread after 1987, many work-permits for Palestinians were withdrawn. Today, fewer than 20,000 permits are distributed.[23] The results have been devastating. Unemployment in the Gaza strip exceeds 60 per cent, factories and workshops have closed due to the loss of purchasing power, families have been forced to sell off their assets to survive, and social welfare indicators among children have worsened.

Discriminatory economic and social policies have been coupled with a failure to invest in social welfare provision, amounting to a failure to recognise the basic rights of Palestinians to health care. Whereas per capita spending on health for an Israeli citizen is $350, the figure for Palestinians is $35.[24] Poverty, contaminated water supplies, and poor sanitation, mean that preventible diseases such as gastroenteritis, respiratory infections, and diarrhoea are major killers of Palestinian children. Symptoms of malnutrition are found in around one-third of Palestinian children and several epidemic diseases have not yet been eradicated, including typhoid and infectious hepatitis. According to the Union of Palestinian Medical Relief Committees, one of Oxfam's project partners, infant mortality rates are some five times higher in the OPTs than in Israel.[25]

Palestinian civic organisations are attempting to address some of these problems. The Palestinian Hydrology Group is working in the northern part of the West Bank, rehabilitating natural springs and constructing cement storage tanks in districts, such as Tulkarm and Jenin, which suffer from chronic shortages. The Union of Palestinian Medical Relief Committees, is part of attempts to establish an embryonic Palestinian health system, and has set up 24 permanent health centres and a mobile clinic system, which provide antenatal care, immunisation, and other preventative health-care services. The twin aims have been to address the pressing health needs of the Palestinian people and to create a self-reliant health-care system.

The Palestinian people have suffered deprivation and insecurity as a result of Israeli occupation. Ultimately, however, the security of Palestinians and Israelis is interdependent. Most people in both communities are now convinced of the futility of endless conflict and have expressed a willingness to live as neighbours. This new mood was reflected in the widespread support for the peace accord signed, before the assembled ranks of the world's press, by the Israeli government and the Palestinian Liberation Organisation on the White House lawn in 1993.

Under the peace accord, intended as an interim step towards Palestinian self-rule, Palestinian authorities have recognised Israel's right to exist in peace. This has removed one of the underlying causes of tension between Israelis and Palestinians. In return, however, Palestinians have been granted little more than restricted municipal authority over Gaza and

Jericho. If this were to be a genuine precursor to the creation of a Palestinian state, such limited beginnings might have been an integral part of a peace process. But that prospect of an independent state is becoming increasingly distant in the face of continued Israeli incursion on to Palestinian lands.

Negotiations on the final res-olution of the land issue, which is of funda-mental concern to Palestinians, have been deferred until 1996. On present trends, there will be very little to negotiate about by then. Since signing the peace agreement, Israeli authorities, having pledged in 1992 to halt settlement activity, have been supporting the expansion of settlements, especially around East Jerusalem (the future of which is central to the peace process). Settlements on the Green Line between Israel and the West Bank have also been expanded eastwards, in effect redrawing Israel's borders ever deeper into Palestinian territory. Seen from a Palestinian perspective, this is destroying the territorial foundations for the independent state to which they are entitled. Meanwhile, for Gazans denied the opportunity of employment in Israel, peace has meant a Bantustan existence of mass unemployment and worsening poverty, albeit under the nominal banner of Palestinian autonomy. The result is widespread disillusionment, both with the peace process and the Palestinian leadership.[26]

Seen through Israeli eyes, it is up to the Palestinian authorities to create the security upon which a lasting peace can be built. Faced with repeated attacks from members of militant Islamist groups, security fears in Israel have deepened since the peace accord was signed. Authorities have responded with the planned construction of a vast barbed wire fence around the Gaza strip, and restricting the movements of Palestinians on the West Bank. Yet such measures inevitably reinforce the social pressures which generate violent responses. The danger now is of both sides becoming locked in a vicious downward spiral of violence, as thwarted Palestinian aspiration and deepening Israeli security fears encourage the rise of extremism on both sides. Left unchecked, this spiral will cause the peace agreement to collapse, which would be a disaster for both Palestinians and Israelis.

The diversion of development resources

Contrary to the hopes generated by the end of the Cold War, conflict-related emergencies are absorbing a growing share of international assistance, diverting it from longer-term development. More than half of the UN's budget is now directed towards emergency relief, compared to a quarter in 1989.[27] Bilateral and non-governmental aid is also being re-allocated. In 1993-94, over 6 per cent of all bilateral assistance, or some $4bn, was spent on emergencies — more than double the level at the start of the decade.[28] New claims from the former Soviet Union and the Balkans have added to the demands on the UN. Former Yugoslavia has now become the site of the UN's biggest peace-keeping operation. Since the end of the Cold War, UN operations have involved its diverse agencies in supplying humanitarian assistance, attempting to reduce tension, protecting civilian populations, and overseeing peace processes.

The scale of international funding for conflict-related emergencies points to one of the central dilemmas facing development agencies. As resources are transferred progressively away from longer-term development work, the capacity of the international community to address the underlying causes of conflict is diminished, making future conflict more likely. The upshot is a vicious circle in which more and more development assistance is being diverted into responding to conflicts, whilst totally inadequate resources are invested in poverty reduction, 'preventive' development, and strengthening local conciliation and peace-building initiatives. Quite apart from the human costs of this diversion of resources, responding to conflicts is considerably more costly than preventing them. For example, the first four months of the US's involvement in Somalia cost more than $750 million. That sum is roughly equivalent to UNICEF's entire budget, much of which is an investment in preventing future crises.[29]

Investing more effectively in conflict prevention is one of the central challenges facing the international community. It is not a question of choosing between long-term development or humanitarian relief, but of finding sufficient resources to do both. In the past, development agencies have seen emergency responses, such as the provision of clean water, public health measures, and the supply of seeds and tools, as a springboard to move from disaster relief to rehabilitation and longer-term development. In some countries — such as El Salvador and Mozambique — the resolution of conflict has at last made rehabilitation and development a real prospect. In others, however, including Sudan, Afghanistan, and Bosnia, continuing conflict makes for a semi-permanent emergency. Under these conditions, there can be no neat progression from disaster relief to development.[30] Interventions have to be geared towards supporting local survival strategies, building on people's capacities, and strengthening whatever local structures exist. Support for the efforts of women to develop coping and survival strategies is central to this task. Equally, longer-term development programmes need to build in emergency preparedness and a capacity to be flexible in responding to rising violence and impending conflict. Increasingly, international agencies and NGOs alike must grapple with the dilemma of working in conflict zones where neutrality is at best difficult to maintain, and at worst not recognised in the vocabulary of the parties to the conflict.

Moral dilemmas of working in situations of conflict

Long-running civil conflicts and the emergence of ever more complex man-made disasters have created new challenges both for the UN system

and for NGOs. Attempts to secure the physical survival of civilians caught in conflict, through the provision of disaster relief, are fraught with difficulty and moral dilemmas. Viewed from the perspective of armed factions bent on terrorising civilian populations, there are no 'neutrals' in a conflict. For Serbian forces terrorising Muslim enclaves in Bosnia, for *Interahamwe* militia bent on the extermination of Tutsis, or for Sudanese factions seeking to destroy the social fabric of areas under the control of rival groups, the delivery of humanitarian assistance is inevitably perceived as an act of taking sides: hence their hostility and obstructiveness towards international initiatives.

What may appear to the perpetrators of terror as a hostile act may appear to the victims of that terror as an excuse for inaction in addressing the underlying causes of their plight. Humanitarian relief, most people would accept, can save lives. But a Bosnian Muslim trapped in the 'safe zone' in Bihac might, with some justification, question the purpose of the 'drip feed' humanitarian assistance provided by Western governments, when the same governments have failed to use the means at their disposal for protecting basic rights, defending 'safe zones', and halting ethnic cleansing.

Governments and the UN face great difficulties in resolving such 'complex emergencies'. Where the structures of society have broken down, where the causes of conflict are manifold and interconnected, involving economic, ethnic, political, and cultural issues, there can be no simple solutions. Support for peacemaking, peace-keeping, reconciliation, and reconstruction, are all vital to restore security. Unfortunately, Northern governments have seldom attempted to address these tasks in an integrated manner, especially where they do not perceive a strategic interest. Instead, they have focused on funding emergency relief, increasingly through NGOs. The danger is that NGOs are becoming a humanitarian cover for failure to address the more fundamental causes of conflicts.

Aid and neutrality

The humanitarian imperative to relieve suffering can involve agencies such as Oxfam in complex moral dilemmas, where the relative merits of action and inaction have to be considered. At what point, for example, does food aid become a means of prolonging a war which is destroying more lives than humanitarian assistance can save? Should aid agencies negotiate access to conflict zones with armed groups who have been responsible for appalling human rights violations? There are no easy answers to such questions, especially for agencies caught up in the logistics of responding to a major crisis. Sometimes people in Bosnia vent their anger on aid workers, who offer food or clothing but seem to have done nothing to try to stop the war.

The difficulties inherent in striking a balance are illustrated by events in Southern Sudan. UN agencies responded to the 1988-1989 famine by developing, in negotiation with the Khartoum Government and the SPLA, a humanitarian aid plan, known as Operation Lifeline Sudan, for delivering assistance through agreed access routes. The plan succeeded in stemming the famine and, despite frequent violations by combatants and obstructions to full access, continues today. Civilian lives have been saved in some areas; however, people in other critical areas, such as the Nuba mountains, have not received adequate aid. The food aid has also been appropriated by armed forces to maintain garrison towns, feed troops, generate income, and expand the authority of rival groups over civilian areas.[31]

Guilty and innocent in Rwanda

Particularly stark dilemmas have faced Oxfam and other agencies in and around Rwanda. There is currently a profound debate over whether to continue providing relief to refugees in camps in Tanzania and Eastern Zaire. The camps in Zaire, holding some 630,000 refugees, are now largely controlled by those who masterminded the killing of up to one million Rwandans between April and July 1994.

Having condemned the genocide and demanded that its perpetrators be brought to justice, Oxfam and other agencies have found themselves in the invidious position of delivering aid through structures controlled by the very people responsible for the crimes committed in Rwanda. Hutu militia leaders control the camps and are using them as a base from which to plan armed incursions into Rwanda, and are forcibly preventing refugees from returning home. It is difficult to imagine a graver abuse of international development assistance. Some agencies, unwilling to work with people who are guilty of genocide, have pulled out. Yet if all agencies withdraw, what would become of the hundreds and thousands of innocent and vulnerable refugees, particularly women and children, whose survival depends on the food and clean water provided by the aid agencies?

There is an additional problem. Nobody disputes the fact that there are many in the refugee camps who are guilty of genocide. But to argue, as some human rights groups do, that aid agencies should deny aid to people in the camps who are suspected of committing human rights abuse, would put agencies in the position of becoming judge, jury, and executioner, passing possible death sentences on individuals who have not had a fair trial. In theory, it is the duty of host governments and UNHCR to determine which Rwandans now living in neighbouring countries are true 'refugees'. Dr Boutros-Ghali proposed to the UN Security Council that a security operation should be authorised to do this. Yet, despite an international campaign, the governments who could deliver the resources see Central Africa as peripheral to their interests and have failed to act on the Secretary-General's advice.

Human rights and relief

Article Three of the Universal Declaration of Human Rights states: 'Everyone has the right to life, liberty and security of person.' While humanitarian agencies have traditionally seen the lack of material resources (food, clean water, sanitation) as the most pressing concern, human rights groups have focused on violations to physical security and civil rights. This compartmentalised approach is no longer valid. The indivisibility of rights means that the right to relief, for example, is neither more nor less important than the right to protection from physical attack. Indeed, the enjoyment of one right is often conditional on the protection of the other. Difficult judgements may have to be made on what action will do most to relieve suffering, both in the short and longer terms. For example, in Kumi in 1989, Oxfam suspended relief operations in protest at aspects of the Ugandan government's anti-insurgency campaign. In this case, government policy was changed and relief operations were resumed.

Despite their different position in this debate, and despite problems of NGOs failing to co-ordinate their interventions, some humanitarian agencies are working together to address common concerns. In Goma, for example, MSF-Holland, MSF-Belgium, Oxfam UK/I, and others, have formed a coalition to develop a common platform and maximize their influence with UNHCR. Aid agencies from around the world are also sharing information and ideas about working in complex emergencies. Such crises, be they in Sudan, Liberia, Somalia or Afghanistan, demand the highest degree of political analysis and critical self-awareness. The debate involves a wide range of people, including human rights groups, UN agencies, UN peacekeepers and multi- and bilateral donors, and should include more people from countries in crisis.

The role of NGOs in situations of conflict

What can NGOs like Oxfam do to help people caught up in situations of conflict? A brief account of some of Oxfam's work illustrates the emergence of new challenges, the continuation of old conflicts, new opportunities for peace, and a wide range of local responses to security threats.

In Bosnia and the Transcaucasus states of Georgia, Armenia, and Azerbaijan, emergency relief has figured prominently, as part of a wider international effort to help people to survive in harsh winter conditions. In Azerbaijan, an Oxfam-supported water engineering project has provided water for 60,000 refugees from the Kalbajar region. Water provision has also been a large part of Oxfam's response in northern Afghanistan, providing for around 200,000 displaced people from Kabul who have fled to Pul-I-Khumri.

Many of the communities with which Oxfam works in Sudan have been displaced several times, losing their cattle, household goods, and crops in the process. For these communities, the primary concern is to reduce vulnerability. Oxfam's programme has focused on women as the most vulnerable group. During 1990-1991, Oxfam gave support to local organisations providing health services to displaced people and orphaned children, and in the following year, to local production of seeds and cereal crops. The programme also started providing basic veterinary services for cattle owners who had moved to Western Equatoria after being displaced from their traditional grazing lands. This veterinary programme, which combines vaccination against rinderpest with training in animal health, provides Dinka cattle owners with a service vital for their livelihoods.

Clean water is a scarce commodity in many of the isolated villages in Lakes Province, many wells having been destroyed or neglected during the war. Local communities, concerned at the threat posed by guinea worm and water-borne diseases, have identified the rehabilitation of boreholes as a major priority. Women attach particular importance to this, both because of the demands imposed on their time by family illness; and because they have to walk long distances to find water. In the Western Lakes area, Oxfam is working with local communities to restore primary health systems which have broken down due to the war, and in distributing seeds, tools, and fishing equipment to enable households to become more self-reliant. Women's groups, such as those belonging to the New Sudan Women's Association, have played a central role in identifying needs and in distribution.

Oxfam now plans to support the efforts of communities wanting to leave insecure camps in Equatoria and return home. Plans have been made to provide some 25,000 displaced Dinka women with the seeds and tools which will enable them to rebuild their livelihoods in Bahr el Ghazal. But local efforts at rehabilitation are highly vulnerable to conflict. During the first half of 1994, for example, a Khartoum government offensive led to the further displacement of 150,000 people, many of them from camps where communities had spent several years rebuilding their lives. This underlines the simple fact that, in the absence of local and international action to achieve peaceful conflict resolution, relief measures are unable to provide a secure foundation for sustainable livelihoods.

Southern Africa was the site of some of the worst emergencies witnessed by Oxfam in the 1980s. Today, there is renewed hope. The peace settlement in Mozambique has enabled work towards rehabilitation, providing seeds and tools for populations returning to Zambezia and Niassa provinces. There are hopes now that a successful outcome to peace talks in Angola will make a longer-term development programme possible in that country also. Such a programme has already begun to emerge in the town of Cubal, where Oxfam has supported an integrated water, sanitation, and health management programme, originally developed in response to a huge increase in the numbers of displaced people arriving from war zones. That programme has had a positive impact on the lives of people in Cubal. If the war continues, it will serve as a model for the development of Oxfam's programme in other parts of the country. If the peace holds, the priority will be to support the return of the half-a-million people who have been displaced from Benguela Province, enabling them to re-establish agricultural production. Such a

programme would involve not merely the distribution of seeds and tools, and provision of safe water supplies but also investment in the restoration of infrastructure and the government's capacity to maintain it. Developments in Angola will depend, to a considerable degree, on whether the international community commits itself to supporting the peace process.

Many of the conflict-related problems faced by Oxfam's project partners do not receive much international attention. In Peru, for example, some 600,000 people have been driven from their homes by civil war and violence in the countryside. Large numbers of these people now live in the city of Ayacucho, where Oxfam's project partners are supporting efforts to establish land rights, providing basic housing materials, and organising therapy for children traumatised by violence.

What these local initiatives have in common is a concern to reduce the vulnerability and stress facing communities trapped in conflict. Ensuring survival is a first step. But the wider objective is to build self-reliance and enhance the capacity of people either to adapt to the insecurities associated with conflicts, or to grasp the opportunities provided by peace.

Winning the peace

Unless the underlying causes of violence are addressed as part of the peace process, the potential for renewed conflict will remain intact. This is powerfully illustrated by the experience of El Salvador, where forms of injustice and inequalities handed down from the colonial period to the present day fuelled the country's civil war. Today, the fighting has stopped; but as the following quotation suggests, the struggle for peace and justice continues:

The struggle is not over; the peace accords have brought a ceasefire, the shooting has stopped and the bombing has stopped, but the roots that gave rise to the war are still there.

These are the words of Miriam Ramos,

Mayoress of the municipality of Perquin. They eloquently summarise the situation in El Salvador. Much has been achieved in terms of ending the armed conflict which paralysed the country for 14 years and creating a framework for peace. The UN has played a central role in these achievements. However, the structural roots from which the conflict sprang remain intact. Social injustice and the denial of basic rights have survived the peace settlement. Grossly unequal land distribution, one of the main causes of the war, has yet to be properly addressed. Unless those issues are tackled and the foundations for a new social order established, there is a real danger that the peace will be lost.

The UN's involvement in El Salvador's peace settlement extended from peacemaking, to peace-keeping and post-conflict reconstruction. Both of the first two tasks were performed with remarkable success — a success made possible by a growing recognition on the part of the El Salvador business elite, the government, and the Farabundo Marti Liberation Front (FMLN) that the civil war had reached a stalemate. Pressure from the US on the El Salvador military to enter negotiations, reversing past policy, reinforced the peace process. Between 1990 and 1992, the UN monitored the ceasefire and sponsored peace talks. These culminated in a series of peace accords, covering demobilisation, the reform of the judiciary, and measures to support post-conflict reconstruction. The UN verification mission (ONUSAL) played a key role in protecting human rights and overseeing compliance with the peace accords.[32] Demobilisation was followed by elections, which saw the FMLN force a second-round run-off in the presidential elections, and establish itself as the main opposition to the ARENA government.

In contrast to peace-making and peace-keeping, the task of post-conflict reconstruction has been less successfully addressed. The peace accords themselves speak of an approach to reconstruction which 'reflects the will of the nation'. They include a programme for land-transfer to refugees and internally displaced people previously living in former conflict zones, and a commitment to supporting community initiatives. However, two years after the accords, many of the beneficiaries of the land-transfer programme had still not received titles to land.[33] In the province of Morazan, where Oxfam is supporting local NGOs working to resettle returning populations, no land at all had been distributed by mid-1994.

Equally disconcerting has been the adoption of a top-down approach to development, which has ignored the wealth of community initiative built up during the war years. The National Reconstruction Plan (NRP) is a blueprint for economic management drawn up by government and donors, with its focus firmly on large-scale infrastructure projects. Pro-government NGOs have received the bulk of funding for community initiatives, while many of Oxfam's partners with expertise in grassroots work with communities in former conflict zones have been by-passed. Municipalities formerly controlled by the FMLN have also faced extreme difficulty in obtaining funds.

Post-war structural adjustment

One of the reasons for the government's failure to build a new model of development from below can be traced to the economic reforms which it has embraced. Under a structural adjustment programme, negotiated with the World Bank and the IMF prior to the peace accords, the focus of economic policy has been upon export-led agricultural growth, the accelerated commercialisation of farming, a reduction in the role of the state, allied to stringent and deflationary controls over government spending.[34] Seen through the lens of history there is something incongruous in this approach to structural adjustment. After all, post-war reconstruction in Europe and Japan was based upon expansionary economic policies designed to restore infrastructure and wider economic activity. Similarly, the state was allocated a pivotal role in developing health, education and social welfare systems. Yet in El

Salvador, where there is a vital need for planned reconstruction, the state is being pushed to the margins of economic life. Moreover, free-market growth prescriptions are being applied in a context where the vast majority of the rural poor are excluded from markets. As Miriam Ramos' observation cited above suggests, this is not a strategy for 'winning the peace'.

The failure to develop a form of structural adjustment more compatible with the needs of poverty reduction in a post-war context, reflects a wider institutional failure. Negotiations between the World Bank, the IMF, and the El Salvador government were entirely separate from the UN-mediated peace agreements. The resulting mismatch between the structural adjustment programme on the one side and reconstruction on the other represents a lost opportunity to establish a framework for poverty reduction. For the World Bank and the IMF, development in El Salvador appears to be first and foremost a matter of liberalising markets, concentrating resources on the most commercially developed areas, reducing inflationary pressure through stringent monetary management, and providing 'bolt-on' measures for poverty alleviation through social welfare programmes.

Building on local initiatives

The alternative approach would be to build upon the 'popular economy': the vast range of activities developed by communities to sustain their livelihoods during the civil war.[35] An example is the Agrarian Reform Coffee Growers' Association (ARCGA), an umbrella group of 17 co-operatives supported by Oxfam. Like other smallholder producers of cash crops, coffee farmers find it difficult to get credit or to sell their produce, and are locked into highly unequal relations with powerful intermediaries, typically selling just after the harvest when prices are low, to meet immediate cash needs. Monopolistic private trading companies control coffee exports. The result is a system which transfers the bulk of the value of coffee produced by smallholders out of the local economy. The ARCG is challenging this system by providing credit through a revolving fund, market information, and processing facilities. A far higher proportion of the final export price stays in the hands of coffee growers and boosts the local economy. With the end of the war, it is precisely this sort of initiative that should be supported if reconstruction is to lay the basis for a longer-term strategy to combat poverty. Yet these small farmer and co-operative initiatives, while technically and commercially viable, cannot get credit through formal channels.

Improved health care and education is also vital. In Chalatenango, a Health Promoters' Association mobilised local communities to develop preventive health care systems during the civil war. Now that the government is refusing to support the maintenance of these systems or to assume responsibility for primary health care, the Association is continuing its work. In the capital, San Salvador, the San Luis community organised basic social welfare provision during the civil war. It is now helping to develop small-scale enterprises to generate local employment and purchasing power.

These examples could be multiplied many times over. What they illustrate is the enormous potential of vulnerable communities to tackle poverty reduction through local initiatives. However, grassroots actions must be matched with government investment to restore social and economic infrastructures. In southern San Vicente, for example, Oxfam project partners identify the need for major road repairs, electricity provision, clean water, and investment in river embankments to prevent seasonal flooding, as major priorities, which are beyond the scope of community initiatives.

Community initiatives provide a framework for a new type of development model, in which poor people act as the motor force for economic recovery and poverty reduction, rather than awaiting the benefits of growth generated by others. Government and international financial institutions have a responsibility to support such initiatives, in the interests of both peace and social justice. But little will be achieved without land reform. El Salvador's highly inequitable system of land ownership, in which a small oligarchy owns over three-quarters of cultivable area, was the central cause of war — and it is the biggest obstacle to winning the peace.

Cost-effectiveness of conflict prevention

There is increasing agreement among policy-makers that preventive diplomacy and comprehensive policies to address the underlying causes of conflict are needed — yet these policies remain conspicuous by their absence.

Without effective conflict prevention, peace and security are bound to remain elusive goals. Once widespread violence is taking place, death, destruction, and suffering are inevitable, and it becomes even more difficult to resolve the underlying causes of the conflict. While the international community has an obligation to ameliorate suffering where conflict occurs, armed humanitarian intervention, sanctions, appeals to international law, and UN resolutions are blunt instruments for achieving peace. There are sound economic as well as moral reasons for investment in conflict prevention. Failure to avert conflict in former Yugoslavia, Rwanda, and Somalia has imposed a huge financial burden on the UN and the international community. In Somalia, for every $1 in food aid which was delivered, $10 was spent on the military and administrative machine which delivered it. On economic as well as humanitarian grounds, therefore, the real battles for peace have to be fought before wars begin.

The fallacy of containment

Winning the battle for peace will require new ways of thinking about conflict. Northern governments are reluctant to commit scarce financial resources to conflicts which have not registered as a source of public concern, or do not represent an immediate threat to their peace and security. The 'CNN factor' reinforces this approach, by focusing public attention upon violence which has already escalated into killing on a large scale. Moreover, the UN system itself is not well adapted to conflict prevention. When that system was established, security was perceived as a military and diplomatic issue. The aim was to defend the territorial integrity of member-states, while renouncing the use of force in international relations, and to respond to crises as they occurred.[36] The end result is a political and institutional framework geared towards responding to conflicts, rather than preventing them from occurring in the first place.

The United Nations Development Programme has challenged this approach by elaborating a broader concept of 'human security', which requires international co-operation to address problems of chronic hunger, environmental degradation, mass unemployment and disease. Through this focus, the UNDP has drawn attention to the profound security threat posed by poverty and social dislocation, and the widening gap between rich and poor countries and rich and poor people.[37]

Despite the favourable prospects for growth in East Asia, the absolute number of poor people in the developing world will continue to grow for the foreseeable future. So will the gulf in living standards between the global underclass and the relatively wealthy. Proximity to centres of prosperity exacerbates the stresses associated with poverty and inequality. As Mexico is integrated into the North American economy, millions of Mexican peasant farmers face destitution. The uprising in Chiapas has already suggested that they will not accept the destruction of their livelihoods without a struggle.

Europe and North Africa
In Moroccan and Algerian cities, which lie close to southern Europe, unemployment rates range from 40 per cent to 70 per cent; poverty levels are worsening, providing highly combustible levels of frustration which, given the

perceived subservience of regional governments to Western states, adds to the attraction of fundamentalist politics. The other attractive option, promoted by tempting televised portrayals of European lifestyles, is migration.

Northern governments are not unaware of the security threats posed by these trends. The European Commission, reviewing relations with the Mahgreb countries of North Africa, commented:

At present, political, economic and social conditions in a number of these countries are sources of instability leading to mass migration, fundamentalist extremism, terrorism, drugs and organised crime.[38]

But while the threats to security may have registered, they have been exacerbated by political inertia. For years, the European Union and the international community ignored Algeria, refusing to reduce the country's crushing debt burden, which immeasurably deepened the poverty of its people, or to provide the development assistance and trading opportunities needed to offer hope for the future. Europe's indifference changed in 1992, when the Algerian government lost an election to fundamentalist parties which, with the European Union's implicit support, it promptly annulled. Violence between the government and its fundamentalist opponents is now claiming between 500 and 1,000 lives a week. In response, a twin-track containment strategy has been adopted. First, there has been a flurry of activity to write-off debt and provide billions of dollars in international aid through the IMF. Second, the NATO alliance has been requested to develop a security network for protecting southern Europe against instability in the region. The tragedy is that the international community seemed indifferent to the impoverishment and marginalisation suffered by Algerians, until Western governments discerned a direct threat to their own interests. Far more could have been done to address the underlying causes of conflict at an early stage. This would have averted the need for implausible and costly military plans now being considered by NATO aimed at ring-fencing North Africa to 'protect' citizens in Europe from political and economic refugees.

The drugs trade

There are parallels with this 'wait for the horse to bolt' approach in the response to the international drugs trade. In countries such as Colombia, Bolivia, and Peru, rural poverty, compounded by debt and the collapse of commodity prices, has made the production of narcotic drugs one of the few viable means to a livelihood for small farmers; meanwhile 'drugs barons' have extended their violent sway over national economies and created a regional drugs economy now estimated to be worth $500bn. The US has attempted to address the issue through a combination of stick and carrot, financing the destruction of coca and supporting one-off payments to take plants out of cultivation. The more effective solution would be to eradicate the poverty which forces producers into drugs cultivation.

Immigration

Containment is also a growing feature of immigration policies in the industrialised world. Often presented through rhetoric stressing the advantages of 'staying at home', these policies are increasingly oriented towards protecting rich countries from problems of conflict and poverty. New and ingenious legal formulations have been found to deny refugees their proper rights. Refugees from Sri Lanka and Bosnian Muslims arriving in some European countries are no longer 'refugees' in law, but 'externally displaced': a subtle legal distinction which allows their deportation.[39] In France, the government has reversed a 200-year-old policy of giving asylum to those in need, adopting in 1993 a 'zero refugee' policy. The interdiction and forcible return of Haitian refugees by the US navy is another example. Not only are the refugee policies of Northern governments becoming less humane, but they also fail to address the underlying causes of the refugee problem: the poverty and social dislocation experienced in much of the Third World. Against this background, the broader measures advocated elsewhere in this report for redistributive policies, debt relief, more equitable management of global commodity markets, and improved development assistance, should be seen as part of a wider, integrated strategy for conflict resolution.

Reducing arms sales

It is sometimes objected that, in a world of scarce financial resources, it is simply not possible for Northern governments to create the social and economic conditions for conflict prevention. Perhaps not — but far more could be done. Redirecting some of the $670bn which Northern governments invest in military expenditure would create new resources for development and poverty reduction. For example, if

Figure 2.2 Weapons sales to developing countries by the permanent members of the UN Security Council

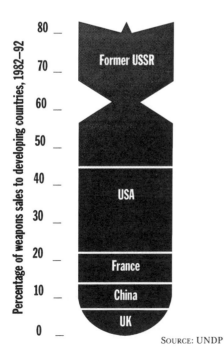

SOURCE: UNDP

Britain were to earmark just a quarter of the savings achieved by bringing its defence spending into line with its European partners by the year 2000, it could meet the 0.7 per cent of GNP aid target, and spend ten times more on meeting priority social needs in developing countries. Reduced military spending would also help to address another of the underlying causes of conflict: the export of weapons to the developing world.

Double standards abound in international relations; and nowhere more so than in the international arms trade. Western governments repeatedly endorse UN appeals for reduced military spending in the South, rightly pointing to its corrosive effect on development. The Security Council issues ringing appeals for world peace. Yet the world's richest countries are responsible for promoting arms exports, sometimes diverting development assistance to do so. Sermons on peace and democracy contrast with policies which inflame conflicts by providing the means for mass death and destruction.

Between them, the five Permanent Members of the Security Council — the US, Russia, China, France, and Britain — account for over four-fifths of the weapons exported to developing countries.[40] These weapons have wrought human destruction on a massive scale. From time to time they have also been used against UN troops, or on soldiers from the supplying country, as they were during the Gulf War and in Somalia. Apart from destroying human lives, arms exports have reinforced the underlying causes of conflict by diverting resources from development. Developing countries now account for 15 per of world military spending, or $118bn annually.[41]

To its credit, the IMF has attempted to draw public attention to the huge wastage caused by military spending, calling for a reduction in expenditure on arms by developing countries. The Fund's managing director, Michel Camdessus, has observed:

In a world of scarce resources we would be derelict in our duty to our membership if we were to ignore the

haemorrhage of financing from productive to unproductive sectors of national economies.

Governments in many developing countries have been derelict in their duty to their own citizens in this respect. But the industrialised countries, too, have been guilty of encouraging military spending.

Part of the problem confronting Northern governments is that they have developed arms industries which rely heavily upon exports to the developing world for their financial viability. Production of the European Union's 'Eurofighter', designed for combat against the former Soviet Union, is going ahead, with developing countries being cultivated as export markets now that European military spending is falling. Over three-quarters of the military exports from Britain, the world's fourth largest supplier, are destined for developing countries.[42] In all, the developing world accounts for over 60 per cent of international weapons trade. These imports are sustained mainly by diverting domestic resources, but military assistance, principally in the form of cheap credit, also plays an important role.

Contrary to the claims of most Northern governments, responsibility for encouraging arms exports cannot be evaded as being a legitimate response to market demand. To some extent, they create the demand by locking countries into ruinous arms races, as each attempts to keep pace with the military hardware of the other. One such arms race is that involving India and Pakistan, diverting sufficient resources to account for one-fifth of global weapons imports.[43] The purchasers must bear the main responsibility for the destruction that will occur should conflict break out, but the suppliers are not without blame for encouraging this huge diversion of resources away from priority social needs.

With the end of the Cold War and a cumulative peace dividend estimated at over $900bn since 1987, the industrial world has an opportunity to scale down its military production capacity by diverting it, through public invest-ment, into socially useful activity.[44] It also has an opportunity to take some responsibility for regulating arms exports to the developing world. Greater public accountability would be a step in the right direction.

Aid and arms

The use of British aid to smooth the way for military contracts with Malaysia drew attention to the limitation of accountability in Britain. So, too, did the Iraq 'supergun' affair. This revealed a web of intrigue, official deception, and covert assistance to provide exports to Iraq during its war with Iran, despite an official prohibition.[45] Private arms traders, operating in a murky world of secrecy, represent a major problem of control in the arms trade. But what the 'supergun' affair demonstrated was the complicity of governments in allowing arms to be shipped into conflict zones, often in defiance of UN resolutions to which they are party. As the head of the public enquiry established to investigate the latter affair observed: 'citizens have a right to know what governments are doing in their names.'[46] This applies even more when public funds are being used for purposes which violate the fundamental rights of citizens in other countries.

There has never been an effective system for monitoring and regulating arms exports, either nationally or internationally. The UN's Register of Conventional Arms, established in 1991, was a step in the right direction. However, it suffers from divergent interpretations and weak reporting procedures. Arms exporters in Latin America and Asia have been particularly recalcitrant in supplying information; and few importers report their purchases. Another serious flaw is that the Register does not cover small arms, landmines, cluster bombs or fragmentation grenades: the very categories of weapons responsible for the majority of casualties in most conflicts.[47]

In Oxfam's view, the UN Register should be reconstituted under a committee of high-level experts reporting directly to the Secretary-General. That committee should be given wide-ranging powers to investigate the arms exports of major suppliers, and to develop uniform and transparent systems of accountability. It should also be empowered to investigate direct and indirect subsidies to the weapons industry, including those given through development assistance budgets. The terms of reference for reporting to the committee should be extended to include all small weapons. Such a system, together with an enforceable code of conduct on international arms transfers, could provide the framework for addressing the second major challenge: namely, a systematic reduction in the volume of military exports. It could also be used as a basis for levying a 1 per cent tax on arms exports, to be used by the UN for conflict-prevention initiatives. Without an open and carefully monitored international agreement, any attempt to limit arms exports would founder as countries sought, through covert activity, to protect themselves against loss of market share.

The UNDP has advocated a 3 per cent reduction annually in military spending up to 2000.[48] If implemented, this would release some $460bn for social development and environmental improvement, providing the resources to demobilise armed forces in the South and relocate workers in the weapons industries of the North. This is a win-win option, which governments ought to endorse. However, arms exporters should also endorse a parallel commitment to reduce by an equivalent amount the value of the arms they export to developing countries and phase out all forms of assistance for military exports. Any linkage between development assistance and arms exports should be prohibited, with immediate effect; and the Development Assistance Committee of the OECD should be asked to prepare comprehensive reports on the current practices of its members in linking aid and arms.

A ban on anti-personnel mines

One category of weapons merits especially urgent action. In theory, the use of landmines against civilian populations was prohibited by the UN Convention on Inhumane Weapons which came into force in 1983. In practice, that convention is a dead letter because it does not apply to civil conflicts, has no monitoring procedure, and no system of sanctions to enforce it. All of which helps to explain why over one million new landmines are planted annually.

According to the US State Department, there are between 65-110 million mines scattered across 60 countries, most of them in unmarked sites.[49] Many of them were indiscriminately scattered from the air, as they were by the Americans in Vietnam and Russians in Afghanistan. Others are deliberately planted in fields and on footpaths by government and rebel forces. What makes them particularly attractive to combatants is their price, which can be as little as $3, and their efficiency in inflicting terror. What makes them particularly hideous from a humanitarian perspective is that they are indiscriminate. Mines are unable to distinguish between the boot of a soldier and the feet of children playing or tending animals, of women collecting water, or men walking to markets.

Every day, more than 20 civilians are killed by landmines. More than double that number are severely injured. For the poor, physical trauma is compounded by the implications of amputation or blindness for their livelihoods.[50] In Angola, which hosts one mine for every person in the country, an estimated 70,000 people have been maimed, blinded or severely disfigured. This is the story of one Angolan victim, José Jamie, a father of six children, who lost both legs just above the knee, recorded by an Oxfam staff member in the town of Luena:

When I met José five days after his accident he was in Luena Hospital in a great deal of pain. He was speaking in a strained whisper, barely audible above the sobbing of his wife. His legs had been amputated and his two stumps bandaged. His wife kept repeating 'how are we going to survive, we have six children.' In a town of over 200,000 people swelled by refugees fleeing the war, the only way of surviving is to grow your own food or rely on UN aid flights. Now José is no longer able to farm his land and UN food is not guaranteed.

José had no idea why the mines had been laid on a path so close to town, since UNITA forces are over 20 miles away. He whispered: 'it's like being dead, without legs what can I do?'

So much suffering is caused to civilians by anti-personnel mines, that in a civilised world, governments would have banned their production and use long ago. Their reasons for not doing so defy belief. The British Government, for example, opposes a comprehensive ban because it believes that anti-personnel mines retain a legitimate military function, and that more sophisticated versions can be programmed to self-destruct. Some mines, it seems, are less reprehensible and altogether more civilised than others. Not, however, if you have the misfortune to tread on one.

Research by the Pentagon[51] casts doubt on the value of anti-personnel mines to the military. The faith placed in self-destruct and self-neutralising mechanisms also seems misplaced. Mines experts estimate a 10 per cent failure rate of anti-personnel mines to self-destruct or self-neutralise, leaving land contaminated and unusable. Whatever the military utility of anti-personnel mines, it is clearly quite disproportionate to the threats they pose to civilians. Their use violates the Geneva Convention, which prohibits acts aimed specifically at harming civilians, and indiscriminate killing. The actions of those who plant anti-personnel mines and those who supply them are in breach of this Convention, and should be treated as such. Governments who, by drawing unworkable distinctions which obstruct a comprehensive ban on the production, possession, use, and export of mines, are similarly in breach of the Convention, and share in the responsibility for the continuing slaughter of civilians by these indiscriminate weapons.

The UN's role in responding to conflict

In the immediate aftermath of the cold War, amid heady talk of a new world order, there was a tendency to regard the UN as the answer to all of the world's problems. But as intra-state conflicts expanded across the globe, and governments allowed one UN mission after another to end in disaster, this optimism quickly changed to pessimism about the UN's ability to get anything right. Ultimately, much of the UN's effectiveness in responding to conflict is determined by member states, and its well-publicised failures reflect the lack of political will of governments and their failure to develop coherent strategies. Like falling dominoes, these failures have had damaging knock-on effects. The fiasco of the UN's intervention in Somalia led to an extreme reluctance to get involved in other conflicts, contributing to the woefully inadequate UN response to genocide in Rwanda. Such cycles of inaction and over-reaction are inherently damaging for international efforts to establish a credible response to conflict. What is needed is a more considered appraisal of the successes, failures, and limitations of the role of the UN, in which its deficiencies are reviewed and practical recommendations for improving its responses are developed.

Preventive diplomacy

The most urgent task currently facing the international community is the development of effective policies for averting conflict. This was recognised by the UN Secretary-General, who stressed the importance of more effective preventive diplomacy in his 1992 *Agenda for Peace*. Yet in reality, if not in rhetoric, the international community continues to regard investment in this area as a diversion from the more pressing concerns of responding to conflicts. This attitude, if it continues, will represent a serious threat to future peace and security.

The dangers of diplomatic inertia are nowhere more apparent than in Bosnia. In 1992, UK Prime Minister John Major opened the London Conference on Bosnia with a ringing declaration of principles: 'The international community will not accept that Bosnia can be partitioned by conquest. Those who suppose that they can secure international acceptance of military advantages gained by force are wrong.'[52] In fact, they have been proved right. Since 1992, the Bosnian Serbs have pursued with impunity their original aim of acquiring almost three-quarters of the territory of Bosnia-Herzogovina to build a 'Greater Serbia'.[53]

Current peace plans drawn up by the 'Contact Group' of Britain, the US, Russia, France, and Germany, will leave the Bosnian Serbs in control of fourth-fifths of the territory they have gained by force — and it will leave as displaced people over one million people who have been 'ethnically cleansed' from their homes. The contrast between the high-minded resolutions of the UN and the international community's inability to stop territorial gains achieved by force of arms, has done immeasurable damage to the credibility of the UN. It has also dealt a blow to international co-operation for conflict resolution, and generated tensions between Western governments.

The virtues of different peace plans and strategies for protecting the Bosnian Muslims are open to debate. What is beyond dispute, however, is that far more could have been done to avert the crisis. For almost three decades, Bosnia's security had rested upon the principle that its three constituent elements would co-exist as equal partners within a republic which, in turn, would be represented in the complex system of federal checks and balances which underpinned the national state. With Germany's unilateral recognition of Croatia in December 1991, the entire system began to fragment into competing and hostile nationalist claims.[54]

Faced with the alternative of an alliance with Croatia (which would have been regarded as a hostile act by Serbia and the Bosnian Serbs), absorption into a Greater Serbia (which linked Serbian communities from Serbia proper across Bosnia and into Croatia), or independence, Bosnia chose the latter, and was recognised by the EU. Predictably, recognition of the Republics without resolving the central political questions of minority rights, acted as a green light for the territorial claims of Serbia and Croatia.

Western Europe and the US could have used their influence to help to identify a peaceful road from the former Yugoslavia, defining new borders, establishing guarantees of minority rights, and adjudicating between rival claims to self-determination. Instead, they announced their support for the two principles of self-determination and territorial integrity, without realising that, for Bosnia, the first principle was bound to contradict the second and lead to war.[55] Once open warfare had started, these political questions were bound to be settled by force of arms, to the advantage of the more powerful sides. The UN declared a series of 'safe areas' and then did nothing to defend them. They proceeded to place an arms embargo on the whole of former Yugoslavia, in effect sharply discriminating against the Bosnian Muslims, who had virtually no weapons, while the Serbs controlled the massive arsenals of the former national army.

The Bosnian conflict represents in extreme form the high costs associated with diplomatic inertia and the pursuit of narrow foreign policy objectives by individual states. But it is not the only example. Had the international community been more attentive to the human and minority rights situation in Rwanda during 1993, when there was clear evidence of human rights abuse, incitement to ethnic hatred, and the training of the *Interahamwe* militia who were later to carry out the genocide, the tragedy in that country might have been avoided.

The UN Secretary-General attempted to address this problem by appointing a Special Representative in October 1993.[56] By then, however, the peace accords made in August between the government and the Rwanda Patriotic Front had already started to unravel, exacerbating tensions. Moreover, his appointment was not followed by concerted international action to make the Rwandan government reconsider the course upon which it had embarked. The UN's failure to act in response to the widespread violence in Burundi in late 1993 probably added to the Rwandan government's conviction that there would be no effective action to restrain its activities.

If the international community believes that conflict prevention is a priority, then preventive diplomacy will have to be taken more seriously.[57] In particular, the UN Security Council must become more alert to early warnings from a range of sources, including governments, NGOs, and the media, and urgently consider preventive action in response. This task might be facilitated by the creation of a new Office of Preventive Diplomacy; or simply by improving existing machinery. The UN should also establish a roster of human rights monitors who can be rapidly deployed to help to calm dangerous situations and provide information to guide the UN in further action. A parallel roster of experienced and competent people is needed for swift deployment as Special Representatives of the Secretary-General to undertake preventive diplomacy.

At the same time, governments, regional bodies, and NGOs, need to do more to strengthen local conciliation and peace-building initiatives, and at all times work to support, not undermine, local capacities and structures, recognising that ultimately the solutions to conflicts have to be found within the societies in which they arise.

The elements for an effective UN response

Responding to complex emergencies has presented formidable new challenges to all the major actors and particularly to the UN. Attempting to provide humanitarian assistance, resolve conflicts, and oversee peace settlements create problems which are far more intractable than those associated with traditional peace-keeping.[58]

There are no blueprints for successful intervention in complex emergencies, each of which throws up its own challenges and problems. There are, however, lessons to be learnt from past policy mistakes. One lesson is that the threat to use force in defence of civilian populations is not effective where there is no intention of doing so. Indeed, such threats become a threat to the

credibility of the UN itself when they are ignored with apparent impunity by armed militia.

This has happened in Bosnia, where UN troops on the ground and occasional NATO air-strikes have been unable to deter aggression against communities in UN-designated safe areas. Differences within the NATO alliance and the Contact Group on Bosnia have compounded the problem. The US Administration has long advocated more intensive use of air strikes and has unilaterally lifted its arms embargo on the Bosnian Muslims. The European Union view is that such an approach offers little more than the hope of a 'level killing field', from which the Serbs would emerge victorious. What is not in dispute is that more concerted use of air-power would effectively terminate the UN's humanitarian mission, illustrating the recurrent tensions between providing humanitarian relief, protecting civilians, and ending conflict.

The US approach is more of an expression of moral indignation than a coherent policy for achieving a just settlement (a fact underlined by US support for a peace plan which recognises the territorial gains of the Serbs). The European alternative is scarcely more credible, not least given the limited ability of the UN to provide humanitarian assistance. What the limitations of both positions underline is the potentially contradictory character of policies designed to address different aspects of emergencies. There are, of course, no easy answers to such genuine dilemmas. However, more decisive action at an early stage of the conflict might have acted as a deterrent to aggression; for instance, the international community might have considered establishing Bosnia as a UN Trust Territory, disarming militia, and defending its borders against external aggression.

Sanctions

Sanctions can potentially play a role in creating the conditions for peace by deterring potential combatants. They could certainly have been applied more rigorously and at an earlier stage against Serbia. However, sanctions and the threat of sanctions have a murky history, and have in the past been manipulated in the interests of major powers. They are notoriously difficult to enforce, and not applied consistently by the international community. For example, Western governments continue to provide Indonesia with military assistance, despite its occupation of East Timor and its well-documented violation of Timorese human rights.[59] In this case, sanctions have never been seriously contemplated, in part because Indonesia represents a lucrative market for Western arms exporters, commercial companies, and foreign investors. In contrast, Western governments have applied highly punitive sanctions against Iraq, seemingly in furtherance as much of US strategic foreign policy objectives as of UN resolutions.

The debate about the use of sanctions is a complex and difficult one, but Oxfam's particular concern is with their social consequences. In Iraq, for example, one UN observer has referred to the conditions they have created as 'pre-famine'. All observers now admit that the conditions in Iraq have become desperate for ordinary people; where they differ is on where the blame lies. Oxfam has responded by helping to supply drinking water in the south, and with an integrated rural reconstruction programme in the north.

However, it is concerned both at the disproportion between the human suffering caused and the objectives of the sanctions; and at the shifting ground which underpins their interpretation. For example, Iraq's recognition of the border with Kuwait was cited as a key condition to be met before consideration could be given to the lifting of the embargo on Iraqi oil sales. However, when Iraq did, in November 1994, recognise this border, the US then stated firmly that this was not enough and that Iraq had to comply with all relevant resolutions. Exactly what constitutes 'relevance' however, is a matter of dispute, between the US and UK on one hand, and the French, Chinese, and Russians on the other.

It seems clear that it is time for an urgent reappraisal of how sanctions are used by the international community. As Dr Boutros-Ghali suggested to the Security Council in January 1995, when sanctions are agreed, the UN should do more to protect humanitarian imports, humanitarian work, and the economies of neighbouring countries.

The need for a rapid response

Another important lesson from past conflicts is that delayed action and incoherent leadership carries with it the potential for disaster. When the killing started in Rwanda, there were over 2000 UN troops in the country, sent there to monitor the cease-fire accord between President Habyarimana and the RPF. The OAU, neighbouring governments, and agencies on the ground, including Oxfam, immediately called on the Security Council to reinforce the contingent. The Council responded by withdrawing the troops, leaving a small rump behind.

The Security Council sought to justify its action by claiming that the UN's 'blue berets' were not equipped to protect lives. Yet the small Ghanaian contingent which remained in the capital Kigali succeeded in protecting some 15,000 asylum seekers. It was not until the end of July, three months after the killing began, that the new contingent of UN peace-keepers arrived.[60] What made the Security Council's inaction doubly inexcusable was the clear evidence, available to the Security Council, that the UN's Convention on Genocide was being violated by a government calling for the extermination of an entire community. The lamentably slow response of the UN was in sharp contrast to the rapidity with which France was able to mobilise a humanitarian force in June 1994 to protect Hutu refugees in the south-west of the country.

So comprehensive was the failure of the UN and its members that the Secretary-General was moved to issue an uncharacteristically stark condemnation. 'We must all recognise,' he said in a report to the Security Council, 'that we have failed in our response to the agony of Rwanda, and thus have acquiesced in the continued loss of human lives.'[61] If there is one single lesson from Rwanda, it is that political inertia must never again be permitted to weaken the capcity of the UN to protect civilians.

Member states should take steps to improve the UN's capacity to prevent or respond to complex, conflict-related emergencies by establishing 'fast-track' stand-by arrangements to provide the UN with the necessary troops, civilian police, logistical support, and equipment to fulfil Security Council resolutions.[62] These arrangements must include field commands and reconnaissance units, and pre-arranged standard fees, so that deployments are not delayed by disputes about finance. In addition, a permanent UN rapid-deployment force for preventive and peacekeeping duties should be created.

The international community could also do far more to strengthen regional capacity for conflict prevention and conflict resolution. This will require financial and logistical support from Western governments. Several African countries, including Zimbabwe and Ghana, offered to send troops to Rwanda if they were provided with the necessary financial and logistical support. Unfortunately, they were not. However, since September 1994, the UK, US, and France have been exploring with the OAU and a number of African governments how Northern governments can support African conflict-prevention and peace-keeping, and similar initiatives could be appropriate elsewhere.

The need for clear objectives

Events in Somalia during 1993 drew attention to another pervasive failure in many UN operations: the lack of clarity with regard both to political and humanitarian objectives and to command structures. The decision of the US to embark on 'Operation Restore Hope', was dictated to a large extent by the public pressure which followed news coverage of the 1992 famine. By the time the troops arrived, over 300,000 Somalis had died. The delivery of bulk food aid did save some lives, but the worst of the food crisis was over.[63] It was replaced by a political crisis, as the UN became entangled in a military conflict with General Aideed, the leader of the largest clan faction, after the breakdown of peace talks. By launching a concerted offensive against Aideed, the UN lost any claim to neutrality, undermining its entire political strategy. It also lost public support, as civilian casualties mounted and reports of human rights abuses by UN troops became widespread. Overlapping military command structures, which resulted in UN forces and the US pursuing different and independent strategies, added to a deepening sense of confusion.

The UN's disastrous military involvement in Somalia ended as it had begun, with media images of the conflict shaping policies. News coverage of the mutilated bodies of US helicopter pilots generated overwhelming public pressure and led the Clinton Administration to fix an early date for US withdrawal. By the beginning of 1994, most UN troops were confined to their barracks. Early 1995 saw the withdrawal of these troops and the looting of what remained of the UN's presence. The failure in Somalia created a pervasive sense of disillusionment over the UN's ability to intervene politically to resolve conflict. It also highlighted the UN's cumbersome command structures and the lack of co-ordination between its different agencies.

The need for improved co-ordination

Part of the problem facing the UN is the sheer size and logistical complexity of many of its operations. To be effective in peace-keeping, these operations require an integrated and coherent command structure, which is capable of responding swiftly to volatile situations. What exists at present is an unwieldy series of chains of command involving the Security Council, national governments, and UN troops on the ground. The time-lag between establishing and deploying intervention forces is also considerable, as was seen in Rwanda.

With regard to relief operations, governments seem to be moving away from a consensus on how to manage UN humanitarian activities. The high hopes in 1991 for a more effective international system gave rise to a British and German initiative in the G7 and UN for the establishment of the UN's Department of Humanitarian Affairs (DHA) in 1992. But the DHA has never been given the staff or resources necessary to co-ordinate the different UN agencies involved in humanitarian aid.

Recent experience confirms that the UN's humanitarian operations are most successful where there is clarity among all the relevant agencies about who is co-ordinating the plan. This can be DHA, as in Rwanda or Angola, or the UN High Commissioner for Refugees (UNHCR), designated as the 'lead agency' in former Yugoslavia. An effective UN humanitarian co-ordinator can provide a single point of reference for NGOs, the host government, and other local agencies, facilitating effective co-ordination. Success depends on their having considerable delegated authority from head office in New York or Geneva and active engagement with local agencies and international NGOs.

What is most important is that, in each crisis, the best system of co-ordination should be rapidly agreed and implemented. The UN's Inter-Agency Standing Committee, chaired by the head of DHA, and including the heads of the relevant UN agencies and NGO representatives, should meet immediately at the outset of each major humanitarian operation to agree precisely how co-ordination is to be accomplished. In some cases, this should quickly result in the establishment of a DHA field office, such as UNREO in Rwanda or UCAH in Angola, charged not with operational responsibilities, but with placing appropriate co-ordinating staff on the ground.

If the UN were being created today a coherent humanitarian system could be established, integrating the diverse structures needed to address complex emergencies. The problem is that emergency responses are being hampered by the activities of competing agencies with overlapping mandates. Moreover, no part of the UN has a specific mandate to address the problems of the huge and growing number of people who are internally displaced. Except where specifically designated, as in former Yugoslavia, the UNHCR does not have responsibility for people displaced within their own countries. This was one of the reasons why the international response to the enormous flow of refugees into Zaire from Rwanda in mid-1994 was slower than it could have been. Though the unprecedented scale of the crisis meant that the capacity of any system would have been severely strained, the faults of the present one were shown up all too clearly.

The crisis in Rwanda has illustrated other problems in international responses to refugee crises. UNHCR's mandate to protect refugees is proving unworkable in the face of the former Rwanda government's violence in the camps around Goma. This is part of a broader picture in which the realities of modern conflict are imposing demands which cannot be met within UNHCR's existing remit. As UNCHR has expanded its operational relief role, as aid is increasingly a resource that is fought over, and as civilians have become the main targets of conflict, the agency finds it ever more difficult to fulfil its protection mandate. These failures suggest it is high time for a thorough and public evaluation of the work of all the UN's humanitarian agencies. One task of the evaluation should be determine whether the DHA has been allowed to play an effective co-ordinating role; and if not, whether more radical reform is needed. One option would be to amalgamate the humanitarian functions of the relevant UN agencies and DHA into a single Department for Humanitarian and Refugee Affairs. This would demand political vision and practical changes, including flexibility for the department to recruit able and experienced people at every level.

Creating the conditions for conflict resolution

Where the UN has intervened as an actor in negotiations for conflict resolution and in implementing peace agreements, it has achieved mixed results. In Angola, its earlier efforts to supervise a peace accord and the transition to elections failed. Under the 1991 Bicesse peace accords, which brought a temporary halt to the Angolan conflict, the UN was given responsibility for implementing the peace agreement, including the demobilisation of UNITA forces and arranging elections. It had neither the means nor the mandate to carry out this task.

In September 1993, when the elections were held, there were only 576 UN officials in Angola (compared to the 7,150 who oversaw the transition in Namibia) and the budget for the operation was around $40m (compared to $400m in Namibia, which has a population one-ninth the size of Angola's).[64] For a country the size of Germany, France, and Spain combined, these resources were derisory. The UN's Representative summarised her invidious position by complaining that the UN 'had been asked to fly a 747 but had been given fuel only for a DC3'.[65]

To make matters worse, the UN's mandate did not give it the authority to demand compliance with the demobilisation elements of the peace accord, increasing the risk of violence after the election. That violence duly arrived when UNITA refused to accept the result and launched a military assault on major cities, re-igniting the civil war.

The only positive aspect of this dismal experience was in the lessons learnt, which were duly applied in Mozambique. There the UN was given a central role in monitoring and verifying the ceasefire, overseeing demobilisation, and assisting the electoral process. Demobilisation was delayed, but completed before the date set for elections. One of the reasons for the relative success of the Mozambique peace process was the active involvement of the international community in the four main commissions established to oversee the peace accords. The Supervisory and Monitoring Commission, which had overall responsibility for guaranteeing the implementation of the agreement, included representatives from Germany, Italy, the UK, the US and the OAU. These countries played a critical role when deadlock threatened the electoral process. In contrast to the UN's operation in Angola, that in Mozambique was well-financed and staffed, with over 7,500 troops overseeing demobilisation.[66] Making the transition from the ending of armed conflict to reconstruction which is able to create the long-term conditions for peace, is the formidable challenge now facing Mozambique and Angola.

Investing in the UN

The nature of conflict in the 1990s and the demands of brokering and implementing peace agreements in countries such as Mozambique and Angola necessitate a strengthening of the internationalist vision of the founders of the UN. Yet political reality, particularly in the wake of the 1994 US mid-term elections, is ever more inwardly-focused, and dictated by domestic opinion polls. Multilateralism is being sacrificed to narrowly-defined national self-interest. In early 1995 the one superpower appears intent on undercutting the viability of the UN at a time of unparalleled need. This isolationism recalls the US decision to stay outside the League of Nations, against President Wilson's wishes, which undermined the League and its ability to prevent the drift into conflict during the inter-war years.

Critics of the UN, especially in the US, often cite its financial costs as a reason for withdrawing support, claiming the money would be better invested at home. Such views are difficult to square with reality. Currently, the cost of the UN's emergency, peacekeeping, and humanitarian operations is around $4bn — about the cost of operating the New York fire-brigade. The US military budget is 70 times larger than the UN budget.[67] By any standards, investment in the UN is a small price to pay for a collective security system.

Unfortunately, however, the UN suffers both from a surfeit of expectations and a deficit of resources, because of a persistent under-financing of its operations. Many member states have accumulated large arrears, among them the world's richest economies such as the US, Japan, Italy, Germany, and Russia. These arrears now amount to more than $1.5bn, with the US owing $220m. Another problem is that humanitarian operations are financed by vol-untary Consolidated Appeals, most of which — especially in Africa — fall well short of their target. The effectiveness of interventions is inevitably reduced as a consequence.

Matters are likely to get worse over the coming years. The Republican-dominated US Congress regards the UN as a costly failure. Reflecting this new mood, the Clinton Admin-istration has unilaterally declared that it intends to cut the US contribution to peace-keeping costs from just under 32 per cent to 25 per cent of the total. This casts doubts over the capacity of the UN to respond to conflicts, let alone to invest in the diplomacy which might prevent them. With the UN system already stretched to breaking point and new demands on its resources mounting, the creation of a more secure financial base is vital. This should include an increase in the size of the Peace-keeping Reserve Fund from the current $150m to $400m, and an increase in mandatory contri-butions for humanitarian assistance to reduce dependence on Consolidated Appeals. Immed-iate payment in full of all arrears may need to be enforced by the imposition of penalties, such as the withdrawal of voting rights, for countries failing to pay; although this would carry the risk of strengthening the arguments of those wish-ing to withdraw from the UN.

Reform of the Security Council

Financial security is one necessary condition for the viability of the UN. Political credibility is another. Many countries continue to see the UN system, and especially the Security Council at the apex of that system, as a vehicle for the pursuit of Western self-interest. Double stand-ards, it is claimed, abound. Bosnian Muslims contrast the UN's response to the Iraqi invasion of Kuwait with its failure to intervene more forcefully in defending their rights; and Africans contrast the comparatively large com-mitment of resources to Bosnia with the lamentable performance of the UN in Rwanda.

Whatever their justification, such criticisms inevitably weaken the UN system. Reform of the Security Council is becoming increasingly important if the UN is to develop a collective security system for the twenty-first century. As the Commission on Global Governance put it:

We believe that the Security Council is too closed a shop. Permanent membership limited to five countries that derive their primacy from events fifty years ago is unacceptable enough. Matters are made worse when working practices reduce transparency.[68]

The Commission on Global Governance has proposed the creation of a new class of Standing Members, followed by a full-scale review of Security Council membership in the first decade of the next century. Three of these countries, they suggest, should be drawn from the developing world, one from each region, and two from the industrial world. Japan and Germany have already staked claims for mem-bership. Another option would be to consider representation through regional groupings, with countries rotating their place on the Security Council. This would have the advan-tage of giving smaller countries, presently excluded from effective participation, a wider stake in the UN system.

Conclusion

Arguably the single most important challenge facing the international community today is that of developing effective policies for prevent-ing and responding to conflict. As we have seen in this chapter, the immediate human costs of conflict are to be measured in the suffering, loss of livelihoods, and death experienced by vulnerable people. But in a world of porous borders, no country is immune to the destabilising effects of growing violence and social disintegration. The crisis of refugees and displaced people forced to flee from their homes, and the deepening insecurity experienced by millions of people in conflict zones unleash destructive force which cannot be contained within national borders. That was well understood by the architects of the UN system, who had the lessons of the inter-war period to drawn on.

Unfortunately, those lessons have been forgotten. Most Northern governments now cling to the belief that conflict-related emergencies can be dealt with on a *ad hoc* basis as they arise , and that the peace and prosperity of their citizens can be protected through elaborate ring-fencing strategies. It is difficult to imagine a less promising prescription for human security into the next century.

Central to the task facing the international community is that of stopping conflicts from occurring. Once large-scale violence has broken out, conflicts become at once more difficult to resolve and more destructive in their impact. Humanitarian action may save some lives, but it is more costly and less efficient in terms of reducing human suffering than conflict prevention. The UN system has a pivotal role to play both in providing humanitarian assistance and in preventing conflict. Yet throughout the post-Cold War era it has suffered from a surfeit of expectation and a deficit in political backing and financial resources.

In this chapter we have outlined some of the reforms which are needed to make the UN a more effective instrument for peace and security. Ultimately, however, any instrument for peace will only be as effective as the political leadership whichguides its action. Against this background, the gathering tide of unilateralism and loss of confidence in the UN on the part of some major western governments represents a serious source of concern.

Even under the most optimistic scenario, however, there are limits to what external intervention can achieve. Long-standing grievances rooted in social inequalities and competing identities must ultimately be resolved within the societies in which they occur, through the initiatives of local people. This underlines the importance of all humanitarian agencies, whether UN bodies, government donors, or NGOs, working to strengthen local structures and capacities and supporting conciliation and peace-building efforts within local communities.

We have stressed in this chapter that policies for conflict prevention must look beyond the UN to address the underlying social, economic and political problems which fan the flames of large-scale violence. There can be no genuine security in a world scarred by poverty and the denial of hope to vast numbers of people. In the words of Nelson Mandela to the World Summit for Social Development: 'security for a few is in fact insecurity for all'. That is why conflict prevention must, as the founders of the UN realised, start with national and international policies, which are aimed at eradicating poverty and giving all the world's people a stake in their society.

3 Structural adjustment

There is only one thing worse than structural adjustment; and that is not adjusting.

KWAFI AKOOR, FINANCE MINISTER, GHANA

ESAP (Zimbabwe's Enhanced Structural Adjustment Programme) has meant that we can only eat two meals a day. We can no longer afford meat, because prices are too high. Everything costs more. I cannot afford to pay the school fees for my son and daughter since they started charging. Government said it was because of ESAP. We can't even go to the clinic when the children are sick because we can't afford the medicines.

ZIMBABWEAN WOMAN, HARARE

I have read that our country is stabilising. That may be true, but we have no jobs. We can't send our children to school. Maybe stabilising is a good thing for the country's we pay debt to, but here life is getting harder.

ZAMBIAN WOMAN

In the old days, we provided soup for a few hundred people. Then, in 1990, we had 'stabilisation'. Prices went up more than 2000 per cent. Look around you, you can see what stabilisation has meant. Look at the children hawking on the streets, when they should be in school; look at the numbers of people we are feeding; look at the numbers sleeping on the streets; look at the conditions in our slums. Has 'stabilisation' made things better?

SOUP-KITCHEN WORKER, LIMA, PERU

Introduction

The United Nations was born out of the two great failures of the inter-war period: the failure to prevent the Great Depression and the failure to avert war. In the eyes of the founders of the UN system, the two events were indissolubly linked. President Roosevelt urged delegates at the 1944 Bretton Woods Conference to recall how 'the great economic tragedy' of the 1930s had caused the 'bewilderment and bitterness which became the breeders of fascism and, finally, war'.[1] The blueprint for global economic governance which emerged from the deliberations at Bretton Woods was designed to prevent a recurrence of that tragedy, and to create the conditions for human security in the post-war era.

The overwhelming preoccupation of the conference delegates was to create the conditions for full employment and improved human welfare.[2] In the 1930s, the international trade and financial systems had imploded, with calamitous results for commodity prices, output, and employment. Governments had compounded the crisis by responding to global problems with deflationary economic policies, further damaging domestic and international prosperity. Speculative and unregulated capital transfers had added to the chaos. Above all, the crisis of the inter-war period revealed the dangers inherent in a global economic system which tied nations in a web of interdependence, but lacked an institutional structure to regulate it. The International Monetary Fund (IMF) and the World Bank were intended to provide that structure.

Although the IMF differed from the agency originally envisaged by Keynes, its most influential architect, its objectives were decidedly Keynesian. According to its first Article, the IMF's basic purpose was 'to contribute...to the promotion and maintenance of high levels of employment and real income and to the development of the productive resources of all members'.[3] The Fund was charged with prime responsibility for assisting countries suffering from short-term trade imbalances in a manner which, with the memory of the inter-war period clearly in mind, enabled them to adjust 'without resorting to measures destructive of national or international prosperity'.[4] The World Bank was set up to create the longer-term conditions for expansion, first by supporting reconstruction in Europe; and then by channelling resources to developing countries. Its over-arching purpose, as described by Keynes, was 'to develop the resources and productive capacity of the world with special attention to the less developed countries, (and) to raise the standard of life and conditions of labour everywhere'.[5]

The changing role of the IMF and World Bank

During the 50 years that have elapsed since the Bretton Woods conference, radical changes have taken place in the world economy. The world the IMF and the World Bank were created to serve no longer exists. Yet their influence is greater than ever; and nowhere more so than in the developing world. As lenders of financial resources in their own right, the IMF and the World Bank directly control billions of dollars. Indirectly, they control considerably more. Most industrial countries demand an IMF-World Bank imprimatur as a precondition for providing development assistance and debt relief to developing countries. Their financial strength and role as intermediaries in North-South economic relations gives the Bretton Woods agencies an enormous influence over governments; and their structural adjustment policies influence the welfare of hundreds of millions of people, most of whom have never heard of Bretton Woods.

Because of their enormous influence, the IMF and the World Bank occupy a pivotal position in international efforts to eradicate poverty. The President of the World Bank at the time, Lewis Preston, acknowledged its obligations in this area. Launching the Bank's poverty reduction strategy in 1992, he stated: 'Sustainable poverty reduction is the overarching objective of the World Bank. It is the benchmark by which our performance as a development institution will be measured.'[6] The IMF has similarly stressed the importance of poverty reduction to its programmes.[7]

These are important commitments. However, in Oxfam's experience, there is a gulf between the policy statements of the Bretton Woods agencies and the design and implementation of their policies. Charged with facilitating expansionary responses to macro-economic imbalances, the IMF has become a guardian of the type of deflationary measures which the Bretton Woods conference sought to consign to history. These policies have undermined the economic growth which is a necessary condition for poverty reduction in the developing world, with damaging consequences for employment and household income. Whereas the Bretton Woods conference envisaged the regulation of markets in the public interest, the IMF and the World Bank have consistently promoted market deregulation as the solution to poverty. This approach ignores the fundamental reality of the market place: namely, that people enter markets as unequal partners, and they leave them with rewards which reflect that inequality. Market deregulation has brought major gains for the wealthy. But for poor communities, such as those with whom Oxfam works, deregulation of markets has often meant further marginalisation. At the same time, the Bretton Woods agencies have failed to protect expenditure on health care, education, and other social proviision needed to eradicate poverty.

This is not to suggest that the objectives of structural adjustment, which include the restoration of financial stability to countries racked by economic crisis, are misplaced. Nor is it to argue for a return to the flawed policies of the past. Fifteen years ago, many governments defended to the death over-valued exchange rates, the blanket protection of industries, and stifling forms of state control over the economy. Today, there is a growing consensus that markets have a vital role to play in development; and that sustainable budgets, realistic currency alignments, viable trade balances, and individual initiative are vital to economic growth and poverty reduction. The issue is no longer one of 'state versus markets', but of which policies are most likely to meet the two equally important objectives of achieving sustainable growth and eradicating poverty.

There are no ready-made, painless solutions to the economic crisis which, in varying degrees of intensity, has affected so many Third World countries since the early 1980s. However, from the standpoint of the poor, the ideologically-driven prescriptions of deflation and deregulation now on offer are not working. The challenge as we approach the twenty-first century is to develop new approaches to adjustment, which are compatible with the objectives identified 50 years ago at Bretton Woods. That means developing expansionary responses to economic crisis; and it means placing poverty

reduction at the heart of policy design. The collusion between the Bretton Woods agencies and governments in designing adjustment policies which transfer the social costs of adjustment disproportionately to the poor, must give way to a new poverty-focused compact for recovery. Such a compact will require far-reaching reforms in the Bretton Woods agencies. It will also require international action to address the debt crisis which, 15 years after it gave birth to structural adjustment, continues to undermine prospects for social and economic recovery.

Structural adjustment programmes

Structural adjustment policies evoke powerful emotions, on all sides of the debate. The IMF, the World Bank, and governments all recognise the social costs of adjustment, but insist that these are symptoms of an economic crisis, for which structural adjustment offers the only cure. There is, in the familiar refrain of countless IMF-World Bank statements, 'no alternative' to adjustment. In the cities and villages of Latin America and Africa, on the other hand, structural adjustment has become a euphemism for suffering, as the quotations at the head of this chapter suggest. Zimbabweans have reinterpreted the acronym for their Enhanced Structural Adjustment Programme, ESAP, as 'Enhanced Suffering for African People'. For people in the South, the argument that there is no alternative to adjustment provokes the almost universal response that there must be. Oxfam believes that they are right — and that there *is* an alternative.

The background: debt and the failures of state intervention

Structural adjustment policies were a response to the severe financial crisis which visited much of the developing world in the early 1980s. [8] The slow down in the world economy, and the lethal interaction of falling commodity prices and rising interest rates, caused by changes in US monetary policy, devastated one economy after another. As export earnings fell, debt repayment obligations rose, leaving much of Africa and Latin America in a state of financial bankruptcy. By the middle of the 1980s, Latin America was transferring some 5 per cent of regional income to its creditors in the industrial world. Between 1980 and 1987, Africa's debt stock rose from the equivalent of one-third of its income to almost three-quarters. By the late 1980s, Africa's debt-to-export ratio (the value of its debt relative to its export earnings) had risen to 500 per cent, which was even higher than that for Latin America.

The debt crisis which evolved in the 1970s and culminated in the early 1980s was precisely the type of event which the IMF and World Bank were created to prevent. Under the original Bretton Woods plan, the IMF would have provided the resources to enable countries to adjust without recourse 'to measures destructive of national prosperity'. In the event, both institutions simply took it for granted that debtor countries should honour their debts in full. Instead of calling for a large-scale debt write-off, they devoted themselves to maintaining creditor claims, in effect acting as debt collectors in indigent states. The preferred solution to the debt crisis was to divert resources on a scale bound to destroy growth and orderly adjustment. The IMF lent money to indebted countries at market interest rates, enabling them to repay creditors. When it became clear that the poorest countries would be unable to repay the IMF, a new system of loans, the structural adjustment facility (SAF), was created to provide more concessional credit; and when the money from this ran out yet another facility was created in the form of the enhanced structural adjustment facility (ESAF), inaugurated in 1987. These concessional facilities are now the main form of IMF credit for low-income countries. For its part, the World Bank provided loans at market interest rates, which were recycled to commercial bank creditors in the form of debt repayments. Subsequently, the

Bank expanded its soft-loan International Development Association (IDA) facility for low-income countries, providing them with what amounted to grants.

The financial resources provided by the Bretton Woods agencies were both inappropriate (since most countries could not afford the repayment terms), and insufficient to enable countries to grow out of recession. However, their response to the debt crisis profoundly changed the relationship between the Bretton Woods system and the developing world. Both agencies assumed an increasingly pivotal policy role in developing countries. The World Bank shifted its focus from project-based lending to the provision of balance-of-payments support for programmes of economic reform. The IMF became increasingly involved in providing 'stabilisation' loans to cover budget deficits.[9] Along with their loans came conditions for policy reforms which, for practical purposes, transferred control over economic policy in those countries to Washington. These policy reforms were broadly aimed at expanding exports and depressing domestic demand sufficiently to maintain debt repayment capacity. As we argue below, this strategy was doomed to failure, in part because of the failure of Western governments to address the debt crisis; and in part because of the inherent shortcomings of the structural adjustment strategy itself.

As the debt crisis deepened, more and more countries came under IMF-World Bank tutelage. Around 30 countries in Africa have had near-continuous programmes with the IMF and the World Bank since the early 1980s.[10] In Latin America, there were 107 IMF-World Bank programmes in 18 countries during the 1980s. These programmes were intended not merely to address the immediate symptoms of the debt crisis, but to initiate wider policy reforms. In particular, the systems of state intervention which had contributed to the economic crisis of the early 1980s were to be radically overhauled.

The need for reform

The case for reform was a powerful one. During the 1970s, the failures of development models aimed at import-substituting industrialisation (ISI), or the displacement of imports through the promotion of local manufactured goods, were becoming increasingly apparent. Fiscal profligacy and extreme corruption were part of the problem in many countries. But the deeper failure of ISI was rooted in its own contradictions.[11] In sub-Saharan Africa, smallholder agriculture was regarded by governments not as an engine of growth but as a source of foreign exchange and finance for industry. State marketing boards levied taxes of up to, and even over, half of the export value of the crops. On average, these taxes were 70 per cent higher in sub-Saharan Africa than in other developing regions.[12] Blanket protection was provided to manufacturing industries, most of which required heavy public subsidies to survive. Overvalued exchange rates were used to lower the costs of industrial and food imports, and to lower the incomes of agricultural producers. In contrast to what was happening in South-East Asia, most industries in Latin America and Africa relied heavily on imports but produced mainly for domestic markets.

In Latin America, industrial growth in the 1960s and 1970s was accompanied by persistent balance of payments deficits, as the cost of imports for local industries outstripped foreign exchange earnings. Those deficits were covered by foreign borrowing. In Africa, the high import-content of industrial growth reinforced dependence on primary commodities to generate foreign exchange, making industrial development ever more vulnerable to the vagaries of world commodity markets.[13] At the same time, heavy taxation of export producers, intended to generate resources for industry, reduced their competitiveness, most disastrously in sub-Saharan Africa, where market shares collapsed. Thus, import substitution became a victim of its own contradictions, by undermining the very foundations upon which its success depended.

Both in Latin America and Africa, governments increasingly resorted to overseas borrowing to cover trade deficits. That borrowing in turn generated inflationary pressure and exchange-rate appreciation, discouraging exports and putting strain on the balance of payments in the process. State regulation of foreign exchange markets and import quotas provided a valuable source of political patronage, as well as windfall profits for powerful vested interests, paid for at vast public expense. By the end of the 1970s, these economic policies engendered the unstable budgetary and trade conditions which were exposed, with disastrous effects, by the surge in US interest rates and slump in commodity prices.

Under structural adjustment, state intervention was to be reduced to a minimum, and the impetus for economic growth was to come not, as in the past, from the domestic market, but from closer integration into the world economy. Governments were to withdraw from the market to provide better incentives for exporters; public spending was to be reduced in the interest of balancing budgets; protectionist barriers were to be withdrawn; and currencies were to be devalued to more realistic levels. These objectives remain central to adjustment policies. In recent years, however, the IMF and the World Bank have claimed that structural adjustment represents not merely an agenda for macro-economic stability, but a comprehensive strategy for poverty reduction.

A range of reforms

The term 'structural adjustment' is shorthand for a wide range of policy reforms. These typically start with an IMF stabilisation programme, which is intended to reduce fiscal deficits (the difference between government spending and revenue) and restore the balance of payments to a viable position. The rationale behind the IMF approach is that both deficits are caused by excess demand, which is reflected in inflationary pressure.[14] Stabilisation programmes are almost always designed to reduce demand, notably by cutting government expenditure, controlling money supply, and raising interest rates, stringent targets being set in all of these areas. Devaluation, which is intended to correct currency over-valuation, restrict imports, and expand exports, is an almost universal part of IMF programmes.

World Bank adjustment programmes are considerably wider in scope than those of the Fund, being intended to establish the foundations for longer-term recovery. Import liberalisation, designed to increase exposure to foreign competition, figures prominently. So, too, does the removal of domestic market 'distortions', such as labour protection, food subsidies, and state control of agricultural marketing. More recently, the Bank's influence has extended into social sector reform, including health financing and the design of social welfare safety nets.[15] In practice, IMF-World Bank programmes are complementary in two respects. First, the principle of 'cross-conditionality' means that the World Bank seldom initiates a programme unless a government has become a client of the IMF. Second, the World Bank, like the IMF, stresses the importance of stringent monetary discipline, the deregulation of labour markets to lower wages, economic policy liberalisation, and a reduced role for the state.

Any assessment of structural adjustment programmes must start out by acknowledging the severity of the problems they are introduced to address. Consider, for example, the case of Zimbabwe.[16] During the 1980s, the country maintained a growth rate which was considerably higher than the average for sub-Saharan Africa, at around 2.7 per cent a year. However, this was lower than the population growth rate, so that living standards declined. Deteriorating living standards were accompanied by an increasingly untenable budget deficit, which the government covered by printing money (which created inflationary pressure) and raising taxes. By the end of the decade, government spending was a quarter higher than revenue, so that the fiscal deficit reached 11 per

cent of GDP. At the same time, there was a recurrent trade deficit, which gave rise to growing debt service obligations. These rose from less than 3 per cent to more than 20 per cent of export earnings during the 1980s. Meanwhile, slow growth was associated with low levels of savings and investment (which was diverted into financing the government deficit), and slow rates of employment creation. In 1990, the year in which the country negotiated a structural adjustment agreement with the IMF-World Bank, employment creation was sufficient to absorb only one out of every three school leavers, so that unemployment had risen to 26 per cent.[17] Social welfare expenditure had already started to come under pressure, jeopardising the gains made since Independence.

By comparison with other countries in Africa and Latin America, Zimbabwe's economic problems were not of chronic proportions. But they illustrate the depth of the economic crisis facing countries which turn to the IMF-World Bank. They also lend weight to the IMF-World Bank claim that macro-economic adjustment is unavoidable. The first victims of chronic instability are to be found not among elites, who have access to foreign currency, but in the shanty towns and villages, where hyperinflation and the collapse of public services exact a very high price.

The costs of adjustment

But while the costs of not adjusting might be high, so, too, are the costs of structural adjustment. The main thrust of IMF stabilisation has been to cut public expenditure, through controls on credit creation, reduced subsidies, and lower public sector wages, while concentrating resources on production for export. Below we argue that stabilisation measures have been inconsistent with the objective of achieving sustained economic recovery. However, they have also resulted in massive social costs, which have been borne disproportionately by women. An example is provided by the experience of Zimbabwe, where the simultaneous reduction of food subsidies and decline in wages which accompanied structural adjustment dramatic-ally reduced household incomes. Between 1990 and 1992, price decontrol increased by half the price of an average food basket for low-income urban families. At the same time, average wage settlements in 1992 were 25 per cent lower than the rate of inflation, implying a further erosion in purchasing power;[18] and unemployment in-creased sharply as structural adjustment and drought combined to cause a deep recession. One study of Kambuzuma, a low-income urban settlement of 40,000 people in Harare, showed the proportion of families living below the poverty line doubling, to 43 per cent. Most households also changed their diets, eating less high protein foods and more carbohydrates. The poorest families cut their number of meals from two to one per day. Women bore the brunt of this household-level adjustment, foregoing meals themselves in order to maintain the food intake of children. Women-headed households were particularly badly affected, reducing their spending on food by one-fifth.[19]

Increasing unemployment, declining real wages, and reduced social welfare provision, have been almost universal features of struct-ural adjustment. In Tanzania, the minimum wage covered only 14 per cent of the cost of the most basic food requirements for a one-person household at the end of the 1980s.[20] In Peru, a 'shock-therapy' programme introduced under President Fujimori in 1990, saw food prices rise by 2,500 per cent in one year, and the number of people living in extreme poverty double. Such trends impose costs on all poor house-holds, but women and young girls suffer dispro-portionately from deteriorating access to food when household incomes fall, because of in-equalities within the household. These in-equalities, largely ignored by policy makers, have a crucial bearing on how the costs of adjustment are distributed.

Additional female employment is one of the mechanisms through which families survive economic crisis. In Latin America, the propor-tion of women in the work-force rose from 22 per cent to 38 per cent during the 1980s, as

increased male unemployment reduced family incomes.[21] There has been a similar trend to-wards increasing female employment outside of the home in Africa. In Zambia, a study of Chawama, a low-income settlement in Lusaka, showed that the number of women working outside the home tripled during the 1980s.[22] Most of this employment expansion has taken place in the informal economy, where female labour is typically concentrated in sectors with the lowest economic returns, and where long hours of work are required to generate small amounts of income. As household managers, women have also been forced to compensate for the decline in social welfare provision which has accompanied economic crisis and structural adjustment. The Chawama study mentioned above discovered that a decline in the provision of public water-points had resulted in women walking greater distances to fetch water. One-third of the women in the compound spent over an hour a day in this task. Declining health sector provision has imposed considerable new demands on women, not least since lower nutritional status increases family exposure to illness. The dilemmas facing women in this area are summarised by a Zimbabwean women living in a low-income settlement in Harare: 'My daughter is sick, but what am I supposed to do? If I take her to the clinic, I cannot afford to pay for treatment — so what is the point? If I stay at home to care for her, how will we buy the food we need to stay alive?'

These words capture some of the less visible costs associated with adjustment. Where adjust-ment policies result in a deterioration in food intake, health care, and public utilities, women are forced to compensate through a combina-tion of paid and unpaid labour. Yet the female labour time spent on family care and the main-tenance of resources does not figure in national accounts.[23] In this sense, the costs to women and family life are invisible. They are, however, very real. The great rise in the number of street children observed in the cities of the developing world, are testament to the growing pressures on low-income households. Once again, the real costs of depriving future generations of education are not reflected in national balance sheets. Nor are the personal costs to women, who are faced with increasingly impossible demands on their time. One detailed study of a low-income community in Ecuador[24] showed that women were typically working in excess of 18 hours per day, and sacrificing time with their children in order to generate income outside the home. On the basis of interviews conducted with the women, the study concluded that about 30 per cent were coping; another 55 per cent were barely getting by, mortgaging the future of their children, and especially their daughters, to survive; and another 15 per cent were exhausted, their families disintegrating and children dropping out of school. The salutary conclusions drawn by the author was that: 'Not all women can cope under crisis and it is necessary to stop romanticising their infinite capacity to do so.'[25]

An agenda for poverty reduction?

There are three main arguments which the Bretton Woods agencies present in defence of their claim that structural adjustment contributes to poverty reduction. The first is that failure to adjust will, ultimately, impose huge costs on the poor, with unsustainable budget and trade deficits leading to hyperinflation, currency instability, and economic collapse. This is uncontroversial, although it hardly amounts to a defence of the specific policies associated with structural adjustment.

The second, more controversial, argument concerns social provision. Both the IMF and the World Bank acknowledge that insufficient attention was paid to this area during the first generation of adjustment programmes in the 1980s. They now claim to have introduced 'social conditionality' into structural adjustment, making provisions to protect expenditure and welfare service delivery in areas of concern to the poor.[26] World Bank investment in health, education, and nutrition, which rose from $1bn for 1987-1989 to over $3bn for 1992-

1994, and reached 15 per cent of total Bank lending, is cited as evidence of reform in this area.

The final argument concerns the relationship between growth and poverty reduction. According to the IMF and the World Bank, structural adjustment programmes, where properly implemented, have not only created the conditions for growth, but for growth which is pro-poor. They contend that state intervention in the rural sector, where the vast majority of the poor live, has lowered prices, reduced market opportunities, and thereby depressed household income. Deregulating these markets, according to the World Bank, has had the opposite effect, raising prices and creating rural employment. In the urban sector, the IMF and World Bank believe that import liberalisation will have the effect of making local industries more competitive, by allowing them to take advantage of imported technologies. Together with the removal of labour market regulations which, in the IMF-World Bank view, artificially raise labour costs, this is supposed to expand employment.[27]

These claims are not supported by the experience of Oxfam's international programme. Few of our partners would question the case for reform, and most are aware of the 'tribute' siphoned off into foreign bank accounts by political elites operating behind a cloak of state intervention. Control over import licenses and foreign exchange quotas have generated vast revenues, some of which are to be found in foreign bank accounts. However, the fact that corruption and misappropriation occurred is not a reason for the withdrawal of the state from areas of social and economic life where the regulation of markets, and public provision, are vital to the interests of the poor. Nor can it justify the failure to protect the welfare of poor people through adequate social welfare provision.

The harsh reality is that structural adjustment policies have not created a framework for sustainable and equitable growth. Their failures are particularly pronounced in four areas:
• Social welfare expenditure has not been

adequately protected. In many countries, health and education provision has been cut back. The introduction of user-charges to finance social welfare systems has meant that essential services are beyond the means of the poorest people.

- Market deregulation has not provided a framework for poverty reduction for the rural poor, and in some cases it has further marginalised them by excluding them from markets. In the manufacturing sector, the deregulation of labour markets has resulted in increased insecurity and lower wages.
- Deflationary stabilisation policies and over-rapid, unco-ordinated trade liberalisation has undermined the investment and employment creation vital to poverty reduction.
- Sustainable and equitable patterns of growth have not been generated under structural adjustment. This is especially true in Africa, where 15 years of adjustment have failed to create a climate for recovery. But even in Latin America, where a fragile economic recovery has taken root, it has been accompanied by growing inequality.

We will now look at each of these areas in more detail.

Passing the costs to the poor

The World Bank claims that improved social welfare provision is at the heart of its structural adjustment operations, and that it has had considerable success in this area. In a statement to the World Summit for Social Development in Copenhagen, its Vice-President responsible for Human Resources Development commented:

As many donors are tightening their belts, foreign aid spending for health, education and other basic needs is no longer in vogue. The World Bank continues to buck this trend because the numbers show that investing in people is not only the key to improving people's lives, it is also good economics....The World Bank's main goal is to help developing countries reach the point where limits to investment in people, no longer hold back growth or keep people in poverty.[28]

The World Bank is right to stress the importance of investment in people. Poor people will not be able to benefit from an improved macro-economic framework if they are illiterate, malnourished or in poor health; nor will they be able to contribute to sustained economic growth.

Given that investment in social welfare is an area in which efficiency and equity are mutually reinforcing, current expenditure patterns give cause for deep concern in all developing regions, and especially in Africa. During the 1980s, real per capita spending on education in Africa fell by one-third; and two-thirds of the countries in the region also reduced health spending.[29] Schools have been left without books and rural clinics without drugs. Staff morale has been sapped by wage cuts and lack of teaching materials. Increasingly, local communities have been called on to fill the gap left by the withdrawal of state support, by paying to maintain schools and clinics, and financing salaries. In the admittedly extreme case of Zambia, it has been estimated that parents pay 80 per cent of the costs of primary education for their children.[30]

Africa is now the only region in the developing world where the percentage of children not attending primary school is projected to rise to the end of the decade. But the future of Latin America has also been jeopardised. Average state spending in the region on primary education fell from $164 per capita at the beginning of the 1980s, to $118 at the end.[31] In South Asia, enrolment rates are improving, but from an exceptionally low base, and with major gender disparities. But even where countries show high initial enrolment rates, poor children — especially girls — are forced to drop out as a result of economic pressure, and are unable to complete primary schooling.

What makes a dismal situation even worse is the bias in public spending towards higher education and urban hospitals, from which poor people derive fewer benefits. This misallocation of resources carries a high social price in terms of lost welfare for poor people. But it also carries a high economic price, since it concentrates resources in sectors where the returns to society are lowest. Misallocation is particularly evident in Africa. Despite having the lowest enrolment rates in the developing world, governments there spend a higher proportion of GDP on education (4.7 per cent) than do governments in East Asia (3.4 per cent), where many countries have achieved universal primary education. This reflects the fact that Africa spends more on tertiary education than any other region.[32]

The World Bank argues that structural adjustment programmes are now reversing

Figure 3.1 Real expenditure per pupil in primary school, Zimbabwe 1987-93

SOURCE: UNICEF

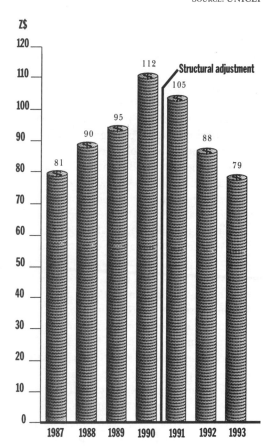

declines in health and education spending, and they are also reorienting public spending to concentrate on primary-level facilities. Unfortunately, in many countries this is not happening, even where the Bretton Woods agencies have attempted to introduce social conditionality.

Structural adjustment in Zimbabwe

Zimbabwe is widely cited by the World Bank as an example of its new, poverty-focused approach to structural adjustment. Under its 1990 structural adjustment programme, the Government of Zimbabwe committed itself to reducing the national budget deficit from 10 per cent to 5 per cent of national income by 1995. There was an agreement with the World Bank that it would do so in a way which would not only protect public expenditure in health and education, but restore cuts made since 1988, when per capita spending in both areas began to decline.[33] According to the World Bank, this was a condition for the release of adjustment finance. In practice, however, budgets for health and education declined dramatically in real terms during the first three years of the structural adjustment programme. Per capita spending on health services fell by one-third, and on education by 29 per cent, to its lowest level since Independence. Per capita spending on primary education fell even faster than spending on other areas of education, suggesting that cuts were falling most heavily on the sector most crucial to poverty reduction. Expenditure on the maintenance budgets for rural water-supply points was also cut severely, reducing the availability of clean water in rural areas.[34]

These expenditure patterns have threatened the impressive social welfare improvements made in Zimbabwe since Independence. Their effects have been deeply felt by many of Oxfam's project partners, who have seen their opportunities for education and health care diminish. There is a widespread and justifiable anger at the failure of the World Bank and the Zimbabwean government to consider more equitable ways of reducing the budget deficit. Public sector reform has been spectacularly slow, with the result that subsidies to the ailing steel industry and other parastatals have not fallen. The build-up of public debt needed to maintain government spending in these areas is diverting resources on a huge scale. Annual interest payments on public debt now absorb an estimated 18 per cent of the budget, the second largest item of expenditure after education. Reluctance to cut spending on defence, the third largest item of government expenditure, accounting for 3.5 per cent of GDP, has further reduced the government's capacity to maintain spending on social welfare.[35]

Social welfare provision in Pakistan

Pakistan is often and justifiably cited by the World Bank as one of the worst offenders in terms of failure to invest in social welfare. Yet the country's structural adjustment programme appears to have coincided with a further deterioration in the country's performance. During 1993-1994, the third year of the programme, the Pakistan Government exceeded even the targets set by the IMF for reducing its budget deficit. The deficit fell by almost one-third in a single year, from 8 per cent to 5.4 per cent of GDP. However, this reduction was achieved not through increased revenue, but through drastic cuts in public expenditure. Since the start of its structural adjustment programme, health expenditure in Pakistan has fallen from 1 per cent of GDP to 0.7 per cent, while education spending has fallen from 2.4 per cent to 2.2 per cent.[36]

Attempting to meet budget targets through expenditure reductions in these areas raises concerns at several levels. In contrast to Zimbabwe, they are being introduced in a context of already grossly inadequate provision. Pakistan has some of the worst social welfare indicators in the world in health and education. In 1990, only one-third of the country's population was literate, and less than a quarter of its women; half of the population does not have access to clean water; and infant mortality and maternal mortality rates are amongst the worst in the developing world. While per capita income in Pakistan is some 80 per cent higher than the average for the 54 countries grouped in the UNDP low-human-development category, its social indicators in each of the above areas are considerably worse.[37] Under these circumstances, public expenditure cuts carry an extremely high price in terms of increased suffering, wasted human potential, and reduced long-term economic growth prospects. Such a price ought to be regarded as too high under any circumstances. In a country where military expenditure absorbs more than the combined health and education budgets, reduced social welfare expenditure suggests a dereliction of responsibility on the part of government.

The responsibilities of the Bretton Woods agencies and of governments

The World Bank has made genuine efforts to persuade governments of the need to protect social expenditures. Unfortunately, these efforts have often been belated and ineffective. For instance, the Indian government in 1991 began implementing budget stabilisation measures agreed with the IMF and World Bank by cutting expenditure in a number of social priority areas. The Department of Rural Development reduced its expenditure budget in the first year of stabilisation. This was followed in 1992-1993 by a 46 per cent cut in the rural sanitation budget and a 39 per cent cut in rural water-supply spending, both priority areas for poverty reduction.[38] In 1992, the World Bank strongly criticised the Indian government for proposing deep budget cuts in health spending, and it may have played a role in limiting the scale of public expenditure retrenchment. The fact remains, however, that real spending on health, agriculture, irrigation, and social services is lower today in real terms than in 1991.[39]

The World Bank's inability to use its influence to secure more effective protection for social welfare provision under stabilisation, has been in evidence elsewhere. In Zambia, one of the 'new model' adjustment operations, the Bank has made strenuous efforts to achieve government commitments on priority social-sector expenditure. However, these commitments were not translated into budget allocations and expenditure. In the 1991 budget, the government pledged itself to raise expenditure on education from 9 per cent to 12 per cent. During the complex political bargaining processes over inter-departmental allocations which followed, the government reduced the education sector share of the budget to 7.7 per cent, its lowest-ever level. Commitments to restore the cuts had still not been implemented by 1993, when the education budget still accounted for only 9 per cent of total expenditure. Moreover, the amount going to primary education within the overall budget has fallen.[40] These trends follow a period of deep and

protracted cuts in social welfare provision, and the failure to reverse the cuts raises serious doubts over the poverty-reduction claims made for Zambia's adjustment programme.

The failure to protect social expenditures under structural adjustment raises a number of important questions about existing approaches to stabilisation and budget allocations. To its credit, the World Bank has attempted to establish agreements with governments, both to protect social expenditure, and to improve its distribution. In practice, these agreements have proved difficult to enforce, and non-compliance has been tolerated in a manner which would be inconceivable were it repeated in relation to, say, money supply or credit control. Yet removing barriers to primary education and health care is no less important to the long-term outcome of structural adjustment than restoring macro-economic imbalances.

Figure 3.2 Health and Education sector spending, Zambia 1981-93   SOURCE: WORLD BANK

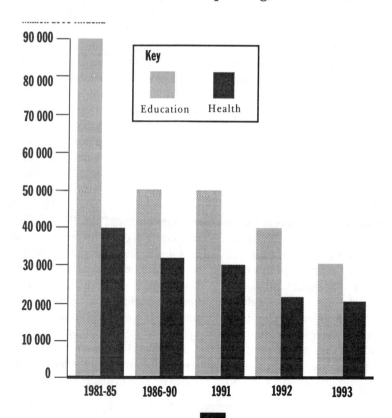

This suggests the need for more transparent and wide-ranging dialogue over how fiscal deficits are to be reduced. Given the influence of political and economic elites, it is hardly surprising that most governments have an in-built tendency to pursue targets for reducing fiscal deficits by cutting expenditure on areas of concern to the poor. It is far easier to cut budgets for rural health clinics than for imported weapons, or for parastatals which are important sites of patronage. And it is far easier to tax the poor, by charging for primary education, for example, than the rich. These are the political realities in which the Bretton Woods agencies operate. Yet it is surely unacceptable for them to fix broad budget targets, in the certain knowledge that they will be a catalyst for reduced welfare provision. In this context, the IMF and the World Bank should accept responsibility for agreeing with governments deficit-reduction measures which protect the poor. Far more emphasis could be placed upon establishing fiscal stability by reducing military expenditure and parastatal subsidies, debt relief, and raising revenue through progressive forms of taxation.

More rigorous social conditionality must also be considered.[41] The respective balance of rights and obligations between the Bretton Woods agencies and governments is a complex issue. The IMF-World Bank view is that governments must take responsibility for setting priorities within agreed overall budget parameters. Both agencies claim that the principles of national sovereignty demand that governments retain responsibility for public spending. This sensitivity towards national sovereignty is less apparent in other policy areas, such as money supply. In Oxfam's view, governments and the international financial institutions share an ethical obligation to protect the interests of the poor during adjustment. In some cases, social costs may be an unavoidable consequence of economic crisis. But the underlying principle for adjustment should be that of 'last call' on the resources of the poor, with poverty-related elements of the budget protected to the maximum possible extent.

The effects of user-fees on health and education

The problems associated with declining public expenditure provision have been made worse by other aspects of structural adjustment, including increased recourse to user-fees to finance services. Faced with budgetary constraints, many governments have imposed charges for health and education services. In an effort to refinance its educational system, the Government of Zimbabwe introduced fees for all urban primary schools and all secondary schools in 1992.[42] Parallel moves in the health sector saw the introduction of more rigorous fee collection in 1991, and a sharp increase in prices at rural clinics and hospitals in 1994.[43] These actions were encouraged by the IMF and the World Bank. Under the structural adjustment programme introduced at the beginning of 1991, targets were set for raising the revenue collected from education fees from Z$40m to Z$120m by 1993. Health fees were to rise from Z$15m to Z$45m over the same period. Both measures were intended to reduce the fiscal deficit by raising the equivalent of 0.7 per cent of GDP. [44]

The cost-recovery programme had adverse effects on the welfare of poor people. In 1992, one survey showed that almost one-third of all patients were unable to afford the full cost of their treatment. Another found that out of a sample of children suffering from diarrhoea who had been treated at home, over half had not been taken to clinics because of the cost.[45] Women's attendance at antenatal clinics was particularly sensitive to increased fees.[46] This was reflected in an increase to 8.8 per cent from 1.6 per cent in the number of babies born in Harare Central Hospital to mothers who had not registered for antenatal care. The perinatal mortality rate for these mothers is five times higher than for mothers who had registered, underlining the extreme dangers for women of exclusion from health facilities.[47]

To its credit, the Government of Zimbabwe withdrew user-fees from rural clinics in 1995 when the evidence of their adverse effects on

Figure 3.3 Maternal deaths recorded nationally at hospitals and clinics compared with Ministry of Health recurrent expenditure per capita, 1987-92, Zimbabwe

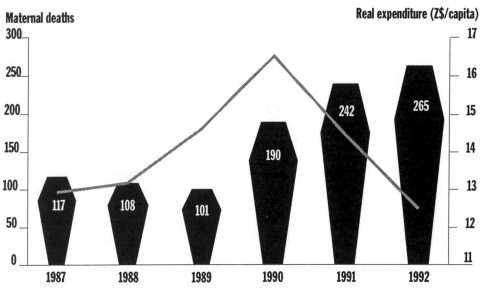

SOURCE: UNICEF

public health became clear. Even before then, the World Bank had acknowledged the high social costs of user-fees and urged their withdrawal, showing a genuine concern to act on its commitment to protect the health of the poor. Unfortunately, however, that concern is not always reflected in World Bank advice. Since the mid-1980s, the Bank has been encouraging countries to increase user-charges, with the twin aim of raising revenue for the health sector and introducing market principles into resource allocation. Although exemption systems have been designed to shield the poorest from payments, in the absence of institutional capacity these have almost universally proved inadequate. The consequences are cogently summarised by a Medical Superintendent at Masaka Hospital in Uganda:

The rural poor do not attend Masaka hospital except in extreme cases. They do not attend because they cannot afford the costs involved including transport, drugs and the minimum fee.[48]

The most significant costs of the reduction in provision and imposition of user-charges have been borne by women, for whom inadequate health care poses acute risks, especially during pregnancy. Women also suffer in terms of increased demands on their time. When health services collapse, it is women who look after sick children and elderly relatives, extending their unpaid labour to cover the real costs of structural adjustment.[49]

There are serious grounds for questioning the use of cost-recovery in health services, even on narrowly-defined efficiency terms. User-fees are not a particularly efficient mechanism for health sector financing, seldom generating more than 5 per cent of recurrent health spending even where they are well established. In many countries, the costs of administering user-fees are probably more or less equivalent to the revenue they generate. Where there is widespread poverty, as in most of Africa and Latin America, the costs of administering an exemption system which actually worked would almost certainly outstrip the revenue from user-fees. Under such conditions user-fee systems are particularly inefficient, since the revenue they generate decreases with the extent of poverty, while the costs of administration increase as the number of people eligible for exemption rises. Claims that user-fees can generate financial resources for investment in health services are technically correct, but largely irrelevant. In almost all cases, the income generated by user-fees is transferred to finance ministries, rather than re-invested in health care. In reality, fees have been imposed with the aim of rationing resources and reducing fiscal deficits by taxing the poor; and their effect has been to reduce demand by pricing services beyond the means of poor people.[50]

Oxfam's anxiety is that the World Bank's advocacy of user-fees and private health care has subordinated a concern for equity and the provision of basic health for all, to the introduction of market mechanisms into health financing. This reflects the underlying philosophy of the Bank, which sees the market as the most efficient way of allocating scarce resources and forcing individuals to exercise responsibility.[51]

The scarcity of financial resources poses very difficult dilemmas in health-care planning. However, there are more equitable and efficient ways of addressing that scarcity, both nationally, through raising additional funding from progressive taxation or reduced military and parastatal spending, and internationally, through development assistance and debt relief. The introduction of what amount to highly regressive forms of taxation such as user-fees should be a last resort, unless they can be effectively targeted at income groups who can afford to pay them.

Social welfare safety-nets

Since the latter part of the 1980s, most structural adjustment programmes have incorporated social welfare safety-nets, aimed at off-setting what the World Bank characterises as 'transitional' effects of adjustment, such as increased unemployment and falling incomes. Variously labelled as 'social emergency funds', 'social dimensions of adjustment programmes', and 'social investment funds', they have been used to protect vulnerable groups, typically through joint interventions by donors, governments, and the NGO community. All the programmes were introduced to ease the costs of adjustment in the short term, while assuming (erroneously in many cases) that economic recovery would diminish the need for assistance in the medium term. Among the motives for these programmes, the objective of maintaining political support for structural adjustment has figured prominently.

In some cases, social dimensions programmes have been reasonably effective. In other cases, they have proved deeply flawed, even as limited social welfare initiatives. But whatever the country-specific experiences, social welfare safety-nets have inevitably proved inadequate in the face of the failure of structural adjustment programmes to create a viable macro-economic framework for poverty reduction.

Politically, one of the most successful programmes has been National Solidarity Programme (PRONASOL) in Mexico. Between 1989 and 1993, the budget for this programme quadrupled to $2.5bn, providing food assistance, social services, investment in water and sanitation, and direct subsidies and credit to small producers. The World Bank has held PRONASOL up as a model to be followed. However, while the programme has provided benefits for many communities, it has also been the subject of extensive political manipulation, with resources being concentrated in accordance with the political priorities of the governing Institutional Revolutionary Party.

Much has been made by the World Bank of the 'demand-driven' character of its social dimensions interventions, most of which place the emphasis on responding to community initiatives. This is a laudable alternative to 'top-down' interventions, which ignore community concerns. But responding to project applications is not, in itself, an effective targeting strategy for poverty reduction. In Bolivia, the Emergency Social Fund (ESF) sought to offset the effects of the unemployment caused by adjustment, providing the equivalent of one-third of public spending by 1991. However, over half of the beneficiaries from this programme, which focused on construction work, already had a job; and the poorest regions of the country received least funding. Another way in which the programme failed to reach the poorest was that only 1 per cent of the jobs created went to women.[52] These failures reflect a wider failure to make ESF funding available to the poor. But perhaps the biggest failings were that the programme was able to reach only a small proportion of the unemployed, and that it came to an end before any sign of recovery had occurred.

One of Oxfam's criticisms of the 'demand-led' approach associated with social dimensions programmes is that, in practice, they often result in resources being distributed to those best placed to make viable applications. In Honduras and Costa Rica, for example, it appears that wealthier municipalities are receiving the largest share of resources.[53] Elsewhere, the prospect of World Bank funding has led to a proliferation of NGOs, some of whom have only tenuous links with local communities.

The dilemma, to which there is no easy answer, is that genuine community initiatives and genuine participation take time, whereas there is an onus on social dimensions programmes to make large grants and to spend funds swiftly. More fundamentally, there is a problem of working with communities to develop alternative strategies for survival in conditions where the poor are becoming increasingly marginalised, and where broader macro-economic policies undermine sustainable livelihoods.

Many social dimensions programmes, especially in sub-Saharan Africa, appear to have been contrived as a hastily designed afterthought to structural adjustment. In Zimbabwe,

the Social Development Fund (SDF) did not come into operation until some 18 months after the adjustment programme was finalised in 1991. No co-ordinator was appointed until 1993, and no additional staff were allocated to existing social welfare offices, despite the massive increase in public demand caused by a combination of drought and structural adjustment policies.[54] There was widespread duplication in procedures for applying for assistance, with separate procedures for food subsidies, health fee exemptions, and assistance with education fees. Forms to register eligibility were several pages long, requiring information unlikely to be available to many people.[55] Not surprisingly, the scheme achieved limited success. Food subsidies have reached an estimated 4 per cent and school fees exemptions around 20 per cent of the eligible population. By mid-1994, three years into the adjustment programme, 45 per cent of the population had not even heard of the SDF.[56]

Social welfare programmes occupy a central role in the World Bank's poverty reduction strategy. But while social safety-nets are important, they cannot resolve long-term poverty problems. This is especially true in countries where economic recession is fostering widespread social dislocation, and where free-market reforms are excluding large sections of the population from any prospect of sustainable livelihoods. What is needed is an integrated approach to social welfare provision, in which the emphasis is placed both on improving the capabilities of the poor, through the provision of health care, education, and productive assets, and on creating an enabling environment in which those capabilities can be realised.

Agricultural markets and liberalisation

The view that structural adjustment automatically brings benefits for the rural poor rests upon a number of assumptions about how rural markets operate. According to the Bank, devaluation (which raises the local currency earnings from export crops) and the elimination of state marketing agencies, which previously taxed producers at sometimes ruinous levels, have restructured markets in a 'pro-poor' fashion. As one Bank document puts it:

Because the majority of Africans — and the majority of Africa's poor — live in rural areas and are self-employed smallholders, adjustment programmes that move the terms of trade in favour of the rural sector and focus on broad-based growth in agriculture offer the most immediate opportunity for alleviating poverty.[57]

In other words, higher prices for the crops produced by the poor will raise their household incomes and reduce their poverty.

Almost nobody today defends the past excesses of marketing boards in Africa, or denies the damaging effect of currency over-valuation on smallholder producers. However, the conviction that market deregulation is sufficient to reduce poverty owes more to ideology than to evidence derived from the experience of poor communities. For many of these communities, market reforms have conspicuously failed to create a framework for enhanced opportunity, increased self-reliance, and poverty reduction.

Structural adjustment in agriculture has had complex and sometimes contradictory consequences, which affect particular groups in different ways. The main effects are mediated through the price system and marketing arrangements. Devaluation and lower levels of taxation on exports have raised the prices generated by the sale of export crops (although the prices of imported inputs have also risen). Meanwhile, parastatal marketing agencies have significantly scaled down their presence in markets, and in some cases been withdrawn altogether. From the standpoint of producers this has meant a change in the intermediary through which they market their produce, with private traders assuming a greater role. The effects of adjustment policies depend upon what people produce, their strength in the market, the distribution of rewards within the household, and the degree to which the withdrawal of the state is followed by the emergence of a competitive private-sector trading system.

Adjustment and commercialisation

One of the central aims of structural adjustment is to improve the balance of payments by encouraging agricultural exports. Commercialisation in this area has been promoted both by macro-economic reforms (such as devaluation and reduced taxation), and by direct investment. Unfortunately, the benefits of commercialisation are often skewed towards large-scale commercial producers, who produce the bulk of marketed production.

In Zimbabwe, the large-scale commercial farm sector accounts for around 90 per cent of the marketed output of crops and livestock. While small-scale communal farmers have dramatically increased their marketed share of some crops, such as cotton and maize, this has been restricted to 20 per cent of the better-off communal farmers.[58] Meanwhile, the vast majority of rural households, which are located in overcrowded, ecologically fragile, low-rainfall areas, have few opportunities to expand production for the market. Most of these households are net purchasers of food, rather than surplus producers. One of the prerequisites for any poverty-reduction strategy in this context is a comprehensive redistribution of assets, including land redistribution, coupled with public investment in the social and economic infrastructure of the poorest areas. Without such measures, the benefits from commercial incentives will inevitably be skewed to the advantage of the wealthier. Yet the World Bank's structural adjustment policy for Zimbabwe has focused upon expanding the production of horticultural crops, flowers, tobacco, and cotton, where the benefits will be concentrated on the commercial farm sector. It is true that, if successful, this strategy will generate some rural employment. But it will do little to enhance the autonomy or reduce the vulnerability of the poorest sections of society.[59]

The boom in non-traditional exports which has accompanied adjustment in many countries illustrates the inequitable distribution of benefits which can flow from market reforms. The promotion of non-traditional exports in Chile resulted in fruit exports growing at over 25 per cent a year in the two decades after 1974. The country is now the largest supplier of seasonal fruit to the northern hemisphere.[60] But while there have been major foreign exchange gains, the bulk of these have gone to the five large fruit companies, four of them foreign-owned, which account for over half of all exports. Fruit exports have created employment, but often on highly exploitative terms.[61] In the Central Valley of Aconcagua, for example, Oxfam supports an organisation for temporary agricultural labourers, who work up to 16 hours a day at harvesttime, and often suffer serious health problems resulting from applications of toxic pesticides. Many of them come from families which were displaced from their holdings in the valley in the late 1970s, when the government lifted the ban on land ownership by foreign corporations and eliminated land-ceiling legislation.

For these labourers, the majority of whom are women, the non-traditional export boom has been a mixed blessing, providing a source of income, but on highly insecure terms. These are the words of Luisa Pina, a labourer in the Central Valley :

We are paid to work ten hours, but during the harvest we work for at least 14 hours with no extra pay. Last year I became sick. It was after we were spraying Temik [a severely toxic pesticide] on the peas. I was told I would not be paid if I could not work, so I continued working. Many other women suffered from stomach complaints. But we all continued working...we cannot live if we do not have work.

The costs to women like Luisa of Chile's economic miracle do not figure in national economic accounts or trade statistics. But they are an example of how market reforms can be a double-edged sword, especially where they are accompanied by the withdrawal of effective state protection for minimum health and safety standards and labour rights.

There can be other costs incurred as a result of ineffective state regulation. In Ghana, for example, the World Bank structural adjustment programme, included measures to boost timber exports. These exports have contributed to the destruction of forest cover, which is receding by between 1.3 per cent and 2 per cent a year. Once again, there have been foreign exchange gains, although these are likely to prove temporary. Timber resources have now been depleted to such a degree that the country is likely to become a net importer in the next few years. Deforestation has undermined the livelihoods of some of the poorest communities in Ghana, who depend on forest resources for food, fuel, and medicines.[62] In many countries in which Oxfam works, structural adjustment policies have contributed to the reckless exploitation not only of forests, but coastal waters, in a way which is degrading two of the primary natural assets of poor people: land and water.

Smallholder producers: who benefits?

Among small-holder producers, price and marketing reforms have differential effects; in most countries there is an inverse correlation between the probability of a household being in poverty and the size of its marketed surplus. Higher producer prices will not have a significant impact on the poverty of farmers who market very little of their output, and who produce mainly for their own consumption. In this sense, the price mechanism is a limited instrument for poverty reduction, since it distributes benefits in a manner which reflects market power. In Bangladesh, 75 per cent of marketed surplus is produced by 15 per cent of farms; with the result that an increase in producer prices will offer only marginal benefits to poor farmers.[63] For households which are net purchasers of food (the vast majority of the rural poor), higher food prices might have negative effects, if they translate into higher prices for consumers. Rough estimates show that on average the rural poor in Bangladesh and India derive 50 per cent of their calorie intake from market purchases.[64] Rural labourers are likely to suffer particularly adverse effects from an increase in food prices.

For smallholder producers of export crops, structural adjustment policies can bring economic benefits, as higher prices and reduced taxation increase the returns on production of coffee, tea, cotton, and other commercial exports. Whether these benefits are realised depends partly on the terms on which producers participate in markets. Evidence from Mozambique and Tanzania, for example, suggests that the gains from higher prices fall disproportionately to traders, who are able to exploit the market weakness of producers, and purchase their produce on highly favourable terms.[65] From a poverty-reduction perspective, the more significant point is that rural poverty is often highest in regions where farmers are unable to grow cash crops for export, whether because of distance from markets, lack of inputs, or ecological constraints.

The experience of Uganda illustrates these diverse effects of market reforms.[66] Under structural adjustment, taxation on coffee exports, the country's main source of foreign exchange, was reduced from over 70 per cent to less than 10 per cent in the early 1990s. At the same time, devaluation increased the local currency value of exports. The combined effect was that the real prices received by coffee producers rose by about 7 per cent between 1987 and 1991, even though international prices fell by half over the same period. Farm-gate prices for cotton, another major export crop, more than doubled. Smallholder producers, such as the coffee producers around Lake Victoria, who account for the bulk of production in both crops, reaped significant benefits. These have been reflected in the rapid growth of production and exports.

By reversing years of disastrous state-marketing practices, structural adjustment measures have, in this case, contributed to the rehabilitation of the agricultural sector and an impressive export-led recovery. They may also have contributed to an increase in wages for agricultural labourers. However, the general rise in prices for tradable goods has not been matched in non-tradable crops, such as cassava, maize, millet, and sorghum, which account for about 70 per cent of total agricultural production. Research by the World Bank suggests that farm-gate prices for these crops fell by 25 per cent between 1987 and 1992. Since the poorest regions, such as the northern part of the country, and the poorest households, depend predominantly on the production of staple food crops, they have not immediately benefited from structural adjustment.[67] The same pattern has been repeated in Ghana, where prices received by cocoa producers in the southern part of the country have increased dramatically under adjustment. However, producers of staple foods in the drought-prone northern savannah region suffered a fall in real income during the second half of the 1980s.[68]

Structural adjustment and women farmers

Whether or not women farmers benefit from structural adjustment depends less upon market prices than upon complex patterns of gender relations. Women and men face different opportunities and constraints in responding to economic policy changes and shifts in prices and incentives. These differences arise from structural inequalities in their respective rights and obligations, which translate into differences in use and control of productive resources.

Policy makers frequently overlook the fact that, in many countries, women farm their own plots in addition to working on the plots of their husbands. The resulting division of labour has important implications for the distribution of benefits from structural adjustment. For example, in Uganda the production and marketing of coffee and cotton is controlled by men, whereas 80 per cent of staple food is produced by women.[69] It follows that the distribution of benefits within the household is likely to be skewed in favour of men. In West Africa, women are more extensively involved in the production and marketing of commercial crops. For instance, women farmers in southern Ghana commonly grow cocoa; in Niger groundnuts provide the main income from women's fields; and in The Gambia women grow and market cotton. However, it would be wrong to assume that men and women operate on the basis of equality. As one reviewer puts it:

In most cases of women growing industrial or export crops on their own account, the scale is of the order of a sideline. Nor do women and men enter production of these crops in the same circumstances.[70]

Their different circumstances include, in many cases, exclusion from credit markets, extension services, and marketing infrastructure. In the Katete district of Zambia, where Oxfam works with smallholder farmers, most women produce food crops, while crops such as cotton and tobacco are male-dominated; women tend to produce cotton only on a very small scale. An Oxfam credit survey carried out in 1992 showed that women were virtually excluded from institutional credit, even where they were producing cash crops.[71]

The assumption that benefits from adjustment are equitably shared within the household is flawed in several respects. Where restricted land rights make it virtually impossible for women to obtain credit, as they do in much of South Asia and sub-Saharan Africa, their ability to benefit from market opportunities is diminished. Moreover, improved incentives for crops controlled by men can diminish the autonomy of women in the household, and increase demand for female family labour. For example, the introduction of swamp rice in The Gambia in the early 1980s decreased the workload of men, but increased that of women.[72] Where female labour is transferred in this way, it can have adverse consequences for food production on women's plots and for household food security. In many cases, however, efforts to encourage commercialisation have failed because women prefer to work on their own plots. One irrigated rice project in Cameroon — SEMRY 1

— illustrates the problem. In this case women refused to abandon cultivation of their own fields to produce rice for commercial markets, even though returns were higher. The reason was that the marketing of commercial rice was controlled by men.[73]

Agricultural markets and poverty reduction

Like the World Bank, Oxfam believes that measures to enhance the productivity and security of the rural poor are vital for poverty reduction. However, increasing agricultural prices is not a sufficient condition for raising the incomes of the rural poor. Improving the returns on assets held by the poor will not make inroads into their poverty if their productive assets are limited, or if supporting infra-structure is lacking. The social consequences of price reforms and their implications for poverty are determined by the realities of power in the market-place, including the distribution of assets, land-tenure arrangements, and differences in power between men and women. Separated from wider measures to address these realities, increased prices are as likely to exacerbate as to reduce inequality and to compound poverty.

None of which amounts to a case for abandoning price reforms, or for returning to the past excesses of state marketing boards. Proper price incentives for agriculture are vital for national food security, rural employment, and wider economic development. But price reforms need to be accompanied by measures that increase the availability of productive assets for the poor, to enable them to benefit from such reforms, and to reduce their insecurity.

Agrarian reform, including land redistribution and land-tenure reform, is a prerequisite in many countries for poverty reduction. In Latin America, where land ownership is highly concentrated, the benefits of rising agricultural prices are unlikely to benefit the poor. Indeed, increased returns to large-scale commercial producers may result in the displacement of labour as a result of increased investment in mechanisation. For Asia, rural landlessness is a major factor in explaining poverty levels. Even in Africa, where land availability is a less pressing problem, landlessness or skewed patterns of land-ownership is a major cause of poverty in countries such as Zimbabwe, South Africa, and Kenya. Allied to landlessness, insecure land tenure and inequitable share-cropping arrangements in much of South Asia contribute to a situation in which higher prices are likely to lead to increased poverty and inequality. Unless such structural inequalities are addressed, market reforms will generate only limited benefits for poverty reduction.

Improving infrastructure is another necessary condition for creating an enabling environment. One of the defining features of poverty in many countries is geographical isolation. Poor people often live in areas badly placed for transport networks, agricultural services, and marketing facilities. Where farmers face difficulties in obtaining inputs or reaching markets, infrastructural investment is necessary to improve productivity. In many cases, however, stabilisation policies result in cuts in public expenditure in these areas, reducing the capacity of farmers to increase output and yields. By contrast, the combination of the rise in prices and increased infrastructural investment which took place in Indonesia during the 1980s resulted in agricultural growth rates which were high even by South-East Asian standards.[74] Similar policies were responsible for the dramatic post-independence increases in smallholder production in Zimbabwe, where the proportion of maize marketed by smallholders increased from less than 10 per cent to over 50 per cent of the total.[75] While the benefits of intervention were restricted to wealthier smallholders, the experience of both countries underlines the important interaction between public investment in infrastructure and market outcomes. The provision of credit and viable lending institutions tailored to the needs of small borrowers is another important part of the prescription for reducing poverty through market reforms.

Unravelling the complex implications of price reforms for women is vital to any poverty reduction strategy. This requires information about the different roles of men and women in crop production and marketing, and about intra-household relations. Yet such issues are seldom considered in the design and implementation of adjustment policies, with potentially adverse consequences for the section of the population most vulnerable to the increased insecurity which can result from macro-economic reform. Similarly, market reforms which leave in place the social and economic barriers to the equal participation of women in the market-place, are likely to diminish rather than enhance their opportunities for greater autonomy.

It is argued by some that the advantages in terms of efficiency of concentrating resources on commercial farmers, outweighs the equity gains which would result from redistributing assets: the 'efficiency versus equity' trade-off to which we referred earlier. In fact, this trade-off is more illusory than real. In South Korea, for example, land reform played an important role in increasing agricultural productivity and expanding rural demand, both of which were crucial to the country's economic success. Redistributive measures can do much to reduce the vulnerability of small farmers, who account for the bulk of the poor in Africa and Asia. But they can also bring wider benefits. There is a substantial body of evidence to show that smallholder farmers have higher levels of productivity per acre than large farms.[76] They also generate that productivity by using their own labour, rather than by investing in capital-intensive systems of production. In addition, increased rural incomes have important linkage effects with the rest of the economy, generating demands for goods and services. One of the most important economic benefits derives from the savings in foreign exchange which can result from increased food production and a lowering in demand for imported cereals. Apart from these economic benefits, traditional, labour-intensive production systems are best equipped to maintain soil fertility and minimise soil degradation.

Deregulating agricultural markets

Price reform is one of the foundation stones of structural adjustment. Another is the liberalisation of agricultural marketing structures. Here, as in other sectors, there has been a concerted effort by the World Bank to remove the influence of the state from the market in favour of private-sector traders, in the belief that this will enhance productivity and reduce poverty. In one recent publication, the World Bank identified the withdrawal of state agencies from the marketing of export and staple food crops as one of the criteria for successful policy reform. Is such an approach consistent with a commitment to poverty reduction? The experience of liberalisation of the maize market in Zambia would seem to suggest that it is not.

The Zambian maize market

Under its structural adjustment programme, the Government agreed to liberalise and privatise the maize marketing system. In 1993, it provided some Kwacha 15bn to a small number of authorised private-sector traders, who were expected to purchase maize at prices above a floor price of Kwacha 5,000 per bag. In the event, however, much of this credit was invested by the traders in government bonds, which yielded far higher profit levels than were attainable from maize marketing.[77] The resulting withdrawal of resources left the maize marketing system chronically under-financed: a classic example of the dangers of unregulated markets. This was in a year when there was a bumper harvest, which could have replenished national food reserves depleted by the drought. Instead, a large proportion of the harvest went to waste, as the marketing system collapsed. Government-authorised traders were unable to pay their agents, who in turn were unable to pay farmers from whom they had purchased maize.

The Government was forced to step into the breach with costly 'promissory notes' to cover the debts owed to farmers. However, many farmers, including Oxfam's project partners in Mumbwa, did not receive payment until five months after harvest, with devastating consequences for the poorest households.

Equally devastating was the entirely predictable concentration of private-sector traders on the more commercially viable agricultural areas located near to transport facilities and markets. The absence of a state marketing system, and failure of private sector traders to fill the vacuum, left women farmers in Oxfam-supported co-operatives in the Petauke, Chipata, and Nyimba districts of Eastern Province unable to market their maize. The Kazimule area of Chipata district, where Oxfam works with two women's groups, is about 45km from the nearest maize marketing centre. Since there is no bus service, the only means of transport is by foot, and the cost of the journey in terms of lost labour time is considerable. Faced with this prospect, many farmers were forced to trade their maize on highly unfavourable terms in a market dominated by a single buyer. Some eventually sold their maize at prices 25 per cent lower than the official floor price. Others were forced into inequitable barter deals. In August 1994, the Zambia Catholic Commission for Justice and Peace reported that poor farmers were bartering cereals for groceries at 'ridiculously low prices', citing the exchange of a 15kg bag of maize for two tablets of soap, worth only a quarter of the value of the maize at the previous year's prices.[78]

One women farmer from a village in Eastern Province summarises her experience under market deregulation in the following terms:

We were told that the ending of government purchase would be a good thing for us...that we would get a good price from the private traders. I have not seen any traders. This year I got the lowest price I can remember — it was not a fair price. How can I afford to pay for school fees and medicine when prices are so low?

The World Bank, which helped to shape the design of the liberalisation programme, has acknowledged the severe problems which emerged in implementation. The conclusion it has drawn is that these problems did not arise from a headlong rush into deregulation, but from the government's concern to establish a floor price. Affirming its faith in the power of market deregulation to benefit the poor, the Bank commented:

The principles behind the maize pricing and market reforms are sound and in the long run will help reduce poverty ... Their (i.e. poor producers) position can only be improved under liberalisation, where they will be in a position to choose freely between competing suppliers and purchasers.[79]

(Keynes' observation that 'in the long-run we are all dead' might have rather more resonance with many Zambian producers.)

It is certainly true that Zambia's maize marketing system was in need of reform. That system set up an unnecessary cycle, in which poor farmers were prevented from milling their own maize locally, which was sold to state monopolies, transported hundreds of kilometres to millers, and transported back in the form of maize meal. Yet the market deregulation measures through which these distortions were addressed proved to be economically inefficient, and highly damaging to the interests of many poor producers.

In Zimbabwe, a similar marketing system to that in Zambia was estimated to reduce the household incomes of the poorest families in communal areas, by raising the cost of their food staple.[80] The Zimbabwe Government's structural adjustment programme has addressed the inefficiencies in the maize marketing system in a constructive way. The state has remained a buyer of last resort, setting a floor under market prices in the more marginal areas. The marketing system has been opened up, so that small-scale millers have been allowed to process maize, ending the monopoly of large urban millers. Small-scale millers are now producing roller meal (a slightly less processed form of maize preferred by most consumers) at prices lower than the previously subsidised price. Recent studies have shown that small hammer mills can supply more than half the demand for maize meal in the main urban centres, providing benefits for the urban population, while reducing demands on public expenditure.[81] This is an example of a market reform process which has worked, without adverse effects on the welfare of poor people.

Stabilisation and small producers

Stabilisation measures have in many countries reinforced the pressures operating on smallholder producers. For instance, in Costa Rica, high interest rates (in excess of 30 per cent) and the reorientation of agricultural production, has diverted credit away from the food-staple sector, in which the vast majority of poor producers operate, into commercial export crops and commercially produced food crops. There is a similar story unfolding in Nicaragua. Between 1990 and 1993 credit provided to the smallholder sector in that country fell by half in the face of a sharp rise in interest rates. Although credit for livestock farming increased, this was oriented towards large-scale producers. Smallholder production of export crops such as cotton, coffee, and oilseeds has fallen, as has production of basic foodstuffs. The result is an increased dependence on food imports and a diminishing ability to pay for them. For a country with one of the world's most crushing debt burdens, this is unsustainable. It is also a prescription for the loss of rural livelihoods, increased poverty, and social dislocation.

The IMF view is that market interest rates are the building blocks for successful adjustment. Both the Fund and the World Bank point to the failures of subsidised credit schemes, arguing with some justification that most have acted as a conduit for transferring public resources into the hands of rural elites. But where small farmers are unable to obtain credit, it is very unlikely that they will be able to benefit from higher prices. Indeed, inadequate credit structures are one of the main reasons why the price reforms introduced under adjustment have failed significantly to increase agricultural production.[82] Of course, simply pumping out subsidised credit in the general direction of small farmers is unlikely to be either economically sustainable or socially beneficial. What is required are institutions specifically designed to enable small farmers lacking collateral to obtain and repay credit. Such initiatives would combine public and private finance in supporting communities, and their success would be dependent on other support services for farmers being in place, including technical and marketing advice and transport infrastructure.

Stabilisation, trade liberalisation, and growth

Almost all structural adjustment programmes regard budget stabilisation and trade liberalisation as of prime importance, although the specific policies implemented vary from country to country. The aim has been to restore macro-economic stability and growth. Policy recommendations in both areas have tended to favour the simultaneous adoption of radical budget reforms, the deregulation of financial markets to encourage foreign investment, and the withdrawal of trade protection, in what is often termed the 'big-bang' approach.

Budget stabilisation

Measured in terms of reducing public sector deficits, structural adjustment policies have made some important advances. According to the World Bank, the 15 countries in sub-Saharan Africa which adhered most closely to the policy targets set by the Bretton Woods agencies reduced their budget deficits by around one-third between 1983-1985 and 1986-1990.[83] However, these cuts were achieved mainly through cuts in spending, rather than increased revenue. The resulting retrenchment

fell mainly on public investment, with adverse consequences for economic recovery.[84] Oxfam has witnessed some of the resulting contradictions. In the Shinyanga area of Tanzania, for example, Oxfam works with smallholder producers of cotton. These producers increased their planting and production of cotton in response to price incentives, only to see much of their crop go to waste as the state marketing system collapsed. They lost desperately needed household income, and the country lost the foreign exchange earnings which the structural adjustment programme was intended to increase.

Stabilisation policies rely overwhelmingly on interest rates to achieve their objectives. The aim is to restrict money supply by squeezing credit out of the economy and deterring government spending. In recent years, the IMF has encouraged the use of government bonds to 'mop up' what is deemed to be excess liquidity in the economy, and reduce purchasing power. Once again there have been some spectacular success stories, if success is measured against the yardstick of reducing inflation. In Zambia, the squeeze on the domestic money supply lowered inflation from an annual rate of over 200 per cent in 1993, to 30 per cent in 1994.[85] The sale of foreign exchange reserves, another measure to siphon money out of the economy, contributed to the dramatic decline in inflation and an unplanned increase in the value of the Kwacha. The IMF duly declared Zambia a model for the rest of sub-Saharan Africa.

What it failed to point out was that real interest rates (i.e. the difference between the inflation rate and the nominal interest rate) in excess of 60 per cent had crippled investment in manufacturing industry, and squeezed virtually all credit out of non-commercial agricultural sectors. These punitively high interest rates made it far more attractive for investors to acquire government bonds than to invest in economic activities. With real interest rates on these bills in excess of 100 per cent in some periods, domestic and foreign investors were able to achieve in absolute security the aim of speculators worldwide: to take a sum of money and double it, without risk. Meanwhile, the textile industry, one of the labour-intensive sectors which adjustment was supposed to help, was starved of the investment it needed to adjust to increased competition from imports. Over one-third of the work force in the industry was laid off in 1993, reducing textile towns such as Livingstone to centres of mass unemployment.

Zambia's experience is a cautionary tale of the dangers associated with the IMF's obsessive preoccupation with lowering inflation, to the exclusion of all other considerations. Paradoxically, however, the IMF's supposedly stringent disciplines have given rise to some notably irresponsible forms of budget management. Prior to IMF surveillance, most governments covered budget deficits by the simple expedient of printing money and allowing inflation to act as a regressive tax. Today, they resort to the equally simple expedient of printing government bonds.

In Kenya, for instance, the government has failed to make a dent in its budget deficit, not least because most of it is directed towards maintaining parastatals, which are centres of patronage for the ruling party. What it has done since the IMF's insistence on the abolition of foreign exchange controls is to generate funds by offering government bonds to foreign investors, who have been attracted by some of the highest rates of return available on world markets. Speculators have made windfall gains, investment has fallen from already low levels (partly because of the rise in interest rates needed to attract foreign speculators), and the country has been left with burgeoning obligations to foreign creditors, to add to those it was already unable to meet. Meanwhile, exporters condemned the government for policies which, by articifially driving up the value of the currency, were rendering them uncompetitive in foreign markets.[86] The ultimate irony is that this exercise in financial irresponsibility is effectively funded by the IMF and foreign donors, since it is they who provide the financial assistance with which the Kenyan government repays its creditors.

Trade liberalisation

Trade liberalisation under structural adjustment is intended to promote export-led recovery by reducing the costs of imports. The stated aim is to promote efficiency through increased competition, while enabling potential exporters to acquire the imports they need to raise productivity. Import liberalisation has been implemented more vigorously than almost any other aspect of adjustment apart from devaluation. Latin America now has lower tariff protection than any other developing region.[87] The average tariff rates in six of the largest countries in Latin America are half those in East and South-East Asia.[88] Much of sub-Saharan Africa has undergone a transformation in trade policy of only marginally less impressive dimensions. In the past, most governments maintained 'positive lists' stipulating what imports were allowed in without regulation; most lists were very small. Under structural adjustment programmes most governments now have 'negative lists', which allow all goods to be imported on open-general license (OGL) schemes, unless expressly prohibited. In Zambia, the OGL scheme covered 95 per cent of imports in 1992, compared to 10 per cent in 1988.

There was a clear case for carefully phased trade liberalisation in both regions. In many countries, protection of local industry had been raised to excessive levels. Tariff structures had fostered dependence on imported capital goods, instead of promoting more self-reliant industrial structures through effective protection of nascent industries. However, rapid import liberalisation has not created the conditions for a recovery in production and employment. Under the deflationary conditions associated with adjustment, a sudden withdrawal of trade protection can destroy potentially competitive industries by exposing them to levels of competition to which they are unable to respond.[89] Foreign exchange shortages and high interest rates mean that industries are often unable to get the imports they need to improve efficiency. Low levels of domestic demand and capacity utilisation often compound the uncompetitive position of local industries.

The end result of trade liberalisation under these conditions is often the opposite of that intended by structural adjustment. Employment in local industry is destroyed in the face of intense competition. Local production suffers, leading to an increased dependence on imports, reduced exports, and persistent balance of payments problems. These are often dealt with by yet more deflationary measures, leaving local industry and employment trapped in a vicious downward spiral.[90]

Compelling evidence for this spiral has recently been provided by Mexico. In the mid-1980s the World Bank provided two major structural adjustment loans to support import liberalisation. These have since been complemented by the North American Free Trade Agreement (NAFTA), which has transformed Mexico into one of the most open economies in Latin America, especially for trade with the US and Canada. The abrupt liberalisation of trade has had dramatic effects, notably in the form of a trade deficit with the US which expanded from $5bn in 1989 to $30bn in 1994. In the latter year, the overall current-account deficit stood at around 8 per cent of national income, higher even than it had been on the eve of the country's debt crisis in the early 1980s.[91] Under normal market conditions, this deficit would have resulted in currency devaluation, which would have driven up inflation and prevented the government from meeting its targets for financial stabilisation. The Mexican government sought to resolve this conundrum by attracting speculative foreign capital through government bonds carrying exceptionally high interest rates. As the current account deficit grew, the interest rates needed to sustain these capital inflows increased, before the bubble finally burst in December, 1994 and the Mexican peso lost half its value in two weeks.[92]

The shock-waves from Mexico's financial crisis spread rapidly to other emergent markets, prompting stock-exchange collapses across the region. But the most devastating effects of the NAFTA have been experienced not by stock-market operators, but by the Mexican poor. The liberalisation of trade with the US exposed fragile domestic industries to levels of competition for which they were ill-prepared. Upward pressure on commercial interest rates reduced investment, especially in medium- and small-scale enterprises, as savings were diverted into speculative bond markets. In 1992 the country's textile industry shrank by 5 per cent, as imports expanded their market share.[93] While new, low-wage jobs were being created in the *maquiladora* zone, employment opportunities overall contracted. In 1993 alone, over 600,000 jobs were lost in the manufacturing sector. Wages have fallen sharply, with minimum wages losing one-third of their value between 1987 and 1994.

The result has been a process of growth through exclusion, with high profits in the financial sector and increased prosperity for the middle classes, obscuring the worsening welfare of the poor. According to one study, almost half-a-million people joined the ranks of the extremely poor between 1989 and 1992. Meanwhile, the already huge gap between rich and poor widened. In 1992, the richest 20 per cent of the population received 54 per cent of national income, compared to 48 per cent in 1984. Over the same period, the poorest 20 per cent saw their share fall from 5 per cent to 4 per cent, mainly due to falling wages.[94] It is likely to fall further in the wake of the country's financial crisis. With the rising costs of imports pushing up inflation, the Mexican government has initiated a new round of stabilisation, in which wages will bear the brunt of the adjustment.[95] Once again, ill-conceived 'big-bang' trade liberalisation and market deregulation have benefited the wealthy, and the costs have been borne by the poor.

The rapid removal of protection from local industries is socially and economically disruptive even in countries with a diverse manufacturing base. That is why governments in the industrialised world, for all their adherence to

free-trade principles, would never countenance trade liberalisation practices on the scale of
those implemented by governments in Latin
America and Africa. The social and economic
costs of rapid and poorly co-ordinated trade
liberalisation are apparent across much of these
regions. In Nicaragua, for example, the virtual
elimination of tariffs under a 1990 IMF-World
Bank programme, coupled with the imposition
of severely deflationary policies, resulted in a 14
per cent decline in industrial production during the period 1990-1993. Employment levels
fell from an average of 106,000 in the latter half
of the 1980s, to 60,000 in 1993.[96] De-industrial-
isation has also been evident in West Africa,
where local industries have contracted in the
face of intense competition.

Serious tensions can emerge between stabilisation programmes intended to restrict demand, and economic reforms intended to
expand output. These tensions focus on the
sequence in which reforms are introduced in
the three areas of trade policy, financial and
monetary policy, and public investment in
social and economic infrastructure. Where
import policy is liberalised without countervailing support for domestic industries, then
unemployment and disinvestment can result.
Similarly, failure to stabilise budgets in advance
of import liberalisation can, as in Mexico, lead
to rapid inflows of capital which artificially
inflate currency values, to the detriment of
industries producing for the local market, of
exporters, and of the poor. All these problems
point to the need for the careful design, co-
ordination, and phasing of reforms in the interests of maximising employment and generating
recovery. Unfortunately, the IMF-World Bank
continue to favour a 'big-bang' approach, preferring to place their faith in sudden trade
liberalisation and the capacity of market forces
to restructure economies for the public good.

Labour market deregulation

Labour market deregulation has figured prominently as an element of structural adjustment.

Both the World Bank and the IMF argue that
past forms of government intervention in fixing
minimum wages and enforcing security of
employment were an impediment to labour
mobility, and a cause of unemployment. As
unemployment has increased under structural
adjustment, they have argued for the withdrawal of obstacles to mobility and the introduction of 'flexible' labour practices. The sparse
regulation of labour markets in South-East Asia
is often cited in defence of the case for
'flexibility'.

This approach suffers from several shortcomings. First, it wrongly isolates labour market
regulation and high wages as a major cause of
unemployment. Wages fell dramatically in
Africa and Latin America in the 1980s, even
where formal labour market regulations were
in place, without improving employment levels.
The collapse of the economic model based upon
import substitution, and debt, were far more
important causes of economic decline than high
wages, in both regions. Second, although the
suppression of the labour movement in South-
East Asia was an accompaniment to economic
growth in that region, it is doubtful whether it
was a necessary feature, and it was of marginal
significance in comparison to wider economic
policies. More recently, the improved recognition of trade union rights in countries such as
South Korea has not had a negative effect on
growth rates. As the ILO has written of Latin
America:

*Developments with respect to labour market
regulation do not provide confirmation of the view
that it is necessary to have an unregulated labour
market in order to be internationally competitive.*[97]

Quite apart from the fallacies in the
arguments used to support 'flexible' labour
practices, such practices have consequences
which are both economically and socially
undesirable. They are economically undesirable because, in many countries, low wages and
insecure employment lead to low productivity,
inadequate training, and high levels of absent-
eeism. There can be little doubt that, in many

countries, wages have fallen below efficiency levels. In Tanzania, for example, by 1988 the average monthly wage was insufficient to provide an adequate family diet. By 1991, it would barely buy enough food for 20 days.[98] Drastic wage reductions also have the effect of reducing demand for local producers, undermining growth prospects, and deepening recession. The World Bank itself has acknowledged that this was one of the reasons for the failure of Bolivia's adjustment programme in the 1980s.[99]

Flexible labour markets are socially unjust because they involve highly exploitative labour practices, especially with regard to women. The trend towards 'flexible' labour markets has often reduced the return to female labour, and the security of employment. One woman working in a garment workshop in Recoleta, the textiles centre of the Chilean capital of Santiago, puts it in these terms:

I have four children. If I did not work, they would not eat. But even when I work sixteen hours a day, I make hardly enough to stay alive. I have no contract and no security. How can I build a future like this?

In Chile, 'flexibility', one of the watchwords of structural adjustment, has meant working harder, for longer hours and less pay, with a loss of job security. Even though unemployment has fallen and women are participating in labour markets on an unprecedented scale, adjustment policies have not eliminated long-standing problems of poverty. In 1992, almost half of all workers earned less than enough to provide for their basic needs. As a recent report by the United Nations Research Institute for Social Development confirmed, the single major cause of poverty in Chile is not unemployment, but precarious, low-wage employment.[100]

A prescription for growth?

The Bretton Woods agencies both recognise the social costs of adjustment. They claim, however, that economic recovery is taking root in those countries which are adhering to structural adjustment policies. Unfortunately, the evidence upon which this claim is based is exceptionally weak. Evidence of the failure of structural adjustment programmes is particularly comprehensive in sub-Saharan Africa. In no other region have such programmes been applied more frequently. Excluding sectoral adjustment loans, there have been more than 160 World Bank and IMF loan agreements covering over 30 countries since the early 1980s: more than for the whole of the rest of the world.[101] Some countries have had the questionable privilege of uninterrupted structural adjustment programmes for some 15 years. Moreover, these programmes have been supported by around $200bn in net development assistance since 1982. Foreign aid doubled as a proportion of regional GDP from just under 5 per cent for the first half of the 1980s to almost 10 per cent for 1998-1992. These aid flows increased Africa's share of global aid to almost 40 per cent in 1991.[102] On a per capita basis, sub-Saharan Africa receives around four times more aid than other low-income countries.

Despite these transfers, average incomes in Africa fell by over 1 per cent a year in the 1980s, and have continued their decline in the 1990s.[103] Investment today is lower in real terms than in 1980, and the region has suffered loss of world market share and foreign investment. There is no shortage of candidates to blame for the crisis. Civil conflict, domestic policy mismanagement, corruption, debt, and deteriorating terms of trade, have all contributed to varying degrees. But so have structural adjustment programmes. Attempting to separate the effects of these programmes from other factors, internal and external, is a hazardous exercise, which is made more complicated by the 'counterfactual' case: what would have happened *without* structural adjustment? The question is impossible to answer. Another complication, strongly emphasised by the IMF and the World Bank, is the non-compliance of governments with the conditions of their structural adjustment programmes. In fact, however, implementation has been more rigorous than is often claimed. According to one World Bank study published in 1990, compliance for all adjustment conditions was in the range of 75 per cent, with particularly high levels of target attainment in fiscal policy, trade liberalisation, exchange rate policy, and wages.[104] Termination of adjustment programmes was a rare occurrence in the 1980s, with only 21 out of 241 programmes being abandoned, and has remained so in the 1990s.

Efforts to gauge the success of structural adjustment programmes have focused on comparisons of countries within various performance categories, ranked according to their compliance with adjustment policies. Studies by the IMF and the World Bank have attempted to establish a correlation between these policies and economic growth rates. This has proved difficult. In one study of adjustment lending in the 1980s, the World Bank concluded that:

Adjustment lending has not significantly affected economic growth and has contributed to a statistically significant drop in investment ratios...Also, adjustment lending programmes did not significantly affect inflation or saving to GDP ratios.[105]

The World Bank's third review of adjustment lending, published in 1992, confirmed the weak correlation between adjustment policies and growth. 'Core' adjusting countries identified in this study succeeded in expanding per capita income at 1 per cent a year: a growth rate at which it would take 70 years to double per capita incomes.[106]

Reviews of IMF programmes have reached similarly unfavourable conclusions, although these have been repackaged to provide a more positive interpretation. For example, in a review of 19 countries (all but four African) which had graduated from the IMF's Structural Adjustment Facility programmes to its Enhanced Structural Adjustment Facility Programmes, the Fund claimed to detect evidence which 'confirme(d) that these countries had improved their economic performance signifi-

cantly', especially when compared to country's without IMF programmes.[107] In fact, the statistical evidence raised more questions than it answered. While countries embarking on SAF did record an increase in growth following the inception of SAF programmes, for the ESAF period the growth rate *fell* from 4 per cent to 2.8 per cent. This was below the average population growth rate, and only marginally higher than for countries without IMF programmes (which had received less donor assistance, and had a worse external trade environment, and more serious budgetary problems). Moreover, despite a strong increase in the growth of export volumes, countries adhering most closely to IMF programmes did not achieve significantly better results in terms of reducing their budget deficits or reaching more viable balance-of-payments positions. An independent review of the IMF study found no significant correlation between adherence to an IMF programme and improvements in macroeconomic stability.[108]

These data are open to different interpretations, but what appears beyond serious doubt is that, apart from the disappointing impact of adjustment on GDP growth rates, there is a strong negative correlation between adherence to structural adjustment and investment, with serious consequences for future growth, employment, and poverty reduction. Comparing the position in 1980 with 1986-1990, countries classified by the World Bank as 'intensive adjusters' suffered a drop in investment from 25 per cent of GDP to 15 per cent. Savings also declined, with a resulting increase in dependence on foreign aid. For Africa as a whole, investment rates fell as a proportion of national income in 25 countries, with investment per head falling by half.

Recent World Bank evaluations presented as a vindication of structural adjustment have taken on a slightly desperate air. In *Adjustment in Africa: Reforms, Results and the Road Ahead*, the World Bank categorises countries according to how closely their economies conform to an adjusted ideal (broadly balanced budgets, sustainable trade balances, and market-based exchange rates). Six countries — Ghana, Zimbabwe, Gambia, Nigeria, Burkina Faso, and Tanzania — are identified on the basis of having made 'large improvements' over the period 1981-1986 and 1987-1991, which are claimed to be associated with higher growth rates. Summarising its conclusions, the Bank asks: 'Is adjustment paying off in sub-Saharan Africa? The answer is a qualified yes.' [109]

From a close inspection of the evidence, it is possible to arrive at precisely the opposite conclusion. For example, Burkina Faso is included, even though it was implementing a 'home-grown' adjustment programme which bore little resemblance to those advocated by the IMF-World Bank; Zimbabwe did not have a programme with the IMF-World Bank for most of the period, and made little progress in reducing its budget deficit; and Gambia's success was built on a tourist boom which was weakly connected to the rest of the economy. In each of these countries growth was either negative or only marginally positive. Indeed, without Nigeria, where the adjustment programme collapsed in 1988, the group of large improvers would have lower average growth rates than countries which were less diligent in following adjustment-style policies. In reality, very little can be discerned from studies such as this. What they confirm is that large initial devaluations of massively over-valued currencies have a major impact in expanding export production. However, few countries have been able to combine stabilisation with balance of payments improvements and economic growth. [110]

One of the worrying findings to emerge from the World Bank's study, is that agricultural production (as distinct from agricultural export production), has a lower rate of growth in countries adhering most closely to conventional adjustment policies. This trend, which has potentially damaging consequences for rural employment, poverty reduction, and food self-reliance, appears to be closely correlated with reductions in the public provision of extension services under adjustment programmes. Exter-

nal factors, notably a marked deterioration in terms of trade, are partially responsible for the failures of structural adjustment. Even here, however, the design of adjustment policies has contributed.

In the early 1980s, the IMF and the World Bank sought to address Africa's trade imbalances by expanding the production of primary commodities, and raising producer prices through exchange-rate and trade reforms. Expansion of exports of primary commodities was similarly stimulated through project-lending and macro-economic reforms in Asia and Latin America. By encouraging a large number of producers to export a small number of commodities into already saturated markets, however, the IMF and the World Bank contributed to the deep depression in world prices. Cocoa provides a clear example. Between 1980 and 1992, West African cocoa producers increased their production from 1.6 million to 2.3 million tons. [111] Because these countries are major suppliers to the world market, the resulting increase in exports contributed to the collapse of world prices, which fell by more than half over the same period. As a result, countries such as Ghana doubled their exports but earned less foreign exchange. [112] While it was necessary to introduce exchange rate devaluation and lower producer taxes to restore the market shares lost since the 1970s, the failure of the IMF and World Bank either to anticipate the consequences of commodity over-supply, or to encourage moves towards international co-operation in managing commodity markets, was irresponsible.

Recent research by the OECD has confirmed that export promotion for primary commodities has been linked to a deterioration in trade performances. In an economic simulation of the effects of a 25 per cent reduction in export taxes, the OECD found that the resulting increase in supplies and decrease in prices would reduce the national income of major coffee and cocoa exporters by up to 0.5 per cent, and cause a deterioration in the terms of trade of around 12 per cent. [113] Ironically, the IMF has blamed adverse terms of trade for the failure of many of its programmes to restore balance-of-payments stability.

The oft-cited exception to the picture of Afro-pessimism is Ghana, which has been the IMF-World Bank's five-star performer for more than a decade. More recently, Uganda has succeeded is establishing high economic growth rates, although from a low economic base. The question is whether or not these growth processes are sustainable: the evidence is mixed. By African standards, the 2 per cent a year increase in average income achieved since 1983 is impressive. But at current rates of growth, it will be another two decades before Ghana joins the ranks of middle-income countries; and another 50 years before the average Ghanaian crosses the poverty line. This is despite international aid transfers equivalent to 8 per cent of the country's national income. Meanwhile, there has been little progress towards diversification, manufacturing exports are negligible, and investment rates, one of the keys to sustained economic recovery, are less than a quarter of those in South-East Asian economies such as Thailand. Without its international aid lifeline, there can be little doubt that, after a dozen years of adjustment, the Ghanaian economy would collapse under the weight of a foreign debt which has tripled to $1.3bn since 1986.

Latin America

The bleak picture which emerges from sub-Saharan Africa is of a set of policy prescriptions which have failed to establish a framework for economic recovery and poverty reduction. In contrast to Africa, however, Latin America is often presented by the IMF and World Bank as a region which, with some exceptions, has made the transition through macro-economic stabilisation and adjustment to sustained growth. Poverty reduction, so the argument runs, will be the natural outcome of this economic recovery, as growth feeds into the creation of employment and rising incomes.

Unfortunately, the evidence does not sustain the argument. Growth rates for Latin America

have recovered from the 'lost decade' of the 1980s, when the region saw its combined income fall by one-tenth. Growth has averaged over 3 per cent a year since 1990, although the recovery has been unequally spread (per capita incomes have declined in Nicaragua and Honduras, for example).[114] Translated into per capita terms, income has increased at the exceptionally modest average annual rate of 1.7 per cent. That is half the growth rate of the 1970s, suggesting that structural adjustment policies may suffer from shortcomings which are more pronounced than those associated with import substitution. At current rates of growth it will take 40 years for average regional income to double.[115] This performance is even less impressive alongside the other benchmark criteria for structural adjustment: inflation and export growth. After falling for three years, regional inflation doubled in 1993, to 800 per cent on an annual basis. At best, the record in this area has been mixed and unstable. Export growth has been feeble in most countries (expecially when measured against the extremely low starting point of the late 1980s), averaging around 4 per cent a year.[116] This has proved insufficient to establish balance-of-payments stability, with trade deficits being covered, as they were in the 1970s, by foreign capital flows. Here, too, the central dilemmas of import-substitution remain unresolved. Viewed from a poverty reduction perspective, Latin American growth patterns are neither strong enough nor equitable enough to bring sustained improvements in human welfare.

In its preliminary overview of Latin American economies for 1994, the Economic Commission for Latin America and the Caribbean (ECLAC) concluded: 'Generally speaking, it is clear that growth rates under 4 per cent...are not high enough to allow major inroads in the battle against poverty or to prevent unemployment from remaining unacceptably high.'[117] The deeper question is whether the existing pattern of growth will ever create the employment needed to reduce poverty. Part of the problem is that employment creation is lagging behind economic growth. Unemployment rose in Brazil, Argentina, and Bolivia. In Peru a growth rate of 11 per cent failed to reduce unemployment, which affects one in ten of the population.

Arguably the most striking feature of Latin America's economic performance has been the huge inflow of foreign capital, amounting to around $184bn over the past three years. These inflows have masked some of the structural weaknesses in Latin America's recovery, notably the huge deficit — amounting to over $50bn — in the region's merchandise trade, but inflows are unlikely to be sustainable in the longer term. Over three-quarters of the funds flowing into Latin America are high-risk, non-investment bonds — more commonly known as 'junk bonds'.[118] The flow is being driven by the attraction of quick profits from investment in government bonds and the sale of government utilities, rather than productive investment in the economy. The resulting growth in financial markets brings major benefits to those associated with them, but few benefits in terms of job creation and increased prosperity for lower income groups. In 1994, direct foreign investment accounted for only $15bn out of $57bn of foreign capital inflows.[119] Quite apart from causing financial instability, the capital inflows have artifically increased currency values, with adverse effects for livelihoods in the real economy. In Mexico, for instance, the over-valued peso made imported foods cheaper, undermining markets for rural smallholders, and encouraging the displacement of local manufacturing production by cheap imports.

The underlying weaknesses in Latin America's recovery are reflected in other areas. During the 1980s, public investment in social and economic infrastructure collapsed. If it is not restored, there is little prospect of economic recovery taking root; and no prospect of its benefits being more equitably spread. During the 1980s, per capita spending on primary education, one of the most important determinants of growth prospects, fell by half, and it remains lower today than in1980. One in five children of primary school age do not attend school;

around one-third of the region's population do not have adequate sanitation or an electricity supply.[120] Economic infrastructure is dilapidated and a deterrent to investment. Yet while there is a growing recognition of the need for restoration, the shifting of government assets and responsibilities to the private sector, and an entrenched reluctance to disturb elite consumption patterns by expanding the tax base, make it difficult to see how public investment is to be financed.

The failure of investment levels to recover raises serious questions over the durability of the economic recovery process.[121] According to the ECLAC, investment rates need to increase from their present level of around 17 per cent of national income to 22 per cent if recovery is to be sustained. Yet there has been only a marginal increase in investment, despite the economic recovery. In 1992, Latin America's investment and savings rates were less than half those for the high-performing Asian countries.[122] This represents an obstacle to poverty reduction which lies at the heart of Latin America's inequitable growth patterns. Despite high real interest rates, domestic savings levels have fallen. One reason is that upper-income groups prefer to use their increasing wealth to buy imported consumer goods, which have been made more easily available through trade liberalisation, rather than to invest it. Latin America's growth is being directed into holidays in Miami, and expensive imported stereos, designer clothing, and other status imports which fill shopping malls from Bogota to Buenos Aires. The disruptive effects of the resulting trade deficit are contained partly through wage restraint, and partly through foreign capital inflows. The high interest rates needed to attract the latter are undermining manufacturing investment and employment creation.

An alternative framework for structural adjustment

There are no ready-made, universal blueprints for successful adjustment to economic pressures. But it is possible to devise a new model for adjustment which combines equity and economic efficiency in a manner which offers hope for poverty eradication into the next century. As we suggest below, international action to resolve the debt problems of the world's poorest countries will be vital if any form of adjustment is to succeed. But so will institutional changes and new policy priorities on the part of the Bretton Woods agencies themselves.

The need for institutional change

The Bretton Woods agencies exercise through their structural adjustment programmes an enormous influence over economic and social policy in developing countries. Yet neither institution is accountable, in any meaningful way, to the citizens of those countries. With some justification, both the IMF and the World Bank are widely perceived in the South as institutions representing Northern interests and offering policy prescriptions designed by Northern governments. The resulting 'democratic deficit' has been summarised in colourful terms by Samuel Huntington, who has written:

In any poll of non-Western peoples, the IMF undoubtedly would win the support of finance ministers and a few others, but get an overwhelmingly unfavourable rating from just about everyone else.[123]

Part of the problem is that the Bretton Woods agencies are governed through a system of 'one-dollar-one vote', with nations allocated voting rights according to their financial stake. Developing countries account for more than three-quarters of the IMF's membership, but they have only one-third of the voting share. Such structures give Northern governments an undue influence. The also create a democratic

deficit in developing countries themselves. While urging developing country governments to become more open and accountable to their citizens, Northern governments appear content to see power over economic policy transferred to agencies which they control. The result is a perversion of the principles of 'good governance'.

If developing country governments are to become more accountable for structural adjustment policies which affect the lives of their citizens, they must be given greater power to shape these policies in the World Bank and IMF. Voting structures in both agencies should be reformed to allow for more democratic representation, in which political influence more closely reflects the composition of their membership. At the same time, the Bretton Woods agencies should be more closely integrated into the UN system. It is often forgotten that both the IMF and the World Bank are supposed to be part of the UN, even though they have developed parallel structures. These structures need reform. Both the IMF and the World Bank have a vital role to play in supporting economic reforms and in helping to create the conditions for full employment. This is what they were set up to do. However, both agencies have assumed a powerful role in shaping social policy. It is far from clear whether they are equipped to play that role; or if they are in a position to evaluate the social impact of macro-economic reforms. These are areas in which the specialised agencies of the UN should be given an enhanced role in the design, implementation, and evaluation of structural adjustment. As we suggested in Chapter 1, these are also grounds for the various social treaty monitoring bodies of the UN to monitor the effect of IMF and World Bank policies on vulnerable social groups. The moral voice of such bodies could play an important role in shaping structural adjustment policies into a broader and more effective strategy for poverty reduction.

Increased openness is also vital to the reform of structural adjustment programmes. Community participation in the social, political, and economic sphere is an important element in the adjustment process, both as an end in itself and because it increases the equity and efficiency of development. At present, however, the entire structural adjustment process is opaque and surrounded in secrecy. Developing country governments bear considerable responsibility for this, not least since they have an interest in blaming 'external' forces for policies which may be socially painful and politically unpopular.

Availability of information

There are a number of ways in which this secretive approach could be changed. In general, information should be made more widely and more readily available. Policy Framework Papers, which set out the overall orientation of adjustment policies and include broad targets, are negotiated, usually without public debate, between the IMF-World Bank and governments. People in Zimbabwe had no inkling that the Bretton Woods agencies were recommending increases in user-fees for health and education, or that their government had agreed to them. If they had, community organisations with experience in both sectors could have provided information to guide policy decisions.

This is part of a wider problem which is linked to the refusal of governments and the Bretton Woods agencies to open dialogue on structural adjustment to wider scrutiny. For example, the Policy Framework Papers, which are negotiated between governments, the World Bank, and the IMF, and set out the policies and conditions attached to structural adjustment loans, are negotiated without public debate, and they are not made publically available. Similarly, the World Bank's Country Assistance Strategies, giving its analysis and policy recommendations, are treated as internal documents. Publication of these documents would contribute to an improved public debate. But the wider objective must be to involve at an early stage representative groups, such as trade unions, NGOs, and women's organisations, in

designing, monitoring, and evaluating adjustment programmes. It is encouraging that senior World Bank officials are now thinking along these lines.

Greater disclosure of information is especially necessary with regard to the IMF, which operates in an extremely secretive manner. Conditions for stabilisation and monetary policy established by the Fund under its Enhanced Structural Adjustment Facility (ESAF) set the macro-economic framework within which adjustment occurs in many low-income countries. However, the two documents setting out these conditions (the Performance Criteria and Structural Benchmark papers attached to EASF agreements) are made available only to the IMF's Board and, on a confidential basis, to a handful of other organisations (such as the EU and regional development banks). Once again, greater openness and accountability would facilitate wider participation in evaluating the likely outcomes of IMF conditions.

The IMF, far more than the World Bank, is responsible for the detailed monitoring and appraisal of economic performance. Under its Article 1V consultations, the Fund carries out surveillance and reports to its Board on macro-economic performance. It also prepares six-monthly reports on countries with ESAF programmes. These exercises suffer from two major shortcomings. First, the reports focus on narrow macro-economic indicators, without evaluating the implications for poverty, livelihoods, and social welfare provision. Second, they are confidential, as are the Fund's *Recent Economic Development Reports*, which provide the most comprehensive accounts of developments under adjustment in almost all developing countries. Once again, these documents should be made more widely available in developing countries, and their scope broadened to include evaluations of IMF programmes with respect to their success in reducing poverty.

Wider participation in the design and implementation of adjustment policies would also allow for more effective monitoring of their effects. Through its poverty assessments, the World Bank has made genuine efforts to involve community organisations and NGOs in evaluating the impact of structural adjustment on poverty. It has also attempted to develop participatory assessment methods, finding out from people their own experience of adjustment. These are new and encouraging departures which should be developed. There is some scope for improvement; for example, the poverty assessment procedure is cumbersome, often involving around two years' work to produce reports which are out of date by the time they are published. What is required is a more effective way of monitoring the effects of adjustment as they are felt by vulnerable groups, for example through periodic participatory surveys, and some way of ensuring that poverty assessments feed directly into policy design. Also, more effective methods are needed to monitor the impact of adjustment on women, especially with regard to their time and workloads. It is important that poverty assessments are made more relevant to the design and implementation of adustment policies. However, there is little evidence at present that the findings from these assessments are influencing the formulation of macro-economic policy.

Reforming stabilisation

Budget stabilisation is a vital precondition for successful adjustment. However, the repeated introduction and implementation of IMF-World Bank programmes in low-income countries suggests that these countries have been unable to restore the conditions for self-sustained growth. In many cases, the programmes have been accompanied by continued economic deterioration, widening inequality, and rising poverty. One reason for these failures is that adjustment policies have tended to exacerbate, rather than eradicate, underlying structural problems in the economy. New forms of stabilisation are needed which combine realistic fiscal targets with equitable ways of

achieving them.

Particularly problematic has been the pursuit of unrealistic targets for reducing inflation, with an over-reliance on deflationary monetarist policies for achieving them. These policies are inconsistent with the aims of poverty reduction and recovery. Very high interest rates have hampered economic recovery and investment activity, with damaging consequences for employment creation. Meanwhile, wages have borne the brunt of the counter-inflationary pressure, resulting in dramatic falls in household incomes. According to the IMF, the lowering of wages and the deregulation of labour markets create the conditions for future employment expansion. However, when wages fall below subsistence level, they are not merely damaging for human welfare: they also reduce productivity and demand.

Adjustment policies should set targets for budget deficit reduction and interest rates which are compatible with economic recovery and employment creation. They should also place more emphasis on revenue expansion, through progressive tax measures, as an alternative to reduced public expenditure on social welfare and economic infrastructure. Current approaches to revenue expansion focus on sales taxes and other measures which can be regressive in their effects. There are other options. For example, under a self-imposed adjustment programme in the 1980s, Burkina Faso was able to increase government revenue from 13 per cent in 1983 to 16 per cent of national income in 1986, while maintaining an expansionary economic environment. It was able to do so by improving tax collection and introducing progressive taxes, such as a wealth tax, a property tax on urban landlords, and fees for use of paved roads.[124] Accompanying reductions in expenditure were achieved through measures such as a ban on the importation of luxury cars by government officials.

Policies aimed at reducing fiscal deficits through increased taxation need to be introduced as part of a convincing 'national project' that persuades the private sector that the government is serious about growth and able to deliver. In this way, tax reform can be introduced in a way which will avoid its acting as a disincentive to investment and employment creation. In Latin America in particular, there are powerful reasons of equity and efficiency for an increase in taxation of the richest section of society to reverse the decline in the ratio of public expenditure to GDP. The richest 20 per cent of the region's population receive around two-thirds of its income, but pay less than 3 per cent of its tax.[125] Increasing income tax on this group would bring benefits in terms of increased revenue to finance the public expenditure upon which sustainable economic recovery will depend. Supported by import duties and sales taxes on luxury items, it would also curtail the consumption of imported luxury goods which is worsening the chronic trade deficits facing the region.

In the Philippines, the Freedom from Debt Coalition (FDC), has built a mass public campaign against the introduction of a regressive sales tax, which will increase prices for basic items, designed to meet IMF budget targets. While accepting the need for a reduced budget deficit, the FDC campaign is aimed at making the rich pay proportionately more through increased income tax, because an increase in rates of VAT would mean that the poor would shoulder more of the burden. They propose an increase from 35 per cent to 56 per cent in the proportion of tax revenue generated by income tax; stricter enforcement of tax collection to prevent evasion (current evasion rates reduce the tax returns from the corporate sector by one-third and from individuals by two-thirds); the withdrawal of tax privileges for foreign-owned companies; and the withdrawal of 'tax holiday' provisions and duty exemption.[126]

Trade policy and the role of the state

One of the central aims of structural adjustment has been to diminish the role of the state in economic life, allowing market forces to dictate economic restructuring. The policy failures of the past have been used to justify this approach. However, there is mounting evidence to suggest that market deregulation has also been profoundly unsuccessful in bringing about sustainable and equitable growth. As the United Nations Conference on Trade and Development has put it: 'Admittedly, there has been much misguided intervention in the past; but that is no reason to throw the baby out with the bath water.'

As with structural adjustment in the broader sense, there is no blueprint for appropriate trade policy; but there are important lessons from South-East Asia which suggest viable alternatives to the 'invisible hand' of the market. Trade policy in South Korea and Taiwan included the extensive but selective use of import tariffs and quotas to protect firms producing for the domestic markets. Export incentives were also provided in the form of cheap credit.[127] These measures formed part of a wider strategy for industrial development, including support for technological innovation and strict controls over foreign investment and capital markets.[128] Governments in both countries played a critical role in directing investment resources into potentially competitive sectors, regulating the markets, and generating new forms of comparative advantage. While there was much greater state capacity in these countries than in many others in the developing world today, this is not an argument for weak states to give up on managing markets. On the contrary, the Asian economic success story underlines the need for both public sector and wider institutional reform.

By contrast, experience under sudden trade liberalisation and the withdrawal of the state is hardly encouraging. Chile is often cited as a model adjusting country which combined relatively high growth rates with a move towards market deregulation and low uniform tariffs during the 1970s and 1980s. However, Chile's 'success' was more partial than is often recognised. The country's manufacturing export growth has been relatively weak (just over 3 per cent a year in the 1980s). Despite two decades of liberalisation, and its large human resource base, Chile's manufacturing exports are only $96 per capita, compared to $3,5000 for Taiwan. Colombia, unlike Chile, retained significant trade barriers and state intervention during the 1980s, yet it grew faster (despite adverse trends in its terms of trade), diversified its exports more rapidly, and improved its indicators of basic human welfare.[129]

If there is a lesson to be learnt in this area, it is that successful exporters have usually been able to combine protection of the domestic market with export promotion. The World Bank itself has acknowledged this in a widely-cited study of economic growth in East Asia. According to the Bank, however, the forms of state intervention which underpinned that growth could not be pursued today, partly because they would be inconsistent with obligations under the World Trade Organisation.[130] This suggests that there is a powerful case for reforming international trade rules as well as adjustment policies.

One area in which reform is particularly urgent is in the regulation of capital markets, which adjustment policies have sought to de-regulate. Evidence from Latin America suggests that speculative capital flows are destabilising recovery prospects by causing severe balance of payments instability. One of the lessons from Mexico's experience is that sustainable recovery cannot be built on junk bonds. There are lessons here from countries such as Chile and South Korea, where governments have actively discouraged speculative capital flows through regulations on profit repatriation and taxes on short-term capital. It is no coincidence that, in contrast to other emergent markets, both countries survived the crash which followed Mexico's financial debâcle relatively unscathed.

Finally, structural adjustment policies need to focus to a far greater extent on developing regional trade opportunities. At present, the IMF-World Bank approach to regional trade policy is the mirror image of their global trade policy: namely, that restrictions should be removed across the board. What is needed is a more integrated approach, in which trade policy and other forms of state intervention are oriented towards the expansion of regional trade and employment. This is especially true in Africa, where intra-regional trade still accounts for less than 5 per cent of the total; and where in some regions, notably southern Africa, there are new opportunities for regional integration.

Social equity and conditionality

Structural adjustment policies have failed to achieve their stated poverty-reduction goals of increasing incomes and social welfare provision for poor people. This is because of an undue faith in the capacity of unregulated markets to operate to the benefit of the poor; and a failure to protect social services delivery.

In Oxfam's experience, market deregulation has often reduced the opportunities for poor people. The deregulation of agricultural markets has served, in many cases, to exclude vulnerable communities and enhance the power of powerful trading interests. In manufacturing, the deregulation of labour markets has made employment more insecure, and reduced wages to below the level of subsistence. As we have argued elsewhere in this report, redistributive strategies are needed so that poor people can acquire the productive assets, such as land and credit, which they need if they are to benefit from market deregulation.

The failure of adjustment policies to protect social provision can be traced to two causes. First, the IMF-World Bank and governments have failed to ensure that social expenditure is protected during adjustment. This suggests a case for more effective social conditionality. It will be argued by some that such conditionality would represent an unwarranted intrusion into political sovereignty. Viewed from a different perspective, health care, primary education, and other forms of welfare provision, are basic human rights, which governments and financial institutions both have an obligation to respect. Moreover, if economic conditionality is being enforced, it is hard to see how there can be grounds for not enforcing social conditionality. But, important as such conditionality may be, it should be developed not through edicts from the Bretton Woods agencies, but through dialogue and binding contracts involving governments, the IMF, World Bank, and UN agencies. Such contracts should focus on the attainment of specific targets for welfare provision and improvement, and be subject to close monitoring and surveillance by NGOs and grassroots groups.

Second, the move towards financing health and education provision through user-fees has had adverse consequences for poor people. The effect of these fees is to place services beyond their reach, with severe consequences in terms of lost opportunities and, in the health sector, lost lives and debilitating sickness. Against this background, adjustment programmes should aim at the progressive and speedy withdrawal of user-fees for primary health and primary education. Alternative forms of resource mobilisation should be developed at the national level and at the international level to replace revenues lost from cost-recovery.

Conclusion

It is now 15 years since structural adjustment policies started to dominate the economic policies of developing countries. Over that period, the Bretton Woods agencies have become increasingly aware of the need for a more poverty-focused approach. This has created the scope for a more substantive dialogue with grassroots groups in the South and with NGOs about the design and implementation of adjustment programmes. But welcome as the public commitment of the IMF and the World Bank to poverty reduction may be, in Oxfam's experience a vast gulf remains between public statements in favour of policies which benefit the poor, and the realities of structural adjustment. In practice, the costs of adjustment are still being borne disproportionately by the most vulnerable sections of society. Moreover, there is little evidence to substantiate

the claim that adjustment policies are creating a framework for more equitable growth and poverty reduction. In many countries they appear to be doing precisely the opposite.

With or without the IMF and the World Bank, many developing countries will continue to undergo painful adjustment processes into the next century. Their problems pre-date structural adjustment, and will not be resolved by external intervention. However, the Bretton Woods agencies, by virtue of their political and financial influence, can play an important role in developing genuinely poverty-focused adjustment strategies. If they are to do so, fundamental reforms in policy design and implementation will be vital, including an early departure from the free-market orthodoxies to which both remain wedded. Failure to embark on these reforms will mark a further betrayal of the principles upon which the Bretton Woods system was founded.

For their part, NGOs, including Oxfam, have a responsibility to engage the Bretton Woods agencies in a more constructive dialogue. Defending past forms of state intervention, which have self-evidently failed the poor, is no more a starting place for such a dialogue than a recitation of the received wisdom of free-market economics. All sides in the debate over adjustment share a common interest in developing a better understanding of the effects of macro-economic reforms on the poor; and in involving the poor themselves in the processes through which adjustment policies are designed and implemented.

4 International trade

We grow food to fill our stomachs and as insurance against hard times. But it is the income we get from coffee that clothes us, pays for school fees, and buys seed and implements. In the old days we got a very bad price for our coffee crop. The traders got most of the profit. Now we get a better price because we have formed a co-operative and we control the marketing. But we don't control the world market, where prices are too low.

COFFEE FARMER, DOMINICAN REPUBLIC

They say free trade is good for our country. They say it will bring new opportunities and more wealth. But where is our opportunity? We cannot compete with this American maize. How can they produce it so cheap? What are we to do? This free trade will be the end of us. Our only opportunity is to leave our land and move to the city.

SMALLHOLDER MAIZE FARMER, MEXICO

In the old days, there were enough fish to support all of our villages. Today, there are fewer and fewer fish. There are giant ships from Japan which come to our shores and take too many fish. We can't survive if it goes on like this.

FISHERMAN, THE PHILIPPINES

Introduction

International trade conjures up images of giant cartels, impenetrable and seemingly endless rounds of GATT negotiations, disputes between the major economic powers, and frenetic activity on the floors of commodity markets. Such images partially reflect reality. But international trade is also to do with people's livelihoods and their most basic social and economic rights. For millions of the world's poorest people trade is part of daily life, and a crucial determinant of welfare. Consider the statements at the head of this chapter; what these accounts suggest is that, from the perspective of the poor, international trade, like economic growth, is neither inherently good nor bad. Trade has the power to create opportunities and support livelihoods; and it has the power to destroy them. Production for export can generate income, employment, and the foreign exchange which poor countries need for their development. But it can also cause environmental destruction and a loss of livelihoods, or lead to unacceptable levels of exploitation. The human impact of trade depends on how goods are produced, who controls the production and marketing, how the wealth generated is distributed, and the terms upon which countries trade. The way in which the international trading system is managed has a critical bearing on all of these areas.

For the past half century, trade has acted as a mighty engine of growth in the world economy. It has also emerged as one of the central threads in a web of interdependence, integrating national economies into an increasingly global economic system. For some developing countries, trade expansion has played a crucial role in economic development, creating employment and opportunity. Others, however, have been increasingly marginalised, with ruinously low commodity prices and protectionism excluding many of the poorest countries from the benefits of world trade. If these countries are to share more equitably in global prosperity, new approaches to trade management are needed. It is also clear that unrestrained free trade is no longer justifiable, if it ever was, as an end in itself. Trade which is built on the foundations of unacceptable levels of social exploitation, which destroys the environments of vulnerable communities, or causes global ecological damage and disregards our obligations to future generations, is not conducive to sustainable development. Yet too much trading activity conforms to these patterns.

As we approach the twenty-first century, there is a need for new trade rules which reconcile the demands of global commerce with people's social and environmental rights. The current system of unregulated international trade is no more capable of safeguarding these rights than any other form of unregulated market. Unfortunately, governments remain wedded to the principle that trade should be deregulated. Indeed, not since its heyday as the economic religion of nineteenth-century Britain, has the doctrine of free trade enjoyed such unassailable dominance. The expansion of commerce through the deregulation of markets is at the core of the mission allocated to the World Trade Organisation (WTO), the body which, with the conclusion of the Uruguay Round, succeeded the General Agreement on Tariffs and Trade (GATT) and assumed responsibility for managing the world trading system. Trade liberalisation is also increasingly

central to economic policy in developing countries. By contrast, issues of sustainable resource management, the regulation of commodity markets, and poverty reduction strategies, are conspicuous by their absence from the international trade agenda.

So, too, are transnational companies (TNCs). In the popular perception, trade is an activity conducted between sovereign countries, each of which controls its own economic destiny. In reality, however, world trade flows are dominated by formidably powerful TNCs. The 'free market' in most of the primary commodities upon which the world's poorest countries depend, is actually controlled by a handful of private companies. At the same time, economic deregulation and new technologies have made TNCs more mobile. Through their trade and investment activities, these companies are shifting resources between economies and creating global production systems, over which governments have little control. The full implications of the growing mobility of capital have yet to be grasped. It is already clear, however, that as borders become more porous it is increasingly possible for TNCs to exploit differences in social and environmental standards with a view to maximising profits. This carries with it the threat of a constant downward pressure on these standards towards a lowest common denominator. Governments have facilitated the increased mobility of capital by progressively withdrawing controls on foreign investment at the national level, and by instituting, under the auspices of the WTO, international trade rules which limit the rights of governments to control the activities of TNCs. Yet there is no countervailing force, either at the national or the international level, to defend the social and economic rights of people. The result is that public welfare and sustainable development have been subordinated to the pursuit of corporate self-interest and commercial profit.

Fifty years ago, the Bretton Woods conference sought to recast a failed global trading system in a new mould. In the words of Harry Dexter-White, the chief US negotiator:

We must avoid the pre-war pattern of every country for itself, of inevitable depression, of possible widespread chaos, with the weaker countries succumbing first under the iron law of the jungle that characterised international economic practices of the pre-war decade.[1]

The discriminatory trade policies of the inter-war years, which had resulted in cycles of beggar-your-neighbour protectionism, were to be consigned to history. Instead of each country for itself, the system envisaged was to be built upon international co-operation and respect for shared rules and values. Non-discrimination, the regulation of commodity markets, and control over international monopolies, all figured prominently in the blue-print for a new order which emerged from Bretton Woods.[2] In the event, that order was never put into operation. But the vision of the Bretton Woods conference remains a powerful inspiration. That vision was based, above all, on a commitment to establishing a system of management of world trade which placed the advancement of human welfare above the reckless pursuit of short-term commercial advantage.

The world has changed since 1944, and it is not possible to resolve today's problems through yesterday's solutions. Some of these problems, such as the concentration of power in the hands of TNCs, were only dimly perceived at Bretton Woods. Others, such as the linkages between trade and environmental deregulation, were absent from the agenda. But what the Bretton Woods conference offered was a simple but radically new approach to trade reform. It was taken as axiomatic that governments should regulate the global market-place in the public interest. Today, the problems posed by international trade are at least as formidable and potentially destructive as those faced at the Bretton Woods conference. Yet governments have offered no viable framework for protecting social and environmental rights in the global market-place of the mid-1990s.

There are no simple answers. Free trade, to the extent that it has been pursued, has failed.

But finding alternative ways of balancing the sometimes competing claims of economic growth, employment creation, sustainable resource management, and social equity, is not easy. Outright protectionism is no more likely to achieve these diverse aims than free trade. Protectionist arguments, like those of free-traders, are often little more than a smoke-screen for the pursuit of sectional gain against the public interest, or for the imposition of discriminatory measures on developing countries. What is clear is that to continue on the present course will impose huge costs on vulnerable communities, and threaten the interests of future generations. New institutions and policies are urgently needed to create an international trading system which will enhance human welfare into the next century.

The new world trade order

During the post-war period international trade flows have expanded by a factor of twelve, to over $4.0 trillion. These flows have played an important role in increasing global prosperity.[3] Since the early 1980s, for example, international trade has grown half as much again as the growth of national products, so that imports and exports have figured increasingly prominently in the economic activity of most countries.[4] On average, trade accounts for around one-third of national incomes for middle-income countries, and one-quarter for low-income countries. But while trade remains an engine of economic growth, international trade relations are undergoing a profound transformation. Most obviously, there is no single dominant economic power. In the 1960s and the 1970s, the US played that role, effectively policing the international trading system and maintaining a momentum behind liberalisation. In the 1990s, there is a multipolar system, with power concentrated in three blocs: North America, Europe, and, increasingly, the Pacific Rim.[5] Within this more diffuse power structure, trade relations are being transformed by:

- increased flows of foreign investment and the globalisation of production under the auspices of TNCs
- trade liberalisation in developing countries
- regional divergences
- new institutional structures.

Foreign investment

Foreign investment is the driving force behind the emergence of an increasingly integrated international economy. Improvements in tele-communications, new information technol-ogies, reduced transport costs, and the removal of barriers on foreign capital, have made it possible for companies to transfer technologies and organise their production and marketing activities on a global basis.[6] The national car, like the national economy, has long been a thing of the past. Even something as apparently all American as the Pontiac Le Mans is made up of parts produced in 18 different countries.[7] Now the Ford motor company has unveiled a massive restructuring plan which will take glob-alisation in the automobile industry a stage further, integrating its European, North American, Asian, and Latin American opera-tions into a single, global, co-ordinated system of production, establishing a model which its competitors will follow.[8] This represents an advanced stage in the internationalisation of production. But it is being repeated on a more modest scale throughout the world.

High streets in the industrialised world provide plenty of evidence of globalisation. Twenty years ago, most of the video recorders exported by the Japanese company Mitsubishi were made in Japan. Now they are all made in South-East Asian countries like Thailand, where Japanese firms account for 7 per cent of manufacturing employment.[9] Top-of-the-range shirts and dresses for chic middle-class con-sumers are manufactured in Bangladesh and China, from cloth exported from Europe and North America. One of France's largest elec-tronics groups now employs three times as many people in Asia as in France. In Mexico,

blue-chip US companies such as General Motors export gear-box components to its *maquiladora* plants in Mexico, for assembly and re-export back to the US.[10] The investment driving these changes has provided employment in many countries, including industrially advanced countries. Holdings by foreigners of companies registered in the EU, the US, and Japan increased from $800bn to $1300bn between 1986 and 1991.[11]

International specialisation in company operations is not new; nor is production in the South by foreign companies seeking to export to the North. It is the sheer scale and pace of globalisation which is unprecedented; and the manner in which foreign investment flows are transforming economic relations. During the 1980s, foreign investment by the industrialised countries increased dramatically. Initially, much of that investment was directed towards other developed countries.[12] In recent years, however, developing countries have figured increasingly prominently in foreign investment flows. In 1993, they attracted some $80bn in such investment. That was approximately twice the amount they received two years earlier and equivalent to total world investment flows in 1986.[13]

Most foreign investment in the developing world goes to a core group of about a dozen countries in Asia and Latin America. China is now the world's second largest host to foreign investment, with $26bn of inflows.[14] In Latin America, Brazil and, until the recent crisis, Mexico, have dominated. But behind these aggregate pictures, changes are taking place in capital flows within the developing world. Rising wage costs in the first generation of newly-industrialising countries (NICs) have prompted the transfer of Japanese investment to Malaysia and Thailand, where wage costs are one-tenth of those in South Korea and Taiwan.[15] More recently, Vietnam has emerged as a new growth point, diverting foreign investment from the second generation of NICs. Since opening its economy to foreign investors in 1988, Vietnam has attracted $7bn in foreign capital.[16] In Latin America, export-processing zones are expanding rapidly in some countries as a point of entry to the US economy. Mexico is the most significant example, but other countries are in competition; in the Dominican Republic, the number of such zones has increased from 18 to 27 since 1988, with foreign investment rising from $0.5bn to $1.2bn over the same period.

The power of TNCs

The increasing specialisation in the international economy is intimately associated with the rise of TNCs. The 100 largest TNCs control over one-third of the stock of foreign investment.[17] World trade itself is becoming an increasingly corporate affair, with around 40 per cent taking place *within* companies.[18] The economic power of these companies is difficult to comprehend. General Electric, General Motors, and Ford, for example, have between them assets roughly double the GDP of Mexico. The largest ten TNCs control assets which represent three times the total income of the world's poorest 38 countries (excluding China and India), with a population of over one billion people.

In the past, foreign investment by TNCs was often determined by a concern to locate production in markets to which import access was denied through restrictive trade barriers. Increasingly, however, it is directed towards re-export and the global integration of production. In China, the share of foreign affiliates of TNCs in the country's exports rose from 9 per cent in 1989 to over 25 per cent in 1993.[19] German chemical giants such as Bayer and BASF have relocated plants from Europe to China's coastal provinces, partly with a view to re-exporting to Europe and South-East Asia. Foreign firms now account for more than half of manufactured exports in Malaysia, Mexico, and the Philippines; and as much as three-quarters in Thailand. Thus developing countries are becoming increasingly important export bases for TNCs seeking a low-wage manufacturing site from which to export to high-wage consumer markets in the industrialised world.

The technological revolution

In the past, there were limits to the transferability of capital. Some of these were politically determined: developing country governments were often hostile to foreign investors, imposing tight controls on profit repatriation and ownership. Other limits were inherent in production technologies, many of which required high levels of skills and maintenance. Today, by contrast, most governments maintain an open door to foreign investors; and the micro-chip revolution has transformed production systems, making it possible for companies to transfer the most productive technologies. As Klaus Schwab, the President of the World Economic Forum, has argued, what is distinctive about the world trade order as we approach the next century is the relative ease with which capital and technology can be transferred across borders.[20] Potentially, this has the power to revolutionise relations between the industrialised and developing world. In the old order, high wages in the North reflected the higher productivity of the technologies used. Coversely, low wages in the developing world were linked to technologies with lower productivity. Limitations on the mobility and transferability of capital kept these two high- and low-wage worlds separate. Now, the ease with which capital can be transferred has severed the link between high productivity, high wages, and the most productive technologies, and made it possible to combine low-wage labour with highly productive technologies.[21]

There is a countervailing force, in that labour in industrialised countries generates higher levels of productivity — a consequence of differences in infrastructure, education, and other factors. However, these differences are being eroded. In the automobile industry, robotic production systems are diminishing the productivity gap between car workers in Mexico and the US. In labour-intensive industries, such as footwear, textiles and, to a more limited extent, iron and steel, some developing countries are outstripping their Northern competitors in the productivity stakes. As these industries expand their exports to the industrialised world they generate foreign exchange earnings, which will in turn finance imports, and drive the cycle of trade expansion. New jobs will be created to produce for expanding Third World markets, locking North and South into a virtuous circle of growth and prosperity. That, at least, is the theory. But it is a theory which ignores the fact that there are winners and losers in the industrial world. The winners are to be found in the more sophisticated, high-wage, knowledge-intensive industries. The losers are located in the low-skill, low-wage sectors, where competition with Third World exporters is most intense. According to one study, competition from Third World imports reduced the demand for unskilled labour in the industrial world by 15 per cent in the 1980s alone.[22] This fall in demand has contributed both to increasing income inequality in North America and parts of Europe, insecurity of employment, and to the growing phenomenon of poverty in employment as a result of low wages.

In the US, the growing discrepancy between the wages of high- and low-skilled workers has contributed to levels of inequality unprecedented in post-war history, with the real incomes of the richest 20 per cent having risen by one-fifth since 1990, while those of the poorest 40 per cent have remained static.[23] In Britain, around one-third of workers now earn less than 68 per cent of the national average wage, a 25 per cent increase since 1979.[24] Such trends are not caused solely by import competition from low-wage economies, but they are powerfully influenced by them. Thus international trade relations raise important issues of poverty and inequality for the North as well as the South.[25]

Regionalisation

Media images of the world breaking into three mutually hostile trading blocs in Asia, Europe, and the Americas, have given rise to a perception of regionalisation as the antithesis of internationalisation. 'Fortress Europe', well-publicised clashes over agriculture and microchips, and economic sabre-rattling by the US against Japan have provided the headlines. In fact, the images are almost entirely divorced from reality; the new patterns of regionalism have been oriented towards liberalisation, economic deregulation, and integration into the global economy.[26]

Latin America typifies this new regionalism. Since the mid-1980s, one country after another has been embarking on economic liberalisation at a rate which governments in the North would never contemplate.[27] Average tariffs in the region were reduced by half between 1991 and 1993 to 12 per cent, less than a quarter of those prevailing in the mid-1980s.[28] Quantitative restrictions have also been withdrawn from countries such as Bolivia and Brazil, where they previously covered a large share of imports.

The North American Free Trade Agreement (NAFTA) has linked Mexico, the US, and Canada into one of the world's largest free-trade markets (second only to the EU) and stretching from Yukon to Yucatan. As a result, the tariffs and quantitative restrictions which have characterised the Mexican economy are being phased out. Moves are now under way to integrate Chile, already Latin America's most open economy, with an average tariff rate of 11 per cent, into the NAFTA. In 1995 a new customs union was created between Brazil (Latin America's largest and, traditionally, one of its most protected, economies), Argentina, and Uruguay. This is likely to form the foundation of a continent-wide free-trade area, linking up with NAFTA and extending to the Andean Group of countries (Venezuela, Colombia, Ecuador, Peru, and Bolivia) early in the next century.[29]

These moves towards liberalisation have substantially increased regional trade flows, as well as trade with North America. Trade among the 11 largest Latin American economies has doubled since 1989, and these intra-regional

flows now account for almost one-fifth of total trade. Brazil, the dominant regional economy, has seen exports to its Mercosur partners rise from 4 per cent to 14 per cent of the total since 1990.[30] Restrictions on capital flows have also been reduced under regional free-trade pacts. This is accelerating the creation of a regional free-trade market linked, through capital markets and trade, to North America.

In Asia too, countries have been removing tariff and other barriers to trade at an accelerating rate. Average tariff levels have fallen dramatically in countries such as Malaysia, the Philippines, and Indonesia. Such moves reflect an impetus to regional free trade within the Association of South East Asian Nations (ASEAN). More significantly, the Asia-Pacific Economic Co-operation (APEC) forum, created in 1993, holds out the prospect of an extended free-trade area, linking the NAFTA with Japan, China, South Korea, and Pacific Rim states such as the Philippines, Malaysia, and Thailand. Under an ambitious plan drawn up by the US, APEC members are now considering a proposal to abolish all trade barriers by 2020, locking more than half the world's population and 40 per cent of its trade into a free-trade zone.[31] With the Pacific Rim countries growing at three times the rate of the Group of Seven countries, the strategic interest of the latter in easier access to Asian markets is considerable.

Far from turning inwards, the European Union has been actively seeking to expand its trade ties with the other blocs. Since 1986, Europe has been the largest trading partner with the four Mercosur countries, with which it is now negotiating a free-trade arrangement.[32] This move is one of a series designed to link Europe more tightly with potential growth points in the world economy, including the ASEAN countries. Meanwhile, the integration of Chile, with its Pacific coastline and strong economic ties with Asia, into Mercosur is creating an embryonic free-trade zone between Latin America and Asia.[33] These evolving ties between Europe and Latin America on the one side, and Latin America and Asia on the other, illustrate how the mosaic of separate free-trade agreements are combining to form an increasingly liberalised global trading and financial system.

That system is being consolidated by the Uruguay Round GATT agreement. Three-quarters of the 117 countries which signed that agreement were developing countries.[34] Under the GATT accord, trade restrictions will fall across a wide range of areas, although the merchandise exports of developing countries will continue to face discriminatory treatment in world markets. Where the agreement could prove even more significant is in boosting foreign investment. For example, the agreement on trade-related investment measures will prohibit governments from requiring as conditions for market access that TNCs meet criteria for training nationals, use a minimum content of domestically produced goods in production, or generate sufficient exports to cover the foreign exchange costs of their operations. Similarly, the General Agreement on Trade in Services will require governments to remove restrictions on the repatriation of profits and capital in the financial services sector. Both provisions will reinforce the trend towards the globalisation of production and investment, especially with the anticipated admission into the WTO of China, Russia and Vietnam.

Trading prosperity and decline

Almost all countries are becoming more dependent on trade to maintain growth and employment. But trade has acted as a more powerful engine of growth for some countries than for others. International trade played an important part in fostering the original South-East Asian 'miracle' and in maintaining the dynamism of economies in the region. At the other extreme, sub-Saharan Africa has suffered continued economic decline, in part because of the unfavourable trade environment in which the region operates.

During the 1980s, South-East Asia's export growth rate averaged 10 per cent a year: more than double the world average. That trend has continued into the 1990s, boosted by the performance of China and Vietnam. It is projected to continue into the next century. By contrast, sub-Saharan Africa's export growth was barely positive in the 1980s and has registered only marginal improvements in the 1990s.[35] With merchandise exports accounting for one-fifth of regional income, this goes some way towards explaining the catastrophic decline in living standards experienced by the region. These contrasting fortunes reflect an interplay of domestic policy with external factors.

Some of Africa's problems can be traced to grossly incompetent economic management. The predatory activities of state marketing boards which over-taxed producers, and persistent currency over-valuation which undermined export competitiveness and reduced local earnings for exporters, led to dramatic losses of market shares in primary commodities. At the same time, debt and generalised economic crisis led to a collapse in economic infrastructure and a process of 'import strangulation', as foreign exchange shortages prevented producers from importing essential requirements.[36] Overall, imports fell by 5 per cent a year in the 1980s. But it is sub-Saharan Africa's continued dependence on primary commodities which has made the region so vulnerable.

As a group, developing countries have dramatically increased their share of world manufacturing exports, accounting for almost 25 per cent, compared to 5 per cent in the early 1970s.[37] South-East Asia generates over 75 per cent of these exports, and there is a direct correlation between the region's reduced dependence on primary commodities and its growth performance. Developing countries in which manufactured goods compose 50 per cent or more of total exports have achieved consistently higher growth rates over the past two decades than primary commodity exporters. Between 1980 and 1992, manufacturing exporters grew at an average rate of 7 per cent a year, or four times faster than commodity exporters.[38] As

Figure 4.1 Sub-Saharan Africa's percentage share in commodity exports, 1971-91

		1971	1991
	Cocoa	81	67
	Coffee	29	15
	Groundnut oil	41	34
	Palm oil	16	3

SOURCE: WORLD BANK

international trade becomes increasingly knowledge-intensive, this divergence is likely to continue.

For sub-Saharan Africa, where primary commodities account for 80 per cent of exports, the consequences could prove disastrous. Only six countries in the region derive 20 per cent or more of their export earnings from manufactured goods.[39] The fundamental weakness of Africa's economies is further underlined by the fact that, with around 10 per cent of the world's population, they account for 0.4 per cent of world manufacturing exports and less than 1 per cent of world trade.[40] Foreign investment flows appear to offer little prospect of transforming this picture. While it is true that foreign investment and flight capital is returning to countries such as Ghana and Uganda, and that South Africa will continue to attract private capital,[41] Africa as a region is becoming increasingly marginalised. Collectively, the region receives less foreign investment than Malaysia, its share of world investment flows having fallen by half to 0.5 per cent since the early 1980s. [42]

Figure 4.2 Percentage growth rate of economy of developing countries according to type of exports

	1970-80	1981-92
Non-oil commodities	3.0	1.4
Fuel	5.1	0.5
Manufactured goods	6.5	6.8
Diversified	5.7	3.6

SOURCE: WORLD BANK

Institutional structure

Another distinctive feature of the current global trading system is the new institutional structure through which it is now being managed. The General Agreement on Tariffs and Trade (GATT) emerged by a circuitous route from the Bretton Woods conference. It was intended to oversee a trade regime built upon the principles of transparency, non-discrimination, and a shared commitment to multilateralism. In practice, the GATT's rules were largely ignored by the industrialised countries, especially after competition from developing country exports intensified from the 1960s. Moreover, the GATT's remit did not extend to areas such as investment, intellectual property management, and the regulation of trade in services.[43]

All this will change with the creation of the World Trade Organisation (WTO). In contrast to the GATT, its successor has wide-ranging powers to enforce compliance with the principles of trade liberalisation. It will also have the power to enforce the liberalisation of foreign investment and the protection of intellectual property rights. As we argue below, the Uruguay Round agreement, which the WTO will oversee, does not address many of the interlocking problems facing developing country exporters, such as commodity price stabilisation; and its rules on investment and intellectual property may compound many of these problems. Meanwhile, the GATT agreement on agriculture, which the WTO will implement, does little to address long-standing problems of subsidised over-production in the industrialised countries.

There is also a growing concern that the WTO does not create a viable framework for the social and environmental regulation of international trade. While the treaty includes a commitment to promoting sustainable development, its rules are focused almost entirely upon the narrower objective of trade expansion.[44] Developing countries have reacted strongly against suggestions that the WTO should be used to establish minimum social and environmental standards, fearing that this could encourage protectionist action. They point out, with considerable justification, that poverty is the real cause of low standards; and they claim that access to Northern markets is vital to raising these standards. Equally, however, the world cannot afford a global trading system which subordinates all other considerations to trade expansion under the auspices of footloose TNCs. What is needed is an international regulatory system which protects the basic rights of people, without jeopardising legitimate trade interests.

International trade and sustainable livelihoods

It is not only deepening economic interdependence which is a striking feature of the global economy. Social and ecological interdependence is no less obvious. The terms of that interrelationship have a crucial bearing on human welfare; and on whether trade acts as a positive force for human development, or as a negative force for increased marginalisation.[45]

All international trade involves some element of specialisation, in which countries, communities, local manufacturers, and traders or foreign investors seek to exploit a competitive advantage. That advantage, which is shaped by economic policies and international circumstances, can derive from public investment in social and economic infrastructure, from natural factors such as climate and the availability of natural resources, or from the skills of the work force and the price of labour. It can also derive from unacceptable levels of exploitation, both of people and of the environment. Inevitably, there are complex trade-offs and dilemmas in determining what constitutes an 'unacceptable' level of exploitation. For example, production for export may cause ecological problems while at the same time creating employment opportunities for highly vulnerable populations. Exploitation and poor labour standards are often associated with export production: but the old aphorism that it is better to be exploited than to be unemployed carries special weight in developing countries.[46] Such dilemmas pervade debates on international trade. But it is increasingly clear that the present terms of world trade are highly disadvantageous to poor countries, while the pursuit of trade expansion without regard to ecological constraints is likely to prove disastrous to present and future generations alike.

Natural resources

Around 25 per cent of world trade involves the import and export of primary products, such as timber, fish, minerals, tea, and coffee.[47] Many of the world's poorest countries are heavily dependent upon such exports for their foreign exchange earnings. However, the export of natural resources often involves environmental and, sometimes, social, costs which do not figure in national accounting systems.

Consider, for example, the massive increase in shellfish exports from developing countries. During the 1980s, consumption of shrimps doubled in the US and Japan, generating a sustained increase in exports from South-East Asia. The foreign exchange gains have been substantial. By 1990, shellfish was the largest non-oil commodity export from developing countries, having surpassed coffee by a comfortable margin. For some low-income countries, such as Bangladesh and Vietnam, shellfish is now one of the largest sources of foreign exchange. However, shrimp and shellfish farming along the coasts of tropical countries is destroying the world's mangrove forests, with disastrous social and economic consequences.

In the Philippines, mangrove swamps have been cleared at an average rate of 3,000 hectares a year to make way for large commercial prawn farms, most of them owned by Japanese companies producing for export to Japan. These swamps now cover less than one-tenth of their original area. The destruction of the mangrove breeding grounds means a progressive lowering of fish catches each year for local fisherfolk. On current trends, the Philippines' remaining mangrove swamps will be destroyed within a decade.[48] In Bangladesh the expansion of shrimp farming has been associated with the forcible displacement of smallholder producers, often involving considerable violence. In addition, the demands of the shrimp industry for fresh water has severely depressed the water table in many areas, creating water shortages and adding to problems of salinity.[49]

Offshore, there has been a parallel depletion of natural resources vital to community livelihoods. Mismanagement and over-exploitation of fish stocks in the industrial world has increased dependence on fish stocks in the South. In the decade up to 1987, the volume of fish exported by developing countries increased four-fold, to almost 70 per cent of world trade in fish stocks.[50] European factory ships now supply their home markets by draining fishing grounds off West Africa of their stocks. In Senegal, the livelihoods of over 35,000 small-scale fisherfolk has been threatened by the encroachment of EU fleets into their traditional fishing grounds. Having failed to manage fish stocks in its own territorial waters sustainably, the EU is now extending its unsustainable practices into the developing world. [51]Governments

receive foreign exchange for fishing quotas, the stocks and the profits flow back to the EU, and local communities suffer a destruction of their livelihoods. This is the unacceptable face of trade in operation. In Chile, where coastal fishing stocks have been depleted by factory ships producing animal feed compound for the EU market, the Federation of Regional Fish Workers has drafted a fishing law which would ban exports of fish from areas reserved to meet the needs of local communities.

Livestock farming illustrates in stark form the potential conflict between trade expansion and sustainable resource use. In Costa Rica, the expansion of beef exports to the North American market was a driving force in the country's trade expansion during the 1960s and 1970s. The price of satisfying the booming US demand for hamburgers was the destruction of the country's rainforest, only 17 per cent of which remained intact by the mid-1980s. Cattle ranches forced smallholder producers off their land on to fragile hillside slopes and into forests, accelerating deforestation and soil erosion. By 1984, over half of Costa Rica's agricultural land was under pasture, even though most of it was unsuitable. From 1979 to 1989, the country lost an estimated 2.2bn metric tonnes of soil to erosion.[52] To make matters worse, these huge social and environmental costs were sustained for an enterprise which was, by any normal market criteria, commercially unviable. Cattle ranching was controlled by a small group of 2000 politically powerful families, who received huge government subsidies, export grants, tax concessions, and subsidised imports.[53] Subsidised credit, most of which was never repaid, enabled commercial ranchers to reap huge profits. Although impressive quantities of foreign exchange were earned, the environmental costs in terms of resource depletion were equally impressive, draining the country of an estimated 5 per cent of its national income each year.[54]

A similar story is continuing to unfold in Botswana, where privileged access to the EU market under the Lomé Convention has en-couraged the expansion of cattle ranching on the country's fragile semi-arid soils. Chronic soil erosion has resulted. Meanwhile, the enclosure, with World Bank assistance, of vast areas has decimated the nation's herds of migrating wildebeest, threatening the security of the vulnerability rural communities which depend on them. Once again, the main beneficiaries are a small group of wealthy ranchers who control the bulk of the exports.[55]

The timber trade and deforestation

The international timber trade's role in rainforest destruction is well-documented. Industrialised countries account for over 90 per cent of timber imports, which are used for a variety of purposes. In Japan, construction companies make disposable moulds out of tropical hardwood. Mahogany from Ghana has proved popular for toilet seats in Europe. Chile exports to the North American furniture industry 100-year-old trees in the form of woodchips. These exports generate foreign exchange, but often at a huge environmental cost. Commercial timber logging has denuded the Malaysian states of Sarawak and Sabah, which supply over 90 per cent of Japan's timber imports, and increased the rate of clearance for natural forests fourfold in the two decades up to 1990.[56] In Sarawak, the local Penan people are engaged in a last-ditch effort to protect the remaining forests, upon which their survival depends. During the 1980s, Ghana's export drive included an expansion of tropical timber exports which reduced its forest area to a quarter of its original size. Like Côte d'Ivoire, the country will soon be making the transition from a net exporter to a net importer of timber.[57] Commercial logging represents a profound threat to food security of local communities which depend on forests for food, fuel, and medicine. It also reinforces wider pressures on forests. Logging is often the beginning of a new cycle of deforestation, as it enables small farmers to convert degraded forest to farmland.

As in other forms of trade in natural resources, the benefits of timber exports are often illusory. In the Philippines, commercial logging removed 10 million cubic metres of timber annually in the 1970s.[58] Foreign companies were given short-term leases to extract timber, which created an incentive to log their concessions as rapidly as possible and leave. By the end of the 1980s, the country had started to import wood. Meanwhile, the economic benefits were considerably over-stated by the under-valuing of the forest ecosystem. The Philippines government received an estimated 11 per cent of the value of timber exports in the form of forest charges and export taxes, with the rest going to timber operators.[59] Set against these gains are the inestimable costs of lost forest resources, such as fruits, nuts, fuelwood, and biodiversity; increased exposure to soil erosion, as fragile slopes are exposed to sun and rain; and lost livelihoods of forest dwellers. Moreover, provinces in the Philippines affected by massive deforestation have become major disaster areas when hit by tropical cyclones.

In Thailand, where logging reduced forest cover from 55 per cent to 28 per cent of the country's land area between the early 1960s and 1988, deforestation contributed to mud slides, floods, and consequent loss of life, none of which registered in the 'loss' margin of the country's national accounts.[60] Studies have repeatedly shown that preserving forests and managing their resources in a sustainable manner not only prevents these losses; but also that it generates returns in terms of employment and income comparable to those generated by commercial operators.[61] But because the goods and services provided by forests to local communities do not have an easily measurable monetary, or market value, they also do not appear in national accounts.[62]

Unsustainable practices

Reducing the environmental toll associated with commodity trade will require action in several areas. Increasing the value of exports could help in many cases, by reducing the volume of natural resources needed to generate an equivalent amount of foreign exchange. Unfortunately, there are several obstacles to this. One is tariff escalation (which we discuss in more detail below), that is, the practice of imposing import duties which rise with the degree of processing undergone. This discourages local processing, which is the most effective way to add value to exports. For instance, Japan and the EU impose a higher tariff on plywood than logs. The aim, in both cases, is to protect powerful domestic timber industries.[63] The effect is to intensify environmental pressures, since logs have a lower unit value than plywood and more have to be exported to generate the same amount of foreign exchange.

Transfer pricing by foreign companies represents another potentially destructive influence on the environment. This is facilitated by intra-firm trade, which enables companies to evade taxes and raise profits by understating the true value of exports of raw materials. Because it is illegal, transfer pricing is not well documented, and it is extremely hard for poorly-resourced regulatory authorities in developing countries to take action to stop it. However, cases have been reported of exports from Indonesia being under-valued by as much as 40 per cent.[64] The effect of transferring a large proportion of the final value of a primary commodity is to increase the tendency towards over-production, as countries compensate for revenue loss by expanding export volumes.

Many of Oxfam's partners are supporting community efforts to resist commercial encroachments on common resources, such as forests and coastal waters. Some are pressing governments to establish limits on export volumes, by reducing quotas for foreign fishing fleets or limiting timber exports. But unless they are backed by international action, local initiatives often have unintended 'displacement' effects. For example, in 1989 pressure from local communities and environmental groups in Thailand resulted in the government imposing a ban on logging. Timber companies promptly shifted their operations to Laos and Cambodia, which have become sites of appalling environmental destruction. According to the UNDP, nearly two million hectares of Cambodian forest have been destroyed since the Thai ban came into effect, with exports running at four times the sustainable harvest level.[65] Thus, positive action in one country has had a negative outcome in another.

International commodity arrangements and fishing agreements could establish parameters for sustainable resource use. The International Tropical Timber Organisation (ITTO) has taken a step in this direction, setting the end of the decade as a target date for all trade in tropical timber to come from sustainably managed forests. In practice, however, progress towards this goal has been derisory, largely because of the absence of political commitment by both exporters and importers.[66] Far more stringent measures are needed, including a ban on imports from countries in which particularly unsustainable forms of timber extraction are practised. Several of the timber companies responsible for the deforestation of Sarawak have now been granted extensive concessions in Guyana. One consortium, which has acquired a 4.1 million hectare concession, plans to export 1.2 million tons of timber from the country by the year 2000. That represents four times the country's entire current timber exports, and is likely to cause massive environmental destruction.[67] Importing countries should take action to prohibit imports in such cases, in defence of communities in the exporting country. They should also act to eliminate the 'throw-away' use of tropical hardwoods, such as Japan's 25 billion pairs of disposable chopsticks and $2bn worth of single-use hardwood moulds.[68] Concerted consumer action could play an important role in fostering more sustainable trade; labelling schemes to identify timber grown and harvested sustainably can persuade companies of the market advantages of sustainable resource management. There is plenty of evidence to suggest that consumers in importing countries are willing to pay more for sustainably logged timber.

Taxing unsustainability

One of the most vexed problems in sustainable trade management is the role of the market. Current prices for many natural products, such as timber, rarely reflect the social and environmental costs of production. This undervaluation leads directly to overuse and depletion.[69] The prices charged by Japanese companies to consumers for shrimps do not reflect the enormous costs to local communities of lost fish stocks, the reduced soil fertility caused by salination, or the associated loss of livelihoods. Similarly, the prices paid by European consumers for furniture made from West African hardwoods bear no relation to the costs borne by local communities. In theory, governments could intervene in markets to ensure that prices more accurately reflect hidden costs, imposing consumption taxes or import levies on unsustainably produced materials; or, in extreme cases, prohibiting imports.

There are two problems with this approach. The first is the obvious one of determining what constitutes sustainable production. Where there is an international agreement, as there is, for example, on timber production or fisheries, this may be possible. But how can governments compare the environmental costs of cocoa produced in, say, Ghana against that produced in Brazil? The answer is 'not without extreme difficulty'.[70] The second problem is that the international trade rules enshrined in the WTO act as a potential restraint on local and international action to protect natural resources. These rules do not allow for the imposition of consumption or import taxes on the grounds of unsustainable production.[71] Nor is it clear whether they permit export controls in the interest of sustainable resource management. While existing rules allow governments to restrict exports for environmental reasons, such restrictions are treated as exemptions to free trade which are only granted under stringent conditions.[72] Recourse to GATT has been used to overturn existing conservation measures, forcing a reversal of Canada's fish stocks management policies in the early 1980s, for example. In recent years, both Europe and Japan have threatened recourse to GATT to overturn bans imposed by the Philippines on the export of unprocessed timber. Meanwhile, efforts by the Dutch government to promote an EU ban on unsustainably logged timber were withdrawn in the face of warnings that it would be inconsistent with GATT obligations.

It is clear that there are major conflicts between the rules of international trade and the demands of sustainable resource management. This is an area in which the WTO itself is in urgent need of reform. Export prohibition can play a vital role in sustainable resource management. So could export taxes and import levies, despite the problems outlined above. Revenues from surcharges imposed for environmental reasons could be pooled and used to finance a fund for sustainable resource management, and to protect the interests of communities which have been adversely affected, provided the necessary institutional reforms were put in place in developing countries. Such a scheme has been proposed by Dutch and UK timber operators, only to be rejected by exporting countries.[73] One objection to such schemes is that they could in effect give an unfair advantage to producers with lower environmental standards. However, that loophole could be closed by importers requiring imposition of an export tax as a precondition for exporters gaining market entry. Countries not imposing the tax could either be charged an equivalent import duty (with the proceeds used for the same purpose), or excluded from the market. Applied in an open and non-discriminatory manner, such export taxes could enhance the prospects for more sustainable trade across a wide range of products.[74]

Pollution havens: environmental and social dumping

Foreign investment is integrating national economies and labour markets into an increasingly globalised system. This has profound implications because of the divergence in living standards and environmental standards between countries.[75] There are at least three sources of concern. First, there is a danger that TNCs will relocate to countries where wages, working conditions, and basic labour rights, do not conform to reasonable minimum standards, even allowing for the fact that countries are at very different stages of economic development. Second, there is a parallel concern that non-existent or weakly applied environmental laws will act as a magnet for foreign companies eager to lower production costs by relocating to 'pollution havens'. Thirdly, there is a fear that these twin pressures towards 'social dumping' and the creation of 'pollution havens' will exercise downward pressure on social and environmental standards worldwide, as the fear of losing foreign investment forces governments to lower standards.

The public in developed countries are increasingly concerned that their living standards and employment prospects will be eroded by competition from countries at lower stages of economic development. Such fears are well-founded. For their part, developing country governments and many NGOs regard any discussion of minimum social and environmental standards as the thin end of a protectionist wedge, designed to insulate Northern markets from Southern exports. In fact, the issues go far beyond North-South differences over trade rules, and raise fundamental questions about the balance between the claims of free trade and basic human rights.

These questions have figured prominently in the debate over the future of Europe. Moves towards the creation of a regional free market were belatedly supplemented by social programmes and the Social Chapter. The aim has been to prevent the unacceptable exploitation by investors of national differences in living standards. However inadequate the mechanisms involved, they reflect a recognition that citizens have a legitimate claim on governments to defend certain basic rights, which might be threatened by the deregulation of markets. They also reflect an awareness that unless minimum standards are established, socially destructive forces might threaten political stability.[76] There is no such awareness reflected in the rules governing international trade.

Social and environmental dumping, NAFTA style

Advocates of trade deregulation argue that there is little evidence to support the claim that social and environmental dumping is taking place on any scale. That argument is not supported by the experience of Oxfam's project partners working in the *maquiladora* zone in Mexico, described by one commentator as 'a facsimile of hell on earth'.[77]

The Mexican border region is the site of more than 2000 manufacturing plants, which operate by importing components free of duty, for assembly and re-export to the US.[78] Blue-chip companies such as General Electric, General Motors, and Du Pont, have all transferred plants to the *maquiladora* zone (prompting Ross Perot to hear 'the giant sucking sound' of US jobs being transferred south of the border). The attraction of the *maquiladora* zone is partly the low wages, which are less than a tenth of those in US plants, and proximity to US markets. Lax enforcement of environmental laws has been another attraction. More than a quarter of the US firms with plants in Mexicali cited environmental costs and more stringent US environmental provisions as reasons for the relocation.[79] In the late 1980s, the introduction of more stringent air pollution controls in California prompted a large-scale exodus of furniture manufacturers to the *maquiladora* zone.[80]

The environmental costs of the *maquiladora* zone have been unacceptably high. According to Mexico's Secretariat of Urban Planning and Ecology, more than half of the *maquiladora* plants produce hazardous waste. This waste is supposed to be transferred to the United States, but compliance is the exception rather than the rule. An official Mexican investigation in 1991

estimated that only one-third of plants complied with Mexican toxic waste laws.[81] The public health consequences, compounded by chronic over-crowding, have been alarming. In one investigation, the US National Toxics Campaign found heavy metals and other toxic discharges associated with birth defects and brain damage being emptied into open ditches. Towns such as Matamoros have an incidence of anencephalic (brainless) baby births running at 30 times the Mexican average. The American Medical Association has branded the *maquiladora* region 'a virtual cesspool and breeding ground for infectious diseases', with hepatitis and tuberculosis rife on both sides of the border.[82] This is a classic example of how environmental problems do not respect national frontiers.

While it may be unrealistic to expect Mexico's environmental laws fully to comply with US standards, either in design or implementation, the practices of *maquiladora* plants are clearly beyond the pale. The same is true with regard to labour. Low wages in Mexico reflect the lethal interaction of rural poverty and government policies designed to transfer the costs of adjustment on to wage-earners. But it is not merely low wages which are attracting foreign companies. Consider the following testimony from a *maquiladora* worker, given before a US Congressional committee in 1993:

My name is Alma Molina, and I live in Juarez...In June 1992 I went to work for Clarostat, a US company with a plant in Juarez. I was among some 300 workers who made electrical switches and sensors. I earned the Mexican minimum wage of $4.50 for a nine-hour day.

A group of us wanted to improve our working conditions, safety and wages at Clarostat. We worked with dangerous chemicals, including phenol and epoxy resin, but no masks were provided. The chemicals irritated our skin. Six of us began to organise a union. We had meetings every two weeks. After a few months I was fired. Four other workers were fired one week later. The personnel manager told me I was being fired because I was trying to organise a union...

Shortly after being fired, I was hired by Electro-componentes, which is a General Electric Company. The GE logo is on the factory. At that plant, 1800 workers make wiring for refrigerators sold in the US...I had been at GE for only seven days when I was called to the personnel office and shown a list with my name on it...The personnel man said that he did not know why my name was on the list, but that he would have to fire me anyway.[83]

Alma Molina's testimony provides an insight into the realities of deregulated trade. Eight out of every ten *maquiladora* workers are women, most of whom are denied even the most basic labour rights. Driven by rural poverty to towns such as Juarez, where some 400,000 people live in shanty towns with no sewerage, clean water, or electricity, women find that the *maquiladora* zone offers a livelihood which enables them to survive, but little else. Efforts to improve working conditions are hampered by company practices such as those described in the testimony above; and by the Mexican government's suppression of the country's independent trade union movement.

Concern over the social and environmental implications of the NAFTA led to the negotiation of two side-accords to address the problem of establishing minimum standards. Both leave much to be desired. For example, the labour side-accord recognises the right to freedom of association and the right to collective bargaining. However, violations of these rights are to be the subject not of punitive trade sanctions, but fact-finding exercises and 'consultations'.[84] The environmental side-accord has provided resources to improve standards in Mexico, recognising the need to establish acceptable minimum standards. However, the Commission established to oversee the accord has no powers of investigation and must rely on evidence supplied by governments.[85] Responsibility for enforcement is also placed squarely on governments, despite the fact that non-enforcement of environmental laws by the Mexican government is a major part of the problem.

A problem beyond Mexico

The experience of Mexico has placed the twin problems of social dumping and pollution havens on to the international trade agenda. The problems, however, extend far beyond Mexico. Pollution-intensive European chemical industries, to take but one example, are relocating on a substantial scale to Asia in general, and to China in particular. When the German chemical giant Bayer announced plans to transfer bulk capacity to Shanghai, the corporation's chief executive explained the move in terms of the disincentives to staying in Europe: 'The main disadvantage we have to face are higher labour costs and expensive social security systems, coupled with widespread regulation of environmental affairs by the state.'[86]

The clear inference for governments in Europe, and even in other parts of South-East Asia, is that the price for retaining investment and employment is a progressive lowering of standards towards Chinese levels. Such threats constitute a potential deterrent to efforts to improve environmental standards. Environmental costs impose a substantial and increasing financial burden, which would rise progressively if public pressure forces governments to introduce higher standards. According to the US Environmental Protection Agency, the costs of pollution control will increase from the equivalent of 2 per cent of national income in 1990 to 2.8 per cent by the end of the decade.[87] The danger is that, as the costs rise, TNCs will simply relocate their investment and jobs elsewhere, providing a major disincentive to government action.

It is sometimes argued that what may appear to be exploitative working conditions when seen through European or North American eyes, is reasonable employment from the viewpoint of developing countries. In some instances, this may be true, in others, not. Women account for the bulk of the employment generated by direct foreign investment, both in manufacturing industries, where female labour is used in assembly plants, and in the production of non-traditional agricultural exports. Employment in these areas can be a source of income and increased autonomy for women. However, employment practices are often unsafe, insecure, and highly exploitative, with women suffering serious wage discrimination.

In the Dominican Republic, for example, around 140,000 people are employed in free-trade zones, the majority of whom are women, who are denied even the most basic security of employment, work for less than the minimum wage, and are obliged to work long hours of overtime without compensation. To gain employment, women are often required to prove that they are not pregnant and to agree not to join a trade union. This is the testament of Andrea, a 25-year-old women:

I have five children and work in the free-trade zone making children's clothes. In lots of factories when the women try to form a union they throw every one out. When you go to fill out the forms many factories ask you if you have been a member of a union, and if you say yes they don't give you work. The rhythm of work is very fast. There is no canteen — most people eat on the patio. The free-trade zone helps the country in some respects — because there are few other alternatives for the people. But the way it operates is almost a crime against the workers.

Andrea's words cogently summarise the dilemma facing women workers in the Dominican Republic. They are acutely aware that the alternative to working in the free-trade zone is unemployment and deeper poverty. But they also feel that the standard practices of TNC employers are unacceptably exploitative — and they are right.

In some cases, foreign investors have sought commercial advantage in a manner which exposes workers to acute health risks, as well as extreme exploitation. This is especially true in countries which have specialised in non-traditional agricultural exports such as flowers and horticultural products. Pesticide inputs are especially high on crops such as strawberries, flowers, and mangoes destined for markets in Europe and North America, where consumers demand uniform and unblemished products. In Ecuador, one of the fastest-growing flower exporters to the US, over two-thirds of workers interviewed in one medical survey in a flower-producing area had suffered health disorders from exposure to toxic chemicals, many of which are banned in Europe and the US.[88] Inadequate provision of protective clothing increases the risk from pesticides. Women are particularly vulnerable to acute poisoning and long-term damage because of the impact of toxic substances on the human reproductive system. Another survey of female plantation workers in Ecuador showed that less than half had received the health and social security benefits they were entitled to under the country's labour laws; 80 per cent had no labour contract; none had been given the statutory maternity leave to which they were entitled; and most were required to work overtime, normally without pay.[89]

Such practices ought to be regarded as unacceptable for all people, regardless of the state of development of their countries. Unfortunately, however, they could be multiplied many times over. In Thailand and China unsafe conditions in factories producing for export to Europe and North America have resulted in horrifying loss of life as a result of fires. In Indonesia, independent trade unions are subject to ruthless repression, helping to keep wages low for TNCs producing training shoes for Western consumers. Whether attracted by inadequate labour provisions, lax enforcement of human rights and labour law, or weak environmental rules, it is clear that unregulated foreign investment and trade flows have the potential to lock all countries into a downward spiral of deteriorating social and environmental standards.

Towards an international framework

Drawing the line between the acceptable pursuit of comparative advantage and unacceptable exploitation is inevitably difficult. It would be wrong, for example, to establish minimum standards which were beyond the reach of poor countries. But it would be equally wrong to turn a blind eye to the dangers inherent in continuing on the current course.

One answer to this dilemma is already emerging in the form of local action. Trade unions in the US and Mexico are building alliances and attempting to strengthen the provisions of the NAFTA labour side-accord, in part by filing test cases. The first of these contested the sacking of 100 workers in two US plants in the *maquiladora* zone, one of them owned by General Electric.[90] Environmental groups from Canada, the US and Mexico have also linked up in a effort to amend the NAFTA by removing the restrictions it places upon governments seeking to conserve resources and promote environmentally clean technologies. Across the developing world, many of Oxfam's partners are involved in struggles to establish basic trade union rights in free trade zones, to restrict commercial encroachments into areas of common resources, and to conserve forests and fish stocks.

Ending social dumping

Much more could be done to suport these initiatives by creating an enabling international framework which establishes reasonable minimum standards. In 1947, the UN Conference on Trade and Employment attempted to extend the principles of the Bretton Woods framework to international trade. A charter was drawn up giving a clear statement of the links between trade and labour standards:

The members recognise that measures relating to employment must take into account the rights of workers under inter-governmental declarations, conventions and agreements. They recognise that all countries have a common interest in the achievement and maintenance of fair labour standards related to productivity, and thus in the improvement of wages and working conditions as productivity may permit. The members recognise that unfair labour conditions, especially for export, create difficulties in international trade, and accordingly, each member shall take whatever actions may be appropriate and feasible to eliminate such conditions.[91]

The International Trade Organisation for which this Charter was drafted never saw the light of day, and the problem of protecting social rights within a multilateral trade framework was allowed to drift off the international agenda. Recently, however, the issue has emerged as a focal point in the dialogue over the future of the World Trade Organisation. While international trade treaties such as the WTO cannot and should not be used to eliminate differences in wages, not all differences in wages reflect what might be termed reasonable market conditions. The persistent and widespread violation of internationally recognised labour standards is a distortion of fair competition, as is discrimination on the basis of gender. Failure to enforce provisions for social security, and health and safety regulations is also unacceptable.

If international trade is to be conducted under the auspices of an equitable, open, and rule-based system, governments must accept a reciprocal obligation to enforce minimum standards. Workers must be free to organise and bargain over their conditions of employment. Existing trade rules already outlaw the use of prison labour to produce exports on the grounds that this is unduly exploitative. They also outlaw dumping where this involves the use of subsidies to gain an unfair advantage in exporting, say, a video recorder. Logically, there is no reason why they should not outlaw dumping associated with the denial of the most basic human rights in employment.[92] These rights include those enshrined in International Labour Organisation (ILO) conventions, such as:

- the right to freedom of association
- the right to collective bargaining
- the abolition of forced labour
- freedom from discrimination and entitlement to equal remuneration
- the right to adequate health and safety regulations in the workplace.

Contrary to the fears of some Third World governments, the incorporation of social provisions in international trade rules will not insulate Northern economies from competition. All countries have to adjust to competition, and it is up to Northern governments to provide the investment needed to facilitate new employment opportunities for vulnerable populations. What a social clause would do is bring greater equity to the international trading system. It would do so by spreading the benefits of growth more widely in exporting countries, and by preventing the most extreme forms of exploitation. A social clause would also safeguard the achievements of citizens' groups in all countries, who now see labour and environmental standards under attack from forces currently beyond public control.

Arguments against minimum social standards betray a number of misconceptions. One such misconception is that these standards represent the imposition of a Northern agenda. In fact, the vast majority of WTO members, including its developing country members, are already signatories to the main ILO Conventions. There is, therefore, no question of imposing new standards. This has been recognised by trade union federations in Asia and Latin America, who have endorsed calls for a social clause in the WTO.[93] Nor would a social clause have to be administered in an institutional context, such as that provided by the WTO, susceptible to manipulation by Northern governments. The WTO should recognise the obligation of all governments to meet minimum standards, and it should allow trade restrictions to be imposed on countries which do not meet those standards within a specified time-frame. But compliance should be monitored by the specialised committees of the ILO, which already review complaints and evaluate governmental performance.[94] Citizens' groups, including non-unionised female workers, should be given the right of individual and collective petition to the ILO. This would considerably strengthen the hand of local communities striving for their basic rights.

The complexities and political problems in attempting to establish minimum social standards are considerable. However, failure to create a social clause in the WTO will inevitably swell the gathering tide of political xenophobia and overt protectionism in the industrialised world, where competition with workers subject to gross exploitation is deeply resented as a cause of unemployment. Moreover, without a credible multilateral framework for social standards, unilateral actions will gather pace. Under existing US trade law, aid and trade preferences are conditional upon compliance with standards set by the US. These standards are applied with great inconsistency, in a manner which reflects US commercial interests (hence the refusal to link trade with China to improvements in its human rights record). It would be far better from the standpoint of developing countries to participate in genuinely multilateral and open arrangements.

Closing pollution havens

The problems associated with 'pollution havens' parallel those caused by the disregard of labour standards. Unacceptably low environmental standards are not a source of legitimate comparative advantage, but a form of exploitation which creates unfair competition.

As in the labour sphere, complete harmonisation of environmental policies is neither practical nor desirable. However, moving towards a minimum parity level for some of the most environmentally-damaging production processes would be a step towards placing international trade on more sustainable foundations. Where the industrialised countries are concerned, there is a strong case for using trade measures in defence of sustainable environmental policy objectives. The energy tax proposed by the EU's Environment Commission was withdrawn partly because of fears of a loss of industrial competitiveness. In this case, it would have been legitimate to use import restrictions to offset that loss, countering any advantages accruing to competitors.

Unlike the industrialised countries, many developing countries would be unable to afford the clean technologies needed to meet higher environmental standards. The Brundtland Commission estimated that in the early 1980s developing countries exporting to the OECD countries would have incurred costs in excess of $5bn had they been required to meet US standards.[95] The sum today would be considerably larger. Not large enough, however, to justify inaction. Financial resource transfers, including debt relief, could be linked to the adoption of technologies which would enable developing countries to introduce higher standards. Similarly, if tariffs were deployed to protect industries meeting higher environmental standards, the revenue generated could be repatriated to developing countries in the form of an environment fund, administered by a multilateral body, for investment in clean technologies.

One of the most formidable barriers to the use of trade policies for promoting more sustainable practices is to be found in the rules of the WTO itself. Existing international trade rules do not allow for governments to implement trade restricting policies in pursuit of environmental objectives. This was underlined by a GATT dispute between Mexico and the US over American restrictions on tuna imports caught by methods which killed large numbers of dolphins. In practice, it is probable that the US trade restrictions in this case, applied under the Marine Mammal Protection Act, did discriminate against Mexico. But the GATT panel which ruled on the case in Mexico's favour did so on two precedent-setting grounds. The first of these was that no GATT member had a right to use trade sanctions because of objections over the manner in which an import was produced. The second was that environmental resources located outside of national borders could not be subject to trade restrictions.[96]

Both principles have far-reaching implications. They call into question the use of trade measures to counter global warming and ozone depletion (the ozone layer being located beyond national borders); and they appear to rule out the use of trade sanctions against unsustainably harvested timber and depletion of fish stocks.[97]

In Oxfam's view, there is an unassailable case for using trade measures as part of a wider strategy for achieving environmental objectives. The framework should be developed not by trade ministers in the WTO, but by a wider forum held under the auspices of the Commission for Sustainable Development, which is more democratic, transparent, and broader in its focus. The forum should examine trade, environment, and sustainable development policies at the national, regional, and global levels, and recommend measures for resolving potential conflicts between free trade and sustainable development. These measures should:

- Establish the primacy of global environmental treaties. The WTO should explicitly recognise that obligations under internationally negotiated environmental treaties take precedence over the commitment to free trade.
- Recognise the right of governments to use trade measures in pursuit of sustainable environmental policies. The WTO treaty should be amended to allow governments to implement trade restrictions where production and processing methods are having adverse environmental consequences, or where these are necessary to maintain higher domestic environmental standards. Obligations on developing countries to comply with industrial country environmental standards should be linked to the provision of financial support, and subject to longer transitional periods than for industrial countries.
- Establish a body under CSD auspices to negotiate, monitor, and adjudicate over environmental standards in international trade, and to explore options for introducing 'green tariffs' to promote sustainable trade.
- Establish minimum environmental standards. These would set minimum international norms of emission control on factories producing for export, which would be codified in international agreements. Such agreements would prevent the industrial countries from imposing unrealistically high standards. Importing countries with higher environmental standards would be permitted

to block or impose tariffs on imports which did not meet these standards.

- Allow the imposition of 'green tariffs' on trade between industrial countries. Where punitive tariffs are applied on environmental grounds the revenues should be invested in jointly agreed funds to finance the transfer of clean technology to the industry concerned.

- Facilitate technology transfer. Any international agreement on standards which did not provide for the transference of technology to developing countries would be rightly regarded as unfair, and probably be unworkable. The initiatives undertaken under the Montreal Protocol and the Bio-diversity Convention to facilitate technology transfer should be built upon to promote sustainable development.

Trading old problems and new: the Uruguay Round

The Uruguay Round represented the most ambitious and far-reaching set of trade negotiations of the post-war era. It took place against a protracted crisis in the external trade environment of the world's poorest countries, with low commodity prices, debt, and protectionism undermining their export prospects. The 1980s also witnessed a marked deterioration in the multilateral trade environment, with developing countries increasingly subjected to the threat of unilateral trade sanctions by the major industrialised countries.

Had the Uruguay Round failed to culminate in agreement, there would have been a real prospect of a descent into 1930s-style trade policies, with the major industrial powers engaging in cycles of retaliation and counter-retaliation. Developing countries, with their limited retaliatory powers, would inevitably have suffered. However, the agreement which emerged from the Uruguay Round is highly unbalanced and weighted in favour of the industrialised nations. This is reflected in the distribution of economic benefits, a projected

two-thirds of which will go to the industrialised countries. Sub-Saharan Africa, the world's poorest region, stands to lose from the agreement.[98]

The distribution of gains reflects the focus of the Uruguay Round on issues primarily of concern to the industrial countries. Long-standing problems facing primary commodity exporters have not been dealt with. Other problems, such as discriminatory protectionism and agricultural over-production, have been, at best, only partially addressed. TNCs were able to use their influence with Northern governments to secure agreements in areas such as intellectual property and investment, which could undermine the prospects for more self-reliant development into the next century.

Figure 4.3 GATT winners and losers (projections to year 2002)

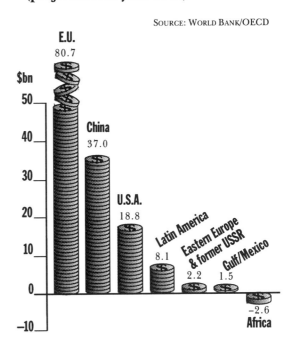

SOURCE: WORLD BANK/OECD

In the following section we examine the failures of the Uruguay Round to address the problems facing developing countries in four critical areas:

- primary commodities
- protectionism in manufactured goods
- agricultural and food security
- the regulation of TNCs and intellectual property rights.

Primary commodities

Trade in primary commodities has grown much more slowly than trade in manufactured goods. But although primary commodities are of diminishing significance in international trade flows, they are of great importance to some of the world's poorest countries and people. Some 30 countries in Africa and 18 in Latin America depend on primary commodity exports for more than half of their export earnings.[99] Such dependence leaves them highly vulnerable to fluctuations in international commodity markets. Some nations are even more vulnerable by being reliant on just one or two commodities.[100] Coffee, for example, accounts for over three-quarters of export earnings for Uganda and Ethiopia.

Instability and exploitation

Revenue from primary commodity exports is vital to the livelihoods of millions of smallholders and workers throughout the world, from the Ethiopian Highlands, to the Punjab and the Andean countries. These cash crops provide households with the income they need to buy seeds, clothes, and fuel, and to pay school fees. They also generate the foreign exchange which countries need to maintain essential imports, and the revenue which governments need to invest in health and education services. Yet for well over a decade, primary commodity exporters have faced a sustained depression in world markets, deeper and more protracted than at any time since the 1920s. Between 1980 and 1993, prices for non-oil primary commodities fell by more than half relative to prices for manufactured goods.[101] The estimated annual loss to developing countries over this period was around $100bn: more than twice the total flow of aid in 1990.

Superimposed on the overall downward trend in commodity prices is an erratic zig-zag line of fluctuating prices, reflecting the volatility of the markets upon which vulnerable commodity producers depend. Prices for commodities such as sugar, coffee, and cocoa are notoriously unstable, making any attempt at planning a hazardous exercise. Prices for cocoa, for example, averaged $2000 per ton between 1980 and 1987, before falling to $649 per ton in 1992, and rising again in 1994. Coffee prices plummeted to an all-time low in the early 1990s, before reaching a six-year high in 1994.[102] Despite these brief price surges, World Bank projections suggest that the index for beverage prices will not reach even its depressed 1989 level before the turn of the century.[103]

Falling world commodity prices are not just trends on commodity flow charts; they can destroy the livelihoods of entire communities. For example, the collapse of world prices for sugar in the mid-1980s, led to famine conditions on the Philippines island of Negros.[104] A farmer in Colombia explained what a fall in coffee prices had meant for his family as follows:

We had no choice but to sell. But we cannot live on what we have earned. This year our entire coffee crop would hardly be enough to feed and clothe the children, let alone to pay their school fees. It is the same for the rest of the families in the village. We have no choice but to leave and find work in the towns. Maybe we could borrow some money and hope that prices will rise next year. If they don't we may as well tear up our bushes.

In fact, many thousands of smallholders have been driven to tear up their coffee bushes to grow coca, illustrating the deadly connection between deepening poverty in the South and social problems in the North. Politicians in the industrialised world often welcome reductions in the commodity price index, citing the benefits of lower prices for consumers and inflation. In fact, the benefits of lower commodity prices are reflected more in increased profit margins in the highly-monopolised food-marketing sector, than in lower consumer costs. The

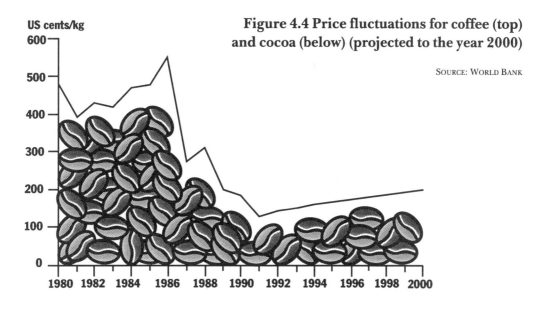

Figure 4.4 Price fluctuations for coffee (top) and cocoa (below) (projected to the year 2000)

Source: World Bank

benefits to consumers in terms of lower inflation are marginal, especially when offset against the human costs to producers.

In its international programme, Oxfam is working with smallholder producers who are attempting to develop more sustainable livelihoods through commodity trade. One of the main problems which these producers face is that, in most cases, they receive a small share of the final value of their production. For raw cotton, the growers' price represents less than 8 per cent of the final product price. For coffee, exporting countries typically retain between 12

per cent and 25 per cent, although growers receive substantially less after the profits of traders and state taxes are taken into account.[105] The bulk of the final value is transferred through production, processing and marketing chains controlled by Northern TNCs, to the industrialised world.

In the Dominican Republic, Oxfam works with some of the country's 70,000 coffee farmers, most of whom farm on ecologically fragile hillsides growing coffee alongside food staples. These producers are developing production and marketing systems designed to retain a higher share of the final value of their produce in the local economy. At the other end of the marketing chain, Oxfam is working with other groups attempting to develop fairer trade relations, by persuading consumers of the case for buying products which return a higher share of their sale value to producers. However, without more fundamental reforms to address the underlying causes of the crisis in international commodity markets, there is a limit to what such initiatives can achieve.

Decline in the prices of primary commodities

There are several factors behind the long-term decline in prices for primary commodities, which some analysts trace back to the beginning of the twentieth century.[106] The low rate of growth in demand relative to production is part of the problem. Demand for commodities such as tropical beverages tends to grow more slowly than income in the industrialised world, so that markets expand less rapidly than for manufactured goods. Market outlets have also been restricted by the development of synthetic substitutes; for example, Zambian copper has been displaced by fibre optics in communications networks. Changing economic structures and production patterns in the industrialised world have also reduced the demand for primary commodities. Financial services and 'knowledge-intensive' production processes, the growth points of most economies, use minimal amounts of raw materials. Meanwhile, efficiency savings have increased, so that the average American car weighs 15 per cent less than two decades ago, again resulting in reduced demand for raw materials.[107]

These trends are probably irreversible. However, some of the causes of over-supply are rooted in more immediate policy interventions. Agricultural over-production and the dumping of subsidised exports by the industrialised countries has been a major factor in depressing world markets.[108] For example, exports of sugar and edible oils by the EU have contributed to the prolonged price depression in both commodities. Structural adjustment programmes have also expanded supplies on to already saturated markets. These programmes were designed in part to expand commodity exports by liberalising trade and foreign exchange markets, so that the incentive to domestic producers increased. As anticipated, export volumes rose. Unfortunately, they were rising everywhere, as a large number of countries producing a small range of exports sought simultaneously to expand their market shares in obedience to the dictates of structural adjustment programmes. The entirely predictable result was another twist in the downward spiral of world prices.

As with many of the international economic problems facing the world's poorest countries, underlying causes are easier to identify than solutions. Over half-a-century ago, John Maynard Keynes, the chief architect of the Bretton Woods system, warned of the dangers and inherent social injustice in allowing commodity prices to fall to levels incompatible with decent living standards. Defending the case for a system of price support, he suggested that the proper 'economic price' should be fixed not at the lowest possible level, but at a level sufficient to provide producers 'with proper nutritional and other standards in the conditions in which they live'. He added: 'It is in the interest of all producers alike that the price of a commodity should not be depressed below this level, and consumers are not entitled to expect that it should.'[109]

Regulating commodity markets

Higher and more stable prices for commodities would bring substantial benefits for producers. This is especially true for producers of tree crops (like coffee) that produce their maximum yield several years after planting. Increased planting during times of shortage when prices rise, as they have over the past year, typically leads to future glut, price collapse, reduced plantings, and the resumption of the same unstable cycle. Latin American coffee producers in the Andean highlands who were tearing up coffee plants three years ago are now replanting them. But the beans produced by their investments are likely to come on stream during the next price trough. Such instability cannot provide a foundation for sustainable and secure livelihoods.

During the 1970s, efforts to regulate commodity markets focused on international agreements between producers and consumers to maintain prices. These agreements sought to defend prices by buying in stocks when prices were low and selling them on the rare occasions that prices rose above a pre-determined ceiling.[110] However, viable international commodity agreements have proved an elusive alternative to the destructive tendencies of free markets. Of five international commodity agreements developed under the auspices of the United Nations Conference on Trade and Development in the 1970s — coffee, cocoa, sugar, tin, and rubber — to defend floor prices through managing 'buffer' stocks, only that for rubber is still in operation. The international cocoa agreement was stripped of its market intervention provisions in 1988, contributing to the steepest price fall since the Great Depression. The international coffee agreement followed suit the following year, with similarly dramatic price effects. Between 1989 and 1990, prices dropped from 114 cents a pound to 44 cents. Today, both agreements continue in name, but without any effective mechanisms for stabilising prices at reasonable levels.[111]

The reluctance of developed countries to provide the financial resources needed to maintain effective buffer stocks has been part of the problem. Chronic over-supply has been another. Consensus on what constitutes a realistic support price has also proved hard to achieve, not least because of a concern on the part of developed countries to exploit the weak position of exporters by driving down prices. Developing countries themselves, however, must bear some of the responsibility for instab-ility in international commodity markets. For example, the coffee agreement broke down partly because Brazil refused to give up some of its market share to Central American and African exporters. Similarly, the cocoa agreement was undermined partly because new suppliers in Asia were determined to expand production and market shares outside of the agreement.

The case for commodity co-operation between consumers and producers, and between producers themselves, is as compelling today as it was for Keynes. Market forces can deal with structural imbalances between supply and demand only through long and painful boom-bust cycles in output. For this reason, the essential objectives of UNCTAD's Integrated Programme for Commodities remain valid: improving terms of trade for commodity exporters, stabilising prices, and encouraging local processing.[112] Appropriate forms of supply-management are also urgently required to restore more balanced markets. Existing funds for compensating producers for short-falls in exports earnings, such as the IMF's Compensatory Financing Facility and the EU's Stabex Fund, could be diverted for this purpose, instead of focusing on the fruitless task of counteracting the losses from adverse price trends. It must be stressed that consumers and producers share a joint interest in managing commodity markets more successfully, not least to avert the potentially destabilising social dislocation caused by persistent excess supply and depressed prices.

Diversification

The longer-term solution for the problems facing commodity-dependent Third World exporters is diversification. However, this is easier to advocate than to achieve, since it requires investment, including funds for education and infrastructure. The UN Secretary-General has attempted to address this challenge by proposing, in the UN's New Agenda for the Development of Africa, a commodity diversification fund for sub-Saharan Africa. That was in 1991. Unfortunately, donors have failed to provide the $50-70m envisaged for the fund, preferring to place their faith in private sector initiatives.[113]

Inadequate investment and lack of international support for diversification is compounded by problems of protectionism. One of the most effective ways in which developing countries can generate employment, increase export earnings, and escape dependence on volatile primary commodity markets is to add value to their exports through local processing. However, this is actively discouraged by import tariffs in developed countries, which increase with the level of processing. For example, Malaysia can export unrefined palm oil to the EU at a tariff rate of less than 2 per cent. But if it processes the palm oil into higher value-added margarine the tariff rate rises to 25 per cent. Similarly, the average industrial country tariff on chocolate is more than twice that on cocoa beans.[114] This system is designed to discourage developing countries from diversifying — and it partly explains why such a small proportion of the final value of primary commodities remains in exporting countries.

The EU has supported in a modest way efforts at diversification under the Lomé Convention. These efforts, however, have been undermined by the trade restrictions enshrined in the same treaty: an example of the contradictory effects of EU trade and aid policies. Under the Lomé Convention, countries in the African, Caribbean, and Pacific group can export locally processed goods duty-free to Europe, provided that all of their products originate in the ACP countries themselves. This rule has prevented Zimbabwe from exporting cloth mixed with South African wool, hampering the development of its textile industry.[115] It has also restricted potential sources of supply in a manner which is totally unrealistic if the aim of the Convention is to promote the competitive position of the ACP countries. Restrictions imposed under the Common Agricultural Policy, present another formidable barrier to the local processing of fruit and vegetables.

The Uruguay Round agreement will do little to reduce the problem of tariff escalation for beverages, oilseeds, and fish, which are of great concern to developing countries. Tariffs will continue to escalate by between 8 per cent and 26 per cent in these areas, reducing the benefits of the agreement for the world's poorest countries.[116] Meanwhile, the trade barriers imposed under the Common Agricultural Policy will remain largely intact. For the world's poorest commodity producers in sub-Saharan Africa, there are justifiable fears that the Uruguay Round agreement will jeopardise trade prospects in European markets. This is because the agreement will lower tariffs for all countries, thereby diminishing the preferences currently granted to Africa under the Lomé Convention. Projections by the OECD in 1994 suggested that the resulting loss in foreign exchange earnings could amount to as much as $2bn annually for sub-Saharan Africa (including South Africa) up to 2002.[117]

Action is needed to improve the trading prospects of the world's poorest countries, including:

- urgent international efforts to re-establish price stabilising international commodity agreements, especially for coffee and cocoa
- increased co-operation between developing countries to initiate supply management measures compatible with more remunerative prices
- a review of structural adjustment programmes and development assistance directed at expanding commodity exports to consider their impact on global commodity markets
- increased investment in complementary measures to compensate least developed countries for shortfalls in foreign exchange earnings, such as those provided under the Stabex scheme in the EU's Lomé Convention agreement with the African, Caribbean and Pacific countries
- support for the UN's proposed commodity diversification fund and increased investment in other diversification initiatives

- the withdrawal of escalating tariffs on primary commodities exported from developing countries.

Banana wars and free trade

For some of the world's poorest and most vulnerable producers, the failure of the Uruguay Round to address problems in international commodity markets will be compounded by its impact on existing trade arrangements. These are the words of Winston Graham, a banana farmer in the Windward Islands.

We are told that the world has changed, that because of GATT there must be a free market in bananas. But the market should not be so free that it can destroy people's lives.

Winston Graham's small farm on a steep hillside in the Windward Island of St Lucia seems a million miles from the plush GATT negotiating rooms in Geneva. But along with thousands of fellow banana producers in the Caribbean, his livelihood is at the heart of an international trade dispute between the EU on the one side, and Latin America and the US on the other. It is a dispute which raises fundamental questions about the values, principles and priorities which underpin world trade.

The immediate issue at stake is trade with the EU, whose citizens consume some 3.5 million tons of bananas annually. Until 1992, the EU banana market reflected the old colonial ties of its member states. Britain, for example, imported two-thirds of its bananas from its former colonies in the Caribbean, including the Windward Islands. But this arrangement could only be maintained by protecting the British market from Latin American exporters, such as Colombia and Costa Rica, where bananas are produced at around half of the cost of the Caribbean on giant, highly mechanised plantations. Thus the Latin American producers (largely TNCs) dominated markets in Germany, but were subject to quotas and tariffs in the British market.[118]

With the arrival of the Single European Market in 1992, such protection became inconsistent with EU law. However, after a protracted debate, in July 1993, Europe introduced a new import policy which set an increased quota for Latin America bananas. Imports above that quota — set at 2 million tons — are subject to higher duties.[119]

The EU's aim was to protect the Caribbean from the social and economic effects of free trade by maintaining a regulated market. Such a policy was justified by the degree of dependence of Caribbean exporters on the EU market. In The Windward Islands (Dominica, St Lucia, St Vincent, and Grenada) bananas are the mainstay of economic life, accounting for 15 per cent of national income and over half of export earnings. Around 57,000 people, a third of the labour force, are directly or indirectly involved in the banana industry. Maintaining a viable banana industry was vital in a region where unemployment is in excess of 20 per cent and where there are few alternatives.

However, the new EU regime was promptly challenged at the GATT by five Latin American exporters. Having already condemned the EU's system of preferences, there was little doubt that the dispute panel set up to adjudicate would rule against the new system. The panel ruled that discrimination against the Latin American countries was a violation of the obligation on the EU to uphold the GATT principle of free trade.[120]

The US has now entered the fray. Following a complaint from the giant banana corporation, Chiquita Brands International, the American Trade Representative has threatened to impose trade sanctions on EU exports unless the European banana market is liberalised. Along with three other companies (Standard Fruit, Dole, and De Monte), Chiquita controls around three-quarters of bananas exported from Latin America.[121]

If the EU were to comply with the GATT ruling and the demands of the US, it would sound the death knell for the banana industry in much of the Caribbean.[122] In Oxfam's view, this would place the dictates of free-trade dogma and corporate self-interest over the interests of people and their livelihoods. There are likely to be more stringent rules for settling disputes under the new WTO regime, which will force the EU to give way and allow Latin American exporters access to EU markets on the same terms as the Caribbean producers. Oxfam is supporting the efforts of farmers of the Windward Islands Farmers' Association to improve the competitiveness of the local industry, and to develop ideas about diversification. But without the maintenance of a preferential system in Europe, such efforts will count for little.

Manufacturing protectionism

If developing countries are to reduce their dependence on primary commodities and expand their exports of manufactured goods, they need access to the markets of the industrialised countries. These countries account for over two-thirds of global imports of manufactured goods and three-quarters of developing country exports of manufactures.[123] As a result, trade policies in industrial countries have an important influence on the economic prospects of developing countries.

Governments in the industrial countries frequently stress their adherence to the principles of free trade. These principles have been adopted in many developing countries across Latin America, Asia, and Africa, as witnessed by the steep decline in trade restricting measures. Countries such as Ghana, Kenya, Tanzania, and Zambia have been phasing out restrictions and tariffs.[124] In contrast, there has been little progress towards dismantling trade barriers in industrialised countries. These barriers have become increasingly arbitrary and discriminatory in their treatment of developing countries. As a result, there has been a widening divergence between the principles espoused by the industrial countries and their trade practices.

The GATT was established on the foundations of three key principles: non-

discrimination, transparency (which meant that countries should use open tariffs rather than less quantifiable forms of protection), and reciprocity (which meant that where importers reduced tariffs, exporters should reciprocate).[125] But these principles are little more than empty words, especially where developing countries are concerned. Behind the rhetoric of multilateralism in international trade rules there is discrimination, unilateralism, and recourse to arbitrary forms of protection. No other area of North-South relations is marked by such a profound divergence between the stated commitment of Northern governments to market principles, and the protectionist nature of their trade policies.

Non-tariff barriers (NTBs)

One of the achievements of the GATT during the post-war period was to reduce the incidence of tariffs in industrial countries. With the conclusion of the Uruguay Round, average tariffs have fallen to less than 5 per cent, compared to over 40 per cent fifty years ago.[126] Since the mid-1970s, however, the international trading system has witnessed the rise of new forms of protection, mainly in the form of non-tariff barriers (NTB), which violate the spirit and, in some cases, the letter, of GATT rules. Among the most common NTBs are quotas, voluntary export restraints (VERs), and a wide range of measures to counter allegedly unfair trade practices.[127] Viewed from the perspective of the importer, the main advantages of NTBs are that they are 'legal' in GATT terms, and that they can be used, in contravention of the GATT principle of non-discrimination, to target individual suppliers.

Developing countries have been the main target of NTBs. One-fifth of all non-fuel exports from developing countries are now covered by NTBs, compared to one-tenth for trade between the developed countries.[128] Contrary to a commitment made at the beginning of the Uruguay Round to 'roll-back' such trade restrictions, they actually increased during the 1980s.[129] VER arrangements, under which countries 'voluntarily' agree to limit exports, or face trade sanctions, are especially pernicious, since they allow developed countries to exploit the weakness of developing country exporters. The US, which led the 'free trade' drive during the Uruguay Round, uses VERs to protect its steel industry from Brazilian imports, its cement industry from Mexican competitors, and its footwear industry from Asian exporters.[130] In Europe, VERs and quotas are applied to everything from teddy bears made in Thailand to videos produced in other parts of South-East Asia.

The Multi-Fibre Arrangement

The most significant NTB facing the world's poorest countries is the Multi-Fibre Arrangement. Negotiated two decades ago as a temporary departure from GATT principles, the MFA has allowed the industrial countries to impose quotas on individual suppliers.[131] It was progressively strengthened during the 1980s. For example, in the early 1980s, the EU introduced a device called the 'basket extractor'. This allowed it to extend MFA restrictions even to products not covered in existing bilateral agreements. Clearly impressed, the US followed suit. All major importers also introduced a range of safeguard devices to curtail increases in imports they might not have considered. The fourth MFA was negotiated during the Uruguay Round, despite the pledge to 'roll back' existing forms of protectionism. In the event, the MFA was rolled forward to cover a lengthy list of new products, including some (such as jute and ramie) of primary concern to the world's poorest countries, such as Bangladesh.[132]

The overall cost of the MFA to developing countries has been estimated at around $50bn a year: roughly equal to the total flow of development assistance provided by Northern governments.[133] The real costs in terms of lost livelihoods in the developing countries are considerably higher. For many of these countries, the textile industry is the first step on the ladder of industrial development. Because it is labour intensive, its growth generates employment opportunities and income, especially for women; and because the technology involved in the early stages of production is relatively simple, investment in the textiles sector is an obvious way for countries to generate the exports they need to pay for imports. The MFA was designed to undermine the comparative advantage of developing countries, with detrimental effects for employment and trade.

Anti-dumping measures

Some trade barriers are more difficult to quantify than others. For example, companies in Europe and North America have frequent recourse to anti-dumping actions. These are supposed to counter the use of subsidies to gain market shares by imposing countervailing duties on exporters. In principle, anti-dumping measures are a perfectly legitimate response to unfair trade practices. In practice, anti-dumping rules are designed to discover dumping where none exists and to exaggerate its severity. They are widely abused by powerful business interests to exclude rivals from markets.[134] For example, European electronics groups have gained anti-dumping protection from South-East Asian rivals, while continuing to import the same items from their own plants in the region. One recent review of anti-dumping cases investigated by the EU and published in 1994 found that 95 per cent had resulted in the exporter being found guilty — a conviction rate unmatched in any other judicial context.[135]

Trade barriers after the Uruguay Round

The Uruguay Round agreement concluded in April 1994, only partially addresses the bewildering array of trade barriers facing developing country manufacturers. While the share of such exports entering industrial country markets duty free will double, the proportion attracting tariffs of 10 per cent or more will remain relatively high — and far higher than for goods traded between the industrial countries themselves. Moreover, some of the product groups of greatest interest to developing countries, including textiles and clothing, footwear and leather goods, will continue to face severe discrimination. Around one-fifth of textile exports will continue to face tariffs in excess of 15 per cent.[136]

Other discriminatory measures will also remain intact for some time, especially if the industrial countries continue their imaginative efforts to undermine both the letter and the spirit of the GATT agreement. The MFA is supposed to be phased out in three stages by 2005. During the first phase, which lasts three years, restrictions are to be reduced by 16 per cent. Unfortunately, instead of grasping the opportunity to remove one of the longest-standing inequities in world trade, the EU appears bent upon discovering ingenious ways of undermining the textile agreement. By tabling an offer to remove restrictions on items which were either not covered by the MFA, or which were covered but not subject to quotas, the EU has signalled its intention to meet its GATT targets in a way which will leave all current restrictions in place until 1998 at the earliest.[137] This contrasts with moves towards liberalisation in developing countries themselves. For example, under bilateral arrangements with the EU and the US, India is reducing its textile tariff by 65 per cent up to 1998 and phasing out quotas thereafter.[138]

Under the new GATT regime, anti-dumping rules have been tightened. But the new rules reflect the demands of US and EU negotiators for a framework that will enable them to respond positively to protectionist demands from industrial lobbies. The GATT agreement will also allow for the continuation of VERs, and permit the selective application of 'safeguard' measures, which can be used to impose duties and quotas on countries which succeed in rapidly expanding their market shares.[139]

Arguably the deepest inequity in the GATT system is the abuse by developed countries of the principle of reciprocity. In theory, GATT rules require all countries to respond to liberalisation by their trade partners with equivalent measures, the aim being to create a dynamic process of trade liberalisation. In practice, this does not happen, for two main reasons. First, because developing countries have been liberalising their economies either unilaterally or in the context of structural adjustment programmes, rather than under GATT auspices, industrialised countries are technically not required to reciprocate. Second, developing countries do not have the economic and political muscle to press their claims against the industrialised countries.

There is considerable scope for improving the Uruguay Round agreement by:

- setting clearer rules for phasing out the Multi-Fibre Arrangement and accelerating the withdrawal of restrictions
- abolishing 'voluntary export restraints' and withdrawing all NTBs which discriminate against developing countries
- establishing clear and uniform rules for anti-dumping legislation.
- establishing a wider principle of reciprocity whereby industrial countries are required to match the liberalisation efforts of developing countries.

Agriculture and food security

The agricultural policies of the industrial countries exercise an important influence on the trade prospects of developing countries, and on the livelihoods of their inhabitants. The industrial countries are the world's largest importers of agricultural produce, and they dominate a number of export markets. These exports compete with those of developing countries on international markets, where they drive down prices. They also enter the food systems of the developing countries, bringing smallholder farmers there into direct competition with farmers in Europe and North America, often with disastrous consequences.[140]

Until the Uruguay Round, agriculture was treated as an exception to the GATT principle that markets should be liberalised. There was no prohibition on the use of export subsidies to dispose of surpluses; and no effective prohibition against the use of import controls to protect farm incomes. This special dispensation existed because the GATT's rules on agriculture were tailored to accommodate the US farm-income support programmes designed during the New Deal, which depended on import controls and export subsidies. The Common Agricultural Policy (CAP) of the EU, which also involved import controls and subsidies to protect farmers, was subsequently accommodated within the GATT, resulting in increasing tension with the US.[141]

Governments in the industrialised countries have used a wide range of mechanisms to protect the incomes of their farmers. Domestic price-support policies, in which farmers receive guaranteed prices for their output, have been backed by a bewildering array of trade restrictions designed to stop imports coming in at lower prices. The overall cost to the OECD countries of these policies amounted to around $350bn in the early 1990s; around six times what they provided in official development assistance.[142] In Europe alone, taxpayers typically spend in excess of $20bn on the CAP, which continues to absorb the bulk of the EU's budget.

The CAP system has resulted in massive overproduction. Until recently, farmers in the EU were paid a guaranteed price for virtually unlimited output. This encouraged productivity gains, as farmers invested in increasingly intensive systems of production. Each acre of cereals farmland in northern Europe produces three times as much today as it did in the 1960s. Thus, while small farmers have been squeezed out, the larger farms which have replaced them have maintained a relentless incease in output, changing Europe from a net importer to a major exporter.[143] Over one-third of European cereals production is now exported. As a result, the EU's share of world markets increased from less than 7 per cent in the early 1970s to almost a quarter in the 1990s. The EU is now the world's largest exporter of sugar and beef, the second largest exporter of cereals, and a major

exporter of edible oils.[144] The costs associated with toring surpluses and disposing of them on world markets now absorb over one-third of the CAP budget.

The effects of subsidised exports

In the 1980s, competition between the EU and the US intensified, as world markets contracted. With surpluses mounting, both 'agricultural superpowers' sought to outsubsidise each other to expand their market share, with disastrous consequences. World prices fell to their lowest levels in real terms since the Great Depression, driving up the costs of farm budgets and export subsidies. By the mid-1980s, agricultural trade conflicts seemed likely to escalate into a wider trade war, bringing the problem of agricultural policy reform to the top of the Uruguay Round agenda.[145]

Agricultural trade problems are widely perceived as a matter of interest solely to the EU and the US. But the most damaging effects of trans-Atlantic trade hostilities have been felt in developing countries, where the most visible victims have been non-subsidised exporters, caught in the crossfire of the EU-US subsidy barrage. For example, falling prices for cereals and oilseeds reduced Argentina's export earnings by 40 per cent between 1980 and 1987. The effects of falling world sugar prices as a result of the twin pressures of a surge in EU exports and reduced market access to the US were transmitted back to producers, including millions of smallholder farmers and agricultural labourers, with the Philippines and Dominican Republic particularly severely affected.[146]

Subsidised exports have also undermined livelihoods by flooding local markets with cheap imported food. The impact of EU beef dumping in West Africa is one example. Pastoral farmers in countries such as Mali, Niger and Burkina Faso sell animals in local markets to generate cash income for household needs. During the latter half of the 1980s, these markets were disrupted by heavily subsidised EU beef, which was being sold at one-third of the normal price.[147] Currency over-valuation further reduced the price of imported beef, although a 50 per cent devaluation in 1994 radically changed this picture. For nomadic peoples such as the Fulani, maintaining their herds on ecologically fragile grazing lands in areas of uncertain rainfall, the effects of low prices are disastrous. As one farmer puts it:

Everything here depends on the income from selling animals. With this climate nobody can count on crop production. If the animals don't sell, or are sold at a derisory price, people lose their savings. They cannot buy enough food, and they cannot afford education or medicine for their children.

In the Andean region, Oxfam has witnessed how heavily subsidised wheat and maize imports from the US have destroyed the livelihoods of local producers of food staples. In West Africa, cheap wheat imports have been displacing traditional food staples in local diets. Wheat imports into the coastal region have been increasing by over 8 per cent a year for the past decade, while per capita production of sorghum and millet has been falling.[148] Wheat-based bread has become a staple food in many countries. By driving down local prices, wheat imports have damaged rural livelihoods and employment. They have also contributed to the creation of an unhealthy and unsustainable dependence in many countries upon food imports. These now use up more than a quarter of export earnings in sub-Saharan Africa, where political elites have long regarded cheap food imports as a way of supporting industrial development.[149]

The UN's Economic Commission for Africa has called for a renewed emphasis upon achieving greater food self-reliance. 'Africa's viability,' it wrote in 1991, 'resides, above all other considerations, in its being able to feed its own people from its internal resources.'[150] The case for improved self-reliance is rooted not only in the inherent dangers for weak trading countries of dependence upon volatile world food markets, but also in the importance of food staples production for rural employment and poverty reduction. These dimensions of food security are often ignored by advocates of agricultural trade liberalisation for the developing world. So, too, are implications of trade liberalisation in markets which are massively distorted by agricultural subsidies. The familiar GATT refrain stressing the need for 'a level playing field' in agriculture remains popular with Northern policy makers. But the playing field in agricultural trade runs all the way downhill from the heavily subsidised farms of Europe and North America to the staple-food systems of Asia, Africa, and Latin America.

Mexican maize and NAFTA

Consider, for example, the implications of agricultural trade liberalisation under the NAFTA. In Mexico, maize accounts for almost two-thirds of agricultural production in some areas of the country, where millions of households farm on steep, ecologically fragile hillsides using traditional methods of cultivation. In areas such as Morelos, Guerrero, and the Tarascan Plateau, deepening rural poverty has already caused a wave of male migration to urban areas, leaving women and children to carry out the bulk of production. Households survive partly by selling small amounts of maize after the harvest and partly through off-farm activity, such as employment on larger holdings.[151] Under the NAFTA agreement, restrictions on US maize imports are being progressively withdrawn, along with price support to Mexican farmers. By imposing a 'free trade' on such unequal contestants in the market, NAFTA is signing the death knell for millions of Mexican smallholdings. Average yields in Mexico are less than a quarter of those in the US,[152] where farmers benefit not only from production subsidies (which account for a third of the value of maize output) but also from a wide range of marketing and irrigation subsidies.[153] It has been estimated that fewer than one in ten Mexican maize producers could compete in an unprotected market. Translated into human terms, this means that the free importation of US maize will displace an estimated 2.4 million peasant producers and their families from the land.[154] The overall effect will be to destroy the social, ecological, and economic foundations of agriculture in some of the poorest areas, resulting in forced migration to cities or to the US.

Agricultural trade reform

The Uruguay Round agreement and the reform of the EU's CAP have been widely celebrated as the start of a new era in world agricultural trade. In practice, however, the changes introduced will be of marginal relevance to world agricultural markets. Briefly summarised, the GATT agreement comprises three elements: a reduction in domestic income support by 20 per cent; a reduction in the volume of subsidised exports by 21 per cent and in the value of such exports by 36 per cent; and the conversion of all import barriers into tariffs.[155]

The implementation of the agreement will produce results which are considerably less impressive than the figures imply. Both the US and the EU claim to have already made the necessary cuts in domestic subsidies, so there will be no additional reductions.[156] The EU has changed the way in which it provides subsidies so that, in the arcane world of GATT semantics, they are no longer treated as subsidies (and therefore not subject to reduction). Under the new CAP regime, farmers are paid income support tied to the volume of land they farm, rather than price support for output. Since income support is treated, under the Uruguay Round agreement, as distinct from an export subsidy, it will be possible to maintain current levels of over-production and export dumping.[157] As in the US, the biggest farms in the EU will have to take a proportion of their land out of cultivation to qualify for price support. Already, however, set-aside, as this system is known, has shown itself to be highly ineffective as a means of cutting production, as witnessed by the increase in the EU's 1994 cereals harvest.

Agriculture is one area of international trade in which there are win-win scenarios for the majority of people in the developed and the developing world. The main beneficiaries of existing price support policies in Europe and North America are large-scale farmers (the largest 20 per cent of whom receive three-quarters of CAP subsidies),[158] agro-chemical suppliers (for whom intensive agriculture provides a huge market), and grain traders (who are given public funds to penetrate world markets). Meanwhile, small farmers continue to go bankrupt in record numbers, and intensive agriculture is destroying natural habitats, and creating health hazards for consumers.[159] There is a growing awareness in the industrial world that food systems are running out of control, although considerably less awareness of the costs of this to developing countries.

A new sustainable agricultural framework is urgently needed in the developed countries. Currently, price-support systems reward farmers in relation to the size of their output and land area. These systems should be restructured to encourage less intensive production and lower levels of output, and more ecologically sustainable forms of production. Taxation on inputs of nitrogen would be one of the most effective ways of reducing productivity. Upper limits should be placed on the volume of production eligible for price support.[160] Using taxpayers' money to finance over-production under a system which increases environmental damage, and benefits mainly a small elite, is bad enough; expecting the same taxpayers to finance the disposal of surpluses on world markets in a manner which destroys the livelihoods of Third World producers is totally unacceptable. The international framework for food security should include:

- a provision in the WTO prohibiting the use of agricultural subsidies
- a provision allowing developing countries to protect their agricultural systems through trade measures designed to enhance rural employment, achieve sustainable environmental objectives and improve food self-sufficiency.

TNCs, foreign investment, and intellectual property rights

Increased recourse to protectionist measures against developing countries has been one of the defining features of industrial country trade policy since the early 1980s. Another has been an increased propensity to use the threat of unilateral trade sanctions to prise open Third World investment markets, and to enforce the intellectual property claims of Western TNCs. The influence of these companies on the outcome of the Uruguay Round is reflected in the agreements on investment, services, and intellectual property, where the sovereignty of Third World governments in relation to foreign investors has been severely eroded.[161]

The United States has been at the forefront in using unilateral trade threats to secure its strategic objectives. Under trade legislation adopted in 1988 — the so-called 'Super' 301 provision of the country's Trade Act — the Administration declared itself judge, jury, and executioner in deciding whether the US's trading partners were adopting 'unfair' trade policies, and what the penalty should be. Super 301, or the 'crowbar legislation' as it came to be known, was used most conspicuously in an attempt to prise open the Japanese market.[162] But while the resulting trade tensions between Tokyo and Washington grabbed the international headlines, it was developing countries which bore the brunt of the US's threatened recourse to trade sanctions. By 1990, more than half of the countries being investigated for 'unfair' trade practices were developing countries.[163]

'Unfair', in this context, referred to a wide range of practices. For example, India was charged with denying American financial corporations access to local banking and insurance markets, which were being protected in the interests of national economic development. The most frequently cited unfair practice was the alleged failure of Third World governments to protect the patents of American companies.

Super 301 was used to force countries such as Brazil, Thailand, Chile and, with more limited success, China, to amend their own intellectual property codes by bringing them into line with those of the US.[164] Charges were filed under the US trade legislation by powerful companies such as American Express, IBM, and Du Pont, and invariably upheld by the investigating authorities.

Governments and TNCs

The GATT agreement enshrines in multilateral trade law many of the policy changes which the US government and TNCs have sought through unilateral trade actions. The Agreement on Trade-Related Investment Measures (TRIMs), for example, will prohibit developing countries from requiring as a condition of market access that TNCs meet minimum requirements for using local materials in the production process. Regulations requiring TNCs to meet minimum export requirements, promote local ownership, or meet minimum capital requirements will similarly be phased out.

Discriminatory taxation against foreign investors will also be forbidden under the new GATT agreement. Restrictions on profit repatriation will be dismantled under the General Agreement on Trade in Services (GATS). Such arrangements will accelerate moves towards the liberalisation of foreign investment codes. In its 1994-1995 budget, for example, India lowered its tax rates on foreign companies as a step towards creating a uniform structure.[165] In many countries, moves towards the liberalisation of foreign investment have been even faster than towards trade liberalisation, and will now be accelerated by obligations under the WTO, enforceable through punitive trade sanctions.

TNCs and investment

There is no political justification or economic rationale for a multilateral investment regime so clearly designed to promote the interests of foreign investors and TNCs. The new rules were largely written by TNCs such as American Express and Citibank, which exercised a powerful influence over the US trade negotiating position.[166] This raises serious concerns about the distribution of power in international trade negotiations; and about the subordination of the principles of multilateralism to corporate self-interest. There are sound economic reasons for developing countries to regulate foreign investment and to subject it to conditions and export requirements which reflect national priorities and efforts to achieve greater self-reliance. Investment flows determined solely by corporate profit objectives are unlikely to achieve the most efficient outcomes for human development, and are likely to prove financially destabilising in some sectors. Moreover, to cite free-market arguments in defence of the investment rights of TNCs ignores the realities of market power, monopoly, and the absence of transparency in the behaviour of most TNCs. As the South Commission has put it:

In a world of monopolies, transfer pricing, and internationalisation of economic processes, measures to regulate foreign investment are not necessarily trade-distorting.[167]

It is true that foreign investment can play an important role in the development process, notably through employment creation, training, and the transfer of technology. Transferred technologies in the form of hardware and machinery can facilitate the production of new, higher-value-added goods, and generate exports. In Singapore, for example, the emergence of a semi-conductor industry was an outgrowth of foreign investment. However, isolated success stories do not justify the enforced liberalisation envisaged in the GATT agreement. The limitations of foreign investment were demonstrated in Malaysia, where Japanese investment boosted exports of electronic equipment; but the local content of these exports has been negligible, there have been few linkages with local firms, and no independent design and marketing capacity has been

developed. Malaysia's technological base remains small and underdeveloped. With the rate of foreign investment beginning to decline in the face of rising wages in Malaysia, and new opportunities for low-wage assembly operations emerging in China and Vietnam, it is questionable whether foreign investment has improved prospects for self-reliant development. Where investment is concentrated on low-skill industries in free-trade zones — as in the Dominican Republic — the economic linkages generated, like the financial benefits involved, are negligible. Almost half of the employment generated by TNCs is in such zones.

Although TNC production and exports generate revenue, this is often counterbalanced by profit remittances and transfer-pricing systems designed to minimise tax liability. The argument for regulating foreign investment is reinforced by the experience of some of the more dynamic developing countries. In both South Korea and Taiwan, for example, foreign investment played a marginal role in supporting economic growth.[168] Such investment as was allowed, was tightly controlled to maximise the benefits of technology transfer and local training. In both countries, governments focused on the need to develop domestic capacity through adaptation, training, and investment in technical education. What these experiences suggest is that a far greater degree of autonomy is required than envisaged under the GATT agreement, so that governments are able to adapt foreign investment to local development needs. Any equitable multilateral agreement must also address other aspects of TNC behaviour, such as transfer pricing, restrictive business practices, restrictions of the free flow of technology, and excessive profit repatriation, that impede prospects for more self-reliant development.[169]

TNCs and intellectual property rights

The strengthening of the international intellectual property rights under the GATT agreement is a similarly one-sided approach, biased towards the interests of the Northern TNCs which control over 90 per cent of the world's patents. Under the Trade-Related Intellectual Property Rights (TRIPs) agreement, developing countries will be required to enforce a patent system modelled on those of the US and the EU. The period of patent protection will extend to 15 years, which is substantially in excess of existing provisions in many developing countries.[170] Viewed from the South, the danger is that, by rewarding monopoly through enhanced royalty collection, the GATT agreement will further marginalise developing countries by raising the costs of technology transfer. None of today's industrial countries were subjected to such restrictive practices during earlier stages of their own development; and it is unlikely that they would have developed their manufacturing bases if they had been.

But the intellectual property agreement does not merely concern the interests of TNCs and governments. It is also of profound concern to local communities in developing countries. During 1992 half-a-million farmers marched in the Indian state of Karnataka to challenge the efforts of TNCs to extend, under the auspices of a GATT agreement, patents to genetic materials. Such a move, they claimed, would rob farmers of the freedom to use, reproduce, and modify their seeds and plant materials. Since farmers control over 85 per cent of seed production in developing countries, the issues at stake are part of wider concerns about food security and sustainable development.[171]

Unravelling the implications of the GATT agreement is made difficult by the arcane language in which it is couched, and by the widely divergent interpretations of what it means. However, Oxfam shares the view that the agreement could be used to deny farmers the right to use certain seed varieties. Under the new rules, WTO members will be required to provide for the protection of plant varieties either through patents, or through an effective national system of royalty collection. In either case, companies will be able to pursue claims on

patented seeds with the full weight of international trade law, and the implicit threat of sanctions against governments, behind them. As a result, farmers could be penalised for saving seeds for planting in future seasons, or for exchange with other farmers.[172]

Such a regime presents a considerable threat to the conservation of biodiversity.[173] One hundred years ago, Indian farmers grew 30,000 varieties of rice. In 15 years' time they will be growing no more than 15, exposing the country to an increasing risk of crop failure. The GATT agreement will accelerate this loss of varieties in all countries by placing a premium on uniformity, with potentially irreversible adverse effects on local food systems. This is inconsistent with the aims of the Biodiversity Convention, which was signed by 50 states at the Earth Summit. Driven by a growing sense of concern over the loss of the world's most vital resources, governments at the Summit pledged to explore fair and equitable ways of sharing the benefits from genetic resources, and of conserving biodiversity.

The Biodiversity Convention has now been overtaken by the GATT agreement, which offers a one-sided approach to intellectual property protection. Genetic resources from the South are being widely used in the North to improve seeds and plants, generating vast revenues in the process. However, the seeds patented after modification in Northern laboratories by TNCs have, in many cases, been developed and modified over centuries by communities in developing countries. Yet the local knowledge, innovation, and ingenuity involved in this process is not regarded, under the GATT agreement, as intellectual property.

The Uruguay Round agreement has considerably expanded the rights of TNCs. These rights now extend beyond the bounds of legitimate corporate concern, into areas where they threaten public interest, as starkly illustrated by the TRIPs agreement. Once again, the GATT agreement in this area was effectively written by powerful corporations, such as Du Pont and IBM, which formed an Intellectual Property

Coalition to influence the outcome of the Uruguay Round.[174] The resulting system prioritises Northern interests, enlarging and strengthening, in the name of 'free trade', the monopolistic rights of sellers of technology. This expansion of rules governing intellectual property rights will have significant adverse effects for developing countries. In particular, it will reduce their capacity to afford, absorb, and adapt new technologies, widening the distance between themselves and the knowledge-intensive production systems of the industrialised world.

As an urgent first measure of reform, it is vital that the GATT agreement is made to complement, rather than supersede, the Biodiversity Convention. The WTO's Committee on Trade and Environment should establish a review procedure for examining the implications of the TRIPs agreement in consultation with the relevant UN bodies, NGOs, and local communities, as well as industry. At the same time, new mechanisms of development assistance are needed to facilitate the transfer of technologies to developing countries, allied to measures which curb the restrictive practices of TNCs in relation to technology transfer. More generally, the globalisation of investment and business requires new structures of public accountability, scrutiny, and control to ensure that the legitimate concerns of consumers, producers, and governments are not overridden by remote multilateral bodies, such as the WTO, which predominantly represent the commercial interests of TNCs.

The UN Restrictive Practices Code is a step in the right direction, but is too weak. Under the original Bretton Woods proposal for an International Trade Organisation, there was to be an anti-trust body with surveillance powers. Such a body now needs to be established as an independent part of the WTO, with the authority to investigate transfer pricing and other malpractice. Co-operation is also urgently required on the issue of taxing multinationals. Faced with the problem of foreign corporations under-reporting profits, the state of California

in the US has developed a 'unitary tax' structure. This establishes its right to tax TNCs by calculating the value of local operations as a proportion of their global activities. As a powerful economic entity in its own right, this is a viable option for California; but it would hardly be feasible for, say, Honduras, to follow such an option. This suggests the need for enhanced regional co-operation and international mechanisms for assessing tax liability.[175]

Public interest would also be strengthened through multilateral agreements and codes of conduct. Efforts to develop a binding code of conduct for TNCs began in the early 1970s, but were effectively abandoned in 1994 in the face of opposition from Northern governments. Such codes can play an important role in supporting the efforts of TNCs attempting to develop socially responsible forms of investment. On the other hand, voluntary arrangements are inadequate where public health and safety is concerned. Several European and US TNCs openly violate codes of conduct agreed with UNICEF and the World Health Organisation for restricting the promotion of infant formula. Their activities are a contributory cause of the deaths of over one million babies annually, who would have lived had they been breast-fed. Such practices ought to be subject to judicial proceedings in the home countries of the TNCs involved. In the case of production processes involving hazardous toxic substances, TNCs should be subject to laws as least as stringent as those applying in their home countries, and be subject to prosecution at home when they violate such laws elsewhere in the world.

An agenda for reform of world trade

Under the Uruguay Round, the power of policing and implementing the international trading system will pass to the World Trade Organisation. This will enjoy a far wider remit than the GATT, with its authority extending into areas such as financial services, investment, intellectual property, and agriculture, previously either beyond trade rules, or weakly covered by them.

Oxfam is in favour of a strong, supranational body to oversee world trade. But it shares with its partners a serious concern both about the rules underpinning the WTO, its accountability, and its relationship to other international bodies and treaties.

Under the post-Uruguay Round regime, the WTO will become a formal part of the Bretton Woods structure, interacting with the World Bank and the IMF, in a triumvirate of institutions which will effectively govern world trade and finance. However, the WTO has a narrowly-defined free-market remit designed to expand trade without reference to wider social, economic, and environmental implications.

One way of redressing this would be to make the WTO answerable to the United Nations, through regular reports to the Secretary-General, the General Assembly, and the Economic and Social Council. While this would not, in itself, imply a fundamental shift in power and authority, it would at least ensure that international trade issues were debated in a context where the views of small states carried more weight. Moreover, the moral authority of the UN and its influence on international opinion would inevitably have a bearing on the policy orientation of the WTO.

Closer integration into the UN system is important for the WTO, not least to address the widespread concern among people and governments in the South that the WTO will become, like the GATT, an instrument through which the industrial countries impose their own strategic trade agendas. While formally democratic, the WTO will reflect the imbalances in trading power between the North and the South, with the world's poorest countries excluded to the margins of decision-making. This is not the way to bring about co-operative management of global economic interdependence.

It is equally important that the WTO's remit does not lead to the marginalisation of social and environmental concerns. The WTO should be required to co-operate closely with UN agencies, including the Commission for Sustainable Development (CSD), the International Labour Organisation, the UN Development Programme, and the UN Conference on Trade and Development. Observer status should also be granted to NGOs and citizens' organisations, whose important role was acknowledged in Agenda 21.

It is to the credit of trade ministers that they are now attempting to examine trade principles which go beyond celebrating the virtues of market deregulation, notably with regard to the environment and labour rights. New frameworks for trade policy are urgently needed in both areas. However, these too must be developed in a broader institutional context. Responsibility for developing and implementing a social rights agenda should reside with the ILO and its specialised committees, which have an established track record in monitoring compliance with standards. Meanwhile, the existing WTO Working Party on Trade and the Environment should be administered under the CSD, and expanded to include environment ministers and environmental experts.

One of the keys to greater accountability in international trade is improved access to information. It is wrong that WTO trade disputes panels should continue in the GATT tradition of meeting in secret and arriving at judgements made available to the public only after a long delay, or not all. In some cases, these unselected and unaccountable panels will have the power to demand changes in policies and standards set by democratically elected legislatures, without reference to public opinion. All meetings of the WTO, including those of its trade disputes panels, should be in public and governments should be required to report regularly to national parliaments on their positions.

Improved structures of accountability are critical to the credibility and the future of multilateralism. But accountability alone will not ensure that trade becomes fairer and more sustainable. As we have argued in this chapter, wider action is needed to address the interlocking problems of low commodity prices, Northern protectionism, and the dumping of agricultural exports. The fact that such issues were not dealt with in the Uruguay Round demonstrated the extent of the domination of the GATT by the industrialised countries. So did their success in forcing on to the GATT agenda, against the almost universal opposition of developing countries, the new issues of trade in investment, financial services, and intellectual property. The agreements in all of these areas could severely hinder the efforts of developing countries to foster more self-reliant and sustainable development.

Finally, mechanisms must be found to regulate the growing power of TNCs. The Uruguay Round agreement will give an important impetus to the foreign investment rights of TNCs. What is needed is an international commitment to restoring the rights of workers to minimum standards of welfare. These rights, based upon existing UN Conventions, should be enshrined in the WTO and implemented alongside wider measures to enforce greater transparency and accountability on the part of TNCs.

Change at an international level is vital; and public pressure, exercised through consumer choice, can also act as a force for change. Consumers can make a difference by buying fairly-traded goods and demonstrating concern to major retailers over the sourcing of products, including the conditions under which they are produced and the prices paid to producers. In this way, consumers in the North can help to bring about tangible improvements to the livelihoods and rights of poor producers. Below, we describe the work of Oxfam and others to bring the issue of fair trade before a Northern audience.

Oxfam's work for fair trade

Oxfam is working for change in international trade at a number of levels. Through its 'Bridge' programme, Oxfam provides a market for Third World producers, paying fair prices and purchasing through organisations which ensure that the bulk of the price reaches the producers. The name 'Bridge' aptly summarises the aim of linking producers in the developing world to their customers in the North on more equitable terms. Oxfam supports the efforts of local producers in various countries to gain more control over their production, for example by improving their access to credit and information.

Today, Bridge goods are sold in over 600 Oxfam shops in Britain and Ireland, and purchased by almost one million people annually. Over 80 per cent of these goods are handicrafts, produced mostly by women. In 1993/1994, over £3m was paid out to 293 producer groups, representing a significant transfer of resources to the poor and an investment in their livelihoods.

By providing a market, Bridge helps to ensure that money gets into the hands of women, whose labour is often unpaid. Apart from the direct economic benefits, this helps to improve the status and self-esteem of the women involved, and provides a means of ensuring that children are fed and clothed. Bridge expects producer groups to adhere to certain criteria: including sensitivity to gender issues, avoidance of bonded labour, support for people with disability, and a responsible approach to child labour. In return, producers receive a fair price and support with marketing, design, and product development.

Aj Quen

Aj Quen, or 'weaving together', is Bridge's main partner in Guatemala. It was established in 1989 by a group of weavers, tailors, carpenters, basketmakers, potters, and other handicraft producers in an effort to break out of poverty and establish a sustainable foundation for livelihoods. Eighty per cent of the producers with which Aj Quen works are women, many of them widows whose husbands have been killed in conflict and violent repression.

In 1993/1994, Bridge purchased £30,000 worth of orders from Aj Quen. This has brought social and economic benefits, even though the average income per producer remains low because the tailoring skills of many of the groups need to be developed.

The purchase of good quality raw materials will help to change this. But the project cannot be measured solely by its economic returns. Each year hundreds of women make long and difficult journeys by foot and bus to take part in annual meetings, giving them a sense of control over the co-operative and their own lives. At the same time, Aj Quen has invested in providing literacy centres, expanding the opportunities for employment outside the home.

Trade in commodities

Around 15 per cent of Bridge's sales come from food products such as coffee, tea, honey, and spices. These are all competitive markets, where Bridge is up against the big-name brands available on supermarket shelves, as well as low-priced private labels. In order to compete, Bridge promotes the fair-trade value of its products to consumers. There is increasing acceptance in the market that producers have a right to a reasonable standard of living, that realistic prices ensure sustainability of production, and that fair trade can be more effective than aid in supporting the development of communities.

As in other countries, the coffee market in Nicaragua is dominated by giant transnational companies. Working through local buyers, known as *amarradores*, these companies attempt to buy their coffee as soon as possible after the November-December harvest, when prices are at their lowest. Smallholder producers have little choice but to sell at that time because they lack storage capacity and have immediate cash needs, for school fees, clothes, and to purchase next year's seeds. Many producers sign advance contracts with the *amarradores* before the harvest.

PRODECOOP has intervened to challenge the powerful bargaining position of the *amarradores*, using a revolving credit fund to provide cash advances which reduce the need for forced sales in the immediate post-harvest period. In 1993, PRODECOOP was paying prices some three times higher than those offered by the *amarradores*. It was able to do so partly because it provides a higher proportion of the final price to the producers, and partly because it has the storage capacity to keep the coffee until prices increase later in the marketing year.

Such market interventions, which figure increasingly prominently in Oxfam's work, bring immediate and obvious benefits to producers. In El Salvador, Oxfam supports the Agrarian Reform Growers' Association, an umbrella organisation comprising 17 smallholder co-operatives. Like PRODECOOP in Nicaragua, the association provides credit and information to smallholder farmers. But it also provides processing facilities, which adds value to the coffee beans before export. This increases the share of trade revenue going to local households and the local economy, and reduces the transfer to large companies in the North.

Cafédirect

Bridge has joined forces with three other alternative trade organisations to market a new brand of coffee, Cafédirect. As its name suggests, the coffee is purchased direct from small farmers, who receive a price linked to the minimum floor price previously defended by the International Coffee Organisation. When Cafédirect was launched during the trough in world coffee prices, producers were paid $1.20 per lb. Had they been selling in the international market, they would have been paid around 65 cents per lb.

Cafédirect costs more than some of its competitors, but it has proved popular with consumers; so popular that it is now stocked in all the main supermarket chains in the UK. Its success underlines the willingness of many consumers to pay slightly more when the benefits go to producers. It also underlines the extent to which consumer power can act as a positive force for change in international trade.

Honey bees

The forests of Zambia's remote North-western Province provide a source of livelihood for an estimated 10,000 beekeepers, whose ancestors have been producing and trading honey since the twelfth century. But in recent decades, they have suffered from a combination of neglect and misplaced policies by companies more concerned with making short-term profits than supporting sustainable livelihoods.

In the early 1990s, Oxfam responded to an initiative by the region's Beekeeping Association to set up a small company, the Uchi Trust, to purchase shares and represent their interests in a company called North-western Bee Products (NWBP), which controls the production and marketing of honey. This has had tangible effects on the prices they receive. It has also enabled them to explore wider marketing opportunities at home and abroad.

For example, NWBP is now promoting sustainable forest management schemes, and has been given an organic certificate for the honey it purchases. This has enabled the company to penetrate Northern markets more effectively by meeting consumer demands for products produced without artificial chemicals. More recently, Oxfam has supported NWBP efforts to encourage diversification into crops such as groundnuts, sesame, and castor. Because honey harvests can vary enormously from year to year, depending on the rains, production of these crops will increase security.

The aim is to maximise the value retained in the forest economy by processing the seeds into oil, which will be marketed through local traders. NWBP is also exploring the possibility of the local community producing timber goods for sale to Oxfam's Trading Division, which has been buying substantial quantities of honey.

Organic production

Honey is one of several organic products marketed by Oxfam. 1994 saw the launch of Maya Gold, an organic brand of chocolate made from cocoa grown in Belize, which is already penetrating consumer markets with some success. Oxfam also sells organic coffee from Peru.

Oxfam Trading is concerned to promote organic brands for several reasons. First, consumer preference is creating a growing market for crops produced without the application of chemicals and pesticides. Second, the marketing of organic produce can provide support to traditional farming systems, where producers are often unable to afford the chemical inputs needed to exploit high-yielding hybrid seeds. Finally, the promotion of organic methods of production offers one route to the attainment of more sustainable and self-reliant agricultural systems.

This is not to suggest that organic production is an easy option. For example, the withdrawal of chemical applications means that weeding and pest control makes increased demands on labour time; and labour is a commodity in short supply during key periods of the agricultural season in most developing countries. However, producers in many of the co-operatives with which Oxfam works are expressing a growing interest in this option and are receiving support for their efforts to meet organic standards.

Removing obstacles to fair trade

It is now widely accepted that fair trade requires intervention to assist producers, to reform local and international marketing systems, and to expand consumer markets. Along with other fair-trade organisations and development agencies, Oxfam is improving its project interventions in support of producers, and investing in more effective marketing. The overall aim is to shorten the chain between producers and consumers, and to maximise the returns to the former.[176]

However, the trade policies discussed in this chapter constitute an obstacle to the creation of a fairer trading system. For example, because the organic coffee imported by Oxfam is processed in Mexico, it is subject to a far higher tariff than coffee beans. Such a tariff discourages local processing and protects the markets of powerful domestic food conglomerates.

People in the North can act as a powerful force for change both by campaigning for fairer trade policies and by exercising their power as consumers. After nearly 30 years of direct involvement in alternative or producer-friendly trading, Oxfam saw the need to help to promote fair trade beyond its own shops and catalogue, in the mainstream consumer market-place. The device specially developed for the purpose in the UK is the Fairtrade Mark. Together with other development agencies, Oxfam is a founder member of the Fairtrade Foundation which administers the Mark. The Foundation licenses the Mark to endorse commercial products which need to satisfy strict criteria on terms of trade and conditions of employment in developing countries. In 1994, its first year, the Mark was licensed to brands of tea, coffee, and chocolate, which are all on sale in major supermarkets.

The fairtrade Mark and its counterparts (Max Havelaar and Transfair in other European countries, and a similar scheme being prepared in Canada) open a new avenue of action and bring a new power to bear in favour of greater justice in trade. They provide a guarantee that the product in question gives 'a better deal' to the workers or small producers, and therefore an opportunity for consumers to exercise positive choice. In this way, shoppers at the check-out point in Northern supermarkets can make common cause with peasant farmers' organisations and producer groups in the South in bringing about fairer trade.

5 Ecological footprints

If it took England the exploitation of half the globe to be what it is today, how many globes will it take India?   GANDHI

Introduction

Hatiya Island, which lies at the mouth of the Meghna River, in the Bay of Bengal, is a dangerous place to live. Not much more than a large sand bar, the island is home to 300,000 people, the majority of them landless. The poor communities who cultivate its fertile soil face many problems. All of the island's inhabitants live with the threat of cyclones and tidal surges, but it is the poorest families who are most vulnerable. In the devastating cyclone of April 1991, more than 90 per cent of the island's inhabitants lost their homes. Their crops and fields were submerged under several feet of salt water. Over night, years of hard work were destroyed. Dwip Unnayan Sangstha (DUS), one of Oxfam's project partners in Bangladesh, was one of the few organisations still able to help stricken people, distributing food and other essential supplies. It continues to support the islanders through longer-term development work, focusing particularly on a campaign for land rights. With help from DUS, people displaced by river erosion from the north of the island have successfully claimed land newly created by silt deposits in the south, and they have been encouraged to protect it from tidal surges by building embankments and planting trees.

The people of Hatiya are well aware of the threats posed to their livelihoods by unequal social relations and an unpredictable environment. But there is another threat of which most are unaware: the threat of global warming. There is substantial agreement among scientists around the world that human activities are warming the surface of the earth. The burning of fossil fuels and, to a lesser extent, the clearing and burning of forests, together with the emission of methane gas, some of which is produced by animals, accelerate the build-up of greenhouse gases. These reflect infra-red radiation that would otherwise pass out of the earth's atmosphere, thus causing global warming. The Intergovernmental Panel on Climate Change (IPCC), a body of more than 300 experts convened by the United Nations, currently predicts that the expected rise in concentrations of greenhouse gases will result in an increase in average global temperature of between 1°C and 2°C by 2030, and nearly 3°C by the year 2100. That may not sound like much, but the scale and speed of the changes are greater than anything witnessed in the last 10,000 years. Since the coldest point of the last Ice Age, world mean temperature has increased by only some 4-5°C. The IPCC predicts that temperature increases will cause sea levels to rise globally by 18cm by the year 2030, rising to an average of 65cm by the end of the next century.[1] Subsequent projections have revised the figure downwards a little, but low-lying regions of the world could still anticipate devastating effects.

For Bangladesh, and other countries unable to afford costly flood-defence systems, global warming is likely to bring an increase in the scale and frequency of the coastal flooding associated with cyclones and storm surges. For present and future generations of people living on Hatiya, this spells potential disaster. Some researchers consider that global warming may already be a factor in extreme weather patterns of the kind which brought the 1991 cyclone to Bangladesh.[2]

The dangers facing communities on Hatiya Island and elsewhere in the Bay of Bengal illustrate the way in which global environmental problems hold particular threats for the poor. In general, poor countries, and poorer groups within countries, have less capacity to adjust to the pressures resulting from environmental degradation. Low-income countries are especially vulnerable since their economies are more dependent on agriculture and natural resources that are sensitive to climate changes. Global warming will lead to a greater frequency of extreme climatic events, and result in much more variable growing conditions. In almost all regions of the world, in major food-exporting regions and in areas that are not self-sufficient in food, it is likely that it will be changes in crop-water patterns that will have the most significant effect on agriculture. Although there will clearly be some winners from this process, when cereal production becomes possible in places it was not before, it seems likely that they will be outnumbered by the losers. According to the IPCC, for example, warmer, dryer conditions could cause losses in agricultural production of up to one-third by about 2030 in the Great Plains of the US and the Canadian Prairies, as the boundaries for cultivating cereals edges northwards by 300 kilometres for every degree centigrade increase in average temperature. This constitutes a threat both to the livelihoods of farming communities in North America, and to the food security of the world's poorest countries in Africa and elsewhere, many of which have become critically dependent upon food imports.

The most serious threat is to vulnerable communities in arid and semi-arid regions, such as the Sahel and the Horn of Africa. If rainfall changes do not compensate for warming, the impact on vulnerable groups in semi-arid areas could be huge: in Kenya, for example, it is estimated that there would be reductions of up to 30 per cent in the area suitable for maize cultivation, which would have devastating effects.[3] Warming would also have a dramatic impact on the availability of pasture for grazing, as reduced moisture leads to a loss of tree cover and vegetation. For many of the pastoral farmers and smallholder producers with whom Oxfam works, therefore, global warming is, quite literally, a matter of life and death. Unlike the industrialised world, most developing countries simply lack the investment resources which would enable them to diversify or adjust to global warming; and they have fewer options in terms of migration. Poorer people in these countries will pay the highest price, since it is they who work on the most vulnerable land or in the most exposed low-lying regions; and it is they who have the fewest resources with which to adapt.

There is now a gathering awareness of the threat posed by global warming to the livelihoods of millions of people in the developing world. The recent UN Global Conference on the Sustainable Development of Small Island Developing States (SIDS) made action to combat the risk of global warming the first recommendation in its Programme of Action. Any rise in sea levels, it advised, would have significant and profound effects. 'The very survival of certain low-lying countries would be threatened.'[4]

Calculating the effects of global warming

Case studies carried out for a Commonwealth Group of Experts show how rising sea-levels could have far-reaching social and economic effects on low-lying coastal areas. Major deltas could be acutely affected since they are, for the most part, very low-lying, unprotected from the sea, densely populated, and important centres of agricultural production. The two deltas with the greatest potential for disaster are the Nile and the Ganges. A sea-level rise of 50cm would inundate an area of the Nile delta currently holding 16 per cent of Egypt's population and an even higher percentage of productive farmland. The threats to Bangladesh are more serious still. Climate change would almost certainly increase the frequency of cyclonic storm surges, one of which killed over 250,000 people in 1970; a one-metre rise in sea level could flood more than 15 per cent of the country's land area, directly affecting over 10 million people.[5]

Efforts have been made to predict more precisely the effects of climate change on Bangladesh, but it is a task fraught with complexities.[6] Delta areas are inherently unstable: each year large areas of land are formed by new alluvial deposition and other areas are eroded by shifting channels. These processes are themselves affected by increased rates of deposition as a result of ecological changes in the upper reaches of the rivers, by increased salination, and a major intensification in agriculture. There is, then, an extremely complex and dynamic set of physical and human changes in the delta, making it difficult to predict with certainty the likely effects of a sea-level rise. What can be predicted is that the potential for disaster is considerable.

The Commonwealth Secretariat has attempted to estimate the impact of an increase in the mean sea level of 1 metre (90cm on static sea level and 10cm subsidence). Its findings include:

- In the coastal areas there would be inundation of 2000km², 16 per cent of Bangladesh's total area and 14 per cent of the cropped area. The socio-economic consequences would involve:
  - displacement of 10 per cent of population
  - loss of land currently producing two million tonnes a year of rice, 400,000 tonnes of vegetables, 200,000 tonnes of sugar, 100,000 tonnes of pulses, and accommodating 3.7 million cattle, sheep, and goats
  - loss of 1.9 million homes, 1,470km of railways, 10,300 bridges, 700km of metalled

road and 19,800km of unmetalled roads
  - output loss estimated equivalent to 13 per cent GDP and loss of assets of 450bn taka ($11bn).
- The Sunderban mangrove forests, in southwestern Bangladesh, stretching over 400,000 hectares, would be destroyed by increasing salinity, then inundation.
- Salinity problems, already serious, could be aggravated with implications for drinking water (especially in Khulna and Chittagong), agricultural yields (especially for vegetables), and industrial facilities (e.g. power stations).
- Coastal structures like the existing 58 polder embankments, which protect areas of land with internally-controlled water management, would need heightening and strengthening, as would drainage systems. The estimated cost is 18bn taka ($4.5bn)
- The above effects do not include the potentially catastrophic consequences of:
  - more extreme and/or more frequent storm surges resulting from tropical storms like those in 1970 that killed over 250,000 people, and in 1991 left over 138,000 dead
  - the impact of different rainfall patterns on river flows and, thus, vulnerability to river flooding, like that in September 1988, which inundated 85 per cent of the land area and affected 45 million people.

Further studies have been published which challenge scenarios such as this, on the grounds that they fail to address both the considerable natural resilience of the Bangladesh coastal zone, and human adaptability to environmental change. While this may be the case, the issue is still of such uncertainty as to warrant using the 'precautionary principle', and examining what may be worst-case scenarios.

Responsibility for global warming

People living in low-lying countries have developed over many centuries ingenious methods for dealing with an unstable environment. But they are now faced with a threat which may be beyond their control. That threat is rooted not in the vagaries of climate, but in the consumption patterns of people in the industrialised world, which are overwhelmingly responsible for emissions of CO_2, the greenhouse gas mainly responsible for global warming.

In essence, the patterns of production and consumption in the industrialised world are threatening the survival of vulnerable communities in developing countries; communities like those on Hatiya Island. Ultimately, of course, they also threaten the welfare of future generations in the industrialised world. There is now a growing awareness, heightened by the 1992 Earth Summit, that our planet's ecosystem is being stretched to breaking point. For many in the South, environmental degradation is already posing a profound threat to security and livelihoods. For people in the North, the threat might seem more remote. However, the reality is that global security is at risk. Having lived for much of the post-war period with the threat of a nuclear holocaust hanging over its head, the international community will enter the next century facing the prospect of an ecological crisis which constitutes a less visible but no less profound threat to survival.

When the UN was founded, it established a system of global citizenship rights to protect present and future generations from the scourges of poverty and war. However, this has not been translated into a practical framework in which governments can be held responsible for the welfare of future generations. The problem of environmental deterioration demands that this be remedied.. Equal rights for future generations, or 'intergenerational equity', ought to be a guiding principle for the twenty-first century. That principle is based on two linked propositions: that no generation has the right to destroy the ecosystem or degrade the ecological resource-base of the planet; and each generation has the right to inherit a planet capable of sustaining health and wellbeing, and with a diversity in its natural and cultural resource base at least equivalent to that inherited by its predecessor.[7] The challenge for citizens and governments now is to convert a set of moral principles into appropriate economic policies and institutions that will safeguard the global environment, and with it, the rights of future generations.

Unequal shares

If it is the rich — most people living in the North, and many Southern elites — who bear prime responsibility for global environmental degradation, it is the poor who are most immediately affected by it, and who are currently paying the greater price for adjusting to the imperatives of sustainable development. This discrepancy is not reflected in the perception of most people and governments in the North, who continue to regard high population growth in developing countries as the major threat to the environment.

From a Southern perspective, however, to attribute responsibility for the global ecological crisis to the developing world is to turn reality on its head and blame the victim for the crime. At issue is the question of unequal economic power, which enables the North to appropriate more than its fair share of global 'sinks', whilst urging environmental protection measures on the South. As one of India's leading environmentalists, Anil Agarwal, has put it:

A person who is living in India like me may feel very strongly about the fact that if the Americans keep on building more power stations based on coal, this leads to global warming, which leads to a sea-level rise, and then drowns Bombay and Bangladesh. Do I have the right to say something about it or not? What are the levers of power that I have? None at all ... I allow the Americans to go to the World Bank and say there will be a green conditionality on Narmada [dam project] but I have no right, no forum, and no power whatsoever to say that there will be environmental discipline on energy consumption patterns in the United States of America. What do I do about that? It has tremendous repercussions for me, extraordinary repercussions for my economy. If global warming takes place and the climate changes, how am I going to adjust to that? ...

If the demand is for global governance in a sense of fair rights to all of us, then let us talk about a right to a clean environment for every citizen in the world, to which every government will have to submit itself.[8]

Environmental impact of Northern consumption

Poor people are denied the fair rights to the environment, to which Agarwal refers, not only by their poverty, but by the unsustainable patterns of production and consumption of the rich. With one-fifth of the world's population, the OECD countries consume almost half the world's fossil fuels, most of its metals, and a large share of timbers. Together they account for over one-third of the warming impact on the atmosphere from emissions of greenhouse gases. An analysis of commercial energy consumption, a useful measure of environmental impact, demonstrates that four-fifths of the world's commercial energy is used by a quarter of its population, living in 42 countries. Meanwhile, one fifth of the world's energy is used by three-quarters of its population, living in 128 countries. On average, each person in a 'high consumption' country uses 18 times more energy than a person in a 'low consumption' country. According to one estimate, the impact of an average US citizen on the environment is 35 times that of the average Brazilian, and 250 times that of the average African. He or she also consumes 227 times as much gasoline and 115 times as much paper as the average Indian.[9]

The same picture is repeated in relation to global warming. During the 1980s, the industrialised countries produced over half of the observed rise of greenhouse gas content in the atmosphere. While developing countries also emit CO_2 in significant and rapidly increasing quantities, they still emit far less per head of population than industrialised countries. Per capita emissions in the US are almost 9 times those of China and almost 18 times those of India, for example. The UK, with just 1 per cent of the population accounts for 2.37 per cent of emissions.

The North's consumption patterns have imposed a high price on developing countries. Some environmentalists in the developing world have drawn an analogy between the exploitation of environmental resources today and the economic exploitation of the colonial period. 'Despite the world process of decolonisation,' writes one agency, 'there is today many times more land being used in the developing world to meet the food and other biomass needs of the Western countries than in the 1940s before the process of decolonisation began.[10]

Consider, for example, the agricultural systems of the industrialised world, which are partly maintained by production in developing countries. Demand for high protein feedstuffs to support livestock production in the Netherlands is met by production in developing countries on a land area eight times larger than that cultivated in the Netherlands itself. The UK requires two acres abroad for every one under cultivation at home.[11] In some cases, vulnerable communities in developing countries have faced devastation as their land is used to provide food for the people and animals of Northern countries. It can, of course, be argued that trade revenues are vital to the South and can be used to import food and essential manufactures. However, not only is loss of food self-reliance a serious problem for poor countries, but it is the poorest who see the least benefits and pay the cost of environmental degradation in lost livelihoods. An example is the switch to soya bean production in Brazil.

The price of beef
The subsidised expansion of the EU's dairy and livestock industry has created a huge demand for high protein animal feedstuffs. That demand has been met in part through the expansion of large-scale, mechanised soya production in Brazil.

Between the mid-1960s and 1990, the area under soya cultivation in Brazil increased from 500,000 acres to 26 million acres. Smallholder producers of beans and staple foods in the southern part of the country have been dis-

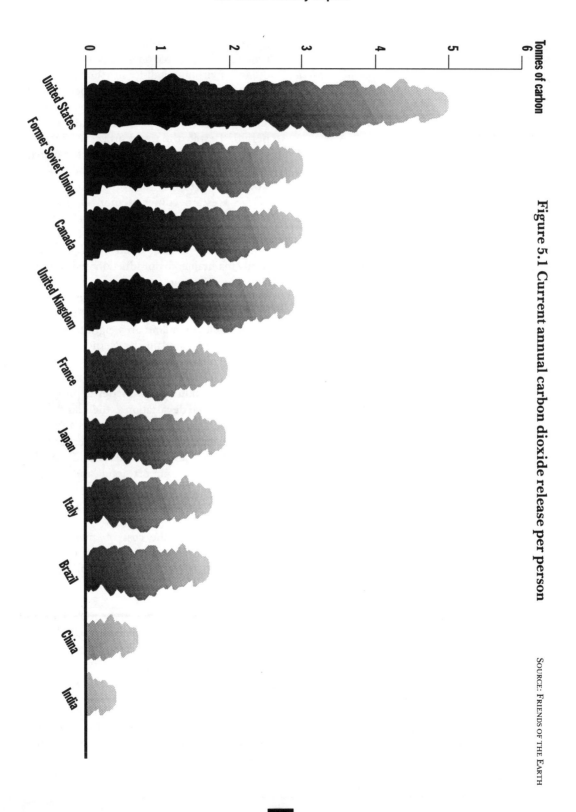

Figure 5.1 Current annual carbon dioxide release per person

Tonnes of carbon

United States
Former Soviet Union
Canada
United Kingdom
France
Japan
Italy
Brazil
China
India

Source: Friends of the Earth

placed to make way for giant soya estates, so that per capita production of beans is less than half of its 1980 level. Many of those displaced have been resettled in the north-east of Brazil, where they have become unwitting instruments of rain-forest destruction. Meanwhile the ecosystem of the Cerrados Plateau, the country's main soya producing area, has been devastated through soil loss and the loss of valuable species. This trading arrangement has brought Brazil major foreign exchange gains, with soya now estab-lished as the country's major agricultural ex-port. However, it is a trading arrangement which has proved considerably more efficient at feeding European cattle than maintaining the livelihoods of poor Brazilians.

Soya production in Brazil provides one example of how consumption patterns in the North can profoundly effect the environment in developing countries. Each kilogram of beef produced in Europe requires five kilograms of high-protein feedstuffs. Supplying those feed-stuffs in the mid-1980s diverted over nine million hectares of land in developing countries. Most of that land was in countries with large populations of rural landless, and where mechanised cultivation of soya is ecologically unsustainable. Despite this, the World Bank has continued to support the expansion of soya cultivation in countries such as Bolivia.

Exports and environmental damage

Oxfam has first-hand experience of working with communities in the South whose environments have been destroyed in the process of producing primary commodities for export to the North: forests have been cleared, fishing grounds depleted, and soils eroded. Even degradation caused by subsistence farming can often be traced back to the displacement of traditional communities onto more fragile, marginal land by landowners and governments oriented towards the production of crops for export. Meanwhile manufactured goods exported by developing countries are kept cheap, in part, by lower, or less stringent enforcement of, labour and environmental standards. The result

is that workers in the South, and particularly women, together with neighbouring communities and the local environment, pay the cost of current consumption patterns in the North in poverty, ill health, and environmental damage. Production for commercial exports can accelerate the cycle of environmental decline, as illustrated by the production of shrimps in Bangladesh for the European market.

Shrimp farming is one of a number of non-traditional cash crops that Southern countries developed during the 1980s and early 1990s. Often of high value, such crops are seen as a way to boost export earnings, and reduce dependence on traditional cash crops, which are subject to wide fluctuations in world prices. International agencies and national governments have pushed to increase these non-traditional exports, often under World Bank-IMF structural adjustment programmes. However, while such exports can increase foreign revenue, this can be at considerable social and environmental costs.

The impact of shrimp farming

Shrimp farming has undergone a phenomenal growth in Asia: during the 1980s production increased seven-fold, from 57,000 tonnes to 441,000 tonnes. Shrimps are big business for Bangladesh, ranking as the country's third largest export earner after garments and jute manufactures.[12]

In many areas of the country, producers have responded to the increased demand for shrimps by converting more land into ponds. This has lead to the transformation of vast tracts of agricultural land into shrimp ponds. The effect on local communities has been dramatic. In some cases, peasant farmers have found their rice crops ruined and their fresh-water supply contaminated by salt water leaking into their fields from neighbouring shrimp farms. In the words of one Bangladeshi farmer:

I dropped to my knees and broke down in tears. I could not believe they could do this to me. I cried to Allah, seeking punishment for the men who had flooded my rice field and made me a beggar overnight.[13]

Even the more amicable land-share arrangements, whereby land is leased to a shrimp farmer for part of the year for the shrimp production cycle, before being returned to the owner for the rest of the year, have had serious impacts. Rice farmers who lease their land claim that the increase in salinity required for shrimp cultivation has reduced rice yields by two-thirds. They also say it will take many years to restore the land's fertility.[14]

The acquisition of land is often achieved by violent means. One frequently deployed method is the deliberate flooding of land belonging to others. This increases soil salinity and reduces its fertility, undermining the livelihoods of smallholder producers. Owners are then left with little choice but to rent their land out at rock-bottom prices.

Diversification is an important policy objective for many developing countries. However, the Bangladeshi shrimp industry highlights some of the problems that arise when economic policies are developed without regard for their social and environmental objectives. In this case there is conflict over the use of land for food production, as opposed to export production. The industry has also reduced local employment opportunities (shrimp farming is capital-intensive, rather than labour-intensive), and is having an adverse impact on the environment. Its benefits are unevenly distributed, so that while considerable gains are made by local entrepreneurs, many other people are poorer as a result. The export of a luxury protein has to be questioned from a country that is unable to feed its own population and is massively dependent on imports of food aid.

Measuring environmental impact

There are different ways of looking at the same facts when measuring environmental impact. For example, the World Resources Institute (WRI) in 1990 compiled a national league-table for greenhouse-gas emissions. Two developing countries, Brazil and China, were included in the top six, because of their high aggregate consumption; such exercises tend to confirm the popular view of developing countries as the perpetrators of the global environmental crisis. But they misrepresent the nature of the problem by focusing attention on overall, rather than per capita, consumption. China has over one-fifth of the world's population, so it is not unreasonable to assume that it will figure as a major consumer of natural resources. On a per capita basis, however, as we have seen, CO_2 emissions in the US are many times higher than those in China and India. With some justification, Anil Agarwal and Sunita Narain, of the Centre for Science and Environment (CSE) in New Delhi, branded the WRI report 'an excellent example of environmental colonialism'.

India and China today account for more than one-third of the world's population. The question to be asked is whether we are consuming one-third of the world's resources or contributing one-third of the muck and dirt in the atmosphere or the oceans. If not then surely these countries should be lauded for keeping the world in balance because of their parsimonious consumption despite the Western rape and pillage of the world's resources.[15]

There are various ways in which the impact of production and consumption patterns of different populations on the environment can be measured. The Centre for Science and Environment (CSE) in India has developed a methodology which takes into account the fact that there are natural sinks or chemical processes which absorb or destroy the greenhouse gases. Approximately half the present CO_2 emissions are absorbed by oceans and land vegetation. Seen from the wider perspective which the CSE approach offers, damage to the biosphere is caused not just by the overall levels of pollution generated, but by the inability of sinks and natural processes to absorb it.

In the CSE's calculations to measure contributions to global warming, sinks are allocated on a per capita basis to each country. The net contribution of each country to the threat of global warming is then measured as the amount by which its total greenhouse gas emissions exceed its allocation of sinks. With this approach, the US shows up as an even greater contributor to the greenhouse gas increase, while China, India, Indonesia, and Mexico disappear from the top 15. Moreover, even the CSE's method understates the responsibility of the industrialised world for global environmental problems, since it looks solely at present consumption patterns. Viewed over a longer time-scale, the industrial production patterns of the North have contributed to the build-up of greenhouse gases to a far greater extent than those of the South.[16]

Ecological footprints

We all leave our mark on the ecological system of our planet, but some of us, as the figures above suggest, leave a far deeper impression than others. This has led environmentalists and development agencies to look at the environmental crisis not in terms of population numbers alone, but in terms of each population's impact, or 'footprint'. William Rees, a Canadian academic who coined the term 'ecological footprint', first used it to describe the tendency of urban regions to appropriate the capacity of 'distant elsewhere'. Footprint analysis can demonstrate vividly the physical dependency of humankind on natural resources. It can be used to produce a first estimate of the present and anticipated natural capital requirements of the human economy, and to reveal the extent to which requirements in one region are currently being met from resources in another. For his own Lower Fraser Valley in British Columbia, for example, Rees calculated that the land required to sustain the population in terms of food and sinks for CO_2 emissions was about 20 times its own land area.[17]

In Rees's model, footprints are a precise calculation expressed in units of land area. This narrow interpretation is of limited use in terms of informing policy analysis, however, since it is seldom appropriate to express all impacts in terms of land units alone. Others are therefore using the concept much more broadly to describe a wide range of environmental, and in some cases, social, impacts of activities in a specific country, which appropriates the resources of other countries in order to maintain its own production, consumption, and investment patterns. Footprints can include the over-extraction and consumption of natural resources, and the impact of that consumption on the environment. There are also wider structural driving forces in the global economy that tend to generate ecological footprints, including trade policies which fail to internalise social and environmental costs, market signals that encourage the adoption of inappropriate high-input, high-output farming systems, and the burden of debt and structural adjustment.

In order to make footprint analysis a more useful policy tool, it is helpful to combine it with the concept of environmental space, which is a calculation of how much of the earth's resources we can use without impinging on the rights of current and future generations. This idea was developed by the Dutch Friends of the Earth in the report *Action Plan for Sustainable Netherlands*. At the heart of the concept is the equity principle: that each person on the planet, now and in the future, has the right to equitable shares of water, food, air, land, and other resources within limited global carrying capacity.

Calculation of carrying capacity, which refers to a given area's ability to support life (in this case, human life) by providing resources and absorbing wastes on a sustainable basis, depends on several changing factors, including consumption levels, technological innovation, and efficiency. Similarly, any calculation of environmental space itself is not fixed: it, too, depends on human numbers and technology. However, it is still a useful tool for setting orders of magnitudes on the levels by which the industrialised countries need to reduce their environmental impact. In terms of agricultural resources, for example, the FoE report estimates that there is a world average of 0.29 hectares available per inhabitant. Unsustainable agricultural practices and population growth could reduce this area to 0.25 hectares. If sustainable methods of production are used, only 0.19 hectares of cropland are needed to produce a basic healthy diet for each person. To live within this space, Dutch use of agricultural land would have to fall by 45 per cent by 2010.[18]

At the 1992 UNCED 'Earth Summit' in Rio de Janeiro, world leaders began to recognise that, in the words of the Agenda 21 action programme, unsustainable patterns of consumption and production in the industrialised countries are the major cause of global environmental deterioration. The Rio Declaration on Environment and Development added:

The developed countries acknowledge the responsibility they bear in the international pursuit of sustainable development in view of the pressures their societies place on the global environment and of the technologies and financial resources they command (Principle 7)

However, the Summit, with its focus more sharply on action in the South rather than the North, made little progress in translating the implications of this recognition into policy commitments, and President Bush's statement that 'the American lifestyle is not up for negotiation' was implicitly echoed by most industrialised countries in their unwillingness to take practical action.

The ecological footprint concept is beginning to enter the political mainstream as individual governments start to acknowledge the need to reduce the environmental burden they impose on other countries around the world. For example, in its National Strategy for Sustainable Development, published in January 1994, the British Government states:

Concerns about sustainability relate not only to a country's own environment but to the environmental impact which its economic activity has beyond national boundaries. The UK ... thus needs to consider the impact of its international activity (trade and investment) globally and in individual overseas countries.[19]

At the 1994 Oslo Symposium on Sustainable Consumption, the Norwegian Premier, Gro Harlem Brundtland, proclaimed that the primary challenge was to 'choose to leave enough "environmental space" for future generations'; and the Dutch Environment Minister, Hans Alders, stated that 'industrialised countries must change their patterns of production and consumption in such a way that less developed economies are given more room for development, both in relative and absolute terms.'[20]

The development of methods to gauge the footprints of different countries could provide a useful policy tool for working towards sustainable development. One obvious advantage is that it would provide some indicator of national responsibilities for particular environmental problems, thereby helping to establish the commensurate obligations of governments. One of the problems in past environmental negotiations has been the horse-trading over who should meet which targets and at what rate; a bargaining process in which developing countries have little power. Provided that the scope of ecological footprint analysis includes both social and environmental impacts, and is linked with the concept of environmental space, it could provide a helpful unifying conceptual framework for bringing together diverse policy areas. Further, it suggests that an appropriate foreign policy would ensure that, at a minimum, the pursuit of sustainable development in an industrialised country does not compromise other countries in their pursuit of sustainability or, better still, that it actively enables other countries to pursue sustainable paths.[21] Finally, it could provide potential political leverage for Southern countries to demand that the principles of equity and responsibility are at the heart of international agreements for sustainable development.

Such action is vital if we are to avert environmental catastrophe. One route to such a catastrophe would be for developing countries to replicate the per capita pollution levels of the industrialised world. Commenting on the dangers of reproducing northern economic models in the South, the UNDP's 1994 Human Development Report observed:

Replicating the patterns of the North in the South would require 10 times the present amount of fossil fuels and roughly 200 times as much mineral wealth. And in another 40 years these requirements would double again as the world population doubles...Poor nations cannot — and should not — imitate the production and consumption patterns of rich nations.[22]

Viewed from a concern with global ecological security, that is unquestionably true. Yet it is neither realistic nor just to expect four-fifths of the world to change the course of their own development in order to protect the earth and its resources, if at the same time, the developed countries continue to monopolise those resources and to damage the biosphere. Industrialised countries must therefore take the lead, both in making dramatic changes in their own production and consumption patterns, and in enabling Southern countries to experience the kind of growth they need to combat poverty, without destroying the environment. This poses difficult choices for policymakers, who are faced with having to make a radical reappraisal of current economic development theories. However, taking the action needed to tackle this should be seen politically as a 'win-win' scenario which is in everyone's interests, since ultimately the legacy of our unsustainable development model will affect all people, North and South.

Policy options for sustainable development

The United Nations Conference on Environment and Development (UNCED) in Rio de Janeiro in June 1992 was the largest diplomatic gathering in history. Thirty thousand people attended the summit, including 9000 journalists and 118 heads of state, and it received a blaze of publicity around the world. Meanwhile, over 500 NGOs and other groups with special concerns and expertise gathered at the parallel Global Forum some 40 miles away to debate many of the same themes. The Brazilian Government spent $33m to refurbish a huge convention hall where the official meetings were to take place, and millions more on keeping the city's hundreds of thousands of slum dwellers out of sight of the official delegates: a special highway was built at a cost of $130m to sweep Heads of State from the airport to their luxury hotels (and the requirement of Brazil's national environmental laws that an environmental impact study be carried out was suspended in order to permit construction in record time).[23]

In spite of unprecedented global attention, the Conference in Rio failed to live up to its promises. The Climate Change Convention set no legally binding targets or time-tables for industrialised countries to stabilise, let alone to reduce, emissions of CO_2 or other gases responsible for global warming. The Biodiversity Treaty was so vague that there appear to be no legal criteria through which compliance or non-compliance can be determined: countries commit themselves generally to conduct biological inventories, establish protected areas, and conduct environmental assessments of development projects. The hoped-for Forests Convention became a series of non-binding 'Forest Principles'.

More promising was the emergence of Agenda 21: a 500-page global action plan for achieving sustainable development. Many of its 40 chapters contain excellent proposals. Unfortunately, they depend upon unrealistic implementation mechanisms and are not backed by the necessary financial resources. Not only is Agenda 21 non-binding, it also depends on an unprecedented transfer of technology and finance from North to South, to invest in a multitude of areas related to environment and development, including health, sanitation, agriculture, the marine environment, technical assistance, and education. The cost was estimated to be $600bn a year, of which the North was to supply $125bn annually. Industrialised countries would therefore need to more than double current levels of development assistance, while Southern countries would somehow come up with an extra $475bn annually in matching funds. Given current economic and political realities, this level of financing seems unlikely, to say the least. Indeed, since 1992, far from increasing, Northern aid budgets for the South have in fact shrunk (as we shall see in Chapter 6). It is not surprising that citizens in developing countries feel betrayed and disappointed by the lack of action, both from their own governments, but chiefly from the North, to follow up the fine words of Rio.

The most curious failure is that the interrelationships between the development process, increasing trade liberalisation, and economic integration, were never seriously challenged throughout the whole UNCED process. It was significant that the corporate sector enjoyed special access to the Secretariat of the Coference throughout, and the influence of transnational corporations (TNCs) was strong enough to block discussion of the environmental impact of their activities. Recommendations drawn up by the UN's own Centre for Transnational Corporations (UNCTC), which proposed stringent global environmental standards for TNC activities, were shelved. Instead the Secretariat adopted a voluntary code of conduct, drawn up the Business Council on Sustainable Development, a corporate lobbying group. Far from being subject to a multilaterally-negotiated, mandatory code of conduct, the TNCs emerged from UNCED without their role in causing environmental destruction and social dislocation even having been scrutinised in the official process, let alone curtailed. The free-market approach was reaffirmed, uniting leaders from the South and North alike. The fundamental questions of what development means, of the impact of market deregulation, and of who benefits from growth, and capital and technology transfers, were simply passed over.[24]

Sustainable growth

Failure to challenge this dominant policy approach is at the heart of the environment and development crisis. Current economic policies assume that growth will improve the environment (via an increase in the resources available for environmental protection), increase employment, and reduce poverty (through trickle down of the benefits of growth). Yet at present none of these assumptions holds true: current patterns of economic growth are all too often destroying the environment, failing to generate sustainable livelihoods, and exacerbating poverty.

What is critical is the quality of growth and the extent to which it is compatible with sustainable development and environmental protection. In its now famous definition, the Brundtland Commission Report of 1987, *Our Common Future*, defined sustainable development as the ability to 'meet the needs of the present without compromising the ability of future generations to meet their own needs'. The definition has been criticised for failing to distinguish either between the vastly different 'needs' in rich and poor countries, or between 'human needs' and 'consumer wants'.[25] Such criticisms are only partly justified, for the Brundtland definition contains two further concepts which are far less often quoted:

- the concept of the essential needs of the world's poor, to which over-riding priority should be given, and
- the idea of limitations: 'not absolute limits but limitations imposed by the present state of technology and social organisations on environmental resources and by the ability of the biosphere to absorb the effects of human activities'.[26]

Whereas the Brundtland report accepts that there are physical limits to material consumption, it concludes that 'technology and social organisation can be both managed and improved to make way for a new era of economic growth.' The International Chamber of Commerce emphasises the mutually reinforcing relationship between growth and sustainability, stating in its 'Business Charter for Sustainable Development': 'Economic growth provides the conditions in which protection of the environment can best be achieved, and environmental protection, in balance with other human goals, is necessary to achieve growth that is sustainable.'[27] For Agenda 21 itself, the links are similarly straightforward: international trade promotes growth, which generates additional resources for cleaning up the environment, which in turn underpins a continuing expansion of trade and growth, and so on, apparently without limit. An 'open trading system' will be 'of benefit to all trading partners', it declares.[28]

There is no doubt that we can improve the efficiency with which we use environmental resources. One clear example is that of Japan, which has experienced an 81 per cent increase in output since 1973, using the same amount of energy. However, given the way in which Japan has located its more energy-intensive production outside its borders, the degree to which this experience is replicable is unclear. The critical question is whether we can improve efficiency fast enough (faster than the rate of economic growth), and cheaply enough (so that overall productivity rises rather than falls). If we can, then it becomes possible to achieve both economic growth and a declining impact on the environment.[29] To do so requires a continuous and exponential increase in efficiency of resource use, backed by stringent environmental policies. This presupposes the existence of the political will either to tighten environmental regulations, or to invest the fruits of growth in expensive environmental protection measures. Yet, in the aftermath of UNCED, that will, with a very few exceptions, appears to be singularly lacking.

How can growth be based on making more sustainable use of environmental resources, rather than mopping up after the damage is done? According to many mainstream economists, the incentive to make more sustainable use of environmental resources is lacking because of 'the failure of markets and governments to price the environment appropriately', taking into account the 'costs of environmental damage to society'.[30] They contend that environmental impact could be significantly reduced

if market prices reflected environmental costs more accurately. Thus, by correcting the environmental blindness of markets through tax policies and other measures, governments can make an important contribution to sustainable resource management.

The 'polluter should pay' principle is central to this approach, and extremely important in attempts to promote more sustainable development. Unfortunately, as most economists would accept, there are huge practical difficulties in giving monetary value to items as diverse as oak trees or the ozone layer, in attempting to price the intrinsic value of natural systems, or the effects of actions today on the environments of future generations. It is hard to decide whose values the prices would reflect, or how to take account of huge disparities in the distribution of resources, or the need to protect marginal producers and consumers. TNCs involved in commercial logging, for example, would be unlikely to place the same value on forests as would the people who live in them.

It is clear that market mechanisms have a crucial role in bringing about changes in environmental behaviour, and that it is important to try to find prices for commodities which reflect their true costs more accurately. The withdrawal of subsidies on energy production and consumption, for example, is a good way of encouraging people to use energy less wastefully; and ecological tax reform is likely to be critical to pursuing a sustainable development path. However, it is unlikely that market-based instruments alone will be capable of placing growth on a sustainable footing at the rates envisaged by the World Bank and others.

The critical question, for policy makers, is whether efficiency and technological improvements are going to be sufficient to deliver sustainability. It is a huge challenge, given the problems we face now, let alone those we might face in future. In its 1992 *World Development Report*, the World Bank forecasts that developing country output will rise by 4 per cent per year between 1990 and 2030. By the end of that period it will be about six times what it is today, with industrial country output tripling over the same period. Total world output would be 3.5 times what it is today. The Bank concludes:

Under a simple extrapolation based upon today's practices and emissions co-efficients, this would produce appalling problems of pollution and damage. Tens of millions of people would probably die each year as a result of pollutants, water shortages would become intolerable, and tropical forests and other natural habitats would be a fraction of their current size. This possibility is clear and real.[31]

Averting this scenario will require technological improvements on an epic scale. The economist Paul Ekins has attempted to measure the scale of the challenge posed by the relatively modest goal of reducing overall environmental impact by half, assuming that current growth trends continue and that world population doubles over the next 50 years, as predicted. He calculates that production and consumption would quadruple over this period. Technological advance would therefore have to reduce the environmental impact of each unit of consumption to one-sixteenth of its present level.[32] The scale of the 'technological fix' required can scarcely be over-estimated. It *may* be achievable: but only with a thoroughgoing revolution in current political and economic priorities.

This conclusion is of particular significance for the South, since poverty reduction will require considerable growth as well as development in developing countries. The terms of the dilemma are clear: the South needs to grow in order to develop, and it is currently dependent on trade primarily with the North in order to achieve this. The North needs to reduce the environmental impact of its production and consumption patterns, and it looks likely that this could necessitate a reduction of trade with the South.

The implications are far-reaching. A critical question must be whether debt-reduction funds for Southern diversification, and increased prices for commodities, via international action to regulate the supply of commodities onto the world markets, or via ICREAs (international commodity related environmental agreements), can be enough.[33] There would have to be an explicit recognition that developing countries should be enabled to pursue more self-reliant growth strategies, by which they reduce their dependence on Northern markets, where demand is maintained through unsustainable consumption patterns. A massive international effort would be needed to facilitate this, including substantial financial and technology transfer from North to South.

Questions about the future relationship between economic growth, trade, and poverty reduction, have been ignored by most analysts. The Brundtland Commission, for example, assumed that a five- to ten-fold expansion of industrial activity would be both possible — and necessary — to raise the material standards of the present world population to European levels by the middle of the next century. Leaving aside important considerations of whether the benefits of such growth would reach the poorest people, ecological footprint analysis suggests that several additional planet Earths would be required to achieve this goal, assuming prevailing material values and the technologies most likely to be available.

Part of the solution to this dilemma must be in improved commodity prices, the withdrawal of discriminatory trade policies, and comprehensive debt relief. Looking to the future, developing countries will need to depend less upon exports to the North, and more upon regional trade and self-reliant growth. There are no simple prescriptions; but there is a growing recognition of the importance of the problems. For example, while the UNDP 1994 *Human Development Report* maintains that there need be no tension between economic growth and environmental protection and regeneration, it does also cautiously acknowledge the scale of change that will be necessary to achieve this goal: 'A major restructuring of the world's income distribution, production, and consumption patterns may be a necessary precondition for any viable strategy for sustainable human development', it observes. However, the report draws back from outlining how such a major restructuring might take place, beyond the introduction of environmental pricing.[34]

Tackling climate change

Developing countries went to Rio with some hope of substantial Northern action on climate change, including appropriate technology transfer to the South. They were disappointed. The Climate Convention which emerged from UNCED is deeply flawed, both in design and scope. Some have suggested that its stated aim: 'To achieve stabilisation of greenhouse gas concentrations in the atmosphere at a level that would prevent dangerous anthropogenic inter-ference with the climate system', is impossible to achieve, since the amount of greenhouse gases emitted into the atmosphere to date already represents a dangerous interference with the global climate, even if all emissions stopped immediately. US lobbying ensured that the Convention's requirement for countries to stabilise CO_2 emissions at 1990 levels by the year 2000 is not legally binding. The industrialised countries are simply required to adopt policies and measures *aimed* at returning emissions of CO_2 and other greenhouse gases to their 1990 levels by the end of the century.

But even if the Convention were binding, it would still be inadequate. In its first scientific assessment in 1990, the IPCC stated that an immediate cut of 60 per cent in CO_2 emissions would be required to stabilise concentrations at present levels. This implied a virtual halving of fossil-fuel use in transport, industry, and elec-tricity generation, at a global level. More recently, it reported that even if CO_2 emissions were capped at present levels, atmospheric concentrations of the heat-trapping gas would continue to increase for at least two centuries, rising well beyond the point at which the Earth's climate would be disrupted, and doubling pre-industrial levels by the end of the next century.[35]

In the light of these warnings, actions to date by the industrialised countries to reduce emis-sions appear derisory. Policy makers are failing

to fulfil their commitments to stabilise CO_2 emissions by the year 2000, let alone making the cuts that are necessary to reduce the risk of significant long-term environmental and social disaster.

The 118 countries negotiating at the first Conference of Parties in Berlin in April 1995 failed to agree a timetable for further reductions, and specifically rejected the proposal from AOSIS (The Alliance of Small Island States) which would have required a 20 per cent reduction of 1990 CO_2 emission levels by 2005. Instead, they agreed the Berlin Mandate, which defers final adoption of targets and timetables for another two years. While this sets in motion a political process which should eventually yield results, the further delay in responding to such a critical issue is clearly regrettable. However, individual governments should not wait until 1997 before acting; there is much they could do now.

CO_2 emissions in the UK: a case study

Along with other industrialised countries, the UK has failed adequately to address the challenge of climate change. The environ-mental group Friends of the Earth has calculated that, taking into account current and historical per capita trends, the UK will have to achieve cuts in its national CO_2 emissions of at least 30 per cent on 1990 levels by 2005, with further cuts after that, to reduce its production to equitable levels. Emissions of CO_2 from the UK were 160 million tonnes of carbon (MtC) in 1990. Of this, more than half was from energy used to provide heat and light and run equipment in buildings, with substantial contri-butions from transport and industrial uses.

Electricity production accounted for another third of CO_2 emissions. At present, very little of the electricity supply is catered for by carbon-free renewable energy sources such as wind, wave, and geothermal energy, although oppor-tunities for wind and wave power electricity generation in Britain are the best in Europe.[36]

The UK Government's report on Climate Change, published at the beginning of 1994 as part of its obligation under the Framework Convention (*Climate Change: the UK Programme*), relies almost entirely on voluntary measures to achieve its target of a reduction of 10 million tonnes of carbon per annum. This is in spite of calls from business leaders for tougher regulations, on the grounds that neither the free market nor 'enlightened self-interest' would work to force a cut in emissions dramatic enough to tackle global warming.

More recently (March 1995) the UK government announced revised figures for the UK emissions of CO_2 which appear to suggest that carbon production will actually fall by the end of the century. However, this seems to have been achieved by confusion over the original predictions of emissions, not by a concerted effort to reduce them. Nevertheless, the government deserves some credit for trying to break the deadlock at the Berlin meeting by proposing a moderate target of cutting 1990 CO_2 levels by 10 per cent by 2010.

The most appropriate mix of policy measures needed to reduce CO_2 emissions is a matter for debate. What is clear, however, is that far more could be done to develop policies to reduce the UK's energy footprint, and to meet tangible and meaningful targets, such as a reduction in CO_2 emissions of 30 per cent from 1990 levels, by 2005. Possible measures include a combination of regulatory and fiscal policies, such as the introduction of tough, mandatory energy-efficiency standards for domestic and office energy-using appliances and, where feasible, industrial processes; upgrading energy efficiency standards in Building Regulations by 35 per cent from 1990 levels; further developing CHP (Combined Heat and Power) plants; reducing private car use; initiating a major programme of investment to upgrade the insulation levels of low-income households; altering energy utility regulations so as to ensure that improving energy efficiency on customers' premises is good business for the electricity and gas companies, and ensuring that the Energy Savings Trust is adequately funded. Investment in renewable energy could

be increased, and an energy tax could be introduced.[37]

Ecological tax reform

Tax reform could play a vital role in achieving targets for sustainable production and resource use, by bringing market prices and costs into closer alignment with the real environmental costs of production and consumption patterns. By changing the way taxes are raised, ecological tax reform could both encourage environmental protection and generate employment. For example, at present, roughly two-thirds of the burden of taxation in the UK falls on the activities of people and the economic 'goods' of employment and business enterprises, while the remaining third falls mostly on consumption, with very little on environmental 'bads' such as pollution and the inefficient use of resources. The economy duly responds to these price signals by over-using natural resources and under-using people (unemployment). By shifting the burden of taxes away from employment (reductions in national insurance charges, lower income and profit taxes), and onto environmental damage and the use of resources (taxes on energy, transport, and pollution, for example), ecological tax reform could make a significant contribution towards reversing the substitution of labour by capital and the increase in the use of energy and raw materials, trends which lead both to an over-exploitation of natural resources and to structural unemployment.

It has been argued that it could be unwise to make governments dependent for their revenue upon an activity which one wants to reduce, since this gives them a strong incentive *not* to encourage its reduction! However, it would not be necessary to make a complete shift from labour to resource taxaxtion. A recent OECD study suggests that significant benefits could arise from relatively small reforms.[38]

Clearly, tax reform of this kind would need to make provision for compensating poorer households, for whom energy costs make up a

significant proportion of their expenditure. However, a combination of government expenditure and other tax reductions targeted on poor households could achieve this. One study has shown that a programme of home insulation in poorer homes could create some 50,000 jobs a year for a decade, and leave the poor better off. For a one-off government expenditure package of about £1bn the environment, the unemployed, and poor people would all achieve significant benefits.[39]

Concerns that increased energy and other taxes on inputs to industry will penalise national competitiveness could be allayed through commitments to return the ecological tax revenues to industry in the form of lower labour costs and incentives for eco-efficient technology investments. This would benefit all the service industries and most manufacturing industries. It would not compensate those that are energy-intensive, however, and special measures would need to be adopted to help them through the transition.

Claims that ecological tax reform would harm employment seem ill-founded. The European Commission's White Paper, *Growth, Competitiveness, Employment* proposes a form of ecological taxation, precisely because of the employment opportunities which it would create, and observes:

The inadequate use of available resources — too little labour, too much use of environmental resources — is clearly not in line with the preferences of society ...people expect for themselves and for their children on the one hand more jobs and a stable income, but on the other also a higher quality of life.[40]

A recent report of the Employment Policy Institute estimated that half a million jobs could be created over 10 years by taxing pollution rather than employment.[41] Friends of the Earth has come to similar conclusions in its study, *Working Future: Jobs and the Environment*, which challenges the conventional wisdom that 'conservation costs jobs', and argues that environmental protection policies are essential to a sound economy.[42] The study provides estimates of how extra jobs could be created by shifting transport investment from road to rail; abandoning nuclear power in favour of renewable energy sources such as wind farms, together with large-scale energy-saving programmes; promoting recycling and organic farming; and introducing regulations to oblige industries to install new technology to clean polluted land and rivers. While the authors admit that tens of thousands of jobs would be lost from the nuclear industry and from factories unable to meet stringent pollution standards, they estimate that there would be a net gain of as many as 700,000 jobs if indirect employment is also included. The report summarises research from across the industrialised world. In the USA, for example, a study revealed that wind and solar energy generated five times as many jobs as coal-fired energy. The OECD has also concluded that environmental protection would generate two million new jobs in industrial countries by 2000.

Opposition to an EU energy tax

Despite the growing evidence to suggest that environmental taxes can be introduced in a manner consistent with protecting employment, efforts to introduce them have typically been thwarted, often through the influence of powerful industrial lobbies claiming that 'green taxation' will lead ineluctably to lost competitiveness and job losses. Efforts to secure agreement on a European-wide energy and carbon tax to reduce CO_2 emissions is a case in point.

The proposal was for a mixed energy and carbon tax, with 50 per cent being levied on carbon content, and 50 per cent on the energy value of the fuel. It was suggested that the tax would be introduced at the rate of $3 per barrel in 1993 rising to $10 per barrel of oil equivalent by the year 2000. A report produced by the EC Commission in October 1992 suggested that the proposed tax would produce a 4 per cent saving in emissions, one-third of the total required. Large-scale exemptions were suggested for energy-intensive industries with a large involvement in international trade such as the steel, chemicals, non-ferrous metals, cement, glass, and paper and pulp industries. The proposal also contained measures which would provide exemptions to those countries with lower than average emissions per head of population. Yet even these modest proposals have been stalled for over three years.

Although there is support from Germany and most Northern European states, it is opposition from the UK Government which is currently holding up progress. In a meeting of EU Environment Ministers on 23 April 1993, the UK was the only country out of the 12 Member states which did not accept the principle that a tax was needed to help the Community to reduce its CO_2 emissions. More recently, at a similar meeting in October 1994, the UK Environment Minister, John Gummer, restated his firm and long-standing opposition to any Community-wide carbon and energy tax.

Yet despite arguments that the unilateral adoption of energy taxes would place energy-intensive domestic industries in an uncompetitive position, the Netherlands, Finland, and Sweden have all introduced new energy and carbon taxes, with the specific aim of curbing CO_2 emissions. (Studies for the UK similarly raise serious doubts over the credibility of the government's case against an energy tax. According to Friends of the Earth, cuts of up to 30 per cent in CO_2 emissions could be achieved in the UK by 2005 through measures including improved energy efficiency, greater energy conservation, higher energy prices for the business and public sectors in line with the EC's proposal for a carbon/energy tax, accelerated development of renewable energy sources, and reduced car use). Moreover, in many cases, investment in energy-efficient technology can itself be a source of competitive advantage, as the experience of both Japan and Germany has underlined. Far from leading to lost competitiveness, carefully designed and implemented taxation measures can act as an incentive to more efficient energy use, to the benefit of the national economy and the global environment.

Transport

The internal combustion engine is now recognised as a significant cause of environmental problems. The products of the motor industry, primarily passenger cars, are globally the largest single source of air pollution. Some 14 per cent of the world's CO_2 emissions come from road transport. Below we highlight issues and policy positions, which are of wider relevance, through a focus on transport policy in the UK.

Over 20 per cent of the UK's emissions come from transport. Between 1970 and 1990, fuel consumption by cars rose by around 70 per cent, car ownership almost doubled, and car mileage grew by around 117 per cent. This sector is now the fastest-growing source of emissions in the UK, with predictions of a further rise of 30 per cent between 1990 and 2005, principally due to a growth in car use forecast by the Department of Transport of between 32 and 51 per cent over the period. The contribution of the government's road-building programme to overall UK responsibility for global warming cannot there-fore be overlooked.

A massive shift away from more road building and more private cars towards investment in public transport is urgently needed. In Britain, the government's *Sustainable Development* strategy, published early in 1994 as part of the Rio follow-up process, claims to be taking steps to introduce a framework which will enable people to reduce dependence on private cars. However, with many road-building plans still in place (despite the success of public protests to halt some), and rail privatisation widely expected to reduce both the quality and quantity of rail services, any such framework is little in evidence. While the measures announced by the government to reduce transport emissions by 5 per cent compared with forecast levels (principally by a commitment to year-on-year real increases in fuel duties of 5 per cent) are to be welcomed, they fall far short of an environmentally-sound transport policy. More progressive measures might include reallocating a substantial proportion of the National Roads Programme budget to investment in public transport, removing the presumption in favour of development from land-use planning law and policy, increasing fuel prices, and setting emission standards for new cars.

Energy in the South

Energy policy lies at the heart of sustainable development. Investing in energy efficiency is a proven strategy for meeting environmental, social, and economic objectives, and together with an expansion of renewable energy sources, and other fiscal and regulatory measures, will be crucial if the current dependence on fossil fuels is to be significantly reduced. This is as true for the developing as for the developed world.

Sustainability in the South, as in the North, depends on a massive shift away from fossil-fuel energy use towards energy efficiency and renewable energy sources. The international financial institutions have significant influence on policy in this area. The World Bank, for example, plays a major role, with energy being the Bank's largest or second largest lending area in recent years, accounting for between 14 and 18 per cent of annual lending in the period 1990-1993. However, in spite of Barber Conable's commitment to the Bank's playing 'a leadership role' in promoting energy efficiency, this has yet to be translated into project funding.[43]

Throughout the early 1990s the Bank focused its lending almost entirely on large dams and thermal power plants, rather than promoting end-use efficiency and conservation. In late 1991, a comprehensive review of the Bank's energy lending by the Washington-based International Institute for Energy Conservation concluded that the Bank was devoting less than 1 per cent of its energy lending to end-use efficiency and conservation investments.[44]

Yet it is well known that current patterns of energy development in developing countries often involve massive social and environmental destruction. Large hydroelectric dams are responsible for the destructin of forests and farmland in many countries, and frequently result in the forced resettlement of rural populations; while the growing use of coal for power production by China and India will make these countries the largest contributors to global warming in the next century if alternatives are not found. The cost of large-scale energy projects is extremely high: in many developing countries between a quarter and a third of all public investment is now being used for electricity generation, diverting desperately needed capital from other priority investments, such as health services and education.

It has been estimated, however, that investments in state-of-the-art industrial equipment, and other energy-saving improvements and appliances, could cut the need for growth in power-generating capacity by as much as 50 per cent in many developing countries. The cost of such end-use efficiency investments is often less than half the cost of the new power plants and dams that would be necessary to generate the equivalent amount of power.[45]

World Bank energy staff themselves have pointed to the enormous economic implications of this neglect of end-use efficiency energy investment scenario:

Estimates suggest that if 20 per cent of commercial energy in developing countries were saved, total gross savings for developing countries would amount to about US $30 billion per annum, or about 7.5 per cent of the total value of merchandise imports. This is about 60 per cent of the net flow of resources out of developing countries for debt service in 1988, and about two-thirds of the official development assistance from OECD and OPEC countries in 1987.[46]

Conclusion

It is clear from the evidence in this chapter that present policies and consumption patterns are not compatible with a commitment to sustainable development and intergenerational equity.

If this picture is to change, urgent action will be required to initiate fundamental reforms in the management of Northern and Southern economies.

Northern governments should follow the Dutch example of assessing the scale and impact of their ecological footprints in key sectors, including energy and agriculture. Governments then need to commit themselves to setting specific, time-tabled targets for reducing the negative consequences of their footprints. Such targets should broadly be based on calculations of equitable allocations of environmental space. Governments would need to report on progress on these targets to the UN Commission on Sustainable Development, together with their reports on implementation of Agenda 21.

Given the urgency of the environmental crisis, governments should demonstrate their commitment to the policies of Agenda 21 by allocating substantial additional financial resources to fund it, together with appropriate technology transfer and acapacity building.

Governments will need to develop policy frameworks across all sectors to meet more stringent targets for energy use. These could include a comination of regulatory and fiscal policies, including a carbon/energy tax, tougher energy-efficiency standfards, programmes of insulation, and investment in renewable enrgy. Governments in the North should commit themselves to reducing CO_2 emissions by 30 per cent from 1990 levels by 2005, and make less polluting technology readily available to the South, so that it is able to pursue a more sustainable, and less carbon-intensive path.

Finally, governments could develop wider tax measures to promote more sustainable forms of production and consumption. The EU, for example, could redesign its taxation policies and structures in such a way as to meet the twin objectives of ending the over-exploitation of natural resources, and helping to create employment.

6 Aid, debt, and development finance

A substantial increase in the resources for fighting poverty in the poorest countries appears entirely affordable. It is a matter of political commitment and the reassessment of donor priorities.

WORLD BANK, 1990

The poor do not want you to impose your programmes to empower us. We know how to empower ouselves. We want your support for our decisions. This is the message from the poor to the governments, the NGOs, and the donor agencies.

KARUNAWATHIE MENIKE, PEOPLE'S RURAL DEVELOPMENT ASSOCIATION, SRI LANKA

Must we starve our children to pay our debts?

JULIUS NYERERE

Introduction

Half a century ago, the Bretton Woods conference acknowledged that many of the world's poorest countries lacked the financial resources needed to expand economic growth and employment. Equity required that these countries should be able to make use of the financial resources of wealthier countries on reasonable terms. The architects of the Bretton Woods system were acutely aware that unregulated capital markets would not provide such terms. The system they designed therefore included mechanisms for transferring, particularly through the World Bank, savings from the industrialised world for investment in the infrastructure and trading activities of developing countries.

Today, long-term development finance remains vital for developing countries, not least to repair the damage inflicted during the debt crisis of the 1980s, when funds flowed in reverse direction from South to North. More broadly, external support is needed in many countries to supplement domestic resources, in order to create employment, raise investment levels, support economic recovery, maintain imports and, above all, to invest in the health and education of people.

Yet external funding, whether from governments, international financial institutions or NGOs, involves much more than a straightforward financial transfer. The relationship between donor and recipient raises fundamental issues of unequal power, the danger of local priorities being unduly influenced or distorted, and of local capacity being undermined. The provision of external aid and technical expertise can distort the economies of recipient countries by creating an unhealthy reliance on foreign exports and imported goods, or by reducing the pressure on governments to embark on painful and long overdue tax reforms.

Foreign donors, ostensibly all committed to the same goal of poverty reduction, face a myriad of contradictions. Aid ministries want to contribute to sustainable development, yet are under pressure to use aid to promote national strategic and commercial interests. The international financial institutions are banks and are constrained by commercial pressures, and by the fact that they are also large bureaucracies, whose ideologies reflect those of their funders. NGOs may enjoy degrees of free-dom that their governments and multi-lateral agencies lack. But they may also be less accountable, and at risk of co-option by particular interests.

Ultimately, external assistance is no solution to fundamental problems of poverty, which are rooted in injustice and the denial of rights. These must be resolved by local people: by grassroots groups, people's organisations, trade unions, NGOs, and business interests, coming together as part of civil society, putting pressure on and interacting with the state to effect change.

Yet this does not deny the critical importance of external assistance to poor people and their governments, whether it comes in the form of aid or invesment flows or debt reduction packages. Such external finance is vitally needed as part of the enabling environment in which people can act together to reduce poverty and secure their basic rights. Unfortunately, most developing countries are not receiving the kind of external support they need.

For many of the world's poorest countries, a chronic debt crisis, largely disregarded in the North because it does not threaten the global financial system, has continued unabated for some 15 years. The depth of that crisis is reflected partly in financial indicators, which point to widespread bankruptcy. At a deeper level, however, the debt crisis is manifest in the suffering of ordinary people: people who are denied health care, education, and opportunities for livelihoods because of the claims of external creditors. These creditors, which include Northern governments and institutions controlled by them, often claim that radical action to reduce

the debt burden of the world's poorest countries would constitute a 'moral hazard', setting a precedent which could threaten the stability of the international financial system. In fact, the debt problems of the poorest countries could, given the political will, be resolved without any such threat. In terms of the UN Charter's commitment to poverty reduction, the real moral hazard is that posed by political leaders in the industrial world who, through their indifference and inertia, have allowed debt to destroy the hopes and opportunities of millions of the world's poorest people.

The surge in private capital transfers to the developing world has brought with it a renewed faith in the efficacy of market forces. Increasingly, the argument is heard that private investment, rather than public finance, holds the key to future prosperity. That is a questionable proposition, even in the countries now acting as a magnet for foreign capital. For the vast majority of the poorest developing countries, which are being bypassed by private capital flows, publicly-financed development assistance remains vital.

International aid programmes could, if adequately financed and properly targeted, play an important role in offsetting the extreme disparities in wealth and opportunity facing people in the North and the South. In their domestic policies, the industrialised countries invest on average around one-quarter of national income on social welfare systems designed to protect the vulnerable and unemployed, and to counteract poverty and extreme inequality. Development assistance provides an opportunity to extend such provision to the international stage. Yet the industrial countries spend only a minute, and falling, share of their national incomes on aid.

To make matters worse, a very large proportion of this very small quantity of aid is irrelevant to the needs of the poor throughout the world. This is because aid programmes are often designed to promote the narrowly-defined interests of the industrialised world, rather than to reduce poverty. Far too much aid

Figure 6.1 Global aid and private investment flows, and developing countries' share of the private investment

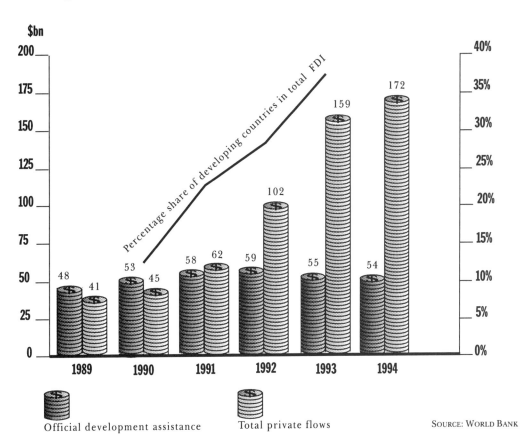

Official development assistance   Total private flows

Source: World Bank

bypasses the world's poorest countries and poorest people, largely because Northern governments are more concerned with cultivating their export markets and building their strategic influence than with reducing poverty.

For most people in the industrialised world this is a deeply offensive use of public funds. They regard aid neither as charity nor as a mechanism for pursuing self-interest, but as a means of extending the principles of solidarity and community in order to reduce poverty. This is the true spirit of development assistance. In a global community, hunger, disease, misery and vulnerability should be no more acceptable abroad than at home. Equity and social justice

demand the provision of a global safety-net to combat severe poverty in the poorest countries. The danger is that, without a radical reform of international aid to achieve this objective, public support for aid will wane, thereby reducing the pressure on governments to maintain aid transfers. Not only would that be a tragedy for human development and the poor, who could derive so much benefit from development assistance; it would also be self-defeating. Northern governments cannot ring-fence their citizens from the conflicts, refugee flows, and violent instability which are the product of poverty and marginalisation. International aid, for all its current faults, remains one of the most important mechanisms for reducing poverty and its destructive effects. Development assistance is one activity where ethical concern and enlightened self-interest coincide.

In this chapter, we examine the problems facing different groups of countries in obtaining external finance. We also outline measures for reforming debt relief and aid strategies in a manner which is pro-poor. Governments, however, are not the only source of aid transfers. Nor are they alone in facing problems in developing genuinely poverty-focused aid programmes. The role of non-government organisations (NGOs) has increased in importance in recent decades. Agencies such as Oxfam have worked with local counterparts in facilitating community-based development efforts, with the emphasis on the participation of local communities, and on enhancing the capacities of the poor. This approach to development starts by listening to the poor themselves, recognises the role and needs of women in the development process, and considers environmental implications and the sustainability of project initiatives.

A problem which NGOs share with governments is that reaching the poor and promoting genuine human development are objectives which are easier to subscribe to in principle than to achieve in practice, as we suggest in the final section of this chapter. Bilateral and multilateral donors and NGOs alike need to listen and learn from local communities, rather than arrive with pre-conceived ideas about the route to sustainable development.

Private capital flows and debt

During the 1970s, international capital markets transferred around $20bn a year to developing countries, financing imports and covering the trade deficits left by rising oil prices. This picture changed dramatically in the 1980s. The rise in real interest rates which occurred after 1979, as Northern governments responded to the second oil price rise with monetarist policies which forced up interest rates, threw North-South financial flows into reverse gear. Between 1983 and 1989, creditors received $242bn *more* from these countries than they provided in new loans.[1] These outflows were maintained at enormous economic and social cost. Imports collapsed, as foreign exchange was diverted into debt repayments, investment slumped, and wages fell dramatically. Social provision deteriorated as bankrupt governments cut spending. In Latin America, the epicentre of the debt crisis, average incomes fell by 10 per cent in the 1980s and investment declined from 23 per cent to 16 per cent of national income, causing widespread unemployment and poverty.[2]

Theoretically, the debt crisis should never have happened. The Bretton Woods agencies were created in part to transfer the savings of surplus countries to deficit countries, in the interests of orderly adjustment. During the first half of the decade, they started lending money to indebted countries, enabling them to repay their commercial creditors. By 1985, however, repayments on IMF loans from developing countries were outstripping new finance, so that the Fund became a drain on resources. After 1989, repayments on World Bank lending also meant that its balance turned negative. Thus institutions created, especially in the World Bank's case, to transfer resources to developing countries, are now doing precisely the opposite.[3] This perversion of the multilateral financial system stands in urgent need of correction.

The 1990s have witnessed a transformation in the overall resource flow picture. Between 1989 and 1994, net transfers to developing countries almost tripled to $227bn.[4] Virtually all of this growth is attributable to private capital flows, mainly in the form of direct foreign investment, portfolio investment in stocks and shares, and funds raised by the sale of government bonds in Euromoney markets. Collectively, these flows are now by far the most dynamic component of finance for developing countries, having quadrupled to $170bn over the past five years. In 1989, private capital flows were roughly equal to overseas development

Figure 6.2 IMF transfers to SILICs

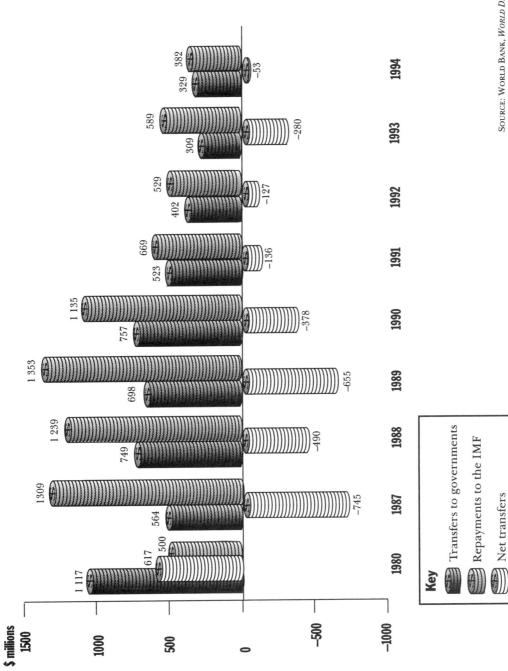

SOURCE: WORLD BANK, *WORLD DEBT TABLES*

assistance. Today, they are some four times larger.[5]

They are, however, heavily concentrated in a relatively small group of about a dozen countries. Most of these, with the major exception of China, are middle-income countries; just five of them (Argentina, China, Mexico, Thailand, and Malaysia) accounted for over half of all private investment in developing countries for the period 1989-1993. The world's poorest countries have been bypassed by these flows of private capital. Sub-Saharan Africa, for instance, receives less than 1 per cent of global investment.

These private transfers are often highly speculative, unstable, and driven by a concern to maximise short-term profit, rather than to support long-term development. They are also easily reversible, as evidenced by the financial crisis gripping Mexico, the country whose threatened default in 1982 brought the expression 'debt crisis' into the language of international finance. Mexico's problems suggest that it may be premature to treat Latin America's debt crisis as past history.

Latin America: from debt crisis to Brady Plan and back

The Brady Plan to reduce commercial debt, launched in 1989, marked a watershed in the international debt strategy for middle-income countries, belatedly acknowledging what had long been evident: that a large proportion of commercial debt was unpayable, even with the financial squeeze applied under adjustment programmes.[6] While enormously complex in implementation, the Plan recognised the simple principle that commercial debt could be reduced with support from the IMF and the World Bank. Creditor banks were invited to accept a range of options for reducing the stock of debt owed to them, in return for a guarantee backed by the IMF and World Bank and the government involved. These guarantees came in the form of 'Brady bonds' with a lower face value than the original debt (which the financial

markets had accepted were unpayable), but with a binding commitment to meet future payments in part with loans from the IMF and World Bank, and in part from the debtor's own resources.

Twelve countries have now completed deals under the Brady Plan, covering some $190bn, or four-fifths of the debt stock owed in 1989. The signing of the first Brady deal coincided with the start of the boom in private capital flows to developing countries, with the countries previously at the centre of the debt crisis figuring prominently among the newly favoured 'emerging markets'. By 1993, Latin America was receiving the equivalent of 3 per cent of reginal income in private capital flows, reversing the outflows of the previous decade, prompting most commentators and Northern governments to draw a line under the 'debt crisis'.

But in fact there is little cause for optimism. Although the Brady Plan played an important part in creating the confidence underpinning the acceleration in private capital flows, it did so by replacing one sort of debt (commercial bank) with another (Brady bonds), and extending repayment periods. The end result is that Latin America's debt stock has continued to rise during the 1990s, and there is little flexibility available for further rescheduling.

Moreover, while the ratio of debt service to exports has fallen, this is partly as a consequence of US interest-rate reductions. Taking into account declining interest rates and the costs to debtors of financing future payments, the Brady Plan had resulted by 1994 in debt reduction equivalent to around $24bn, or 6 per cent of total debt.[7] With repayments on debt still absorbing almost one-third of export earnings, Latin America still has a serious debt problem, even if the debt crisis has receded.[8] The region remains highly exposed to the risk of a renewed crisis in the event of balance-of-payments difficulties. If a repeat of the 1980s scenario is to be avoided, it is essential for the international community to create a framework for financial stability in the region.

Figure 6.3 Latin American and Caribbean debt

SOURCE: WORLD BANK/OECD

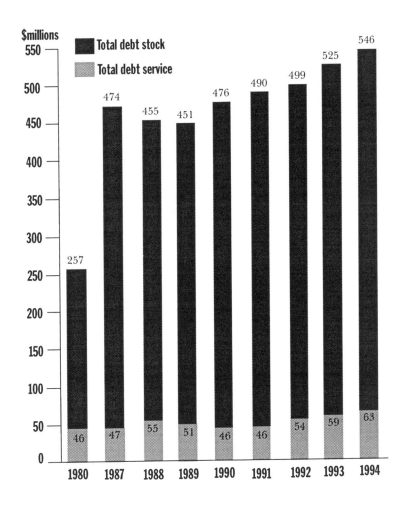

Private capital movements have helped to disguise the depth of the debt problems left unresolved by the Brady Plan. They have not, however, established a viable framework either for the provision of long-term development finance or for financial stability. Indeed, the private capital markets into which some developing countries are being integrated may unleash volatile financial forces which are capable of destroying fragile economies.

The fundamental problem is that a large proportion of the foreign capital pouring into emerging markets is speculative in nature, and entirely disconnected from the real economy. Much of the explosion in private capital flows generated through the sale of government bonds and through portfolio investment represents high-risk short-term speculative activity, and institutional investment by pension funds and money market managers. Contrary to the popular perception, such flows have less to do with opportunities for productive investment and employment creation than with the pursuit of the fast-buck in money markets. This is especially true for portfolio investment, through which fund managers transfer funds through stock exchanges or invest them in privatisation deals, often with highly destabilising consequences.

In May 1991 Mexico embarked on one of the largest-ever privatisation programmes in Latin America when the government sold $2.4bn of shares in Telmex, previously a state monopoly. The shares were sold for $27 before climbing to $75 in early 1994, earning vast fortunes for foreign speculators. As these speculators traded in their shares to take their profits in early 1995, when a financial crisis loomed large, the value of shares fell to $34.[9] This is one example, repeated many times over, of the discrepancy between the forces which govern stock market behaviour, and the realities which shape the real economy in which ordinary people live and work.

Low interest-rates in the US, reducing the gains to capital there, have played an important part in boosting the attractiveness of emerging markets during the early 1990s. During 1993, most of these markets went into steep decline, underlining the fact that, in a global currency market where vast sums can be moved at the touch of a button, money can move out as fast as it moves in.[10] Since most of the capital flowing into Latin America has no connection with production, governments there have attempted to prevent its outflow by raising interest rates to ever more atmospheric levels, with disastrous consequences for the economy.

The collapse of the Mexican peso

With its peculiar brand of incompetent economic management and commitment to financial deregulation, Mexico has been transformed during the 1990s into a 'junk bond' economy. Massively high interest-rates persuaded foreigners to hold almost $30bn in government securities at the end of 1994, compared to $2bn in 1990.[11] The financial crash at the end of 1994 forcefully demonstrated the potential for instability that such speculative capital flows create. As the country's trade deficit deepened

during the 1990s, the Mexican government relied increasingly upon issues of government bonds to attract foreign currency.

These dollar-denominated bonds carried interest rates in excess of 16 per cent, imposing huge repayment obligations, which were covered by issuing more bonds. The whole arrangement propped up an artificially over-valued exchange rate, which in turn allowed investors to protect their profits when transferring them back home. But the over-valued exchange rate had the effect of sucking in more imports and discouraging exports, forcing up the trade deficit to 8 per cent of GDP and increasing dependence on foreign private capital.[12]

Mexico's attempt to finance its trade deficit through speculative capital finally collapsed when, in December 1994, it became clear that the country did not have the reserves to meet payments on $28bn worth of dollar-denominated government bonds. The peso promptly lost 50 per cent of its value, leading to a US-led rescue effort. Some $50bn dollars were pledged to stave off Mexican bankruptcy, $18bn of it by the IMF.[13] Having provided the resources to bale out the commercial banks threatened by Mexican default in 1982, the Fund is now part of a wider international effort to bale out the assorted speculators who gambled with such profitability on Mexico's capital markets.

The size of the rescue package, which exceeds the annual flow of overseas development assistance provided by the OECD countries, ensures that these speculators will be repaid. The terms on which the rescue package is being provided ensures that it will be Mexico's poor who pay the highest price for their government's embrace of the twin theologies of free trade and financial deregulation. Strict conditions attached to the loan demand wage cuts and public spending reductions, and will inevitably lead to a drop in living standards and increased poverty; a scenario reminiscent of the 1980s debt crisis.

Mexico's future is uncertain. While immediate default may have been staved off, the spectre of insolvency continues to loom large, with implications that go far beyond Mexico. Most immediately, the crisis has raised serious questions over the entire NAFTA exercise, which demands that Mexico's economy be exposed to intense competition at a time when reconstruction and selective protection is vital.

The crisis in Mexico has affected stock exchanges of other emerging markets, most of which were already in decline. Banking systems across Latin America have been left in a highly unstable condition, and other exposed economies, notably Argentina, have been forced to embark on emergency programmes with the IMF. There are important differences between the present crisis and the debt crisis of the early 1980s, since it is not just commercial banks who are exposed. But this could be a further source of instability, given that financial markets, persion-fund managers, and other sources of speculative capital, are considerably less subject to government influence than are commercial banks.

Debt in low-income countries

As the threat facing the commercial banking system has receded during the 1990s, the problem of Third World debt has drifted imperceptibly off the agenda of the Group of Seven industrialised countries. But for the world's poorest countries, the debt crisis continues to wreak social and economic havoc. These countries remain overwhelmingly dependent on official aid flows for their financial survival. However, the flow of aid is stagnating in real terms, and likely to decline further as major donors trim their aid budgets. For this reason, efforts to increase the financial resources available to the poorest countries must focus partly on trade and partly on debt reform. Measures to ease the crushing debt burden of these countries are now vital if their marginalisation within the international economy is to be reversed.

Nowhere is this more necessary than in sub-Saharan Africa. The facts speak for themselves: measured as a percentage of GDP, sub-Saharan

Africa's debt is higher than for any other developing region. Repeated rounds of debt rescheduling have succeeded in reducing the ratio of debt to total export earnings, but only to around 250 per cent, which is still as high as in the middle-income countries during the worst years of the debt crisis. Between 1990 and 1993, the region transferred $13.4bn annually to its external creditors.[14] This is four times as much as governments in the region spend on health services. In fact, it is more than their combined spending on health and education. It is also substantially in excess of the $9bn a year which UNICEF estimates as the total cost of meeting basic human needs for health, nutrition, education, and family planning.[15]

This would be bad enough; but unfortunately, it is not the full picture. If African governments were meeting their scheduled repayments, they would by paying out more than twice as much. In fact, arrears are accumulating at an alarming rate, and Africa's debt stock is continuing to grow despite the haemorrhage of resources from the region. The stock of unpaid interest and principal of debt owed to official creditors stood at almost $38bn in 1993 — more than double the level in 1990. Since 1988, about two-thirds of the increase in debt stock for sub-Saharan Africa can be traced to the accumulation of interest on arrears. For the severely-indebted low-income countries (SILICs) as a group, debt service payments account for 18 per cent of export earnings, while scheduled payments account for 45 per cent. Thus while actual repayments are well below the average for middle-income countries, arrears accumulation in the SILICs indicates widespread financial insolvency.

Uganda's debt problem
Of the 32 countries categorised by the World Bank as severely-indebted low-income countries, Sub-Saharan Africa accounts for 25. One of the most severely indebted is Uganda.[16] In 1994, the country is scheduled to pay $162m in debt service payments, which represents over four-fifths of the country's export earnings. This

Figure 6.4 SILICs debt stock and arrears

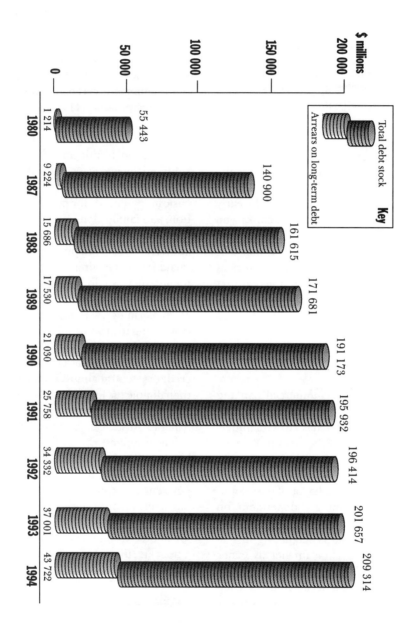

SOURCE: WORLD BANK

compares with $120m which the government spends on health and education combined. Uganda's debt burden is self-evidently unpayable, and universally recognised as such. The debt-service-to-export ratio for the country is more than three times higher than what the World Bank's considers to be the maximum for sustainable debt.[17]

The more telling measure of the unsustainability of Uganda's debt burden is to be found in its human welfare indicators, which are among the worst in the world. The country's death rate is about twice the average for low-income countries. Infant and child mortality rates (at 117 and 180 respectively per 1000) are also exceptionally high. Among children under the age of five, the main killers are preventible illnesses such as malaria, diarrhoea, pneumonia, and malnutrition, reflecting inadequate provision of primary health care and sanitation.[18] Yet despite these appalling indicators, per capita spending on debt repayment is more than double per capita spending on health. If these repayments were to be stopped and the money transferred to the health sector, it would be possible, on the World Bank's estimates, to provide basic health care to all Ugandans.

The debt crisis in other regions

Countries in other regions also figure prominently in today's global debt crisis. With a foreign debt that has reached nearly $11bn, Nicaragua has the highest per capita debt in the world and a repayments profile that defies the imagination. Converted into individual debt, every Nicaraguan woman, man, and child owes the country's external creditors over six times what they can expect to earn in a year. In order to meet the repayments due on that debt over the next seven years, a sum equivalent to twice the country's entire foreign exchange earnings would have to be transferred. To this would have to be added interest payments on overdue balances. Taken together, these transfers would represent the equivalent of almost half the country's total national income.[19]

While debt reduction measures have addressed some of the more immediate problems of middle-income countries, many continue to face acute problems. For example, Peru's outstanding debt represents a far higher proportion of its export earnings (around 400 per cent) than the average for severely-indebted low-income countries.

Debt problems have seriously damaged the social and economic life of Jamaica, for example. While nominally a middle-income country, more than half of Jamaica's population live below the poverty line, and levels of malnutrition have doubled over the past decade. Unemployment and growing recourse to drugs marketing as a means of survival have combined to make Jamaica the crime capital of the Caribbean, with a murder rate second only to Colombia.[20] Migration to the US, legal and illegal, has offered another escape route from poverty for Jamaica's growing under-class. The economic causes of this social breakdown are to be found partly in the country's debt, payments on which have resulted in transfers to creditors of over $1.2bn since the mid-1980s. In the 1993 budget, almost half of all government expenditure was directed towards debt repayment. Meanwhile, maternal mortality rates are increasing, per capita spending on primary education is lower than in the mid-1970s, illiteracy levels are rising, and public services are disintegrating.[21]

Oxfam has witnessed the devastating consequences of debt in many of the countries in which it works. As the state's capacity to provide is eroded by the transfer of resources to repay debts, NGOs have supported the efforts of local communities to provide essential health care, education, water, and sanitation. The wider economic consequences of unpayable debt burdens are often less visible, but they are no less devastating in their impact. For example, the diversion of foreign exchange to external creditors reduces import capacity. As a result, local industries are left without essential items, cutting productivity, undermining employment, reducing fiscal revenues for the state, deterring investment, and generating inflationary pressure (as the output of goods and services declines). Social and economic infrastructure in urgent need of investment is starved of resources; dispensaries are left without essential drugs, transport grinds to a halt from lack of fuel, and repairs and maintenance work are not carried out.

To these costs can be added the deterrent effect which mounting stocks of unpayable debt is likely to have on foreign investors. According to Northern governments, one of the reasons for not providing wide-ranging debt relief is that investment confidence will suffer. The fallacy in this argument is that there is unlikely to be any investor confidence in countries with massive and unpayable debt burdens. Investors are cautious people who know that governments trying to meet unrealistic debt repayments will be forced to raise taxes (some of which will fall on them), or print money (which will generate inflationary pressures). Under these circumstances foreign investors will stay away (as they have in Africa), and domestic investors will put money into short-term trading activities in the informal economy, or invest their capital out of the country.

Such considerations partly explain the failure of investment to recover in sub-Saharan Africa. In addition, devaluation has serious consequences for countries with large external debt problems, since it raises the costs of debt service payments. Thus debt overhang is a major obstacle to the realisation of two of the central aims of structural adjustment: to encourage investment and to make realistic currency alignments.

There is a further cost to severely-indebted countries in the diversion of scarce administrative and policy-making skills. It has been estimated that some 8000 debt-rescheduling negotiations took place between 1980 and 1992 in Africa alone.[22] Some of the most able civil servants in the region have thus been forced to waste their skills on negotiating the terms on which their country's unpayable debts will not be paid.

Bilateral and multilateral debt in low-income countries

The SILICs all carry an unsustainable debt burden. However, the nature of that burden varies from country to country, and this has important implications for the design of debt-relief measures.

Bilateral debt

Debt owed to official creditors accounts for the largest share of debt stock and repayment obligations. In 1994, this category represented 61 per cent of total debt stock for the SILICs, with the Paris Club of Western government creditors accounting for two-thirds of the total.[23] Countries of the former Soviet Union and some Latin American countries are significant official creditors, as well as major debtors in their own right. The stock of official debt has risen rapidly since the early 1980s, and it continues to increase for the reason outlined earlier: that is, non-payment on the part of debtors. At the end of 1992, interest payments capitalised in rescheduling accounted for more than half of the debt owed to the Paris Club by low-income countries. The growth in bilateral debt stock has been accompanied by a hardening in its terms, with a reduction in concessional debt. As a result, scheduled repayments are increasing. Projections for 1992-1997, show that sub-Saharan Africa, for example, is scheduled to pay four times as much on average as it paid official creditors in 1991.[24] Since most of this increase will be unpayable, it will be rescheduled and added to the ever-growing stock of debt, fuelling a cycle of increased repayment obligation, a further build-up of arrears, and higher future repayments.

Multilateral debt

The growing burden of official debt repayments reflects the willingness of official creditors to tolerate a build-up of arrears. In fact, it is a willingness enforced by the growing demands of multilateral debt, owed to the World Bank, the IMF, and regional development banks. In

Figure 6.5 Proportion of debt by creditor category

Long term debt outstanding 1994 (total $171 886 m)

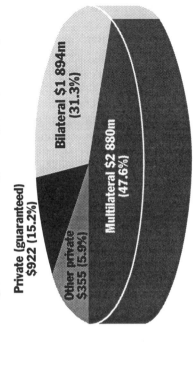

Multilateral $44 332m (25.8%)

Bilateral $100 078m (58.22%)

Private (guaranteed) $23 164 (13.47%)

Other private $4 312 (2.5%)

Long term debt servicing 1994 (total $6 051m)

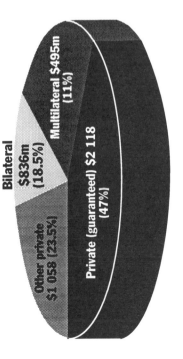

Bilateral $1 894m (31.3%)

Multilateral $2 880m (47.6%)

Private (guaranteed) $922 (15.2%)

Other private $355 (5.9%)

Long term debt outstanding 1980 (total $43 401m)

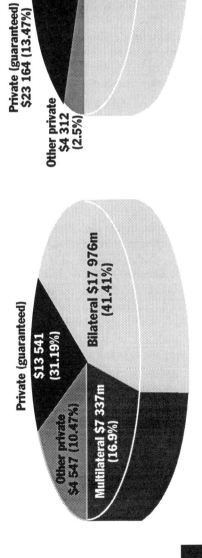

Private (guaranteed) $13 541 (31.19%)

Bilateral $17 976m (41.41%)

Other private $4 547 (10.47%)

Multilateral $7 337m (16.9%)

Long term debt servicing 1980 ($4 507m)

Bilateral $836m (18.5%)

Multilateral $495m (11%)

Other private $1 058 (23.5%)

Private (guaranteed) $2 118 (47%)

the early 1980s, multilateral debt represented a small fraction of the total debt stock of low-income countries. This picture began to change when the World Bank and the IMF increased their lending during the debt crisis. The stock of multilateral debt owed by SILICs has more than quadrupled since 1982 to $49bn, one quarter of their total debt stock.[25] Because multilateral agencies are preferred creditors and have first call on repayments, they absorb an even higher share (roughly half) of debt service payments. In many SILICs, payments to multilateral creditors leave governments with no capacity to service bilateral debt, hence the increasing arrears.[26]

The rapid build-up of obligations to multilateral creditors has created problems at two levels. First, it has contributed to the growing problem of arrears on bilateral debt, creating an ever more unsustainable debt position for a growing number of countries. Second, the recycling of multilateral debt is diverting a large amount of development assistance from poverty alleviation programmes to debt servicing. For example, the World Bank has provided International Development Association (IDA) soft loans, financed by grants from Northern governments, to enable countries to repay hard loans falling due to the International Bank for Reconstruction and Development (IBRD). IDA is the major source of development finance for low-income countries; but a significant proportion of its funds are now being recycled. IDA lent $2.7bn to SILICs in 1994, $1.9bn of which returned to the World Bank in the form of debt-service repayments.[27] Given the desperate financial plight of these countries and their need for reconstruction finance, such transfers are clearly inadequate.

This is especially true for countries with substantial repayment obligations to the IBRD, including Tanzania, Kenya, Honduras, Nicaragua, Bolivia, Jamaica, and Honduras (all of whom paid more than 5 per cent of their export earnings on IBRD repayments in 1992).[28] In 1993, repayments on hard loans from the World Bank cost Honduras $89m —

equivalent to almost one-quarter of total debt repayments in that year. Donors have supported World Bank efforts to reduce the overhang of IBRD debt by providing supplementary finance for its 'Fifth Dimension' programme, under which repayments to IDA are used to cover the costs of interest payments on IBRD debt. This is clearly preferable to imposing unrealistic demands on developing countries. But it is yet another example of aid budgets being diverted to finance the IBRD.

In contrast to the World Bank, which has at least maintained a positive transfer of resources to the low-income countries, the IMF has contributed to the drain of resources from low-income countries. In 1986, the Fund created its Structural Adjustment Facility (SAF) to enable countries to repay loans falling due on its extended fund facility credits (which carried market interest rates) advanced in the early 1980s. These were repayable over ten years, with payments beginning after five, at 0.5 per cent rates of interest. By 1988, these SAF loans were running out, so the IMF requested donor support for an Enhanced Structural Adjustment Facility. The new facility combined interest rate subsidies with new loans on terms similar to the SAF, in an effort to facilitate debt repayments. In contrast to the IDA, however, where repayments start after ten years and do not have to be concluded for 40, SAF and ESAF have refinanced only 40 per cent of debt repayments to the IMF by low-income countries.[29]

The consequence of this complicated picture of borrowing from Peter to pay Paul is that, since the mid-1980s, the IMF has been receiving more in the form of payments on past debts from the world's poorest countries than it has been providing in new loans. For sub-Saharan Africa, the net transfer to the IMF has amounted to $3.8bn since 1987: a huge burden in view of the region's chronic trade and financial problems.[30] One of the worst affected countries is Uganda, where repayments to the IMF will exceed $200 million for the period 1993/94-1997-98. By the latter year, payments to the IMF will account for over one-third of total debt-service and represent 20 per cent of export earnings. This comes on top of a negative transfer of resources to the IMF of $90m for the period 1987-1990.[31]

Estimates of the number of countries facing acute problems in relation to their multilateral creditors vary. However, taking a ceiling of 10 per cent of scheduled debt service payments for multilateral creditors, one study suggests that as many as 21 SILICs and around five middle-income countries are facing difficulties. The study concludes: 'From being the solution as lenders of last resort for new money between 1982 and 1985, multilateral lenders have now become the problem for most indebted countries.'[32]

Multilateral debt obligations are making a mockery of efforts to provide longer-term development finance. In effect, donor money provided by the World Bank under IDA is simply crossing 19th Street in Washington, to the accounts of the IMF. Meanwhile, donors are using their bilateral aid budgets to facilitate repayments to the IMF and to assist the World Bank in reducing IBRD obligations. The absurdity of existing arrangements for debt recycling is graphically illustrated by the case of Zambia. In 1993, the international donor community provided the equivalent of $110 for every Zambian through aid budgets intended to promote poverty reduction and long-term development. Out of that sum, around $70 went straight into the accounts of multilateral creditors, partly to finance $100m in repayments on past debts owed to the IMF.

Towards a resolution of the debt crisis

The protracted nature of the debt crisis in low-income countries is a testament to the failure of Northern governments to develop coherent strategies for debt reduction. Reform measures have been half-hearted and ill-conceived, reflecting a concern to maximise repayments rather than minimise the social and economic disruption caused by debt. Even under the most

favourable debt-reduction options currently available, the majority of SILICs would continue to face unsustainable debt burdens.[33]

Below we outline a strategy for reducing the official and multilateral debt burden of the world's poorest countries. Such a strategy would offer the prospect for sustainable recovery and release resources for investment in human development. Creditors have a responsibility to share in the burden of debt reduction, not least since so many of the loans which brought about today's debt burdens were as irresponsibly lent as they were spent. However, creditors and debtors alike share a responsibility for ensuring that debt reduction is linked to the attainment of objectives for improving human welfare. For most countries, these objectives have been established under National Plans of Action for realising the goals set by the World Summit for Children. In Oxfam's view debt reduction provisions should be tied to agreements which ensure that a proportion of the new financial resources which will be available to governments will be devoted to human investment in areas identified in National Plans of Action.

Official debt

Until 1994 the rescheduling of official debt owed to the Paris Club was carried out under the Enhanced Toronto Terms. These allowed for the reduction by half of the debt stock responsible for interest repayments falling due within 12 to 18 month rescheduling periods. The resulting savings for debtors were minimal, since the stock of debt involved was small, resulting in savings of less than 2 per cent on repayments.[34] Along with other NGOs, Oxfam supported as a step in the right direction efforts by the British Government to extend the terms of debt relief to cover the entire debt stock of countries, and to increase to two-thirds the amount of debt eligible for write-off.

Under the 1994 Naples Terms, named after the site of the Group of Seven meeting which agreed them, the Paris Club has broadly agreed to the UK's proposal. It has also accepted that for countries facing 'exceptional problems', higher levels of debt write-off are necessary. Under the new terms, countries with a per capita income of less than $500 or a debt-to-export ratio exceeding a fixed ceiling will now be eligible for debt reduction of 67 per cent, provided they have remained in compliance with IMF programmes for a minimum of three years. This is an improvement. However, the Naples Terms are inadequate in a number of respects.

Most obviously, the debt reduction element is too small to restore the majority of SILICs to a position of financial solvency. Nicaragua, for example, owes only one-quarter of its debt to Paris Club members, but it has no capacity to service that debt in view of its obligations to multilateral creditors. For countries in this position the decision of the Paris Club marginally to increase the average rate of debt reduction is a matter of almost total irrelevance, since it will merely slow the rate at which the mountain of unpayable arrears increases. In situations such as this, where debt-service ratios are clearly untenable even under the most favourable rescheduling terms, there should be an automatic write-off of between 85 per cent and 100 per cent of debt stock.

Another problem with the Paris Club approach is the requirement that countries maintain a three-year programme with the IMF to become eligible for debt relief. This rule is arbitrary and inequitable in the extreme, especially for countries which have pursued sensible macro-economic policies without recourse to the Fund. Countries such as Tanzania, which has periodically broken off its programmes with the Fund, or which adopted ESAF programmes after 1992, will not be immediately eligible for full reduction of debt stock. Moreover, the generalised failure of IMF programmes suggests the need for donors to investigate more flexible criteria.

But perhaps the most serious flaw in current approaches to debt relief is that they do not address the debt problems of low-income countries in an integrated manner. In part, this is because creditors have refused to address, or even acknowledge, the problem of multilateral

debt; and in part because of the anachronistic conventions which are embedded in Paris Club approaches to debt reduction.[35] One such convention is the application of a 'cut-off' date for the stock of debt eligible for rescheduling and reduction. Debt contracted after that date, which usually coincides with the first visit of the country in question to the Paris Club, cannot be reduced. Since several countries accumulated a large proportion of their debt after their first visit to the Paris Club, the benefits of the Naples Terms will be limited.

The shortcomings of present debt reduction strategies were illustrated early in 1995 when the Paris Club dealt with Uganda's debt problems under the new Naples Terms. Because Uganda's cut-off date was fixed in the early 1980s, only about a quarter of its official debt stock was eligible for rescheduling. The multilateral debt stock, which accounts for the bulk of Uganda's repayments, was excluded from the operation. The end result was that Uganda's total debt stock was reduced under the Naples Terms by less than 3 per cent: a sum which will have a negligible impact on financial transfers. Once again, a more sensible approach would have been to write-off Uganda's entire debt to the Paris Club — an option which was ruled out by the IMF's insistence that the country was not facing liquidity problems!

Three measures are urgently required to enhance official debt reduction measures:

- For most countries, including the vast majority of the SILICs, debt write-offs in the range of 90 per cent to 100 per cent of the entire debt stock are needed. Similar terms should be considered on a case-by-case basis for chronically indebted middle-income countries, such as Jamaica.
- Cut-off dates should be adjusted with a view to maximising the benefits from debt relief, rather than, as happens at present, minimising the costs to donors.
- The linkage between debt relief and adherence to an IMF programme should be broken, with the Paris Club agreeing more appropriate and flexible rules for eligibility.

Multilateral debt

Uganda's problems typify a wider failure on the part of Northern governments and the international financial institutions they control to address the issue of multilateral debt. The received wisdom is that multilateral debt cannot be reduced without jeopardising the stability of the global financial system. (Similar arguments were frequently deployed on behalf of commercial banks during the 1980s, until they were forced, partly by the IMF and World Bank, to accept market realities.) Today, the damaging role of multilateral debt must be recognised and dealt with in a constructive and flexible fashion.[36] That debt is diverting development assistance on an unacceptable scale and undermining investment and prospects for economic recovery.

The international financial institutions themselves have acknowledged the need for formal debt reduction, through their various programmes for debt recycling. Some of these programmes — such as the World Bank's 'Fifth Dimension' scheme and measures to reduce IBRD debt through IDA transfers — have been relatively successful. Others — notably the IMF's arrangements — have been an almost unmitigated failure. It is high time for a new framework for multilateral debt management to be devised. This should include the complete withdrawal of the IMF from financial involvement with SILICs. These countries need long-term development finance provided on IDA terms, rather than short-term balance-of-payments support.

While the Fund has a potentially valuable advisory role to play in important areas of economic management, it is not a development agency, and it continues to provide finance on inappropriate terms. To make matter worse, the Fund has acquired through its concessional lending facilities a policy influence which is incommensurate with its negative financial contribution and inconsistent with the needs of low-income countries. The conditions attached to ESAF are among the most stringent in any area of multilateral finance, with loan releases based upon the attainment of short-term monetary targets monitored on a quarterly basis. Even if the conditions were more appropriate and more flexibly applied, such an influence would be disproportionate to the Fund's financial stake in most indebted countries.

The ultimate aim of a debt strategy for the IMF should be the conversion of its outstanding debt stock in SILICs into IDA terms, and its transfer to IDA accounts. Currently, most Northern governments and the IMF itself rule out any move in this direction, claiming that the Fund does not have the authority to write-off resources which belong to its members. All that is required to give it that authority, however, is a political decision on the part of Northern governments. The alternative for these governments is to continue transferring aid resources to the IMF, which is an option likely to damage the credibility of their aid programmes. In any case, now that bilateral development assistance budgets are coming under increasing pressure, there is little prospect of sufficient aid resources being found to resolve the problem of multilateral debt through aid transfers.

Fortunately, there are simple alternatives to proceeding down the present route. Northern governments and the IMF have consistently over-stated the difficulties of reducing multilateral debt. Essentially, the problem is one of accountancy rather than financial credibility, involving financial provisions against non-payment on outstanding debt. That problem could be resolved in one of two ways: by transferring resources from outside the Fund (i.e. continuing to divert aid), or generating them from within. In Oxfam's view, the latter option is preferable.

Two mechanisms are available. The first is to authorise the IMF to issue a new tranche of Special Drawing Rights (the reserve currency which the Fund holds in trust for its members). There is now broad agreement that this is long overdue, but there is some disagreement over the size of the issue needed. The IMF itself has proposed an increase in SDRs by the equivalent of $40bn. Less than 10 per cent of this would be required to write-down the costs of all IMF debt in sub-Saharan Africa (excluding Nigeria). The other option would be to generate resources for the same purpose by selling off part of the IMF's gold stocks, which are now an insignificant part of its asset base. One variant of this proposal has been advocated by the British Government, which wants the Fund to sell part of its gold stocks, invest the proceeds, and use the resulting revenue to subsidise repayments to the IMF.[37] The overall objective of the UK proposal is to soften the terms of ESAF, rather than facilitate a more ambitious reduction in debt stock. However, the principles upon which it is based could provide a framework for more radical moves towards debt reduction.

Although the World Bank has dealt with IBRD debt more effectively than the IMF has dealt with repayments on its hard loans, it could do more. In particular, it could use some of the IBRD's extensive reserves, now amounting to more than $17bn, to finance the conversion of all remaining IBRD principal and interest repayments owed by SILICs (with the exception of Nigeria and a handful of other countries) into IDA terms. The argument that this would undermine the financial position of the World Bank is untenable, since the sums involved account for no more than $2.5bn. The World Bank could also review the position of middle-income debtors facing problems with the IBRD more sympathetically. Jamaica, for example, could derive major benefits from relatively modest reductions in its obligations to the IBRD. Considering the depth of the country's poverty and its financial plight it is certainly in need of such action, which should not be ruled out by rigid classification criteria.

Regional development banks, such as the Africa Development Bank(ADB) and the Inter-American Development Bank (IDB), figure prominently in the problems of some chronically indebted countries. The management of the ADB made serious mistakes in continuing to lend on hard terms, long after it was clear that countries would be unable to pay. The result is that several countries, including Cameroon, Tanzania, and Uganda, now face unrealistic repayment obligations. These countries need to receive concessional finance through the ADB's soft-loan facility, which is seriously under-funded by donors.

Development assistance

The importance of aid is both exaggerated and understated. It is exaggerated because human welfare in poor countries is influenced far more by the external trade environment, debt, and domestic policies than by international development assistance. By creating market opportunities through trade and writing-off debt, Northern governments could do more to enhance human welfare than they could ever achieve through their aid budgets. At the same time, the importance of aid is understated because its significance goes beyond its financial value to recipients. It has the potential both to bring about positive change and to do more harm than good.

The unequal power relationship between donor and recipient can distort local priorities and undermine local capacities. For example, the provision of expert advice to design a health-care system may reduce the incentive for governments to develop their own health expertise. Moreover, despite stated commitments to poverty reduction, and the promotion of sustainable development, the aid policies of donors are also shaped by other factors, including strategic interests and commercial considerations. Yet these inherent contradictions do not add up to an argument against providing much-needed development assistance to poor countries; rather, they underline the importance of ensuring that aid is used effectively to enhance local capacity to tackle poverty.

Aid quantity

At almost $69bn in 1993, official development finance from bilateral and multilateral agencies represents around 40 per cent of the net flow of resources from the OECD countries to developing countries.[38] Globally, aid represents a small proportion of the developing world's income, but is of considerable significance for many low-income countries. As a group, these countries receive about half of their external finance in the form of aid. For some regions the share is much higher; in sub-Saharan Africa aid flows represent on average 13 per cent of national income. These flows play a critical role in facilitating imports, supporting public investment and, increasingly, repaying debt. Without international development assistance, many countries would lack the resources needed for reconstruction and to improve human welfare.

For this reason, recent trends in aid flows represent a source of considerable concern. The deep cuts in bilateral aid transfers recorded in 1993-1994 could mark a watershed in overseas development assistance. After more than 20 years of steady if unspectacular growth, bilateral aid from the 21 OECD countries providing development assistance fell by 6 per cent in real terms (adjusted for inflation), with aid grants to (non-African) low-income countries falling by 25 per cent.[39] In its annual review of aid flows for 1994, the Development Assistance Committee of the OECD put a highly optimistic interpretation on this reduction, suggesting that it was 'a bout of weakness, rather than an incipient collapse' in aid provision. It is difficult to share this sanguine view. Several major donors drastically reduced their aid budgets in 1993, blatantly disregarding pledges to move towards the target of 0.7 per cent of GNP in the process.

The US, one of the countries most distant from the UN target, reduced its aid expenditure by 19 per cent. With conservative Republicans in control of both houses of the US Congress for the first time in 40 years, the foreign aid programme is being subject to intense scrutiny. Proposals before the early 1995 session of Congress include substantial reductions in development assistance to the global South. Some would achieve these by virtually eliminating aid to Africa and concentrating the foreign aid programme on areas of strategic interest, such as the Middle East, and Russia and the CIS.

Another proposal, put forward by Senator Jesse Helms, perhaps the most radical of the critics of foreign aid, would eliminate the US Agency for International Development, incorporating some of its activities in the State Department and establishing a quasi-independent foundation to fund long-term development activities. While the idea of replacing the USAID bureaucracy with a funding agency is intriguing, the implications of Helms' proposal for the levels of US develop-ment assistance are not yet clear. Helms has been a fierce critic of the US foreign aid programme, and it is assumed in Washington that his proposed International Development Foundation would have fewer resources for poverty alleviation programmes than USAID currently allocates. Helms would also ask the Foundation over time to generate its resources from private sources. In other words, he is proposaing the gradual privatisation of the development programme of the supposed leader of the world's democracies.

Elsewhere, official aid budgets are also being squeezed. The Australian government withdrew a commitment to raising its aid budget to 0.4 per cent of GDP by 1995. In Canada, overseas development aid as a percentage of GNP is down to 0.34 pcr cent from a high of 0.49 per cent in 1991-92 and, based on government projection, the level is expected to fall to 0.3 per cent by 1997-98. In the last six years, the ratio between defence and aid expenditures has become more and more unfavourable to aid: while the defence budget will fall by 4.9 per cent from a base of $11.9bn in 1994-95, the reduction in aid by 15 per cent from a base of approximately $2.5bn is much more severe. The voluntary sector has received a disproportionate amount of the cut, and since 1991-92 has been cut by 28 per cent. In Europe, lower contributions from EU member-states to the European Development Fund (EDF), the second largest source of concessional finance for Africa, will be cut by 5 per cent between 1994/95 and 1997/98. The British bilateral aid programme for Africa is projected to fall by about 17 per cent over the same period.

To add to this gloomy prospect, both Britain and Germany have made it clear that they will reduce their contribution to the European Development Fund, which contributes one-quarter of the EDF's $13.2bn, when existing pledges run out in 1998 In Germany, the finance ministry wants to cut contributions by 30 per cent before that date.[40] This raises the spectre of sub-Saharan Africa having one of its main aid lifelines cut at a time when the region is being bypassed by private capital flows.

There are some exceptions to the overall downward trend. For example, in 1993 the government of Ireland reversed a seven-year trend with a decision to increase Ireland's Official Develop-ment Assistance by 0.05 per cent of GNP annually to achieve the UN goal of 0.7 per cent of GNP, with further substantial increases in 1994 and 1995. But for most major donors, significant cuts in future aid spending look likely.

It must be stressed that future reductions will occur against a backdrop of already inadequate aid provision, in which hopes of achieving the UN aid target of 0.7 per cent of GNP are beginning to appear increasingly illusory. In 1993/1994, the industrial countries collectively provided 0.30 per cent of their GNP in aid, the lowest level recorded for two decades. At the same time, new demands on aid budgets are reducing the resources available for investment in long-term development.

The most important of these demands derives from conflict-related emergencies, diverting a growing proportion of development assistance into humanitarian relief. In 1988, less than 3 per cent of bilateral aid was spent on emergencies and relief; today, it is 11 per cent. Several donors, notably Austria, now allocate a substantial

proportion of their aid budgets to domestic programmes for refugees, even though these programmes were previously financed under other budget heads. Such measures reduce the resources available for poverty reduction in developing countries, as does the use of part of the aid budget for debt rescheduling. In 1992, this represented over 2 per cent of official development assistance.

While the resources available for poverty reduction programmes have been falling, the number of claimants recognised as eligible or potentially eligible for aid has been rising. Aid disbursements to Central and Eastern European countries and newly-independent states of the former Soviet Union stood at $7bn in 1994: equivalent to around 12 per cent of aid to developing countries.[41] There is some debate over whether, as governments claim, these resources have been additional to existing aid budgets. What is clear is that, when resources are scarce, choices have to be made over their allocation — and that donors have chosen to find resources for development in Eastern Europe, but not to increase their development assistance to low-income countries.[42]

The failure of aid

Increased aid is not in itself a panacea for poverty. If it were, sub-Saharan Africa would be well on the road to social and economic recovery. Since the early 1980s, Africa's share of the total development assistance budget has increased from 27 per cent to 37 per cent. More than $200bn in aid has been poured into the region, representing a higher share of regional income than even the transfers from the US to Europe under the post-war Marshall Plan. Yet economic recovery has proved elusive, and human welfare indicators continue to worsen. What lessons can be learnt from Africa's experience?

Firstly, and most obviously, aid flows cannot compensate for a dramatically worsening external trade and financial environment. Large as the transfers to Africa have been, they are much smaller than the losses the region has suffered from deteriorating terms of trade.

Secondly, the effectiveness of aid is reduced when it becomes a mechanism for financing debt repayments rather than development. In 1993, sub-Saharan Africa received $18bn in overseas development assistance, but half of it went straight back out in the form of debt servicing. As the demands of multilateral creditors have grown, aid has increasingly been reduced to a mechanism for recycling debt, rather than alleviating poverty.

Thirdly, the effectiveness of aid is determined partly by the wider policy environment. Aid is not effective where civil strife undermines the security needed for long-term development. Nor is it effective where economic policies are flawed. In this respect, Africa has suffered from the worst of all worlds. Bad domestic government (the maintenance of over-valued exchange rates, a failure to pursue coherent budgetary policies, and corruption), and structural adjustment programmes, which have placed an undue emphasis upon market deregulation and deflation, have seriously undermined the effectiveness of aid. So, too, has the absence in many countries of the institutional capacity needed to utilise aid effectively, and to prevent it from ending up in the foreign bank accounts of local elites. Unless these wider issues are addressed, public disillusionment with aid for Africa is likely to deepen over the coming years, with potentially disastrous effects on the lives of African people.

Aid quality

Most aid donors in the industrialised world declare poverty reduction to be among the primary purposes of their aid. For example, the British Government, in a 1994 report to Parliament, states that: 'It is right that a part of the nation's wealth should be used to help poorer countries and their peoples improve the standard of their lives.' [43]Such phrases could be drawn in abundance from almost any of the glossy brochures in which governments publi-

cise their aid programmes. References to protecting the environment, enhancing the position of women, protecting human rights, and improving health and education, are also widely cited as aims for aid. But unfortunately, aid programmes seldom reflect the rhetoric used to describe them. Spending priorities show little evidence of a commitment to poverty reduction. Nor is there any evidence of the sustained political commitment to poverty reduction which will be required from governments if rhetoric is to become reality.

There are three questions which must be asked in any assessment of the impact of aid on poverty reduction:

- Is aid sufficiently oriented towards the countries in which poverty is most concentrated?
- Is it sufficiently targeted on priority areas most likely to benefit the poor?
- Are resources used efficiently, or wasted in an effort to promote commercial advantage?

Country allocation

One of the major reasons for the inadequate poverty focus of aid programmes is that resources are not concentrated in countries where they are most needed. According to the UNDP, donors send less than one-third of development assistance to the ten most populous countries, in which two-thirds of the world's poor people live; the poorest 40 per cent of the population of the developing world receive less than half as much aid per capita as the richest 40 per cent.[44] One of the reasons why aid may tend to be concentrated on better-off and middle-income countries is that they have greater absorptive capacity for aid, and are better equipped to negotiate effectively. This points to the necessity of building up absorptive capacity in the poorer countries.

Of course, geographical spending patterns and country allocations provide only a rough measure of aid quality; just because aid is spent in a poor country does not guarantee it is well spent. And countries with average incomes substantially higher than the poorest countries often have levels of poverty which are as widespread and as deep as in the poorest countries. Between them, Brazil and Mexico have more people living in absolute poverty than sub-Saharan Africa, even though their incomes are higher. Despite these provisos, there is a correlation between the effectiveness of aid in poverty reduction, and its allocation to the countries where poverty is most pervasive.

Judged on the basis of this criterion, the British aid programme compares favourably with other OECD countries, with around 80 per cent of total expenditure being directed towards low-income and the poorest middle-income countries. The US programme, by contrast, appears to be governed more by a concern to support strategic allies than to reduce poverty. Between them Israel and Egypt absorb over half the US aid budget, being provided with over $5bn annually; three times the US aid budget for the whole of sub-Saharan Africa.[45] This generosity is a recognition of their adherence to the Camp David agreement and their support for US foreign policy in the region. Israel, where (outside of the Palestinian community) poverty is negligible, receives $626 per person. By contrast, Peru receives $30 per person, even though average incomes are one-twelfth of those in Israel, and seven million people live in absolute poverty.

The US aid budget reflects, in stark form, the subordination of poverty reduction objectives in aid provision to 'national security' considerations. During the Cold War, such considerations resulted in a bizarre distribution of aid, which was seen largely as an instrument for pursuing strategic interests. Hopes that the end of superpower rivalry would improve matters have so far been only partially realised. High military spenders, notably in the Middle East, continue to receive disproportionate amounts of aid, part of which is designed to maintain markets for military exports. Aid to Eastern Europe and the former Soviet Union is similarly seen in strategic terms by most donors.

Measured in terms of the country allocation of its spending, the World Bank's International Development Association (IDA) can lay claim to being one of the better-focused mechanisms for development assistance. Virtually all IDA spending, which amounted to $5.5bn in 1994, is concentrated on low-income countries, compared with around half for bilateral development assistance. IDA funds are almost equally divided between Africa and Asia. For sub-Saharan Africa, IDA is now the major source of long-term development finance and balance of payments support. However, there are many problems associated with IDA lending. Projects financed by IDA have resulted in the forcible displacement of local communities, and environmental damage; and a significant proportion of IDA lending is tied to structural adjustment programmes, and through them to IMF conditionalities, undermining IDA's capacity to support poverty reduction. Despite this, any reduction in IDA flows would have severe consequences for many low-income countries, especially at a time when bilateral aid budgets are being reduced. Moves by some donors, notably the US, to scale-down their support for the three-year replenishment of IDA represents a serious threat to international poverty reduction efforts.

Aid and human priorities

Even where aid is spent in poor countries, it typically lacks a poverty focus. Bilateral donors collectively spend only 7 per cent of their aid budgets on priority areas such as primary health, basic education, water and sanitation provision, and nutrition programmes.[46] Even when aid is spent on health and education services, it tends to fund schemes that disproportionately benefit the better-off. For instance, Britain's Overseas Development Administration (ODA) claims that it spends about one-third of its aid budget on areas of basic needs, such as health and education. In fact, however, less than one-fifth of the 1992 aid budget for education was directed towards primary education, with the bulk of the remainder going to universities, technology centres, and secondary education.[47]

Given the critical importance of primary education in social and economic development, and in enhancing opportunities for women, this represents a misallocation on a huge scale. Most aid donors have endorsed in principle the conclusion reached by the 1990 Jomtien conference on Education for All that education expenditure should be oriented towards basic education. Yet these donors spend only about 1 per cent of their aid budgets in this area.[48] For every dollar of aid spent on primary school children in Africa during the 1980s, $575 was spent on university students.[49] Such expenditure patterns are clearly not consistent with the objective of achieving a basic level of education for 80 per cent of children by the year 2000, as agreed at the 1990 World Summit for Children. Yet there is little sign of donors changing their priorities.

It is a depressingly similar story in other areas.[50] For poor households, inadequate provision of water and sanitation is a major cause of exposure to water-borne diseases, and a demand on the physical strength and labour time of women who collect water. Yet water supply and sanitation for urban areas receives four times as much development assistance as for rural areas, and much of it goes to providing relatively high-cost tap water to private homes.[51]

Primary health care systems are at the forefront of the fight against poverty. Public provision in this area reduces the incidence of debilitating diseases which affect people's ability to make a livelihood. Without well-run primary health care facilities, women are denied the opportunity to control their own fertility, with adverse consequences for their own and their children's health, and their own opportunities for education and employment. They are also exposed to unnecessary risks during pregnancy and their children are more likely to die. Along with investment in women's education, investment in their health is the most important factor in reducing infant and maternal mortality rates, and in reducing family sizes and demographic pressure. And investment in health promotion is by far the most efficient form of health

finance, both because it brings benefits to more people; and because it is cheaper to prevent disease than to cure it. Yet donors continue to regard investment in primary health care as a peripheral concern. The primary health care facilities which could prevent or treat 80 per cent of the diseases afflicting poor people receive 1 per cent of international aid flows.[52]

Most donors continue to fund teaching hospitals, which provide high-cost services to relatively prosperous urban populations. Japan, for example, spent over one-third of its aid health budget on teaching hospitals in the late 1980s.[53] The failure to develop a poverty-focused aid programme has been particularly evident in the case of Japan, which is the second-largest OECD donor. It reflects the conviction of successive Japanese governments that economic growth achieved through export-oriented industrialisation will 'trickle down' to the poor. Sectorally, Japan has given priority to supporting large-scale economic infrastructure in areas such as power, transportation, and large dams. Investment in areas such as basic education, water supply, and primary health accounts for only around one-fifth of Japanese aid. The country's aid programme also has a bad record in relation to the environment and the protection of people's land rights, as shown in its support for the Sardar Sarovar Dam in India and the Koto Pandjang Dam in Indonesia.

It seems that aid donors, like recipient governments, have an in-built preference for investing scarce resources in areas where the social and economic returns to society are lowest. As we have pointed out elsewhere, the rapid social and economic development of the high-performing countries of South-East Asia was achieved, in part, through a concentration of government welfare expenditure at the lowest levels. That investment brought immediate benefits to people's lives. It also brought longer-term economic benefits and helped to facilitate the relatively equitable distribution of the benefits of economic growth. The contrast between the approach of governments in

Figure 6.6 Official aid from donor countries, 1993, showing percentage for social priority areas

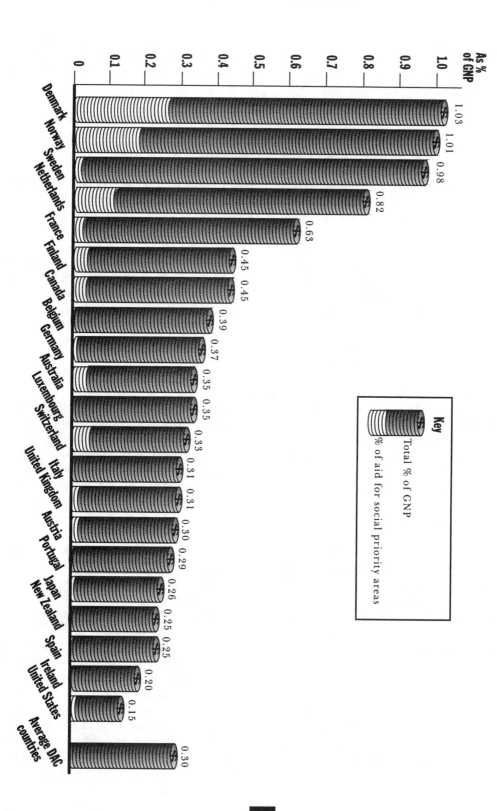

SOURCE: OECD/UNDP

South-East Asia and aid donors is stark and instructive. While the former concentrated on efficient provision for the poor, the poorly-targeted aid programmes of the latter have failed to help the poor. Without a change in priorities which brings aid practice into line with poverty-reduction objectives, resources funnelled through government aid agencies will continue to make at best a marginal contribution to improving human welfare.

Spreading aid thinly

The wide geographical spread of aid budgets is another factor affecting their quality. Several OECD donors, including the EU, Canada, and the UK, provide assistance to over a hundred countries. Britain provided bilateral assistance to 135 countries in 1991-92, with 80 per cent going to 20 recipients.[54] Although such a spread might bring commercial advantages and influence, few donors have the capacity or the expertise to maintain coherent aid programmes in dozens of different countries; nor do they have the means to undertake effective monitoring.

To make matters worse, donor co-ordination within countries is often weak, leading to duplication and waste. From the point of view of developing countries, dealing with multiple donors (whether official or NGOs) imposes considerable demands in terms of the diversion of skilled administrators. Nepal receives aid from 19 bilateral donors and 13 multilateral donors, most of whom operate on different budget cycles and procedures.[55] In countries where there is an acute shortage of trained graduates in the civil service, it is impossible effectively to integrate aid into national strategies for poverty reduction. What often happens in practice, especially in the poorest countries, is that donors themselves assume financial and administrative responsibility for large areas of policy. In order to maximise the effectiveness of development assistance in reducing poverty and assisting states to use aid effectively, there is a strong case for improved donor co-ordination and greater specialisation

both between countries, and between sectors within countries.

Aid and commercial self-interest

If the strategic foreign policy objectives of donors can conflict with the aim of poverty reduction, so too can the pursuit of commercial self-interest. Most aid donors use part of their budgets to promote exports by their own industries, linking aid contracts to domestic procurement. Some do so on a very large scale: around 75 per cent of British aid is tied to the purchase of British goods and technical assistance, one of the highest rates in the OECD.[56] In some cases, development assistance grants and loans are also added to commercial loans to fund part of the costs of tendering for projects, subsiding the commercial sector.

Donors tie aid for a variety of reasons: creating employment, promoting trade, cultivating new markets, and generating profits for business. The result is a vast diversion of public funds from poverty reduction. Because the tying of aid insulates donors from competitive pressures, developing countries end up paying above the market rate for goods and services. One recent estimate suggests that these extra costs to aid recipients represent more than 15 per cent of the aid provided. According to the World Bank, untying all aid flows would generate economic benefits to developing countries amounting to as much as $4bn per year, which is more than the entire UK aid budget.[57] The price inflation associated with aid tying represents a direct subsidy to exporters in the OECD companies, who constitute a formidably powerful lobby influencing aid priorities.

While tied aid is good news for exporters, it is bad news for just about everybody else, including the OECD tax-payers who finance aid budgets. Using public funds to create protected markets for subsidised exporters is a grossly inefficient form of investment. (It is also against the free market philosophy which OECD governments encourage the recipients of their aid to embrace.) In addition, tied aid may result in the purchase of inappropriate goods and services, as the choice will depend upon what is available in donor countries, rather than what is needed in developing countries. The clearest example is to be found in the provision of technical assistance. Of the roughly $12bn in development aid spent annually on training, project design, and consultancy, over 90 per cent is spent on foreign 'experts'.[58] Sub-Saharan Africa has probably received more bad advice per capita from such experts than any other region, and international agencies, from NGOs, to the World Bank and the UNDP, criticise technical advice as one of the least effective forms of assistance. It is often poorly planned and monitored, with little attention given to building capacity in developing countries.

The Aid Trade Provision

The hazards of aid-tying are illustrated by the Aid Trade Provision (ATP) of the UK's bilateral aid programme. According to the British Goverment, the ATP generates three times as much in earnings as it costs taxpayers to finance. It is supposed to support, in the words of the Minister for Overseas Development, 'sound projects that will contribute to sustainable development and which are of particular industrial and commercial importance to Britain'. Powerful industrial conglomerates have been instrumental in promoting the use of aid to win overseas contracts. The same conglomerates have received the lion's share of the benefits in the form of lucrative contracts, mainly for infrastructural projects such as power generation and construction.

Concern over the use of overseas aid to finance commercial activity was highlighted by a project to construct a hydro-electric power station on the Pergau river in Malaysia. This project was the largest ever financed under the ATP, at an estimated cost of £234m over 14 years. It illustrated in graphic form everything that is wrong with tied aid. An assessment of economic viability of the project carried out by the ODA concluded that there were cheaper and more efficient means of supplying energy,

and that the project was 'a very bad buy' for Malaysian consumers and British tax-payers alike.[59] In 1994, the former Permanent Secretary of the ODA told a parliamentary enquiry investigating the project that it had been an 'abuse of the aid system'. So why did the government choose to proceed? One reason, according to the account given by the Prime Minister, was that the project was viewed 'in the wider context of maintaining billions of pounds of British exports to Malaysia'.[60] Another reason was that the ATP provision was linked to a 1988 trade protocol, which provided for over $1bn of British arms exports to Malaysia.[61]

The Pergau affair underlined the dangers inherent in the commercialisation of aid budgets. At a time when aid to the poorest countries was falling, the government was willing to use more development assistance to promote, through an inefficient energy project, the commercial interests of UK companies, than it was providing through bilateral aid to the whole of Latin America. The linking of aid to military contracts was equally disturbing, not least since it represented a violation of the declared principles of the British aid programme, and was kept hidden from public scrutiny. Sadly, the Pergau affair was not an isolated example of waste and inefficiency. An evaluation of ODA-funded power projects in Bangladesh found that UK companies, supported by the ATP, had conspicuously failed to create demand for local suppliers, preferring to maximise imports of their own products. As in other areas, commercial interest rather than a poverty focus was allowed to dictate aid provision. In 1992, a review conducted under the auspices of the ODA concluded that the ATP was directing scarce aid resources into projects of questionable value, and away from the needs of the poorest countries and people; nor was it bringing substantial benefits for the British economy. The review summarised its findings in the following terms:

There have been benefits to the UK economy from the ATP scheme. These are difficult to quantify, but it is unlikely that the overall benefits of ATP which have accrued to the UK economy have matched its costs...ATP projects (also) had a less beneficial impact on recipient countries than other bilateral aid projects which had been evaluated, particularly when comparing success rates for projects in the same sectors and country.[62]

Phasing out tied aid

While some governments, including the UK government, have expressed a concern to reduce the level of aid-tying, progress towards this objective has been minimal. Under guidelines agreed in 1992, the OECD countries agreed that tied aid should not be used to support projects which were commercially viable in their own right.[63] Non-viable commercial projects remain eligible for aid support, provided they are 'sound from a development perspective'. Such guidelines could help to phase out the worst examples of aid-tying. In practice, however, they are sufficiently vague to allow for widespread abuse (for example, there are no clear criteria for judging a 'sound' development project). Another problem is that they appear to endorse the right of governments to avoid open tendering for development projects. In fact, donors are using their aid budgets to promote commercial interests in an increasingly aggressive manner. As the OECD's Development Assistance Committee has concluded:

There have also been changes in some facilities, from defensive to aggressive strategies, seeking commercial advantage rather than reacting to what are perceived as unfair competitive practices by others.[64]

As this statement suggests, all governments are now to some extent trapped in a problem of their own making, using aid subsidies to protect markets from competitors receiving subsidies in other OECD countries. The only way to deal with this problem will be to agree binding multilateral rules, under which all governments agree to phase out aid-trade tying in favour of competitive procurement practices.

Aid, human rights, and good governance

Since the early 1990s, aid donors have sought to use their financial influence to act as a catalyst for change in a wide range of policy areas. Conditions attached to aid now typically include measures to promote 'good governance' — a catch-all phrase which means different things to different donors. The 'good governance' menu includes such things as democratic pluralism, accountability and transparency in government, poverty reduction, respect for the rule of law and human rights, and movement towards a non-regulated economy. Disagreement between donors on the emphasis to be placed on different elements of this package and on how to monitor progress, has resulted in vague and confused messages being sent to Third World governments and citizens. 'Good governance' aspirations have been compromised by double standards, whereby donors demand stringent conditions from aid recipients but do not apply the same conditions to themselves; and, in some cases, the pursuit of mutually incompatible objectives.

An example of incompatibility is to be found in the requirements that developing country governments comply with structural adjustment programmes. However, the effect of many of these programmes has been to reduce state health and education provision, to exacerbate inequalities, and further marginalise poor people through inappropriate forms of market deregulation: the opposite of the objectives set for aid programmes. There appears to be little logic in donors financing primary health care provision in, say, Zambia or Pakistan, when governments there are slashing expenditure to meet budget targets set under the structural adjustment programmes, with which the same donors demand compliance. Despite this, unquestioning support for structural adjustment remains one of the pillars of bilateral and multilateral development assistance. An example of double standards is that structural adjustment programmes demand that developing country governments open up their markets; whereas Northern governments continue to keep theirs firmly closed.

Almost all donors stress the importance of using aid to foster civil and political rights, but ignore almost completely the promotion of economic, social, and cultural rights.[65] The Lomé Convention of the European Union, for example, requires human rights considerations to be taken into account in development co-operation with the African, Caribbean, and Pacific states. Proposals from the European Commission tabled during the mid-term review of Lomé 1V, the current agreement, sought to reinforce the linkage between human rights and development co-operation, which, it said, should be aimed at 'fostering democratic values, the rule of law and good governance'.

The Commission is attempting to establish more stringent conditions for monitoring progress in these areas, and to use European aid to encourage moves in the right direction. Unfortunately, different donors appear to have different and changeable standards for determining what the right direction might be. In 1992, the Dutch Government responded to the massacre of unarmed Timorese protestors by Indonesian troops by stopping aid. Other OECD donors, sensing the prospect of lucrative contracts, promptly stepped in to fill the gap. Britain, which had increased aid to Indonesia from £7m in 1986 to £21m in 1991, criticised the Dutch move on the grounds that it would undermine Europe's ability to influence the human rights performance of the Indonesian Government. By apparently allowing commercial considerations to outweigh human rights objectives, confusing signals are being sent as to the nature of 'good governance' conditionality.

Forceful measures to promote 'good governance' have been the exception rather than the rule. In Africa, the most notable exception is Kenya, where in 1992 donors publicly presented the government with an ultimatum to hold multi-party elections or face aid cuts. Widespread corruption and human rights abuse

were cited as additional reasons for using aid conditionality as a catalyst for change. In the event, the Kenyan government held elections and proceeded to finance its election campaign in part by using multilateral funds provided for development and printing money (in breach of its agreement with the IMF). Ethnic tensions were exploited to divide the opposition and secure re-election on the basis of a minority vote, after which the aid tap was turned back on and the government returned to power, with corruption and other malpractice continuing much as before. Once again, it is difficult to discern precisely what 'good governance' is supposed to mean when it is pursued in such a self-evidently contradictory manner.

Social conditionality

An area in which donors have been less inclined to enforce aid conditionality is poverty-oriented spending patterns. There is no evidence, for example, that governments which use scarce resources for large-scale military expenditure are less favourably treated than others. (Spending patterns suggest they are, if anything, *more* favourably treated.) Nor do governments which invest more resources in areas of social welfare provision of benefit to poor people receive greater support as a reward.

Can and should aid be used to put pressure on governments to reform their spending policies in favour of the poor? Oxfam believes that new forms of conditionality could help to bring about positive policy reforms. Instead of a broad sweep of incoherent objectives under a 'good governance' umbrella, some specific social policy objectives could be constructively pursued through a dialogue with governments over spending priorities. Governments and donors could, in principle, agree incremental steps for raising investment in primary health care, basic education, and the provision of water and sanitation. Such steps could be relatively easily facilitated through a financial partnership, in which governments and donors undertake joint commitments to meet agreed targets. The UNDP has argued for a new devel-

opment compact in which developing countries agree to raise their spending on social priority areas to 20 per cent of budgetary expenditure, and aid donors provide a similar proportion of their aid budgets for this purpose. This '20:20 compact' was broadly endorsed at the Social Summit in Copenhagen, although only as a vague and voluntary target.

Apart from providing tangible, measurable, and realisable policy objectives, such a contract would involve obligations on both sides, rather than the imposition of donor objectives on aid recipients. Most donors reject such an approach on the grounds that it would undermine the national sovereignty of developing country governments. They have been considerably less reluctant about eroding sovereignty in other areas; through their support for structural adjustment programmes, donors have obliged governments to impose fees for primary education and basic health facilities, to devalue their currencies, set interest rates at levels dictated by the IMF, privatise whole industries, and liberalise markets.

Measuring aid quality

Part of the problem with development assistance is that relatively little is known about the distribution of the benefits it brings, or its impact on the lives of poor people. The impact of investment in primary health care and primary education in countries and regions with high levels of poverty, is relatively easy to monitor. But is a power station a poverty reduction project? Not at first sight perhaps; but if it creates employment and provides electricity to poor people at affordable prices, and does not cause environmental damage, investment in power generation can bring important benefits to the poor.

For example, Britain's ODA has provided over £100 million for Greater Dhaka power distribution project in Bangladesh, the aim of which is to strengthen and extend the electrical power system in Dhaka. An initial evaluation of

the project conceded that it had not been targeted at groups in poverty.[66] However, it had created incidental, and largely accidental, spin-off benefits. Residents in some slum areas were provided with electricity, facilitating the expansion of home weaving and the recycling of waste scavenged by poor children. However, they were required to pay more than the official tariff to their landlords and other operators making their electricity connections. A genuinely poverty-focused approach would have attempted to consider the most effective ways of delivering electricity to poorer communities as part of the project design.

Setting aid priorities

To their credit, some donors are now attempting to develop more rigorous methods of evaluating the impact of their development assistance. In an effort to monitor how aid funds are allocated, the UK's ODA has established a Policy Information Marker System (PIMS), which is intended to measure performance against seven priority objectives.[67] These range from direct poverty reduction activities (for example, investment in child health and education) to enhancing productive capacity through infrastructural investment, and promoting market-based economic reforms. One problem with the PIMS approach is that it understates the impact of the British aid programme on poverty. Because investment in productive activity is not counted as 'poverty-reducing', its benefits or costs to the poor are not recorded.

A wider problem is that the impact of aid cannot be assessed against arbitrary categories which bear little relationship to the experience of poor people. 'Economic reform', to take one of the 'non-poverty-reducing' categories included under PIMS, is not neutral in its effects on the poor, and it has a direct bearing on the effectiveness of measures expressly designed to promote social welfare. Aid-based investment in primary health care counts for little where economic problems or changing budgetary priorities are contributing to the collapse of wider public investment in health.

The World Bank's poverty focus

The World Bank has been in the forefront of efforts to measure the effects of its programmes on poverty. Project lending is now measured partly against the extent to which it supports poverty reduction strategies. Where projects include specific mechanisms for identifying and reaching the poor, where the primary purpose is poverty reduction, or where the proportion of poor people participating in the projects significantly exceeds the proportion in the population as a whole, the World Bank now includes them in its 'Programme of Targeted Interventions' (PTIs).[68] In its assessment for 1993, the World Bank stated that 26 per cent of all lending fell into the PTI category, rising to 40 per cent for IDA. However, the extent to which these projects directly benefit the poor is less clear.

The same is true of structural adjustment programmes which are assessed against the criterion of whether or not they incorporate 'poverty-focused measures'. According to the World Bank, 24 of the 49 adjustment programmes agreed in 1992 and 1993 fell into this category.[69] All but one of the 1993 programmes were included partly because compliance with poverty-focused reforms was made a condition for releasing funds. The problem with the World Bank's evaluation criteria is that they take it as axiomatic that the introduction of free market reforms are poverty-reducing. Thus Côte d'Ivoire's adjustment programme merits inclusion under the 'poverty-focused' category because 'deregulation will help create jobs for young entrants into the labour force, as well as for the poorest segments of society.' In some cases deregulation has had precisely the opposite effect.

Another problem is that the evaluation procedures confuse the *terms* of adjustment agreements with their implementation. For example, the structural adjustment programme in Zimbabwe is counted as poverty-focused, partly on the grounds that it provided for the restoration of current expenditures on health and education as a condition for releasing funds. In the event, even though expenditure under both budget heads fell sharply under the adjustment programme, funds were released.

An agenda for aid reform

The ultimate measure of aid effectiveness must be whether it enhances the capacities of the poorest, their education and skills, their health, their ability to control their own lives, and their opportunities to develop secure livelihoods. These are the outcomes which the majority of people in the industrialised world want to see. It is a testimony to the depth of public support for development assistance that, even in the face of repeated evidence of misplaced donor priorities, 'aid fatigue' has yet to set in. Support will start to wane, however, unless governments embark on far-reaching reforms of development assistance.

These reforms should begin with the introduction of greater transparency. Aid funds which are at present devoted mainly to subsidising commercial exports, should be shifted to the budgets of more appropriate government departments, such as trade and industry. Where aid is used to finance military exports and achieve strategic foreign policy objectives, it should be transferred to the budgets of defence and foreign affairs departments. What remains in aid budgets should then be measured against the only valid criterion: is aid helping to empower people to improve their own lives and overcome the worst aspects of absolute poverty? Much of what currently passes for development assistance would fail this acid test. Yet donors have enormous scope for reallocating their aid, and could take immediate steps to earmark more funds for priority areas. Progress towards this objective should be monitored and publicised by the OECD's Development Assistance Committee, on the basis of detailed social priority spending accounts provided by donors.

Increasing the flow of aid

If aid is to make a positive contribution to poverty eradication into the next century, improvements in aid quality will need to be reinforced by increased and more secure flows of development finance. The 0.7 per cent target fixed by the UN remains relevant, and donors should establish firm time-tables for achieving this objective. At present, any moves in this direction will have to be voluntary. There is a powerful case, however, for introducing a more obligatory element into aid efforts, ensuring that the burden is distributed equitably and that annual flows are predictable.

One study has attempted to estimate the revenues which might be generated by a progressive international income tax on rich countries, rising from 0.20 per cent at the lowest average national income band, to 0.37 per cent at the highest.[70] Based on 1990 figures, the study found that such a tax would create more revenue than the aid contributed by OECD countries in that year. If the tax increased gradually to achieve an average transfer in line with the 0.7 per cent target, aid flows could double. Their real value would increase even more if the revenue from the tax were transferred in the form of grants, rather than the current mixture of grants and export credits; and if they were administered by an international authority under UN auspices which prohibited aid-tying. However, it is clear that the idea of taxing rich countries would be fiercely resisted, thus limiting its practicability.

Another option which merits serious consideration is the tax on international currency transactions proposed by Nobel Prize-winning economist James Tobin in 1978. Such a tax would act as a deterrent on the vast flows of speculative capital, currently estimated at $1 trillion per day, which are destabilising economies in the industrialised world and developing world alike. Clearly, any such tax would have to be supplemented by national and international action to bring financial markets under more effective control. But even levied at the most marginal rates, it would generate a major source of revenue with which to tackle global poverty, without taxing constructive economic activities.[71]

The multilateral system run by the Bretton Woods agencies, originally set up to transfer resources to low-income countries, is being subject to criticism from a variety of sources. Community organisations in the developing world and Northern NGOs point to the social and environmental failures associated with the policies of the agencies. From a different perspective, there is an increasingly influential lobby, represented by the Republican-dominated US Congress, which sees investment in development as a costly irrelevance and drain on resources. In the view of this lobby, private capital rather than public finance is the appropriate vehicle for transferring resources to developing countries. In a 1994 report outlining reform proposals for the Bretton Woods system, the influential Volcker Commission, chaired by the former US Federal Reserve chairman, argued for a decisive shift in the balance of World Bank activities, with the focus on investment in private sector development and the enhancement of private capital flows.[72]

There are serious dangers in such an approach. Many low-income countries will not for many years be able to obtain commercial financing for investment on the scale required for poverty eradication. For them, continued access to concessional IDA lending is vital, not least because it is untied. Without IDA funding, the poorest countries would be forced either to turn to commercial markets, borrowing on terms they are unable to afford, or to make do with more limited access to foreign exchange.[73] As it is, the limited resources available under IDA have forced some countries, such as India, to turn prematurely to commercial markets. It has also resulted in more stringent conditions for countries which are eligible for IDA support.

With IDA's three-yearly replenishment in doubt because of opposition in the US Congress, concessional resource flows are likely to decline; whereas what is needed is for IDA to be replenished, but with a much stronger and measurable focus on poverty-reduction; and an increase in the share of IDA in overall World Bank lending from its present base of 30 per cent. This increase might take the form of creating an intermediate facility which charges slightly higher interest rates for countries in less parlous financial circumstances. Even in countries which can afford to borrow on capital markets, private finance is unlikely to facilitate the social and infrastructural investment needed to sustain recovery.

Reform of the IMF

Reform of the IMF is equally urgent. The Fund was created to provide countries faced with foreign exchange shortages with the liquidity they needed to overcome temporary balance-of-payments problems. A new reserve asset, known as Special Drawing Rights (SDRs), was subsequently created to provide that liquidity, with governments effectively transferring part of their reserves to the IMF. These in turn could be used by governments facing balance-of-payments constraints, to help them to import what they needed to grow out of recession. In practice, the Fund's stock of SDRs has always been too small to enable it to perform this role,[74] and with new member countries in the former Soviet Union and Eastern Europe making new demands, they are now hopelessly inadequate.

The IMF's Managing Director, Michel Camdessus, has proposed a new issue of SDR's, amounting to more than $40bn.[75] This would help developing countries, many of whom face chronic foreign exchange shortages, to increase their own reserves without resorting to extreme deflationary measures or putting a brake on growth by cutting essential imports. Innovation in the way in which SDR quotas are distributed would also bring benefits. Under present arrangements, SDRs are allocated on the basis of a country's financial stake in the IMF, so that the richest countries get the largest share. Given that it is developing countries which have the greatest need for finance, the industrial countries could transfer some of their allocation. Once again, the IMF has tentatively proposed moves in this direction, but they have been rebuffed by the industrialised countries. Finance ministries in most of these countries continue to claim that any measure which increases international liquidity will generate inflation. After a period which has witnessed the lowest international commodity prices since the 1920s and with much of the world locked into deflationary policies, recession or slow recovery, this argument is untenable.

World Bank projects

The World Bank is the main source of finance for project-based lending in developing countries. Over the years its focus has gradually extended from infrastructural projects to a wide range of activities in industry, agriculture, and the social sector. The Bank has also adopted impressive social and environmental guidelines, intended to protect vulnerable communities from adverse effects. While the scope of the World Bank's activities make a comprehensive assessment of the effects of these guidelines impossible, Oxfam's experience suggests that, in many cases, they have not been translated into practice.[76]

Resettlement

In the face of mounting public pressure, the World Bank introduced a comprehensive resettlement policy in 1980 designed to protect the rights of displaced people. Where possible, displacement was to be avoided or minimised. Where it was inevitable, the World Bank pledged to ensure proper compensation for the communities affected and assistance for resettlement. However, problems in implementing the new policy were highlighted by the Narmada (Sardar Sarovar) dam project in India.

In 1992, the Morse Commission, set up to investigate problems with resettlement in the dam area, concluded: 'involuntary resettlement resulting from the Sardar Sarovar Projects

offends recognised norms of human rights.'
The report went on to criticise plans to displace
at least 100,000 people, in 245 villages, living in
the area affected by submersion. It noted that
the impact of canal systems, which would affect
a further 140,000 farmers, had largely been
ignored. But the most serious indictment was of
the Bank's internal procedures. The report
concluded that 'no adequate appraisals of
resettlement and rehabilitation, or of environmental impact' had been made, and that the
decision to proceed was taken 'on the basis of
extremely limited understanding of both
human and environmental impact, with inadequate plans in place and inadequate mitigative
measures under way'. Morse went on to criticise
World Bank staff in the India Department for
deliberately misleading Executive Directors
and Bank management in Washington on the
scale of resettlement, and on problems over
non-compliance with agreements.[77]

Other evidence suggests that this was not
simply an isolated example. Over the last seven
years alone, World Bank projects have forcibly
displaced 2.5 million people. In a recent review
of projects affecting about 2 million people over
the period 1986-1993, the World Bank admitted that virtually all of them had failed to ensure
that displaced people regained their former
standard of living. The World Bank review
acknowledged 'the potential for violating
people's individual and group rights makes
compulsory relocation unlike any other project
activity.' Yet it goes on to record serious under-
estimates of the numbers likely to be displaced.
In India, where Bank guidelines were seldom
applied, it admits 'the overall record is poor to
the extent of being unacceptable.' Some of the
problems were traced in the review to slack
project preparation by Bank staff, and lax
management attitudes. This resulted in clearance routinely being given to projects that did
not meet Bank safeguards, and the deferral of
action to remedy non-compliance by borrowers.[78] But a deeper problem, which the report
ignored, is the fact that these project failures
have continued without an effective response

from the Bank's Executive Directors, who have
systematically neglected to bring them to the
attention of national legislatures.

The World Bank has a better record than
many donors in evaluating its projects, and
pledging to learn from its mistakes. But in
Oxfam's experience it appears that the Bank
has done so with variable success. This has been
underlined by a new project to construct a
$770m dam in the remote and ecologically-
unique Arun valley in Nepal which threatens to
repeat the bad practices of the past, and could
produce irreversible damage. Relatively few of
the people living in the valley, who are from
diverse ethnic and cultural backgrounds, will
have to be relocated. But Nepali NGOs are
concerned that compensation rates for families
losing land are set too low, and that families are
being persuaded to accept cash instead of
replacement land. If this is the case, many will
be left destitute after a few years and forced to
leave. Nepali NGOs also fear severe social
dislocation caused by the building of roads and
arrival of construction workers. With the
opening of the road, forests will be accessible for
illegal logging activities, carrying a potential
threat of deforestation, and soil erosion. This in
turn will threaten the future viability of farming
on the region's ecologically-fragile hillside
slopes.

The World Bank claims that the Arun Dam
has an excellent environmental protection
scheme,[79] and is pressing the Board to approve
the project. Oxfam partners believe that the
Bank has seriously exaggerated the export and
employment opportunities which the project
will bring, raising questions about its economic
viability. The Bank has admitted that little has
been done to consider alternative schemes,
such as small and medium-scale private-sector
projects, which would be better designed to
meet local needs.

The protection of land rights
A further problem area is the protection of the
land rights of indigenous communities. This is
illustrated by the Rondonia Natural Resource

Management Project (PLANAFLORO) in the Brazilian Amazon. The project, was approved hastily before the Earth Summit, despite warnings from NGOs that the state government of Rondonia had shown no commitment to enforcing its social and environmental provisions. These included, as a precondition for the World Bank loan, a commitment by the state government to halt illegal logging activities in Indian areas, and to stop invasions of ecological reserves by land speculators. Neither of these conditions were met. Oxfam warned that, unless the Bank took its own loan conditions seriously, PLANAFLORO would only repeat the mistakes of the past. This is precisely what has happened.[80]

Part of the rationale of PLANAFLORO[81] was to mitigate the effects of a previous $457m integrated rural development project called POLONOROESTE, a major component of which was the paving of a 1,500km road. That road accelerated migration into the largely untouched western Amazon, devastated Indian communities, and provoked large-scale, indiscriminate deforestation. The failure of the project's plans to protect Indian lands and the environment was subsequently attributed by the Bank to Brazil's 'inappropriate policy framework', weak institutions, and inadequate monitoring. Barber Conable, the Bank's President, admitted in 1987 that POLONOROESTE was 'a sobering example of an environmentally sound effort that went wrong'.[82]

When the $167m PLANAFLORO was unveiled at the Earth Summit, the Bank confidently asserted that 'the current project incorporates the lessons learned by both the government and the World Bank during the past decade about the necessary ingredients for sustainable development'.[83] Yet two years after its approval, PLANAFLORO seems set on the same disastrous course as its predecessor, with problems of non-compliance by the federal and state governments, and their official implementing agencies. The environmental protection agencies, despite receiving project funds, are not defending Indian areas and ecological reserves; the boundaries of many of the conservation units are being arbitrarily reduced; logging has intensified; and the state zoning regulations, which underpin the whole project, are being systematically violated.

The policy framework, which undermined POLONOROESTE, has not been amended. Moreover, the government land agency continues to recognise forest clearance as evidence of 'improvements', and on this basis awards definitive titles to land speculators. Peasant farmers, Indians, and rubber tappers are suffering in the process. Yet the Bank, although insisting it cannot afford another failure in Rondonia, seems unable to ensure compliance from the Brazilian authorities.

The Bank has repeatedly stressed the importance of the participation of local NGOs in project decision-making, but in June 1994 the NGO Forum of Rondonia wrote to Lewis Preston calling for the project to be suspended. The Forum complained that NGO participation had been limited to superficial discussions of the annual work plans of the implementing agencies, that 'grass-roots proposals were not being incorporated', and that Bank missions had ignored NGO advice and, crucially, failed to address the discrepancy between government policies and the state zoning regulations.[84]

The World Bank inspection panel

In September 1993 the World Bank established an Inspection Panel to investigate complaints from communities affected by its projects. The introduction of independent and effective scrutiny would be welcome. Unfortunately, the Inspection Panel, as currently constituted, will be neither independent nor effective. Firstly, the Executive Directors of the World Bank can arbitrarily block investigations into complaints. Secondly, the Panel can only make recommendations. It cannot demand compliance or compensation, which will be determined by the Executive Directors. Moreover, procedures are ambiguous and do not specify whether complainants will be able to comment on the

response of Bank staff to their complaints. Finally, successful complaints will result only in corrective action by the Bank, rather than compensation to communities affected.

The shortcomings of the inspection panel were underlined by its very first case. In February 1995 the Inspection Panel, reviewing the Arun III Hydroelectric Project in Nepal, recommended to the World Bank's Board that the project should not be approved until there had been time to assess complaints from Nepali NGOs, who claimed that the Bank had failed to comply with its own policy on environmental assessment, disclosure of information, involuntary resettlement, and the treatment of indigenous people. Otherwise the Panel feared that there was significant potential of 'direct, serious long-term damage'. The Board's response was to agree to a limited three-month study, while proceeding with the project on the same time-table.[85]

An agenda for reform

Oxfam and its partners believe that major reforms are necessary in World Bank project lending operations, including:

- Remedial action for people affected by past projects. This should cover not only people displaced by large projects but those whose way of life was severely disrupted by in-migration, through Bank support for road construction or colonisation projects.
- The cessation of loans for projects involving displacement, unless:
  - the environmental and social implications of the project have been properly explained, considered and approved by the affected communities;
  - the affected communities have been given access to the project's Environmental Impact Assessments, which despite new World Bank guidelines often remain undisclosed, and have been directly involved in drawing up the resettlement and rehabilitation plan, including mitigation plans for adverse environmental effects;

- the communities involved understand and have agreed criteria for paying compensation and settling disputes;
- finance for resettlement, rehabilitation and environmental protection is secured before the project is approved;
- an independent panel has been set up to monitor compliance with the loan agreements, and to protect the rights of affected populations; the panel should have powers to halt disbursements and delay construction of infrastructure;
- national laws, guaranteeing the rights of displaced populations are enacted and in force before the Bank proceeds with a project loan.

Participation and decentralisation

In its vision statement *Embracing the Future* published in July 1994, the Bank states its commitment to: 'increase local involvement in the design, preparation and supervision of Bank-Group financed activities'. To date, its main activities in this area have involved support for decentralisation. In Oxfam's experience, decentralisation and participation can be useful instruments for supporting community involvement. But success depends critically on the prevailing local conditions and the development of genuinely consultative mechanisms for dialogue.

The decentralisation model was followed by the World Bank in the Mexican Municipal Funds Program (FMS), which it helped to design. This project, which is part of the National Solidarity Program in Mexico, aims to increase the capacity of municipal governments to respond to development needs with greater efficiency and accountability. Although the FMS has achieved some successes in funding local projects among poor communities, it has been subject to political manipulation by Mexico's governing Institutional Revolutionary Party (PRI). Even so, the Bank is more optimistic in its assessment of this strategy than is justified by the evidence. An internal report about the functioning of the FMS in the state of Oaxaca, prepared for a World Bank Workshop on participation, noted that project selection under FMS did not necessarily prioritise the most pressing basic service needs; and a large minority of FMS projects seemed to have little impact on poverty alleviation, despite the fact that the funds were to be spent on projects that 'benefit the largest number of least favoured residents'. In 1991, in Oaxaca, for example, over 25 per cent of the project funding went into the category called 'urbanisation' (which included paving the town square and building park benches).

Whatever the successes and shortcoming of the FMS, its transferability to other countries is very much open to question. For example, in Brazil the Bank has seen 'municipalisation' as a mechanism for addressing problems associated with its projects. The PLANOFLORO project discussed earlier is an example. In this case, the World Bank has proposed transferring administrative responsibility from a state government notorious for corruption and the protection of vested interests, to municipal bodies. Unfortunately, municipal bodies in the project area share many of the problems associated with state bodies. Similar problems have emerged with the Small Farmers' Support Project in northeast Brazil. This project is administered by local authorities, most of which are dominated by landed interests and have proved unresponsive to the needs of small farmers and landless labourers. What these cases illustrate is that, however laudable the aim of decentralisation, 'municipalisation' has all too often been a euphemism for disempowering the poor in the interests of the wealthy.

This is not to deny the importance of transferring decision-making towards accountable, local political structures. But while the benefits of locally-based participatory development are beyond dispute, real participation requires effective consultation with the communities affected, and is incompatible with a top-down approach to development. Yet World Bank staff are constrained by inflexible procurement and disbursement procedures, are mainly based in Washington, and have few real incentives to carry out participatory work, given the pressure to achieve lending targets.

In short, despite the efforts of reformers within the Bank, its practice is likely to continue to fall short of its aspirations without more fundamental reforms in its decision-making structures. In particular, the Bank, which generally has little field presence itself, needs to attach more weight to the views and experience of local, representative organisations in developing policy and in project-design, implementation, and monitoring. A 'process approach' to projects is needed, in which objectives are developed in the light of experience, and there is a readiness to accept changes proposed by local communities.

The need to listen to poor people and to be flexible in responding to their views has also been a critical area of learning for NGOs. In the next section, we take a critical look at the role of NGOs, the lessons they have learnt and the challenges they now face.

The role of NGOs

The end of the Cold War and the consequent rise in conflict, the globalisation of the economy, and the growing feminisation of poverty, have brought about many changes in the environment in which Northern NGOs work. These include an increased privatisation of welfare services, a devaluation of social reproduction, and increased need for 'aid' and 'humanitarian assistance', and an emerging view that a strengthened civil society, of which NGOs are a part, is essential to the healthy functioning of the state. In addition, the declining importance of the nation state, as large trading blocks emerge and transnational companies and capital flows grow, has been accompanied by questions being raised about the concept of sovereignty, as well as sovereignty being violated on the grounds of protecting human rights.

NGOs have not simply stood on the sidelines and watched these developments, but have been part and parcel of this evolution. Some would even argue that they have been major actors in bringing it about.[86] The problem is that NGOs on the one hand, have not always understood the wider trends in which they have been implicated, and thus have underestimated their catalytic role; while on the other hand, they have often had a mistaken belief in their own operational importance.[87] As a consequence, they can end up doing things that should be the responsibility of others, often governments and sometimes multilateral organisations, and not doing those things for which they are often well placed, such as lobbying at national and international level, and raising public awareness.

NGOs have become an increasingly significant source of development assistance. According to OECD estimates, NGOs in industrialised countries transferred $5.6bn to developing countries in 1993, only slightly less than multilateral donors.[88] At the same time, there has been a spectacular increase in NGOs in developing countries, with the number of registered NGOs in Nepal alone rising from 220 in 1990 to 1210 in 1993.[89] The World Bank estimates that NGOs in India now handle 25 per cent of all foreign aid, and the combined efforts of NGOs across the developing world are estimated to reach some 250 million people.[90] The tendency to channel official aid through NGOs is likely to continue, with an increase in direct funding of Southern NGOs.

The reason why donors are choosing to channel more aid through NGOs is that they are perceived to be more efficient and cost-effective than governments. NGOs are believed to have a better record in reaching the poor, working in participatory ways, strengthening local institutions, and being flexible and innovative. Although NGOs, including Oxfam, would like to think of these as defining characteristics, they need to be wary of what more critical commentators see as a 'fashionable predilection for seeing NGOs as the panacea' for the more intractable problems of development,

on the part of bilateral and multilateral donors.[91]

Panacea they are not. In this and earlier chapters, we have looked critically at the role of governments and international financial institutions. At the same time, we are acutely aware of the need to be equally critical of our own interventions. NGOs, in common with the World Bank, official donors, and other development actors, are confronting complexity, diversity, and uncertainty. There are no simple answers, and there are huge dangers in trying to impose blueprints for development, whether from capital cities like Washington or the head offices of NGOs. There is a need for NGOs to get much better at evaluating their impact and learning from both successes and failures.

There are a bewildering variety of NGOs. They include people's or community-based organisations, whose members directly benefit from their actions; intermediary NGOs whose primary aim is to support the work of others; and donor NGOs which provide funds to either of the first two groups. Many organisations fall into more than one category. International or Northern NGOs may both be donors and play an operational or intermediary role in the South. People's organisations may form federations which develop into support structures with paid staff. Our focus here is primarily on Northern NGOs and how they can better support Southern NGOs and grassroots organisations.

Changing roles and challenges

The roles of Northern NGOs have changed considerably over a number of decades. Many started with an operational role in providing relief, welfare or services and then made a transition to a second phase during which they were primarily funding agencies supporting longer-term community development projects through a range of intermediaries and community-based organisations. Some, like Oxfam, have maintained both these roles, while now increasingly adopting 'third generation' strategies, including a much greater emphasis on advocacy to tackle the root causes of poverty, networking, and strengthening the organisational capacity of Southern partners.[92]

At the same time, NGOs are increasingly under pressure to fulfil the role of sub-contractors in the delivery of privatised welfare and humanitarian relief. There is a risk of NGOs becoming contractors at the expense of developing local capacity. Moreover, it reinforces the tendency of NGOs to become increasingly dependent on funds from Northern governments and multilateral agencies, raising serious questions about the extent to which they are becoming donor-led in their funding priorities, and about their independence and ability to campaign against government policies. Some agencies, such as Oxfam America, have made a policy commitment not to receive government funding in order to safeguard their autonomy.

Increased funding from official donors also further complicates the already difficult issue of accountability to multiple stakeholders. This is a major challenge because of the very different perceptions of donors and Southern partners and beneficiaries about the causes of poverty and therefore the most effective response. Whereas many of the former tend to see poverty as caused by lack of material means (aggravated by climate, 'overpopulation', and ignorance), Oxfam's partners are in no doubt that poverty is rooted in injustice and the denial of rights.

A significant investment in public education is needed in order to close this increasingly untenable gap. Northern NGOs raising funds in a highly competitive environment need to be honest about the extent of the difficulties they face, as well as demonstrating their successes. The messages NGOs give out about their 'speed, efficiency, and effectiveness' contradict the very nature of much of the work they do, or support, which is neither quick nor easy, and needs a significant investment in programme support and management to be effective. Moreover, as NGOs are taking centre stage in

the midst of complex humanitarian emergencies, the consequences of their decisions, or recommendations to others (such as for the UN to intervene in a particular situation) start to have potentially huge ramifications.

All these issues raise difficult questions about the mandates of NGOs. What gives them the right to speak on behalf of the poor? How transparent and accountable are they to beneficiaries, partners and donors? A particularly uncomfortable question for NGOs is whether they are making a significant contribution towards finding development alternatives or only towards alternative rhetoric.[93]

The three case studies which follow attempt to answer some of these questions, and are chosen to illustrate very different approaches in different contexts, as well as different lessons drawn from Oxfam's experience. The first, from Burkina Faso, illustrates both the successes and limitations of the participatory approach adopted by an Oxfam project and its limited impact on underlying problems. The second case study, of a research initiative aimed at influencing the design of a large governmental flood protection scheme in Bangladesh, shows how NGOs are attempting to 'scale up' their impact; and the different understandings of what 'participation' means. The third case study looks at the Campaign against Hunger, Misery and For Life in Brazil, and interaction between NGOs, civil society, and governments.

Environmental protection in Burkina Faso

Declining food security and the closely connected issues of soil-erosion, environmental degradation and population growth have long been endemic in much of the Yatenga region of Burkina Faso. Attempts by a variety of external agencies to improve the situation focused mainly on different water-harvesting techniques. In the early 1960s a European soil conservation agency attempted to build several kilometres of earth bunds using bulldozers. Subsequently, the World Bank funded a local government initiative which involved village groups in constructing earth bunds along

contours determined by topographers. Both of these initiatives failed although local farmers remember them vividly:

Even if they are well maintained, earth bunds are a complete menace, because they flood upland soils and dry up land below, turning it into rock. Stone bunds are better, because they are not easily damaged and require less maintenance. They also allow water to pass through, which enables you to grow crops in front as well as behind. (Ousmanne Ouedraogo a farmer of the village of Noogo)

They sent us fake engineers who came to destroy us with their huge machines. They only came to destroy our trees and leave. They did not even ask the opinion of local people. (The Rassam Naaba, Minister of Youth under the traditional administration system, who currently works for the animal husbandry department)

Returning from a visit to the Negev desert in Israel in 1979, the Oxfam assistant field director was convinced that more could be done in Burkina in soil and water conservation. As a result, Oxfam started researching possible ways of improving water retention, building up soil and slowing run-off. Discussions with local villagers in the Yatenga included the possibility of using stone bunds. Later, Oxfam staff suggested planting trees on the bunds for reafforestation purposes. However, it quickly became clear that farmers were not interested in planting trees. Instead, with some success, they were experimenting with growing cereals beside the bunds.

The major technical challenge was how to determine the contours along which to place the stone bunds, in order to avoid increased erosion through gullying. The solution they found was borrowed from another NGO in Senegal. It involved a very simple transparent plastic tube tied to two wooden poles. Water is poured into the tube and two people then pace the ground, whilst holding the poles and watching the water levels. When the water is level, the contour line is determined. This cheap and simple innovation meant they could dispense with the services of topographers, and

local farmers were empowered by a technology they could control.

An Oxfam-commissioned study[94] carried out in 1993 reveals that the project succeeded in increasing cereal production (average increases in yield between 1981-4 ranged from 12 per cent to 91 per cent), and in stimulating farmers to try out the technique for themselves. It succeeded because farmers themselves were asked for their views and opted for stone bunds, rather then uncritically copying the system of earth bunds used in the Negev. Oxfam development workers also showed flexibility in agreeing to change the immediate objective of the project from tree planting to increasing cereal yields. According to project co-ordinator, Mathieu Ouedraogo:

A participatory approach was taken to identify solutions to problems as they emerged during implementation, rather than anticipating problems and prescribing solutions in advance.

However, despite these successes, there were clear limitations to the project. Stones are hard to come by, as is labour, and a means to transport the stones. The bunding only touches one aspect of the farming system; other initiatives such as composting and the use of manure are also required. As is often the case, the solution to one problem created other unexpected problems. This makes it vital that any development initiative is designed to strengthen the skills of local people to devise their own solutions. As a local farmer put it:

We have two thorns: one in the foot and the other in the backside. Help us to remove the one in our backside first. Then we can sit down to remove the one under the foot ourselves.

Yet the evaluation suggests that, particularly in the early years when the project was run by an expatriate, it may have reinforced people's loss of confidence in themselves.

A significant failure of the project was that it did not take into account the inequality between men and women in the local communities. As a result increased demands were made on the women, particularly through their involvement in collecting and transporting stones. Women interviewed agreed that they had benefited from increased cereal yields, and some said that the project had provided them with a new source of income and improved their social interaction. However, the project failed to address the areas of daily life that concerned women most, particularly the collection of fuel-wood and water. For that reason, the project's 'participatory approach' clearly had limitations.

Finally, the question has to be asked to what degree the project has attempted to grapple with the underlying causes of poverty in Yatenga. Any analysis of the causes of environmental degradation invariably raises problems about land tenure, and conflicting interests over land use, for example between farmers and herders; and the impact of macro-economic policies determined by governments and international financial institutions.[95]

Moreover, within communities and within households, use and control of resources varies enormously on the basis of gender, class, age and ethnicity. These power imbalances are in turn determined by macro-level socio-economic and political factors, making it essential for NGOs to analyse how such external factors relate to micro-level household relationships, and vice versa, even if it is only to ensure that new initiatives do not fail because factors in the external environment preclude their development.

The Yatenga project has succeeded in involving some of those most affected by environmental degradation in defining problems and possible solutions. However, it has not yet been able to strengthen the capacity of local people (men or women) to enter into policy dialogue with decision makers about macro-economic and political factors affecting their rights and livelihoods.

Lesson:: Let the poor seek solutions to their own problems

The Burkina Faso experience underlines the importance of taking active steps to involve the beneficiaries, especially women, in project design, of being flexible, building on local solutions and not attempting to impose ideas from outside. It also tallies with the conclusions of one of the few independent studies of NGOs' overseas work which was undertaken by the UK-based Overseas Development Institute.[96] This drew on 16 case studies of NGO programmes in India, Bangladesh, Uganda and Zimbabwe and concluded that:

NGOs play a significant role in efforts to alleviate rural poverty, even if their projects do not always reach the very poorest, are costly to implement and encounter problems of sustainability.

This study also identified a number of common factors behind successful NGO interventions. They included genuine participation and empathy with beneficiaries, strong and effective leadership and management, decentralised decision making, committed and well-paid staff, good relations with government, and a favourable external environment. Ironically, despite the fact that a favourable environment was considered a key success factor, NGOs were judged to underestimate the wider environmental context in which they operate. The study found that

Any positive changes in the lives of the poor are primarily attributed to the development projects initiated by NGOs, even though they might result from factors external to the project.

This underlines the dangers of 'projectitis': fixating on project interventions to the exclusion of grappling with the complexities of the real world. NGOs need to have a thorough grasp of the local context and to have properly analysed the specific nature and causes of poverty their project seeks to address. Because of the complexity of the problems, any 'intervention', 'grant', or 'project' is going to have both negative and positive effects, many of which are unpredictable. So activities designed to solve problems can only be approximations towards a better response and need to be continually improved on. This requires a greater degree of modesty on the part of NGOs, an ability to admit error, and a commitment to learn from experience.

People's participation and the Flood Action Plan in Bangladesh

As we have seen, flooding and tidal surges caused by cyclones are a serious problem in Bangladesh. Many different flood protection schemes have been tried. To date the most ambitious of these is the Flood Action Plan, on which construction has yet to begin, which has to date involved 26 or more studies, costing some $150m.

The scale of the project means that it will have a major impact on the lives of several million people, as well as on the natural environment. In response to growing concerns about the plan, particularly about the limited involvement of local people in its design, NGOs in Bangladesh, including Oxfam, decided to commission an independent study into popular participation in the Flood Action Plan.

The researchers had to start by disentangling very different views on what is meant by people's 'participation' and define criteria for assessing its effectiveness. For example, they had to determine whether people were consulted from the very outset in defining the problem, whether they had access to adequate information, and whether those managing the project were in any way answerable to the communities affected.

Participation

Over many years people had resisted inappropriate attempts at flood control by cutting embankments, in the same way that farmers in Burkina Faso had destroyed or broken earth bunds. Because of the actions taken by local people, by 1992 the project managers became convinced of the need to acknowledge people's right to be involved, and produced guidelines for their participation.

However, when local people were consulted about their preferred options, their choices were overruled. For example, public consult-ation in the Tangail area showed farmers were more interested in dry-season crops than the flood-protected monsoon crops proposed in the project. In response, the project managers began to express fears that the process was getting out of hand and would disrupt the project cycle. The project managers had a mental block to hearing local people's views when they contradicted their own preconceived notion that the critical issue was flood-control. This made them completely unreceptive to other ideas on how best to make the livelihoods of local men and women more secure. They also failed to consult some of the most vulnerable groups affected by the project.

Wider issues and the role of NGOs

These limitations and those of the Flood Action Plan as a whole meant that it was not addressing some of the wider social and political factors which had made earlier flood control projects fail. The study has been worthwhile in bringing about some changes in the project's approach. However, involvement in trying to influence the Flood Action Plan has been limited to a few NGOs, mainly those based in the capital, Dhaka. This was because NGOs were pre-occupied with their own micro-level activities, and doubted their ability to influence a 'technical' programme. Moreover, many feared getting drawn into head-on confrontation with powerful vested interests.

In order for NGOs to have an impact, they would probably need to work both within and outside the programme, at several levels simultaneously, building better links between international and local NGOs and developing different skills for dealing with non-traditional clients. All of which requires enhanced collab-oration, networking and the pooling of skills and information between NGOs.

Lesson:the need to define genuine participation and to encourage learning

The research into the Flood Action Plan jointly commissioned by NGOs in Bangladesh illust-rates some of the new avenues open to popular organisations and NGOs seeking to protect the interests of poor communities. The study has had a significant impact in raising awareness about the Flood Action Plan and promoting debate about popular participation. It also points to ways in which NGOs can attempt to scale-up their impact by trying to influence the design of large projects funded by governments and multilateral agencies.

The Flood Action Plan study shows that very different things are meant by the term 'participatory', making it very hard to determine what is or isn't 'genuine participation'. As a result new criteria need to be developed in order to assess the quality of participation. These criteria should deal more explicitly with issues of difference such as gender and class, and in many contexts, race and ethnicity, and the degree to which external agencies are enhancing the capacity of different groups to determine their own future.

Looking beyond the specific parameters of the Bangladesh study, it is clear that participatory approaches cannot thrive without significant cultural change within organisations. NGOs are not immune from the problems confronting other bureaucracies, including complacency, hierarchy, inertia, and poor information flow. These can lead to loops of self-deception as feedback from activities is distorted or manipulated by individuals seeking to protect themselves. Senior managers in the 'if it ain't broke, don't fix it' mode will tend to go along with the positive news and carry on regardless until the something 'breaks'. As Robert Chambers has suggested, this kind of institutional blindness has led to the most remarkable feature of development efforts over the last few decades: how wrong 'we' were when 'we' thought we were so right.[97]

One of the crucial changes that is required is a greater emphasis on learning within NGOs and a sharing of learning between NGOs. Recent work in other disciplines and in the private sector suggests that 'front-line' programme-level learning systems need to be developed to improve the effectiveness of relief, development, and advocacy work. This approach to more decentralised learning needs to be based less on large one-off evaluations and more on smaller, regular assessments of programme development that make it easier to identify problems early and makes changes.

NGOs are also increasingly under pressure from donors to develop better systems for assessing the impact of their work. This should include seeking more reliable guidance as to whether things are going well or badly, from the community-based organisations and NGO staff involved, who are already monitoring impact in their own way. Above all, the beneficiaries should be asked for their assessment, as it is increasingly clear that sustainable changes in the lives of poor women and men must be based on their own values and priorities, and their freedom to assert their needs.

Brazil's Campaign against Hunger, Misery and for Life

The global trend identified throughout this book is of an increasing divide between those who have a clear social, economic, and political stake in society, whose voices count; and those who have not. This divide is particularly stark in Brazil, where some 32 million people (20 per cent of the population) are unable to meet even their basic food needs. This inequity is now being actively challenged by a new force in civil society: a broad-based anti-poverty campaign. The aim of the Campaign against Hunger, Misery and for Life is to raise awareness within Brazilian society of the rights and responsibilities of individuals and social groups, and of the need to tackle poverty. It began in 1993, following on from the Campaign for Ethics in Politics, which was instrumental in bringing about the impeachment of President Fernando Collor.

The campaign now brings together a broad spectrum of Brazilian civil society including NGOs, trade unions, private sector companies and banks, church groups, students, teachers, and other professionals into a broad anti-poverty coalition. Oxfam's involvement, along with other international NGOs, has been in providing very small amounts of seed money in the early stages.

The aim of the campaign is to bring about change by involving people in practical action at the local level, for example through job creation schemes or making food donations, and in mobilising them to put pressure on municipal, state, and federal authorities to tackle some of the structural problems which cause poverty. It has achieved government support, including the setting up of a National Food Security Council, with representatives of NGOs amongst its members.

There are now over 3,000 local committees, with some 30,000 volunteer workers. Through the campaign as many as 2.8 million Brazilians (from a total population of 150 million) have participated in the local committees, 3.5 million have made cash donations, and 21 million have donated food or clothes.

The campaign news bulletin (E-mail bulletin of Servicio Brasileiro de Justicia e Paz) gives the following examples of some of the thousands of local initiatives undertaken:

- Around 4500 prisoners in jails in Rio de Janeiro each donated a meal to the campaign. The 2.5 tons of food collected through this effort were distributed among Citizens' Action Committees near the prisons, and fed 200 families for two weeks.
- The trade union federation, CUT (which has 1950 affiliated unions and represents more than 17 million workers), has taken up the campaign, with one union calling for members to each donate one hour of work.
- The local committee in Itumbiara, in the state of Goias, is using 91 hectares of land owned by the electric power company Furnas Centrais Electricas to plant beans, rice, corn and vegetables. Part of the produce is given to 800 needy families and charities and the remainder is sold to finance the costs of the programme.
- Local committees in the state of Minais Gerais have concentrated on jobs and housing, for example with Bank of Brasil employees in Montes Carlos donating cash to build 34 homes for needy families.

The campaign has been extremely successful in challenging apathy about poverty and in galvanising ordinary citizens to take responsibility in responding to the denial of rights of their fellow citizens. As Herbert de Souza (known as Betinho), founder of the campaign explained:

In 1993, misery gained a name, a place, and an address. National hunger, the product of a society proficient in excluding the many and benefiting the few, invaded prime-time television and showed its ugly face even to those who had refused to look, and put itself on the national agenda. Hunger made citizens and society begin to take responsibility for a problem that up until now had been treated only as a question to be resolved by those who are hungry and by those who govern. This change of perception, the understanding that hunger and misery are items on society's agenda, is a major development in the public life of a country that, when it looks at itself in the mirror, sees itself as apathetic, unethical, indifferent, selfish, and cunning. In every gesture of solidarity, every kilo of food donated, every new effort in the Citizens Action against Misery and for Life, Brazil has demonstrated that it still can be put off the road to disaster.

The new campaign focus in 1994 was on creating employment and gaining acceptance of the principles of work for all and a just wage. In a country with 2.4 million unemployed and some 12 million receiving less than the minimum wage, this is a tall order. Some of the Citizens' Action Committees have been successful in creating community work for local unemployed people.

During 1995 the campaign is highlighting the plight of Brazil's 4.8 million landless rural workers and the fact that, while 1 per cent of property owners control 44 per cent of the land, 67 per cent of landholders occupy just 6 per cent. The campaign has succeeded in keeping poverty issues on the agenda and has stopped the state from back-tracking on issues like agrarian reform. As a result, the government now sees more of a role for civil society on poverty issues and has, for example, invited NGO involvement in new poverty programmes. The campaign is raising critical questions about the relationships between NGOs, civil cosiety, the market, and the state, getting people to debate them and begin to redefine them.

Lesson: NGOs, the state, and civil society can work together against poverty

The Campaign is an unusual example of the extent of public response to the erosion of social and economic rights, and of co-operation between civil society and state. It has awakened a spirit of solidarity and public responsibility, which is important agains a background of growing fear, violence, insecurity, and lack of hope. It also serves as an important reminder that NGOs are only one actor amongst many. If NGOs are serious about trying to bring about change, rather than attempting to substitute for the state or the private sector, they need to enter into new partnerships, as has happened in Brazil.

Neo-liberal economic policies have been premised on a reduced role for the state, with NGOs seen as the preferred channel for social welfare provision. Many NGOs, by their actions, if not in their policy statements, have supported this trend. Others, including Oxfam, see the role of an enabling state as critical and will not get involved in service provision, unless building local capacity and strengthening institutional development is integral to the programme. There are now welcome signs of a new recognition amongst official donors that governments, not markets, have the a major role to play in providing essential social services to the poor.[98]

The debate often remains couched in either-or terms ; but the neat separations between citizen and state, markets and government, NGOs and official donors, are not as clear cut as they appear. For example, the citizen and the state 'make' each other to a lesser or greater degree, and the stance that each takes defines the stance of the other.

In the West notions of liberal democracy are based on the idea that society only exists in so far as it satisfies individual ends and in the process of these ends being met harmony will emerge through the invisible hand of the market. Politics in this situation exists to reconcile competing interests. It becomes less and less about creating the conditions for citizens' groups to identify solutions for the common good and more and more about claimant politics as different groups struggle for their own advantage. Developing a national or global consensus on critical issues of poverty and the denial of rights becomes increasingly difficult.

At the same time, there is now a global search for a new development paradigm, which involves all the critical actors and gives greater meaning to the notion of citizenship, and to the potential for individuals and groups to effect change. As in the case of the Brazilian campaign, throughout the developing world citizens' groups and new social movements are organising for change and trying to identify alternative development policies.

Women, particularly in Latin America but also in other parts of the world, have become key actors in forming social movements that question the traditional way of engaging in politics and society. Women's attempts to become full 'citizens' have come to include struggles for political rights, social and economic rights, reproductive rights, and the elimination of all forms of discrimination. In situations of conflict, women have often been at the forefront of peace-making initiatives. For such struggles to succeed in the long term an environment for effective participation is required. This can be achieved both through the struggle itself, for example, in gaining equality before the law; and through institutional reform, civic education the acquisition of literacy and organising skills, and achieving secure livelihoods.[99]

Equally important in these social movements is the search for identity:

The objective...is not only equality of rights but rather the right to be different. The struggle is against discrimination, and in favour of a more equitable distribution in the economic market and, in the political realm the struggle is for citizenship. The right to be recognized as different is one of the deepest needs in post-industrial and post-material society.[100]

Without such social movements, without an environment for them to develop, the consequent loss of identity and idea of the common good leads to a loss of faith not only in our political systems but also in ourselves. In some societies the result is fundamentalism, nationalism, tribalism, and ultimately, violence.

NGOs by no means have all the answers. Their greatest strengths are their values and their proximity to the poor. But they need now to become more 'strategic', and to form new alliances with each other, as part of wider civil society, and with other development actors. This is essential if they are to play an effective role in strengthening the ability of poor people and their organisations to participate more fully in society. They also have an important role in helping state structures to become more responsive and to change. This means taking on an advocacy role and, for Northern NGOs, engaging within their own societies in public education and campaigning to change behaviour and perceptions. If NGOs fail to live up to these challenges in the twenty-first century, or lose sight of their values and commitment to social justice, they will become more part of the problems than of the solutions.

7 An agenda for change

People are not developed, they develop themselves.

JULIUS NYERERE

Working for an alternative approach to development has to be seen as a process... It implies continuous changes, as well as uniting people from across the entire social spectrum in a common purpose. There are many obstacles to be overcome, one of the main ones being to deal with the present situation, while simultaneously working to build an alternative to it.

EDUARDO KLIEN, OXFAM DEPUTY REGIONAL REPRESENTATIVE, CENTRAL AMERICA

Though the challenges are great and the situation is complex, we have hope that we can change conditions and build a better tomorrow.

DECLARATION FROM SOUTHERN WOMEN'S ORGANISATIONS
PRESENTED AT WOMEN LINKING FOR CHANGE CONFERENCE, THAILAND, 1994

The challenge of poverty

There can be no greater indictment of our world than the fact that one in four of its inhabitants is consigned to poverty. This represents a denial of rights and a wastage of human potential on a massive scale. If the present pattern of development is allowed to continue unchallenged, the future is a frightening prospect, of a world of deep divisions, of societies segregated between the 'haves' and the 'have-nots'; between those with skills and opportunities, jobs and wealth, and those with none; between those who 'count' in economic, social, and political terms, and those who do not. This is a prescription for deepening instability.

The only enduring solution is to tackle poverty and injustice, so that all people have a stake in society. For without a cohesive spirit of social justice no society can achieve security and stability for its members. This requires not only the state, but individual citizens, as part of an active civil society, to take responsibility for ensuring that all can enjoy their full rights.

Creating a world order which realises the ambitions of the UN Charter and the goal of ending poverty will require a transformation in attitudes, policies, and institutions. It will necessitate a renewed sense of vision on the part of political leaders, and a willingness to sacrifice short-term political expediency in the interest of achieving long-term human development gains. It will mean creating equal opportunities, and sharing wealth in a more equitable manner, both nationally and internationally. It will also require a transformation of the post-war institutions of global governance, which have become increasingly irrelevant to the challenges of today.

Oxfam's vision of transformation is rooted in the energy and creativity of people who are looking for alternatives and shaping a new agenda. It is based on a conviction that people have the power to effect change — whether they are part of a women's group in Mali organising to obtain credit, indigenous people in Brazil struggling to secure their land rights, Windward Islands banana producers trying to keep open their lifeline to the European market, or citizens in developed countries, who can exercise consumer power in the supermarket by buying fairly-traded goods, or lobby their governments to write off debt as part of a wider poverty-reduction strategy.

Community-based groups of peasant producers, shanty-town dwellers, women's groups, indigenous and ethnic minority groups, trade unions, and NGOs are all working to achieve change, whether in the household, or the community, at district, regional, national, and international levels. On the basis of its work with such groups, Oxfam is convinced that real change must come from the bottom up. Far from being powerless victims of poverty, poor women and men show extraordinary resilience in challenging inequitable power structures. Their success in bringing about positive change will depend on the creation of effective democracies and strong civil societies, which enable people to have a voice, to campaign, and to assert their rights. At the same time, a new sense of responsibility for the rights of others is needed, together with an emphasis on building new alliances to achieve change.

Fundamentally, what is required in order to realise Oxfam's vision of basic rights for all is the creation of an enabling environment at the local, national, and international level, in which people can act as agents of change. In this, the role of the state is critical. It also requires a fundamental redirection of policy on the part of other foci of power, including the UN, international financial and trade organisations, transnational corporations (TNCs), official aid donors, and NGOs.

The five critical elements of that enabling environment are:

- democratic participation
- enhanced opportunity
- increased equity
- peace and security
- a sustainable future.

Oxfam's agenda for change

Participation

Across its international programme, Oxfam works with community groups who are attempting to influence the policies affecting their lives. These range from women in Afghanistan trying to get a say in framing any new constitution, to Zambian grassroots organisations writing to finance ministers in Washington about the impact of debt and structural adjustment on their lives, and black communities in Colombia lobbying the government over their constitutional rights. All, in their different ways, are contributing to the creation of a vibrant civil society. Such initiatives can form the bedrock of genuine democratisation and more participative social structures. However, action is also needed at a national level.

There is no one form of democracy appropriate to all people and transferable between countries; but transparent and accountable government, and respect for the rule of law and for civil and political rights, are crucial ingredients of democracy and participation. Some governments claim that the dictates of economic growth demand the suspension of such rights until a higher level of development has been attained. But while several countries, notably China, have achieved high rates of growth while maintaining oppressive political structures, it does not follow that autocracy is necessary for development. More importantly, civil and political rights are inalienable rights which all people are entitled to enjoy, irrespective of the stage of economic development in the country in which they live. In Oxfam's view, economic growth without respect for these rights does not constitute sustainable development.

Institutional development

To provide a framework for democratic participation, it is essential to strengthen instutions at all levels, from village associations to an independent judiciary capable of implementing the rule of law.

Equality of opportunity

Genuine participation also requires equality of opportunity. It is time for governments to take effective steps to implement all the principles agreed at the Vienna Human Rights Conference — particularly that the human rights of women and of girl children are an inalienable, integral and indivis-ible part of universal human rights — and eliminate all forms of discrimination, against women and other disadvantaged groups. They should ratify, and withdraw all reservations to, the Convention on the Elimina-tion of Discrimination against Women. Similarly, steps to remove discriminatory measures based upon ethnicity, caste and religion are also vital.

A stronger institutional framework to safeguard rights

The UN remains the one global institution able — by virtue of its Charter and universal membership — to play a decisive role in poverty reduction. Charged with finding solutions to international social and economic problems, and promoting and protecting human rights and fundamental freedoms, the UN will be able to carry out its role only if the steady erosion of its power and authority is reversed. With the Secretary-General's Agenda for Development, the UN is set to put its own house in order, streamlining its procedures and cutting out waste and duplication. But reform will be useless unless matched by a renewed commitment from all governments to the UN's democratic ideals. This implies both political support and secure financial backing. If we allow

the only multilateral forum for genuine debate, consensus-building, and standard-setting to decline, it is the world's poor and oppressed who will be the losers.

- The ECOSOC (Economic and Social Council) should have a strengthened role for monitoring the impact of global macro-economic policies on social development and basic rights. At the start of each session — the high-level segment — more time should be allocated for discussion of global macro-economic trends, including the impact of the policies and programmes of the international financial institutions on poverty.

- Participants in the high-level segment of ECOSOC should include finance ministers, representatives of the Bretton Woods institutions, other UN specialised agencies, and the chairpersons of the relevant treaty monitoring bodies, such as the Committee on Economic, Social and Cultural Rights, and NGOs.

- ECOSOC should adopt a system of periodic national reports which would streamline existing reporting requirements on governments and move towards a more balanced and integrated approach to civil, political, economic, social, and cultural rights, and implementation of the Earth Summit agreements.
  In order to ensure that such reports do not become token exercises, citizens' groups and NGOs should be encouraged to present additional relevant information to ECOSOC.

- Governments should support the long overdue creation of a complaints mechanism, open to individuals and groups, to investigate alleged denials of basic rights under the International Covenant on Economic, Social and Cultural Rights.

Accountability of the international financial institutions

There is increasing acceptance that IFIs as part of the UN family have obligations both to promote social and economic rights (which they themselves acknowledge) and to further the social development goals identified by the

United Nations. The World Bank and IMF wield enormous influence over social and economic policy in developing countries, yet for too long they have operated outside the UN's human rights framework.

While recent IMF and World Bank initiatives to conduct poverty assessments are welcome, they should not be viewed as an internal exercise, divorced from the reality of existing programme aims. Such assessments would clearly benefit from input from other UN specialised agencies and expert bodies. It is crucial that the effect of the Bretton Woods policies on vulnerable groups are opened up to wider scrutiny.

- ECOSOC should develop a system of monitoring of global macro-economic trends, structural adjustment programmes, projects supported by multilateral financial agencies, and the implications of trade rules enshrined in the World Trade Organisation, as well as the trade and investment activities of TNCs.

- A report on global trends and the impact of international financial institutions on poverty should be presented each year to the UN General Assembly.

- More disclosure of information is needed to empower community organisations, NGOs, professional groups, and the media, to take part in discussion on critical policy issues.
Moves by the World Bank and other multilateral agencies to develop participatory approaches with community groups and women's organisations on the design, implementation, and impact of their projects and policies on the poor, are encouraging. However, publication of important policy documents, including World Bank Country Assistance Strategies, is crucial, as is effective input into their content by such groups.

- If developing-country governments are to be held more accountable for structural adjustment policies and investment loans which affect the lives of their citizens, they must be given greater power to shape these policies in the World Bank and IMF. Consequently, the voting structures of the IFIs need to be reformed to allow more democratic representation, which more accurately reflects the composition of their membership.

Citizens' movements and campaign groups

The problems of poverty and denial of rights can seem insurmountable. Yet taking campaigning action to get poverty issues on the agenda and generate public pressure for change, as the Brazilian Campaign against Hunger, Misery and for Life has successfully done, or developing a co-ordinated approach to advocacy between groups in the South and North, can be both motivating and effective in changing attitudes and policies.

- Northern and international NGOs should concentrate more on building the advocacy capacity of community-based organisations and Southern NGOs working for change at national and international levels.

- To be effective in attempting to relieve poverty, NGOs should develop advocacy, research, networking, and policy dialogue with governments, multilateral agencies, and the corporate sector, as an integral part of fulfilling their mandates.

Opportunity

The eradication of poverty demands that poor men and women have control over the productive assets and resources on which their livelihoods depend. But to be capable of making use of opportunities, they also need enough to eat, clean water to drink and wash in, health-care, education, shelter, political freedom, and protection from violence.

Health-care, primary education, and other forms of welfare provision, are basic human rights, which governments should be protecting. Moreover, there is compelling evidence to show that investment in health, education, and basic-needs provision, apart from the immediate benefits, also makes good economic sense. Yet deep expenditure cuts and withdrawal of the state from social-service provision, together with the introduction of user fees, have disadvantaged the poorest people. Women are particularly adversely affected by cuts in health-care provision because of their higher exposure to health risks. Young girls are the first to be withdrawn from education in the face of economic stress.

Community groups are organising themselves to improve basic services. They range from community-based organisations in Zambia building their own health posts and schools, and lobbying government to staff them, to women in shanty towns in Peru organising soup-kitchens for destitute urban migrants. Such efforts need the support of governments and financial institutions, who should protect expenditure in areas of concern to the poor.

Provision of health-care and education

- Governments should redirect resources so that at least 20 per cent of government expenditure is allocated to providing services of maximum benefit to the poor, including primary health-care and education, clean water, and sanitation.

- Official aid donors, as part of a '20:20 compact' with recipient governments, should improve the poverty-focus of their aid so that a minimum of 20 per cent is directed towards these social priorities, and phase out the tying of aid by the year 2000.

- To ensure that the poorest people can benefit from service provision, governments should immediately withdraw user fees for primary health and basic education services.

- International financial institutions should introduce effective social conditionality, so that disbursement of structural adjustment loans is made conditional on government action to improve provision of basic services, including the withdrawal of user fees. That action should be agreed in local dialogue between governments, UN agencies, community groups, and IFIs.

National poverty-eradication plans

Governments should prioritise the development of poverty-eradication plans, making time-bound commitments to eradicate absolute poverty, as agreed at the World Summit for Social Development. They should encourage the active participation of NGOs and citizens' groups in the elaboration of these plans and in progress towards achieving the targets set.

Resources for enhanced opportunity

There are a range of ways in which new resources could be found to create opportunity and an enabling environment for poor people. These include:

- **Increased aid:** Official aid donors should establish a timetable for reaching the UN target of 0.7 per cent of GNP for their aid budgets.

- **Progressive taxation:** Governments should introduce progressive and equitable taxation systems, with a focus on taxing income and assets. While any system of taxation must balance considerations of revenue raising against the need to encourage investment, most governments could do far more to expand their tax base.

- **Reduced military spending:** Significant reductions in expenditure on the military and on parastatals could translate into increased public investment in socially useful and productive activities.

- **Debt reduction:** An international conference on debt should be convened by the UN Secretary-General and charged with developing a concrete strategy for reducing the debt-servicing burdens of severely-indebted low-income countries (SILICs) to levels compatible with social and economic recovery by:

  - writing-off between 80 per cent and 100 per cent of the entire stock of official debt owed to governments represented in the Paris Club;

- converting the entire stock of debt owed by SILICs to the IMF into IDA terms, with repayments beginning after 20 years at nominal interest rates ;

- financing this operation from within the IMF, which could be done either by selling off part of the Fund's gold stocks and using the revenue thus raised to reduce debt, or by setting aside part of a new issue of Special Drawing Rights for this purpose;

- using World Bank reserves to convert into concessional terms the outstanding stock of 'hard' debt owed to it by SILICs;

- withdrawing the condition that governments are eligible for debt relief only by complying with IMF stabilisation programmes, and establishing instead more appropriate forms of conditionality.

All these debt-relief measures would be linked to concrete commitments by governments to increase provision in social priority areas through debt-for-development contracts negotiated with citizens' groups and the relevant UN agencies.

- **Concessional loans:** The poverty focus of IDA and the financial resources available through IDA XI should be increased, and an intermediate facility established for countries which have 'graduated' from IDA status but remain unable to obtain financial resources from private capital markets.

- **International taxation:** Most people in the industrialised world would be reluctant to have state welfare provision financed by voluntary contributions, since this would make essential service provision insecure and uncertain. Similarly, a case can be made for putting aid on a more secure footing, through the introduction of a progressive income-tax on OECD countries. Tax-based transfers would undoubtedly meet with political objections, particularly in countries where governments are committed to

lowering taxation. However, in Oxfam's view, international aid should be seen as a financial entitlement, and as part of a compact between citizens in the industrial and developing worlds, as it is in the interests of industrial countries to enhance human welfare in the South. Moreover, in practice aid is already a tax-based transfer. Establishing a formal system would merely ensure that the burden was shared more equitably, and would make the provision of aid more secure. An international tax on currency speculation could serve the dual purpose of providing resources for development and deterring a form of financial activity which is deeply destabilising for all countries.

Equity

Inequity in the distribution of wealth and productive assets is a formidable obstacle to reducing poverty and creating social cohesion. So, too, is the battery of disadvantages faced by women. A nation cannot genuinely claim to be 'developing' where half of its population is marginalised and suffers discrimination. Nor can it expect economic growth to bring improvement in human welfare where vast numbers of people lack rights to the use of land and other productive resources. Patterns of development which exclude poor men and women are not merely socially unjust and politically unsustainable, but also inefficient. One of the central lessons from South-East Asia is that redistributive measures, including land reform, and moves towards more equitable wealth distribution (and investment in primary health and education), can lead to dynamic economic growth.

At an international level, low commodity prices, protectionist trade policies in the North, inadequate regulation of TNCs, and unsustainable patterns of resource use, make international trade less an engine of growth than an engine of economic decline and environmental destruction, for many countries.

Community organisations are working at grassroots level to address inequality. Women's organisations across the developing world are working to remove the deep-rooted structures of gender discrimination. In Bangladesh, for example, Saptagram is tackling the violation of women's land rights and enabling women to obtain credit. In Brazil, landless peasants and Indian communities are trying to secure their land rights; and in Chile, women employed in sweatshops are organising to improve their working conditions. Small producers in co-operatives and producer groups across the world are trying to improve their position in the market, and consumers in the North are choosing to buy fairly-traded coffee, tea, and other commodities to help to secure the rights of small producers. To strengthen their efforts, action is needed in the following areas:

Gender equity
A major priority must be the elimination of all forms of discrimination against women, particularly in relation to land, credit, and control over productive resources; and implementation of the various ILO conventions to protect the rights of employees, including giving women the right to equal pay, free association, and maternity protection.

Agrarian reform
Reform of the rural sector is needed to create more equitable patterns of land ownership and make more efficient use of resources, including measures to:

- redistribute land in favour of poor men and women (in areas marked by extreme inequality in access to land) and prevent extreme concentration of land ownership;

- protect the rights of share-croppers and agricultural labourers;

- safeguard customary land rights and access to common property resources (including forests, fish stocks and waterways);

- enhance the land and inheritance rights of women.

Management of markets
If poor women and men are not to be disadvantaged in local and national markets, these must be managed in the interests of equity by:

- providing targeted investment in credit, extension services, and economic infrastructure for poor women and men;

- providing market information to help poor producers participate in markets on more equitable terms;

- regulating markets to prevent local, national, and independent monopolies working against the social interest;

- enforcing reasonable and non-discriminatory employment practices in compliance with minimum standards set by the ILO, particularly in the areas of living wages, and safety and security of employment.

Redesign of structural adjustment programmes

Structural adjustment programmes need to be redesigned in order to achieve macro-economic stability through progressive fiscal policies and wider redistributive measures which enable the poor to participate in economic growth and ensure that the costs of adjustment are borne by those in a position to pay. The central theme of stabilisation should be that of 'last call' on the resources of the poor. The aim should be to:

- create an expansionary economic environment oriented towards social and economic recovery, employment creation and poverty reduction;

- allow for the selective protection of labour-intensive industries, state intervention to manage agricultural markets in the interests of the poor, and effective protection of labour standards;

- include more effective monitoring of the effects of structural adjustment on vulnerable groups and on women in particular, through the involvement of community-based groups and Southern NGOs in monitoring the design and implementation of economic reforms.

Refocusing the role of the IMF

The IMF's role should be re-assessed, to ensure that it plays a part in poverty eradication. The IMF should withdraw from structural adjustment programmes in low-income countries, with stabilisation measures integrated into consolidated longer-term recovery plans.

The IMF could take an enhanced role in providing balance-of-payments support on concessional terms to developing countries through a new issue of Special Drawing Rights.

Recasting the existing world trade order

There is an urgent need for reform of the international trading system, so that trade becomes an engine of equitable economic growth. The major priorities are:

- international co-operation to stabilise commodity markets at remunerative levels;

- the withdrawal of all discriminatory trade barriers, including tariff and non-tariff measures, targeted at developing countries;

- the introduction into the WTO of a social clause, based on ILO standards, establishing minimum conditions for participation in the multilateral trading system;

- new international trade rules to reconcile the potential conflicts at national and international levels between free trade and sustainable resource management;

- the organisation of an international conference held under UN auspices to negotiate rules on the regulation of foreign investment and protection of intellectual property, with a view to replacing the inequitable arrangements agreed under the GATT Uruguay Round;

- a comprehensive prohibition of agricultural export subsidisation, and the redesign of the agricultural policies of industrialised countries to encourage less intensive production,

and to redistribute income support from the largest producers to small-holders;

- measures to improve the accountability of TNCs and prevent their activities from eroding citizens' rights, including the setting up of a global Anti-Trusts body, under the auspices of the WTO, to recommend and monitor action by governments where markets are distorted by monopoly power; action is also needed to strengthen governments' ability to prevent transfer pricing, and enforce socially and environmentally responsible patterns of investment through effective codes of conduct;

- a binding and strictly enforced WTO prohibition on the recourse to unilateral trade sanctions against developing countries.

Harnessing consumer power

Consumers in industrialised countries can play an important role in helping small producers to get a fairer return on their labour, by buying fairly-traded products and using their power as consumers to put pressure on retailers and suppliers to supply fairly-traded goods.

Peace and security

There is no greater challenge facing the international community than that of creating the conditions for peace and security. Without genuine development and poverty reduction, there can be no lasting peace. But without peace, efforts to eradicate poverty will fail. Poverty, widening social divisions, environmental stresses, and the long-standing suppression of the rights of different social, ethnic, and cultural groups are fuelling conflict, violence, and crime. Civilians, particularly poor women and children, are bearing the brunt of that violence, as rape victims, amputees, and refugees who have suffered the loss of their family and community networks, and their livelihoods.

At the same time, in countries as diverse as El Salvador, Cambodia, Lebanon, and Mozambique, people are facing new challenges as they seek to rebuild their societies after decades of war.

Communities across the world are grappling with these problems. In Southern Sudan, pastoral communities have adapted their survival strategies to cope with the reality of 'permanent emergencies'; in Bosnia, groups are providing counselling and support for women rape victims; and in El Salvador, community organisations built up during the civil war are now involved in struggles for land, health-care, education, and a fairer return for producers. Ultimately, the only lasting solutions will be found within societies and through action at different levels to create the conditions for peace and security through greater equity, opportunity, and participation. However, far more can also be done at an international level.

Currently, the international community is floundering in attempts to find an appropriate response to conflict, having gone from counter-productive intervention in Somalia to inaction in the face of genocide in Rwanda. Much more effort is needed to identify an appropriate role for external actors in conflict, whether the UN, regional bodies, official donors, or NGOs. Below, we list some critical elements of a more appropriate international response.

Conflict prevention

More resources should be invested in helping to strengthen local and regional conflict-mediation and conflict-prevention initiatives.

The UN Security Council should respond promptly to early warnings of impending conflict and put much greater emphasis on preventive diplomacy and speedy deployment of human-rights monitors. This will involve the UN Secretary-General in streamlining UN machinery to provide timely information to the UNSC, possibly through the creation of an Office for Preventive Diplomacy and developing a roster of trained human-rights monitors.

Improved UN response to conflicts

When conflicts break out, the UN must be able to respond quickly and effectively. This requires:

- member states to establish 'fast track' stand-by arrangements (to provide the UN with the necessary troops, civilian police and logistical support), and the creation of a properly financed and adequately staffed permanent UN rapid-deployment force, deployable by the UNSC;

- financial and logistical support from member states to strengthen regional capacity for conflict prevention and peacekeeping duties;

- all UN interventions to have clear political and humanitarian objectives; troops to be under streamlined UN command structures and strictly observe human rights;

- a thorough and public evaluation of the work of all the UN humanitarian agencies and of the effectiveness of the co-ordinating role of the Department of Humanitarian Affairs, if necessary, exploring options for radical reform;

- the provision by member governments of adequate finance for UN operations (including humanitarian relief, conflict-prevention, peace-keeping, peace-making, and post-conflict reconstruction).

Post-conflict reconstruction

Greater priority should be given to supporting post-war reconstruction efforts in a manner which addresses the underlying causes of conflict and creates the conditions for permanent peace.

Reduction in arms sales

In order to establish an enforceable code of conduct on international arms transfers, a high-level expert committee needs to be created, reporting to the UN Secretary-General, to administer the UN Arms Register, with wide-ranging powers to investigate arms exports, and subsidies to the weapons industry, and to develop transparent systems of accountability.

The UN Register of Conventional Arms should be extended to cover all small weapons and used to levy a one per cent tax on arms exports that would be channelled into financing UN conflict-prevention initiatives.

A ban on anti-personnel mines

A comprehensive and worldwide ban on the manufacture, stockpiling, export, and use of anti-personnel mines should be introduced.

Action to tackle human rights abuse

Consideration should be given to creating a permanent International Tribunal for genocide, war crimes, and other serious violations of human rights.

A sustainable future

There can be no sustainable future without peace and prosperity. Poverty is a major destroyer of the environment, since it forces local communities into unsustainable survival strategies. Poor people, and particularly women, who have to walk increasingly long distances to collect water and fuelwood, are all too aware that it is they themselves who bear the brunt of local environmental degradation. A range of community groups are taking action across the developing and developed world to try to conserve resources and protect the environment, such as Beja groups in Sudan taking action to cope with a rapidly changing and risk-prone environment, and the Zabaleen community in the slums of Cairo, who survive by collecting and recycling the city's waste. Their action is paralleled by that of local environmental action groups in the North, who are involved in recycling waste, and regenerating run-down inner city areas.

Citizens' action in industrialised countries is particularly important, because it is there that the bulk of the damage is being done to the global environment, through high levels of energy consumption and wasteful life-styles, which are emulated by the elite in developing countries. By the same token, the industrialised world has no right to demand environmental sustainability in the South until it sets its own house in order — and until it provides the

financial resources needed to realise the objectives agreed at the Earth Summit.

It is therefore essential that countries in the North assume their full share of the cost of protecting the global environment, and that governments take tangible steps to reduce the depth of their ecological footprint on that environment by:

- following the Dutch example of assessing the scale and impact of their 'ecological footprint' in key sectors, including energy and agriculture, and committing themselves to setting specific, time-tabled targets to reduce the negative impact of their footprints; reporting on pro-gress to the UN Commission on Sustainable Development, together with reports on implementation of Agenda 21, agreed at the Rio Earth Summit;

- demonstrating their commitment to Agenda 21 by allocating additional financial resources to fund its implementation, together with appropriate technology transfer and capacity building;

- introducing measures to meet more stringent targets on energy use, including a carbon/energy tax, tougher energy efficiency standards, programmes of insulation, investment in renew-able energy sources, redesigning the taxation system to tax over-exploitation of resources, rather than employment and investment;

- committing themselves to reduce CO_2 emissions by 30 per cent from 1990 levels by 2005;

- introducing environmental policies that use market mechanisms, including environmental taxes, import and export controls, and recourse to the 'polluter pays' principle, so that environmental costs are more accurately reflected in market prices.

Local environmental action

Action by local environmental groups and individual citizens in the North is needed to conserve energy, improve the local environment and make more sustainable use of resources through recycling.

Ultimately, action by citizens and social movements in both South and North, coming together to put pressure on governments to act, provides the best hope of securing rights and ending poverty.

Notes

Introduction

1 Cited in Kirdar V and Silk L *A World Fit for People* New York University Press, 1994.
2 United Nations Children's Fund (UNICEF) *Annual Report* 1994, p.6.
3 United Nations Development Programme (UNDP) *Human Development Report*, 1994.
4 International Monetary Fund *International Financial Statistics*, 1994.
5 Oxfam *Africa: Make or Break*, 1993.
6 'Latin America Survey' *The Economist* 13 November 1993.
7 UNICEF *Annual Report*, op. cit. pp.24-25.
8 UNICEF *The State of the World's Children* 1994.
9 Children's Defence Fund *The State of America's Children's Yearbook* 1994, pp.2-5.
10 House of Lords Select Committee on the European Communities *The Poverty Programme*, HMSO, London, 1994.
11 On poverty and inequality in the UK see Joseph Rowntree Foundation *Inquiry into Income and Wealth* 1995 vol. 1; Glyn A and Miliband D *Paying for Inequality: The Economic Cost of Social Injustice* Rivers Oram Press, 1994; Oppenheim C *Poverty: The Facts* Child Poverty Action Group, 1993, chapter 2.
12 Galbraith J K *The Culture of Contentment* Penguin, 1992.
13 ibid.
14 Joesph Rowntree Foundation *Inquiry into Income and Wealth*, op. cit.
15 Feeny P 'The UN World Conference on Human Rights, Vienna' *Development in Practice* 3:3, 1993.
16 UN *Human Rights: A Compilation of International Instruments* vol. 1, 1993.
17 Tawney R *Equality* George Allen and Unwin, p.56.
18 World Bank *World Development Report* 1990.

Chapter 1 Poverty and livelihoods

1 Mcnamara R *The McNamara Years at the World Bank: Major Policy Addresses of Robert S McNamara 1968-81*, World Bank, Baltimore 1981.
2 See Chambers R and Conway G *Sustainable Rural Livelihoods: Practical Concepts for the Twenty-first Century* Institute for Development Studies (IDS) Discussion Paper 96, February 1992.
3 UNDP *Human Development Report 1990*, p.33.
4 Hall L 'Land tenure and land reform in Brazil' in Prosterman R et al *Agrarian Reform and Grassroots Development* Lynne Rienner, p.206.
5 CIIR *Brazil: Democracy and Development*, Comment series, 1992, p.22.
6 ibid p.23.
7 UNDP *Human Development Report 1994*, op. cit. p.99.
8 Palmer R *Land and Social Domination in Rhodesia*, Heinemann 1977.
9 ibid.
10 World Bank *Country Economic Memorandum: Zimbabwe* 1995 (forthcoming).
11 Robinson M *Evaluating the Impact of NGOs in Rural Poverty Alleviation*, ODI Working Paper 4649 p.6, 1992.
12 See Amin N and Chipika J T *The Differentiation of the Peasantry in Zimbabwe* Department of Economics, University ofZimbabwe Discussion Paper 13 February 1990.
13 Stoneman C and Thompson G *Background Paper on Trade and Food Security in Zimbabwe* CIIR 1993, p.3.
14 UNICEF *Children and Women in Zimbabwe*, Harare 1994, p.32.
15 See Loewenson R *Modern Plantation Agriculture: Corporate Wealth and Labour Squalor* Zed Books, 1992.
16 Government of Zimbabwe National Steering Committee on Food and Nutrition *Food and Nutrition Issues*, paper, 1990.
17 Moyo S et al *The Root Causes of Hunger in Zimbabwe* Zimbabwe Institute for Development Studies Working Paper 4 1985.
18 Thamarajakski R 'Agricultural growth, rural development and employment' *Economic and Political Weekly* 24:12, 1985, pp.5-8.
19 World Bank *Zambia: Poverty Assessment*, 1995.
20 South Commission *Challenge to the South* OUP 1990, p.89.
21 World Resources Institute (WRI) *World Resources 1994-95*, pp.52-53.

22 CIIR *Brazil* op. cit.

23 MacDonald N *Brazil: A Mask Called Progress* Oxfam 1991, pp.33-46.

24 Oxfam *A Case for Reform: Fifty Years of the IMF and World Bank*, Oxfam Policy Department 1995.

25 Association for Land Reform and Development *Proposal on Land Resource Development*, Bangladesh November 1994.

26 Association for Land Reform and Development *Voice of the Landless* Ogami, Bangladesh, 1993.

27 Informal Sector Service Centre *Report on Kamaiya Program* January 1994, Katmandu.

28 Shiva V *The Violence of the Green Revolution* Zed Books 1991.

29 Bouton M *Agrarian Radicalism in South India* Princeton University Press 1985

30 Durning A *Poverty and the Environment: Reversing the Downward Spiral* Worldwatch Paper 92, WRI 1989.

31 Jodha N 'Common property resources and the rural poor in dry regions of India' *Economic and Political Weekly* 5 July 1986.

32 Beauclerk J et al *Indigenous Peoples: A Fieldguide for Development* Development Guidelines Series Oxfam 1988.

33 Kurian J and Achari T 'Overfishing along Kerala coast' *Economic and Political Weekly* 35-36, 1991, pp. 2011-18; Durning A *Poverty and the Environment*, op. cit.

34 WRI *Resources, Population and the Philippines' Future*, Paper 4, 1988.

35 Davidson J and Myers J with Chakraborty M *No Time to Waste: Poverty and the Global Environment* Oxfam 1992.

36 Gilbert A and Guyler J *Cities, Poverty and Development* OUP 1992.

37 World Bank *Zambia: Poverty Assessment*, op. cit.

38 ibid.

39 Cornia G *Macroeconomic Policy, Poverty Alleviation and Long-term Development: Latin America in the 1990s* UNICEF Innocenti Papers 1994.

40 Thorp R *Challenges for Peace: Towards Sustainable Social Development in Peru*, Report of the Pilot Mission on Social and Economic Reform of the Inter-American Development Bank, Social Agenda Policy Group, Washington June 1995.

41 UNICEF *Children and Women in Zimbabwe*, op. cit. p.32.

42 Diaz A *Restructuring and the New Working Class in Chile* UNRISD Discussion Paper, October 1993, p.23.

43 Oxfam 'Exchanging livelihoods' mimeo information pack, July 1994.

44 World Bank *Uganda: Growing Out of Poverty* 1994.

45 UNDP *Human Development Report 1991*, p.50.

46 UNICEF *State of the World's Children 1992* OUP 1992.

47 Desai S 'Women's burdens: easing the structural constraints' in Sen G et al *Population Policies Reconsidered* Harvard University Press 1994, p.147.

48 See Merchant K and Kurtz K 'Women's nutrition through the life-cycle' in Koblinsky M *The Health of Women: A Global Perspective*, Westview Press, p.62-66,

49 See, for example, World Bank *Priorities and Strategies for Education*, Education and Social Policy Department, October 1994.

50 Mooch P 'Education and agricultural productivity' in *International Encyclopedia of Education* Pergamon 1994.

51 World Bank *East Asian Miracle* 1993, p.50.

52 World Bank *Priorities and Strategies* op. cit. part 1.

53 World Bank *Investing in Health, World Development Report* 1993, p.42.

54 World Bank *Priorities and Strategies*, op. cit.

55 ibid.

56 ibid.

57 WRI, *World Resources*, op. cit., pp.45-46.

58 Dreze J and Sen A *Hunger and Public Action* Clarendon Press 1989.

59 Guttman C *In Our Hands*, Saptagram 1993.

60 Rocheleau D 'Women, trees and tenure' in Formann L and Bruce J *Whose Trees? Proprietary Dimensions of Social Forestry* Westview Press 1989, pp.255-260.

61 UN Centre for Social Development *World Survey on the Role of Women in Development* 1989, p.104.

62 Pitanguy J *Violence Against Women: The Hidden Health Burden*, World Bank Discussion Paper, Population, Health and Nutrition Department, World Bank, 1994.

63 Guttman C *In Our Hands*, op. cit.

64 WHO 1991 *Summary Report and Recommendations of the Meeting on 'Women's Perspectives on the Introduction of Fertility Regulation Technologies'*, Special Programme of Research Development and Research Training in Human Reproduction and the International Women's Health Coalition, WHO Geneva.

65 UNFPA *Briefing Kit* 1993.

66 Ehrlich A and P *The Population Explosion* Simon and Schuster, 1990.

67 Sen A 'Population: delusion and reality' *The*

New York Review of Books 22 September 1994.

68 Hansen S 'Population: its challenge to economic and social scientists' in *International Social Science Journal*, September 1994, pp.336-340.

69 Dasgupta P 'Population, resources and poverty' *Ambio* 21: 1, 1992, pp.95-101.

70 UNFPA *The State of World Population* UN 1993, p.39.

71 Sadik N *The State of World Population* UN 1990, pp.14-17.

72 Summers L 'The most influential investment' *People and the Planet* l2:1, 1993, pp.10-12.

73 Sen A 'Population: delusion and reality', op cit.

74 UNICEF *The State of the World's Children*, OUP 1994, p.25.

75 Walt B 'Honduras: population, inequality and resource destruction', in National Research Council *Population and Land Use in Developing Countries*, Washington, 1992.

76 Agarwal B *Cold Hearths and Barren Slopes: The Woodfuel Crisis in the Third World*, Riverdale, 1986, p.21.

77 Human J 'Friends of trees and living beings' *Oxfam News* Summer 1992.

78 Scoones I *Living With Uncertainty: New Directions for Pastoral Development in Africa* ODI, April 1994.

79 Paul J B 'In pursuit of sustainable livelihoods' Oxfam, Mimeo, 1994; see also Almond M 'Pastoral Development and Oxfam in the Sudan', mimeo, 1990.

80 On the relative advantages of smallholder agriculture see the submission by Heyer J and Williams G to the Government of Tanzania, Presidential Land Commission, Oxfam, mimeo 1992; see also International Fund for Agricultural Development (IFAD) *State of World Rural Poverty*, 1992.

81 Williams G 'Taking the part of the peasant: rural development in Nigeria and Tanzania' in Gutkind P and Willerstein I *The Political Economy of Contemporary Africa*, Sage 1985.

82 World Bank *Country Economic Memorandum: Zimbabwe* 1995 (forthcoming).

83 Sengupta S and Gardner H 'Rural poverty and public policy in West Bengal' in Drèze J and Sen A *India: Economic Development and Social Opportunity* Clarendon Press 1995.

84 ibid.

85 UNICEF *The State of the World's Children*, OUP 1995.

86 Carciofi R and Getrangolo C *Tax Reforms and Equity in Latin America* UNICEF, Innocenti Papers, January 1994; see also Cornia G *Macroeconomic Policy, Poverty Alleviation and Long-term Development*, op. cit.

87 Thorp R *Challenges for Peace*, op. cit.

88 Savadogo K 'The impact of self-imposed adjustment: the case of Burkina Faso, 1983-89' in Cornia G et al *Africa's Recovery in the 1990s* Macmillan 1992, p.57.

89 UNDP *Human Development Report 1994*, p.48.

90 Saferworld *The True Cost of Conflict* November 1994, p.3.

91 International Broadcasting Trust, *The War Machine*, IBT 1994, p.11.

92 'Fuel; price crisis' *West Africa* 10-16 October 1994, pp.1572-1573.

93 ibid.

94 Mathai W *African democracy: Statement Presented at the United Nations World Hearings on 9 June, 1994*, UNDP 1994, p.7.

Chapter 2 A world at war

1 Roberts A and Kingsbury B *United Nations, Divided World: The UN's Role in International Relations* Clarendon Press, 1993, p.507.

2 Hobsbawm E *The Age of Extremes* Michael Joseph 1994

3 UNICEF *State of the World's Children*, New York, 1993.

4 UNDP *Human Development Report*, New York, 1994; US Committee for Refugees *World Refugee Survey* Washington, 1995; Ramsey A 'Major armed conflicts' in *Stockholm International Peace Research Institute Yearbook, 1993: World Armaments and Disarmaments*.

5 Adams M and Bradbury M *Conflict and Development: Organisational Adaptation in Conflict Situations*, Oxfam Discussion Paper 4. Paper presented at Development in Conflict Workshop, Birmingham University, November 1994.

6 De Waal A 'The genocide state' *Times Literary Supplement* 1 July 1994; see also Waller D *Rwanda: Which Way Now?* Oxfam Country Profile Series 1993.

7 Ignatieff M 'The Balkan tragedy' *The New York Review of Books* 13 May 1993.

8 African Rights *Rwanda: Who is Killing, Who is Dying; What is to be Done*, London, May 1994.

9 Vassall-Adams G *Rwanda: An Agenda for International Action* Insight Series, Oxfam 1994.

10 UN *Situation of Human Rights in the Former Yugoslavia* Economic and Social Council, New York, 1993.

11 El Bushra J and Piza-Lopez E *Development in Conflict: The Gender Dimension* Discussion Paper

3, Oxfam 1994.

12 ibid; see also Womanaid *Extracts from the Warburton Report* London, January 1993.

13 Mortimer E 'A shell too far in Sarajevo' *Financial Times* 12 February 1994.

14 Brittain V 'UNITA: outpolled but not overpowered' *New Statesman* 4 March 1994.

15 Keen D *Refugees: Rationing the Right to Life; The Crisis in Emergency Relief* Tavistock, London, 1992.

16 UN Development Fund *Women in Crisis: The Impact of the Conflict on Women and Children in Southern Sudan*, New York, April, 1994

17 ibid.

18 On the distribution of landmines and associated problems see Human Rights Watch *Landmines in Mozambique*, 1994; Human Rights Watch *Landmines: A Deadly legacy*, New York 1993; McGrath R *Landmines: Legacy of Conflict* Oxfam 1994.

19 UN *The Scourge of Landmines*, UN Focus, October 1993.

20 Human Rights Watch *Landmines in Mozambique*, 1994.

21 Media and Communications Centre *Israeli Obstacles to Economic Development in the Occupied Palestinian Territories* Jerusalem, April 1994.

22 Nashashi K and Kanaan O 'Which trade arrangements for the West Bank?' in *Finance and Development* 31:3, 1994, World Bank, Washington.

23 Ozanne J 'Gazans struggle in the wake of border closure' *Financial Times* 24 October 1994.

24 Barghuthi M 'Democracy: a precondition for Palestinian survival' *Middle East International* 17 March 1995

25 Union of Palestinian Medical Relief Committees *Palestinian Health*, Jerusalem 1993.

26 Said E 'The Palestinian case' *Washington Post* 25 December 1994.

27 Duffield M 'Complex emergencies and the crisis of developmentalism' *IDS Bulletin*, 25, 3, 1994, Sussex University.

28 OECD *Development Co-operation Report, 1994*.

29 Grant J *Jumpstarting Development*, UNICEF, New York, 1994.

30 Duffield, op.cit.

31 de Waal A 'African encounters' *Index on Censorship* 6, 1994, London.

32 Munch G 'Beyond electoralism in El Salvador: conflict resolution through negotiated compromise' *Third World Quarterly* 14:1, 1993.

33 Murray K et al *Rescuing Reconstruction: The Debate on Post-war Economic Recovery in El Salvador* Hemisphere Initiative,Massachusets, May 1994.

34 de Soto A and Castillo G *Obstacles to Peacebuilding*, UNDP, New York, 1994.

35 Ardon P *From Disarmament to Democracy*, Oxfam, Nicaragua, November 1993.

36 Roberts A and Kingsbury B op. cit.

37 UNDP *Human Development Report* New York, 1994.

38 Gardner D 'Europe looks for Northern conflict' *Financial Times* 28 October 1994.

39 Frelick B 'The year in review' in US Committee for Refugees *World Refugee Survey*, Washington, 1994.

40 Jackson B 'Promoting real security: implications for policy in the North' in Tansey et al (ed) *A World Divided* Earthscan, London, 1994.

41 UNDP op. cit.

42 World Development Movement (WDM) *Biting the Bullet* 1994; International Broadcasting Trust (IBT) *The War Machine* London, 1994.

43 UNDP op. cit.

44 ibid.

45 'Arms to Iraq via Jordan' *The Economist* 7 May 1994.

46 IBT op. cit.

47 On the UN's Arms Registry see Saferworld *Arms and Dual Use Export Controls* Bristol, June 1994.

48 UNDP op. cit.

49 US State Department *Hidden Killers: A Report on International Demining*, Washington, 1993.

50 'Ban the mine' *The Economist*, 25 December 1993.

51 *The Military Utility of Landmines: Implications for Arms Control*, US Defence Department, The Pentagon, June 1994.

52 Quoted in Vassal-Adams G 'The war in the former Yugoslavia', Oxfam mimeo, March 1993.

53 Glenny M 'What is to be done?' *New York Review of Books* 27 May 1993.

54 Glenny M *The Fall of Yugoslavia: The Third Balkan War* Penguin London, 1993; Cow J 'Deconstructing Yugoslavia' *Survival* 33:4, 1991.

55 Ignatieff M 'The Balkan tragedy' *The New York Review of Books* May 13, 1993.

56 Vassall-Adams G *Rwanda: An Agenda for International Action* Oxfam, 1994.

57 The UN Secretary-General has stressed the need for more effective preventive diplomacy. See Boutros Boutros-Ghali *An Agenda for Peace: Preventative Diplomacy, Peacemaking and Peace-keeping* UN, New York, 1992; see also Catley A *The Pursuit of Peace: A Framework for International Action* Saferworld, Bristol, 1994; Cross-Party Independent Inquiry *Military Intervention for Humanitarian Purposes*, London, 1993.

58 Weiss T G 'Intervention: whither the United Nations?' *Washington Quarterly* 17:1, 1994.

59 CIIR *East Timor* Comment Series, 1994.

60 Vassall-Adams G *Rwanda* op. cit.

61 quoted in ibid.

62 Cross-Party op. cit. 1993; Catley A op. cit.

63 Vassall-Adams G 'The Somalia crisis' Oxfam, mimeo, 1994.

64 Vines A *One Hand Tied: Angola and the UN* CIIR Briefing Paper, June 1993.

65 Anstee M J 'Angola: the forgotten tragedy' *International Relations*, XI, 6, 1993.

66 Africa Recovery *Mozambique: Out of the Ruins* Briefing Paper, New York, May 1993; McCormick 'Mozambique's cautious steps towards lasting peace' *Current History* May 1993.

67 Childers E (ed) *Challenges to the United Nations* CIIR, 1995.

68 Global Justice Commission *Our Global Neighbourhood* OUP 1995.

Chapter 3 Structural adjustment

1 Quoted in Rich B *Mortgaging the Earth* Earthscan, 1994.

2 On the aims of the Bretton Woods conference see Holland S *Towards a new Bretton Woods* Spokesman 1994; Cavanagh J et al *Beyond Bretton Woods* Pluto 1994.

3 IMF *Articles of Agreement* IMF 1993. p.2.

4 ibid.

5 Quoted in Moggeridge D (ed) *The Collected Writings of John Maynard Keynes* Cambridge University Press 1980.

6 World Bank *Implementing the World Bank's Strategy to Reduce Poverty: Progress and Challenges* World Bank 1993.

7 Osunsad F *IMF Support for African Adjustment Programs*, IMF External Relations Department 1993.

8 On the debt crisis see Roddick J *The Dance of the Millions: Latin America and the Debt Crisis* Latin America Bureau, London; Commonwealth Secretariat *The Debt Crisis and the World Economy*, London 1984.

9 Bird G *International Financial Policy and Economic Development* Macmillan 1987.

10 World Bank *Adjustment Lending and Mobilisation of Private and Public Resources for Growth* Country Economies Department 1992.

11 Williams G 'Why structural adjustment is necessary and why it doesn't work' *Review of African Political Economy* 60 1994.

12 Valdes A 'The policy response of agriculture' in World Bank *Proceedings of the World Bank Annual Conference on Development Economics 1989*, pp. 263-268; on the role of agricultural marketing boards see Bates R *Markets and States in Tropical Africa* University of California Press 1981.

13 Williams 'Why structural adjustment is necessary' op. cit.

14 IMF policy is explained in Killick T and Malik M *Country Experiences with IMF Programmes in the 1980s*, Overseas Development Institute Working Paper 48, 1991; also see Killick T *Does the IMF Really Help Developing Countries?* ODI Briefing Paper, April 1993.

15 Mosley P et al *Aid and Power* Routledge, 1991; the World Bank's own account of its approach to adjustment is summarised in World Bank *Report on Adjustment Lending; Policies for the Recovery of Growth* World Bank 1990.

16 The following account draws on Government of Zimbabwe, *Zimbabwe: A Framework for Economic Reform (1991-95)* January 1991.

17 World Bank *Report on a Proposed Credit to the Republic of Zimbabwe* 4 June 1993 p.2.

18 IMF 'Zimbabwe background paper', Paper for members of Executive Board, 10 May 1993, p.7.

19 Kanji N and Jazdowska N 'Structural adjustment and women in Zimbabwe' *Review of African Political Economy* 56, 1993.

20 Jamal V 'Changing poverty and employment patterns under crisis in Africa' International Labour Organisation, mimeo, July 1994.

21 Oxfam *Poverty and Inequality in Latin America* Policy Department Briefing Paper, 1994.

22 Moser C *Urban Poverty and Social Policy in the Context of Adjustment*, World Bank, Urban Development Division, July 1994.

23 Palmer I 'Gender equity and economic efficiency in adjustment programmes' in Afshar H and Dennis C *Women, Recession and Adjustment in the Third World*, OUP 1990.

24 Moser C 'The impact of recession and structural adjustment policies at the micro level: low-income women and their households in Guayquil, Ecuador' *Invisible Adjustment* Vol 2 UNICEF New York 1989.

25 ibid; on the impact of adjustment on women see also Commonwealth Secretariat *Engendering Adjustment for the 1990s* London 1989.

26 World Bank *Implementing the World Bank's Strategy to Reduce Poverty: Progress and Challenges* 1993.

27 See World Bank *Poverty Handbook* 1991; Ribe H et al *How Adjustment Programs can help the Poor* World Bank Discussion Paper 71, 1991; IMF/World Bank *Strengthening Efforts to Reduce Poverty* 1992; on the increased pressures on

women's time cause by declining family income and welfare provision, see Elson D *Male Bias in the Development Process* Manchester University Press 1991.

28 Choksi A *The Challenge of Investing in Human Capital, Human Resources Development and Operations Policy* The World Bank, March 1994.

29 Jespersen E 'External shocks, adjustment policies and economic and social performance' in Cornia G et al (eds) *Africa's Recovery in the 1990s* Macmillan 1992, pp.26-39.

30 World Bank *Zambia: Poverty Assessment Vol 1*, Human Resources Division 1994.

31 World Bank *Latin America and the Caribbean a Decade after the Debt Crisis* 1993.

32 World Bank *Priorities and Strategies for Education* Education and Social Policy Department, October 1994. On education expenditure patterns in Africa, see also Sahn D 'The impact of macro-economic adjustment on incomes, health, and nutrition: sub-Saharan Africa in the 1980s' in Cornia G et al *From Adjustment to Development in Africa* St Martin's Press 1994.

33 World Bank *Implementing the World Bank's Strategy to Reduce Poverty*, op. cit.

34 UNICEF *Children and Women in Zimbabwe: A Situation Analysis*, UNICEF Harare 1994; Chisvo M *Government Spending on Social Services and the Impact of Structural Adjustment* UNICEF-Harare, 1993.

35 Hawkins T 'Sense of drift in economy' *Financial Times* 7 December 1994; Holman M 'Zimbabwe economy worries donors' *Financial Times* 26 January 1995.

36 Norman O 'Macro-economic trends and the structural adjustment programme', Queen Elizabeth House, Oxford University, mimeo 1995.

37 UNDP *Human Development Report 1994*, New York 1994.

38 Oxfam (India) *Structural Adjustment in India: Issues and Implications*, January 1994.

39 Harris J et al *Economic Reforms in India: Potential Impact on Poverty Reduction and Implications for Social Policy* Development Studies Institute, London School of Economics December 1992, p. 21.

40 World Bank *Zambia Poverty Assessment*, op. cit.

41 This issue is discussed in Stewart F *Globalisation, Poverty and International Action* UNDP New York 1994.

42 Government of Zimbabwe-UNICEF *Findings of the Third Round of Sentinel Surveillance for Social Dimensions of Adjustment Monitoring* Ministry of Public Service, Harare, 1993.

43 Lennock J *Paying for Health: Poverty and Structural Adjustment in Zimbabwe*, Insight series, Oxfam 1994.

44 Government of Zimbabwe *Zimbabwe: A Framework for Economic Reform*, op. cit. Table 1 (Policy Matrix).

45 The adverse effects of user-fees on attendance at rural clinics in Zimbabwe is recorded in: Government of Zimbabwe/UNICEF *Findings from the First, Second and Third Rounds of Sentinel Surveillance for Social Dimensions of Adjustment*, Ministry of Public Service, 1992-3; Renfrew A *ESAP and Health; The Effects of the Economic Structural Adjustment Programme on the Health of the People of Zimbabwe* Mambo Press, Harare, 1992.

46 Hongoro C and Chandwana S *The Effects of User-fees on Health-care Delivery* Blair Research Institute, Harare, 1994.

47 Lennock J *Paying for Health*, op. cit.

48 Oxfam 'The Impact of user-fees in Uganda Kitovove Hospital' mimeo, October 1994.

49 Palmer I *Gender and Population in the Adjustment of African Economies* ILO Geneva 1991.

50 On the damaging effects of user-fees see Greese A 'User-charges for health care: a review of recent experience' *Health Policy and Planning* 6:4, 1991, pp.309-19.

51 Gilson L *Government Health Care Charges: Is Equity Being Abandoned?* London School of Hygiene and Tropical Medicine, 1988; Bennet S 'Public and private health care in developing countries' mimeo, Health Economic and Financing Programme, Cornell University.

52 Jorgensen S et al *Easing the Poor through Economic Crisis and Adjustment: The Story of Bolivia's Emergency Social Fund* World Bank 1991.

53 Stewart F *Protecting the Poor During Adjustment in Latin America*, Queen Elizabeth House Working Papers, Oxford University 1992.

54 Chisvo M and Munro L *Review of Social Dimensions of Adjustment in Zimbabwe*, UNICEF-Harare, 1994.

55 Kaseke E and Ndaradri M *A Situation Analysis of the Social Development Fund* Ministry of Public Service, Labour and Social Welfare, Government of Zimbabwe, 1993.

56 Government of Zimbabwe/UNICEF *Report of the Fourth Round of Sentinel Surveillance for SDA Monitoring*, Ministry of Public Service, 1994.

57 Husain I 'Does structural adjustment help or hurt the poor?' Presentation to World Bank Poverty Workshop, Madrid, 23 October 1993, Africa Region, World Bank, 1993; also Jusain I *Poverty and Structural Adjustment: The African Case*, Human Resources Department, World

Notes

Bank 1993.

58 Food Studies Group 'Agricultural marketing and pricing in Zimbabwe' Queen Elizabeth House Background Paper for World Bank Agriculture Sector Memorandum, mimeo, 1990.

59 See the forthcoming World Bank *Country Economic Memorandum on Zimbabwe: Achieving Phased Growth*, World Bank 1995.

60 World Bank *Global Economic Prospects and the Developing Countries* 1994, p.33.

61 Barrientos S 'Flexible women in fruit: the success of the Chilean export model', mimeo, Business School, University of Hertfordshire, 1994.

62 Abugre C 'Behind the crowded shelves: an assessment of Ghana's structural adjustment experience', mimeo, Institute for Food and Development Policy, San Francisco, 1993; and Development Gap *The Other Side of Adjustment* Washington, 1993.

63 Ahmed R *Agricultural Price Policies: The Case of Bangladesh,* International Food Policy Research Institute, Research Report 27, 1981.

64 Pele V 'Terms of trade, agricultural growth and rural poverty' in Mellor R (ed) *Agricultural Change and Rural Poverty*, Johns Hopkins, 1985.

65 Gibbon P et al *A Blighted Harvest: the World Bank and African Agriculture in the 1980s* James Currey 1993, chapter 4; and Addison T *A Review of the World Bank's Efforts to Assist African Governments in Reducing Poverty*, World Bank Education and Social Policy Department 1993.

66 The following account draws upon World Bank *Uganda: Agriculture* World Bank Country Study, 1993.

67 World Bank *Uganda: Growing out of Poverty*, World Bank Country Study, 1993.

68 Volshalt L *The World Bank and Poverty Reduction in Uganda*, Centre for Development Research Working Paper 94, 1994.

69 Palmer I *Gender and Population*, op. cit. p.26.

70 Banda G *Food and Farm Product Marketing* Oxfam Lusaka, September 1993.

71 Dey S 'Development planning in The Gambia' *World Development* 10:5, 1982

72 Jones G *The Impact of the SEMRY 1 Irrigated Rice Project* US AID, Washington 1983.

73 Addison T and Demery L 'The economics of rural poverty alleviation' in Commander S (ed) *Structural Adjustment and Agriculture* James Currey, 1989, p.75.

74 World Bank *Zimbabwe Agriculture Sector Memorandum* 1991, p.45-47.

75 International Fund for Agricultural Development *The State of World Rural Poverty: An Inquiry into its Causes and Consequences* IFAD, Rome, 1992.

76 World Bank *Zambia Poverty Assessment*, op. cit. pp 85-96.

77 Quoted in *A Case for Reform: Fifty Years of the IMF and the World Bank* Insight series, Oxfam 1995.

78 World Bank *Zambia Poverty Assessment*, op. cit. p.93

79 Jayne T and Chioro M 'Unravelling Zimbabwe's food insecurity paradox' *Food Policy* 16:4, pp.319-329

80 Government of Zimbabwe/UNICEF *The Impact of Maize Market Liberalisation in Zimbabwe's Urban Areas*, Government of Zimbabwe, Ministry of Public Service, March 1994.

81 Mosley P *Decomposing the Effects of Structural Adjustment,* University of Reading, Discussion Papers in Development Economics 4, 1994, p.23

82 World Bank *Adjustment Lending* op. cit. Table 59.

83 UNCTAD *Trade and Development Report 1993*.

84 World Bank *Zambia Poverty Assessment*, op. cit. pp.79-82.

85 Crawford L 'Kenya central bank comes under attack from angry exporters' *Financial Times* 10 October 1994.

86 UNCTAD *Trade and Development Report 1995*, op.cit.

87 Guasch J and Rajapatirina J *The Interface of Trade Investment and Competition Policies: Issues and Challenges for Latin America* World Bank December 1994.

88 Stein H 'Deindustrialisation, adjustment, the World Bank and IMF in Africa' *World Development* 20:6 1992; Stewart F 'Are short-term policies consistent with long-term development needs in Africa?' in Cornia G et al (eds) *From Adjustment to Development in Africa*, op. cit.

89 UNCTAD *Trade and Development Report 1995*, op. cit.

90 'Under the volcano' *The Economist* 7 January 1995.

91 Fidler S 'Zedillo's programme in question' *Financial Times* 23 December 1994.

92 Hereida C and Purcell M *The Polarisation of Mexican Society*, Development Gap, Washington 1994, p.8.

93 ibid. p.10.

94 Scott K 'More trouble for Mexico' *The Guardian* 15 March 1995; Fidler S 'Tough Terms for US loan to Mexico' *Financial Times* 21 February 1995.

95 CRIES *Towards a National Solution to the Crisis: Adjusting Adjustment in Nicaragua*, Managua 1994.

96 ILO *World Employment Report 1995*, Geneva.

97 Diejomach V ad Kleyburg J *Report on Developments in the Employment Situation in Africa* ILO Eastern Africa Advisory Team 1994.

98 Horton S 'Bolivia' in Horton S et al *Labour Markets in an Era of Adjustment*, World Bank 1994.

99 Diaz A *Restructuring and the New Working Classes in Chile: Trends in Waged Employment, Informality and Poverty* UNRISD, Geneva 1994.

100 World Bank *Adjustment Lending*, op. cit.

101 OECD *Development Cooperation*, Development Assistance Committee, Paris, 1994.

102 UNCTAD *Trade and Development Report*, 1993, op. cit.

103 World Bank *Report on Adjustment Lending 11*, op. cit. For a review of 'compliance' with structural adjustment see Cornia G *Is Adjustment Conducive to Long-term Development?* UNICEF, Economic Policy Series 21, 1991.

104 Elbadawi I et al *World Bank Adjustment Lending and Economic Performance in Sub-Saharan Africa*, World Bank Policy Research Working Paper, October 1992, p.4. Independent reviews of the impact of structural adjustment policies on investment have reached similar conclusions. See, for example, Mosley P and Weeks J 'Has recovery begun? "Africa's Adjustment in the 1980s" revisited' *World Development* 21:10, 1993, pp 1583-1603.

105 UNCTAD *Trade and Development Report 1993*, op cit. p.96

106 IMF *Economic Adjustment in Low-income Countries: Experience under the Enhanced Structural Adjustment Facility*, Occasional Paper 106, September 1993.

107 Killick T 'Can the IMF help low-income countries? Experience with its structural adjustment facilities', mimeo, ODI, London 1994; Bird G *The IMF and Developing Countries: Evidence from the Past and Proposals for the Future*, University of Surrey Working Paper, 93/6 1993, similarly concludes 'the track record of fund-supported programmes is not good', although both authors cite non-compliance as a pervasive problem.

108 World Bank *Adjustment in Africa: Reform, Results, and theRoad Ahead*, World Bank Policy Research Report OUP 1994.

109 For a critical review of Adjustment in Africa, see Sepehri A 'Back to the future?' *Review of African Political Economy* 62, 1994, pp. 559-568.

110 World Bank *Global Economic Prospects*, op cit. 1994, p. 49.

111 Stewart F 'Are short-term policies consistent with long-term development needs?' op. cit,

p.119.

112 Evans D and Edstrom J *Trade Policy Reform and Tropical Beverages: The Fallacy of Compositism in Policy Advice*, University of Sussex, IDS, May 1993.

113 Oxfam *Economic Reform and Inequality in Latin America*, Policy Department Briefing, February 1995.

114 Weeks J 'The Latin American economies in the 1980s and 1990s', School of Oriental and African Studies, mimeo, 1995.

115 ibid.

116 CEPAL *Preliminary Overview of the Latin American and Caribbean Economy* Santiago, December 1994, pp 1-5.

117 UNCTAD *Trade and Development Report 1994*, pp.33-35

118 CEPAL op cit

119 Oxfam *Economic Reform and Inequality*, op. cit.

120 Green D *Silent Revolution: The Rise of Market Economics in Latin America*, Latin America Bureau, London, 1995 pp.7-8

121 *The Economist* 'Latin America Survey' 13 November 1993 p.25.

122 Huntington S 'The clash of civilisations?' *Foreign Affairs* 27:3, 1993 p.34.

123 Savodogo K and Wetta C 'The impact of self-imposed adjustment: the case of Burkina Faso' in Cornia G et al *Africa's Recovery in the 1990s*, op. cit. p.59.

124 Cornia G *Macro-economic Policy, Poverty Alleviation, and Long-term Development*, UNICEF, Innocenti Occasional Papers EPS 40, 1994, p.47.

125 UNCTAD *Trade and Development Report 1994* pp.49-75.

126 See Wade R *Governing the Market*, Princeton 1990; the World Bank has acknowledged the crucial role played by the state in South-East Asia in *The East Asian Miracle*, World Bank Policy Research Report OUP 1995.

127 UNCTAD *Trade and Development Report 1993* pp123-126.

128 World Bank *The East Asian Miracle* op. cit.

Chapter 4 International trade

1 White H D 'Preliminary draft proposal for a United Nations Stabilisation Fund' in Horsefield J K *The International Monetary Fund 1945-65, Vol 3, Documents*, IMF 1969, p.37.

2 On the background to the International Trade Organisation which was originally envisaged as an element in the Bretton Woods system, see Whalley J (ed) *Dealing with the North*,

Notes

Western Ontario, 1987.

3 GATT *International Trade 1993-94, Vol 1*, Geneva.

4 IMF *Annual Report 1993*, pp. 4-6.

5 On the shifting balance of economic power see Latter R *The Interdependent Triad: Japan, the US, and Europe*, Wilton Park Papers 19, 1989.

6 Long T and Hines C *The New Protectionism* Earthscan 1993, part 3; and World Bank *Global Economic Prospects and Developing Countries* 1992, pp. 31-36.

7 'The world's best cars are made all over the world' *International Herald Tribune* 14 February 1989.

8 'Ford's global gamble' *The Economist* 23 July 1994.

9 'Survey of the global economy' *The Economist* 1 October 1994, p.27.

10 Coote B *NAFTA: Poverty and Free Trade in Mexico*, Insight series, Oxfam 1995.

11 'Survey of the IMF, world economy, and finance' *Financial Times* 24 September 1993.

12 ibid.

13 World Bank *World Debt Tables 1994-95*, op. cit.

14 ibid.

15 de Jonquieres G 'The tigers face a challenge' *Financial Times* 12 December 1994.

16 UNCTAD *World Investment Report 1994*, Geneva, p.78.

17 Barnet R and Cavanagh J *Global Dreams: Imperial Corporations and the New World Order*, Simon and Schuster, New York, 1994, chapter 1.

18 Oman C *Trends in Foreign Direct Investment*, Proceedings of meeting held on 20 December 1991, Inter-American Development Bank, Washington, 1991.

19 UNCTAD *World Investment Report*, op. cit.

20 Schwab K and Smodja C 'The new rules of the game in a world of many players' *Harvard Business Review*, November 1994.

21 Stewart F 'The new international division of labour' *World of Work* 8, 1994, pp.28-29.

22 Wood A *North-South Trade, Employment and Inequality*, OUP 1993.

23 Prowse M 'No easy answers to job questions' *Financial Times* 21 July 1993.

24 Low Pay Unit, *Poor Britain in the New Review*, LPU London, p. 6.

25 The role of international trade in reinforcing poverty and low wages in the North is discussed by Lang T and Hines C *The New Protectionism*, passim, op. cit. From a more sanguine perspective see 'Third World job stealers' *The Economist* 2 April 1994.

26 Oman C *Globalisation and Regionalisation: The Challenge for Developing Countries*, OECD, Development Centre January 1994.

27 On trade liberalisation in Latin America see World Bank *The Interface of Trade, Investment, and Competition Policies*, Policy Research Working Paper 1393, December 1994.

28 UNCTAD *Trade and Development Report*, op. cit. p.114.

29 On regionalisation in Latin America see Oman C *Globalisation and Regionalisation* op. cit. pp. 48-57.

30 'Four into one might go' *The Economist* 13 August 1994.

31 de Jonquieres G and Montagnon P 'APEC: future global powerhouse or mere talking shop?' *Financial Times* 14 November 1994; 'Different aims, common cause' *Financial Times* 18 November 1994.

32 Gardner D 'EU plans trade zone with South Americans' *Financial Times* 25 November 1994.

33 Pilling D 'NAFTA accord back on Chile's agenda' *Financial Times* 27 May 1994.

34 Stevens C *After the GATT Uruguay Round* Institute of Development Studies Policy Briefing Paper, April 1994.

35 On the export growth performance of different developing regions see World Bank *Global Economic Prospects and the Developing Countries* op. cit. pp. 20-21.

36 Oxfam *Africa: Make or Break* Oxfam 1993 pp. 7-11.

37 GATT *International Trade 1992-93*, Geneva 1993.

38 World Bank *Global Economic Prospects 1994*, pp. 32-33.

39 Fraser M *Africa's Commodity Problems: Towards a Solution*. A report by the UN Secretary-General's Expert Group, UN 1990.

40 World Bank *Sub-Saharan Africa: From Crisis to Sustainable Growth*, Washington 1989, chapter 1.

41 Holman M 'Glimmer of light in a dark continent' *Financial Times*, *Emerging Markets Survey*, 20 February 1995.

42 UNCTAD *World Investment Report* p.91.

43 Watkins K *Fixing the Rules* CIIR London 1992.

44 See Madden P *The Road from Marrakesh: Regulating World Trade for Sustainable Development* Christian Aid, April 1994; Worldwide Fund for Nature *Sustainable Development and Integrated Disputes Settlement in GATT*, Geneva, 1994.; Third World Network 'After the Uruguay Round' in *Resurgence* 45, 1994; Malaysia (special issue on the WTO) Ragharan C 'Marrakesh and after' *Third World Economics* 88-89, May 1994; Friends of the Earth *Notes on the Proposal for a New WTO*, FoE, London 1994.

45 On the links between trade and environment see Esty D *Greening the GATT* Institute for International Economics, Washington 1993; Arden Clark C *International Trade, GATT and the Environment* WWF, Geneva May 1992; Housman R *Reconciling Trade and the Environment*, UNEP, New York 1994.

46 It also carries considerable weight in the industrialised world; see, for example, 'Free trade or foul' *The Economist* 9 April 1994.

47 World Bank *Global Economic Prospects 1994*, op. cit. chapter 2.

48 Hellier C 'The mangrove wastelands' *The Ecologist* March 1988; Asian Development Bank *Economic Policies for Sustainable Development*, ADP, Manila 1990, p. 49. See also Broad R and Cavanagh J *Plundering Paradise* University of California Press 1989 pp. 37-38.

49 Coote B *The Trade Trap* Oxfam 1992.

50 Haggart K 'The global scramble for fish' *Panoscope* London 1992; Campbell T 'Fishermen pay a high price for free trade' *New Pacific* Winter 1990.

51 European Research Office *Fisheries Views in Europe* Briefing Paper WD 1994.

52 Durning A and Brough H 'Reforming the livestock economy' in Brown L et al *State of the World 1992* World Resources Institute Washington 1992, p.74.

53 Carriere J 'The crisis in Costa Rica: an ecological perspective' in Goodman D and Redclift N *Environment and Development in Latin America*, Manchester University Press 1991 pp. 188-190.

54 World Resources Institute *World Resources 1994-95* WRI Washington, p.37.

55 See The Ecologist, *Livestock Schemes and the World Bank*, World Bank Briefing 1993.

56 Ryan J *Plywood versus People* World Watch, Washington, January 1991.

57 Durning A 'Ending poverty' in Brown L *State of the World* op cit.

58 Cruz W and Repetto R *The Environmental Effects of Stabilisation and Structural Adjustment Programmes: The Philippines* WRI Washington, pp. 20-21.

59 Boado E 'Incentive policies and forest use in the Philippines' in Repetto R and Gillis M (eds) *Public Policies and the Misuse of Forest Resources*, World Resources Institute 1989 pp. 184-186.

60 WRI *World Resources 1992*, Washington, p.49.

61 Repetto R 'Deforestation in the tropics' *Scientific American* 262: 4, 1990; Peters C et al 'Valuation of an Amazonian rainforest' *Nature* 339, 1989.

62 Miller K et al 'Deforestation and species loss' in Tuchman J *Preserving the Global Environment*, W W Norton, pp. 91-93.

63 Arden Clark C *South-North Terms of Trade* op. cit.

64 ibid.

65 French H *Costly Trade-offs: Reconciling Trade and the Environment* Worldwatch Papers 113, March 1993, p. 13.

66 Arden Clark C *Conservation and Sustainable Management of Tropical Forests: the Role of ITTO and GATT*, WWF Discussion Paper, Washington 1990.

67 The Ecologist *Sapping the Forest: Structural Adjustment in Guyana* World Bank Briefing Series, 1993.

68 Goodland R et al 'Tropical moist forest management' *Environmental Conservation* 17: 4, 1990, pp. 314-316.

69 This issue is discussed in Weizsacker E *Earth Politics*, Zed Press 1992, pp. 115-127.

70 The social and economic problems of environmental accounting are discussed in Jacobs M *The Green Economy* Pluto Press 1991, chapter 6.

71 Shrybman S 'International trade and the environment: an environmental assessment of the General Agreement on Tariffs and Trade' *The Ecologist* 20: 1, 1990.

72 Arden Clark C *The General Agreement on Tariffs and Trade, Environmental Protection and Sustainable Development*, WWF, Gland, 1991.

73 Keddeman W et al *An Import Surcharge on the Import of Tropical Timber in the European Community*, Netherlands Economic Institute, The Hague, 1989.

74 Arden Clark C *South-North Terms of Trade*, op. cit.

75 On this see French H *Costly Trade-offs* op. cit. pp. 29-37.

76 See, for example, Wise M and Gibb R *Single Market to Social Europe* Longman 1993, chapter 6.

77 George S *The Debt Boomerang* Pluto 1992, p.26.

78 See Coote B *NAFTA: Poverty and Free Trade in Mexico* op. cit.

79 French H *Costly Trade-offs* op. cit. p.31.

80 Sanchez R 'Health and environmental risks of the maquiladora in Mexico' *Natural Resources Journal*, Winter 1990.

81 Coote B *NAFTA* op. cit.

82 Lennon P 'Profits of doom on the border of blight', *The Guardian* 21 August 1992.

83 Cited in Coote B *NAFTA* op. cit. p.25.

84 International Labour Rights Education and Research Fund *Protecting Labour Rights in Connection with North American Trade* March 1993.

85 Housman R *Reconciling Trade and the Environment: Lessons from the North American Free Trade Agreement* UNEP. Geneva 1994, chapter 3.

86 'German chemical giants target China' *Financial Times* 25 January 1994; Shanghai alone has attracted 120 of the world's largest 500 TNCs, see UNCTAD *World Investment Report 1994* op. cit. p.70.

87 French H *Costly Trade-offs*, op. cit.

88 Thrupp L *Challenges in Latin America's Recent Agro-export Boom* World Resources Institute, February 1994.

89 ibid.

90 Coote B *NAFTA* op. cit.

91 Evans J 'Economic security and minimum labour standards' in Hutton W and Kuttner R et al *Jobs and Growth* Fabian Society 1995, p. 50.

92 On the concept of a social clause for international trade see Liemt G *The Multilateral Social Clause in 1994* International Coalition for Development Action, August 1994, Discussion paper; see also Jackson A *A Social Charter and the NAFTA: A Labour Perspective* Canadian Labour Congress 1994.

93 International Confederation of Free Trade Unions *International Workers; Rights and Trade* Geneva September 1994.

94 Liemt G *The Multilateral Social Clause* op. cit.

95 World Commission on Environment and Development *Our Common Future* OUP 1987.

96 GATT *United States: Restrictions on Imports of Tuna* Geneva, 3 September 1991.

97 Christensen E 'GATT sets its net on environmental regulation' *Inter-American Law Review* Winter 1991-92.

98 On the distribution of benefits from the Uruguay Round see Page S *Prospects for Developing Countries: Trade and Capital* ODI 1994.

99 On the importance of primary commodities see Low P and Ramiro G 'Tropical products in the Uruguay Round' in UNCTAD *Uruguay Round: Papers on Selected Issues* 1989.

100 Coote B *The Trade Trap* op. cit. chapter 2.

101 World Bank *Global Economic Prospects 1994* op. cit. p.32.

102 Luke B 'International commodity agreements: have they a future?' mimeo, paper prepared for Oxfam 1994.

103 World Bank *Global Economic Prospects 1994* op. cit. chapter 2.

104 Coote B *The Hunger Crop: Poverty and the Sugar Industry* Oxfam, 1987.

105 Barratt Brown M *Fair Trade: Reform and Realities in the International Trading System* Zed Press 1993, p.68.

106 See Jackson B *Poverty and the Planet* Penguin 1990, chapter 4.

107 World Bank *Global Economic Prospects 1994* op. cit.

108 CIIR *Agriculture and Food Security*, CAP Briefing 9, 1989.

109 Keynes J M 'The international control of raw materials' in *The Collected Writings of John Maynard Keynes*, Vol. XXVII, Macmillan 1980, p.123.

110 On the efforts to manage international commodity markets see Singer H and Amari J *Rich and Poor Countries: Consequences of International Disorder* Unwin-Hyman, chapter 4; Marcels A *Commodities in Crisis: The Commodity Crisis of the 1980s and the Political Economy of International Commodity Prices* Clarendon Press 1992.

111 Luke B *International Commodity Agreements* op. cit.

112 See Trocaire *UNCTAD VII: Problems and Perspectives*, Trocaire North-South Issues Series 11, 1987.; de Silva L *Weighted Scales in North-South Trade* Non-Government Liaison Service Briefing Paper, Geneva 1989.

113 Katsouris C 'Donors wary of African diversification fund' in *Africa Recovery* 8 1/2, April-September 1994, UN p.10; see also Fraser et al *Africa's Commodity Problems* op. cit. p.69-70.

114 On tariff escalation in tropical commodities see Cable V 'Tropical products' in Finger M and Olechowski A *The Uruguay Round: A Handbook on the Multilateral Trade Negotiations* World Bank 1987.

115 European Research Office *The Home 'Rules of Origin': The Case for Relaxation* ERO, Brussels 1994.

116 UNCTAD *Trade and Development Report 1994* op. cit. pp. 139-141.

117 Goldin I et al *Trade Liberalisation: Global Economic Implications* OEC/World Bank, Paris 1994; see also Madden P and Madely J *Winners and Losers: The Impact of the Uruguay Round on Developing Countries* Christian Aid 1994.

118 The EU's banana market is explained in Commission of the European Community *The Single-market Banana Regime*, Brussels 1993.

119 ibid.

120 'GATT condemns EU over bananas' *Financial Times* 20 January 1994.

121 'EU rejects US threat on bananas' *International Herald Tribune* 11 January 1995.

122 Watkins K 'Yellow peril of the top banana' *The Guardian* 14 August 1992.

123 GATT *International Trade 1993-94* Vol 1 op. cit.

124 Whalley J (ed) *The Uruguay Round and Beyond* Macmillan 1989. passim on trade liberalisation in the developing world.

125 Watkins K 'GATT and the Third World' in *The New Conquistadores, Race and Class* 234: 1 July-September 1992.

126 Laird S and Yeats A 'Tariff-cutting formulas - and complications' in Finger M et al *The Uruguay Round* op. cit. p.89.

127 On the rise of non-tariff barriers see Fritsch W et al 'Market access for manufactured exports from developing countries' in Whalley J (ed) *Dealing with the North* Western Ontario 1987; see also Oleckowski A 'Non-tariff barriers to trade in Finger M (ed) *The Uruguay Round* op .cit. pp. 121-127.

128 UNCTAD *Trade and Development Report 1993* op. cit. p.40.

129 ibid.

130 On the use of non-tariff barriers in US trade policy see Pearson C 'Free trade, fair trade? The Reagan record' in Pearson C and Riedel J *The Direction of Trade Policy* Blackwell 1990, pp. 24-60.

131 On the Multi-Fibre Arrangement see Gable V 'Textiles and clothing in a new round of trade negotiations' *The World Bank Economic Review* 1, 1987; Guo D 'The developing world and the Multi-Fibre Arrangement' in Whalley J (ed) *Dealing with the North* op. cit.

132 World Development Movement *Developing Countries in the Textiles and Clothing Trade* WDM 1990; see also International Organisation of Consumers' Unions *The Multi-Fibre Arrangement and Developing Countries* IOCU Brussels 1991.

133 UNDP *Human Development Report 1994* p.66.

134 Hindly B and Lal D *Trade Policy Review 1994* Centre for Policy Studies 1994; Hindly B 'Dumping and the Far East trade of the EC' *World Economy* 11, 1988.

135 'Report finds EU trade policy wanting' *Financial Times* 20 September 1994.

136 UNCTAD *Trade and Development Report 1994* part 3 provides an assessment of the Uruguay Round.

137 World Development Movement 'The phase out of the MFA', submission to European Commission 19 September 1994; 'EU action on Textiles pact a travesty' *Financial Times* 18 September 1994.

138 Sidhva S and Dunne N 'Indian textile and clothing deals welcomed' *Financial Times* 5 January 1995.

139 'Battle lines' *The Economist* 24 December 1995.

140 Oxfam *The Common Agricultural Policy:*

Implications of Reform for Developing Countries Oxfam Briefing Paper 5, June 1992.

141 CIIR *Agriculture and Farm Trade in the GATT* CAP Briefing 20, CIIR 1989.

142 OECD *Agricultural Markets and Trade* Paris 1993.

143 Australian Bureau of Agricultural Economics *Agricultural Policies in the EC* Canberra 1985.

144 Pryke J and Woodward D *The GATT Agreement on Agriculture* CIIR March 1994.

145 Institute for International Economics *Reforming World Agricultural Trade* Washington 1988.

146 Repetto R *Trade and Environment Policies* WRI Issues and Ideas Briefing series 1993.

147 Madden P *Brussels Beef Case: EC Beef Dumping in West Africa*, Viewpoint 3 Christian Aid April 1993.

148 Westlake M 'GATT wars threaten African food security' *Africa Recovery* 4, 3-4, UN 1990.

149 See Beckman B *The Wheat Trap* Zed Press 1987.

150 Economic Commission for Africa *African Alternative Framework* Addis Ababa 1989 p.11.

151 de Alcantara *Economic Restructuring and Rural Subsistence in Mexico: Maize and the Crisis of the 1980s* UNRISD Discussion Paper 31, 1992, pp. 19-21.

152 Appendini K 'Liberalisation and the maize sector in Mexico', mimeo, Proceedings of UNRISD Seminar, March 1993.

153 ibid.

154 Pereira A *The Social and Political Effects of Agricultural Modernisation* Department of Political Science, School for Social Research, New York 1994, p.19.

155 The Uruguay Round agreement in agriculture is summarised in Gardner B *The GATT Uruguay Round: Implications for Exports for the Agricultural Superpowers* CIIR 1993.

156 This helps to explain why world prices will be only marginally influenced by the GATT agreement. See Pryke J and Woodward D *The GATT Agreement on Agriculture* op. cit.

157 World Wide Fund for Nature *Agriculture in the Uruguay Round: Implications for Sustainable Agricultural Development* WWF Gland 1995; see also Jenkins R *Capping GATT and Gatting CAP* Sustainable Agriculture, Food and Environment (SAFE) December 1993.

158 See House of Lords *Development and the Future of the Common Agricultural Policy : Select Committee on the European Community* Vol 11, 1991.

159 On the environmental damage associated with existing agricultural policies see Baldock D *Agriculture and Habitat Loss in Europe* WWF

1990.

160 See, for example, Sustainable Agriculture Food and Environment, *Missed Opportunities and New Hope* SAFE, London, June 1992.

161 On the influence of TNCs in the Uruguay Round negotiationssee *Multinational Monitor* November 1990.

162 On the growing recourse to unilateral threats in US trade policy see Bhaquati J *The World Trading System at Risk* Harvester/Wheatsheaf 1991, chapter 4 passim and pp. 126-141.

163 UNCTAD *Trade and Development Report 1991*.

164 Watkins K 'GATT and the Third World' *Race and Class* op. cit. Despite the Uruguay Round agreement, the US has retained its unilateral trade measures; see 'Mr Clinton's trade agenda' *Financial Times* 14 January 1994.

165 Oxfam (India) *The Dunkel Draft: Issues and Implications for India* Occasional Briefing Paper 3, 1994.

166 On the role of the business lobby in the GATT negotiations on investment see 'Big business wakes up to the Uruguay Round' *Financial Times* 29 September 1990; 'US companies lobby hard on trade' *International Herald Tribune* 30 November 1990; 'US business seeks better outcome in GATT talks' *Financial Times* 24 September 1990.

167 South Commission *The Challenge to the South* OUP, 1990, p.252.

168 Lall S 'The role of foreign direct investment in Est Asia' paper prepared for UNCTAD, June 1994.

169 These issues are discussed in Puri H and Brusick P 'Trade-related investment measures' in UNCTAD *Uruguay Round: Papers on Selected Issues* 1989; see also 'Antitrust and global markets' *Financial Times* 19 July 1994.

170 Keyola KK *Final Dunkel Act: new Patent Regime* National Working Group on Patent Laws, New Delhi, 1994.

171 'Seeds of discord' *The Economist* 2 April 1994; Jain S 'Seeds of discontent' *India Today* 30 November 1993.

172 Shukla S 'Resisting the World Trade Organisation' *Economic and Political Weekly* 12 March 1994, pp.589-90.

173 See Hobbelink H *Biotechnology and the Future of World Agriculture* Zed Press 1991.

174 See Weissman R 'Patent plunder: tripping the Third World' in *Multinational Monitor* op. cit; see also 'Patent differences holding up deal' *Financial Times* 13 November 1990.

175 On mechanisms for regulating TNCs see Gleckman H and Krut R *Business Regulation and Competition Policy* Christian Aid 1994; UNCTAD *Studies on Restrictive Business Practices*

Trade and Development Board 1993.

176 See Barratt Brown *Fair Trade: Reform and Realities in the International Trading System* Zed Press 1993.

Chapter 5 Ecological footprints

1 IPCC, 1992. The major greenhouse gases are carbon dioxide, methane and nitrous oxide, and a range of 'man-made' industrial fluorocarbon chemicals: CFCs, HCFCs, HFCs, and PFCs. Of these, carbon dioxide contributes most seriously to global warming.

2 Foley G *Global Warming: Who is taking the Heat?* Panos, London, 1991.

3 Parry M *Climate Change and World Agriculture* Earthscan 1990. See also the recent report Rosenzweig C et al *Climate Change and World Food Supply* Environmental Change Unit, University of Oxford, Research Report 3, 1993. See also Downing T E *Climate Change and Vulnerable Places: Global Food Security and Country Studies in Zimbabwe, Kenya, Senegal, and Chile*, Environmental Change Unit, University of Oxford, 1992.

4 UN Global Conference on the Sustainable Development of Small Island Developing States, Barbados, April 1994.

5 Commonwealth Secretariat *Climate Change: Meeting the Challenge*, London 1989, p.6. A recent study challenges previous findings: Kausher A et al *Climate Change and Sea Level Rise: the Case of the Coast* Bangladesh Unnayan Parishad, Dhaka 1993.

6 See, for example, Ericksen N J et al *Socio-economic implications of climate change for Bangladesh* Bangladesh Unnayan Parishad, Dhaka, 1993.

7 Weiss E B (ed) *Human Rights, Sustainable Development and the Environment*, Instituto Inter-Americano de Derechos Humanos, Banco Inter-Americano de Desarollo, Brazil 1992.

8 Anil Agarwal, quoted in 'UNCED in Perspective' in *Costing the Earth: Striking the Global Bargain at the 1992 Earth Summit*, WDM, London, 1991.

9 World Resources Institute Report, 1992, and Parikh J et al, *Consumption Patterns: the Driving Force of Environmental Stress* Indira Gandhi Institute of Development Research, Bombay, 1991.

10 *The State of India's Environment 1984-5: The Second Citizens' Report*, New Delhi, 1985.

11 Ross T C and Hildyard N *The Politics of Industrial Agriculture* Earthscan 1992.

12 Abacus Data Services Ltd, for the Department

of Trade and Industry, 1994.

13 Bangladeshi rice farmer, *Panoscope* April 1994, quoted by Fox N.

14 Monan J *Bangladesh: The Strength to Succeed*, Oxfam, 1989.

15 Agarwal A and Narain S *Global Warming in an Unequal World: A Case of Environmental Colonialism* Centre for Science and Environment, New Delhi, 1991.

16 Karas J H W *Back from the Brink: Greenhouse Targets for a Sustainable World* Friends of the Earth, London, 1992.

17 Rees W 'Ecological footprints and appropriated carrying capacity' in *Environment and Urbanisation* 4, October 1992. Sinks refer to natural resources which absorb gases: in this case, forests absorbing CO2, for example.

18 Van Brakel M and Buitenkamp M *Action Plan for a Sustainable Netherlands* Milieudefensie, 1992. This section owes much to the work of Nick Robins at IIED, who also draws attention to some of the dangers of misuse of these concepts, for example, to justify authoritarian population policies.

19 *Sustainable Development: The UK Strategy*, HMSO 1994, p.105.

20 *Sustainable Consumption Symposium: Report* Ministry of Environment, Norway, 1994.

22 UNDP *Human Development Report 1994*, p 18.

23 Rich B *Mortgaging the Earth* Earthscan 1994.

24 Hildyard N 'Foxes in charge of the chickens' in Sachs W (ed.) *Global Ecology*, Zed Books, London 1993, p.31.

25 Paul Ekins 'Making development sustainable' in Sachs W op cit, p. 91.

26 Brundtland Commission *Our Common Future* OUP 1987, p.8.

27 ICC *Business Charter for Sustainable Development*, Paris 1990.

28 UN, Agenda 21, Chapter 2.

29 Ekins P and Jacobs M in Bhaskar V and Glyn A (eds) *The North, the South and the Environment* Earthscan 1995.

30 See, for example, World Bank *World Development Report, 1992*.

31 ibid p.11.

32 'The sustainable consumer society: a contradiction in terms?' *International Environmental Affairs* 3; 4 Fall 1991, p.250.

33 Henk Cox of the Free University of Amsterdam (1993 and 1992) has proposed the creation of International Commodity-Related Environmental Agreements (ICREAs) to address the problem of declining commodity prices and environmental destruction. See, for example, Cox H M 'The "non-polluter gets paid principle" for Third World commodity

exports' *European Journal of Development Research* 3:1, June 1992.

34 UNDP *Human Development Report*, 1994, p18.

35 *IPCC Report*, September, 1994.

36 Friends of the Earth *The Climate Resolution* London, 1994.

37 ibid.

38 A recent OECD study suggests that significant benefits could arise from relatively small reforms: Majocchi A 'Employment effects of eco-taxes: a review of empirical models and results', paper presented to OECD Workshop on implementation of environmental taxes, Paris 1994. See also Jacobs M *The Green Economy* Pluto, 1991.

39 Barker T (ed) *Green Futures for Economic Growth* Cambridge Econometrics 1991.

40 EC White Paper *Growth, Competitiveness, Employment*, 1993, p.146.

41 Barker T *Taxing Pollution Instead of Jobs*, Employment Policy Institute 1994.

42 Friends of the Earth *Working Future: Jobs and the Environment*, London, 1994.

43 Rich B *Mortgaging the Earth*, op. cit. p. 169.

44 ibid.

45 ibid.

46 *Implementing Energy Efficiency Activities in Developing Countries: A Cross-country Examination of Energy and Environmental Issues, Constraints and Options*, World Bank Energy Sector Management Assistance Program, activity initiation brief, April 1990, pp3-4. Quoted in Rich, op cit, p.171.

Chapter 6 Aid, debt, and development finance

1 Brown A et al *Change for the Better: Global Change and the Environment* Commonwealth Secretariat 1991 p.69.

2 CIIR *World Development Crisis*, Comment Series, 1988.

3 UNDP *Human Development Report* New York 1994, p.63.

4 World Bank *World Debt Tables 1994-94, Vol 1* Washington 1995. Table 1.1 p.7.

5 ibid.

6 The Brady Plan is explained in ODI *Recent Initiatives on Developing Country Debt*, Briefing Paper, April 1990.

7 Woodward D 'Latin American debt: an assessment of recent developments and prospects', mimeo, Oxfam, 1994.

8 Fidler S 'Question mark over debt remains', 'Latin American Finance', *Financial Times* 11 April 1994.

Notes

9 Cockburn A 'War and peso' *New Statesman* 24 February 1995, pp.18-20.

10 'The risk in Asia' *The Economist* 28 January 1995; 'Mexico's peso crisis cools investors' taste for emerging markets' *International Herald Tribune* 13 January 1995.

11 World Bank *World Debt Tables 1994-95*, op. cit. p.13.

12 Fidler S 'Miracle or mirage for Mexico?' *Financial Times* 13 January 1995.

13 'Putting Mexico together again' *The Economist* 4 February 1995,pp.85-86.

14 Derived from World Bank *World Debt Tables 1994-95*, op. cit. p.216.

15 UNICEF *The State of the World's Children* New York 1994, p.51.

16 The following is based upon Oxfam *Multilateral Debt as an Obstacle to Recovery: The Case of Uganda*, Oxfam Briefing Paper 7, March 1994.

17 Johanes R *Towards Resolving the Debt Problem of Special Programmes of Assistance Countries* World Bank, Washington 1993.

18 World Bank *Uganda: Growing out of Poverty, World Bank Country Study* 1993, pp.11-14.

19 CRIES *From Debt Burden to the Search for Development Alternatives* Regional Coordination for Social and Economic Research, Managua 1994.

20 Levy H 'From debt to development' Association of Development Agencies, Kingston, Jamaica, mimeo November 1994.

21 ibid.

22 Helleiner G *Debt Relief for Africa*, UNICEF Staff Working Paper 11, 1993, p.11.

23 Overseas Development Institute (ODI) *Poor Country Debt: A Never-ending Story?* Briefing Paper 1, 1995.

24 Martin M *Official Bilateral Debt: New Directions for NGO Action* Eurodad, Brussels 1993.

25 Mistry P *The Multilateral Debt Problems of Indebted Developing Countries* Eurodad, Brussels, October 1993.

26 All-party Parliamentary Group on Overseas Development *Africa's Multilateral Debt: A Modest Proposal* ODI 1994.

27 World Bank *World Debt Tables 1994-95*, op. cit. p.42.

28 Mistry P *The Multilateral Debt Problems*, op. cit.

29 ibid.

30 Oxfam *Africa: Make or Break* Oxfam 1993, p.17.

31 Oxfam *Multilateral Debt as an Obstacle to Recovery*, op. cit.

32 Mistry P *The Multilateral Debt Problem*, op. cit. According to UNCTAD, 19 SILICs face debt problems with multilateral creditors; see UNCTAD *Trade and Development Report 1993*.

33 This has been acknowledged by the World Bank. See *World Debt Tables 1994-95*, op. cit. p.43; see also Summers L 'The lessons of debt' *Financial Times* 3 August 1992.

34 Berthelot Y 'New approaches to reduce Africa's debt burden' *UNCTAD Bulletin* 20, June 1993, p.11.

35 'Borrowed time' *The Economist* 22 May 1993.

36 NOVIB *Towards Debt Reduction by Multilateral Institutions*, Position Paper, Amsterdam, September 1994.

37 Speech by British Chancellor of the Exchequer Kenneth Clarke to Commonwealth Finance Ministers' Conference, 27 September 1994, Treasury; see also Norman P 'UK relief plan goes for gold' *Financial Times* 26 September 1994.

38 OECD *Development Cooperation Report 1994*, p.56.

39 ibid. p.73.

40 'Britain to cut aid to poorest states' *Financial Times* 15 February 1995.

41 OECD *Development Cooperation Report 1994*, op. cit.

42 *Independent Review of International Aid: The Reality of Aid, '94* ActionAid 1994, p.14.

43 Overseas Development Administration (ODA) *Departmental Report to Parliament*, 1994, CM 2502.

44 UNDP *Human Development Report 1994*, op. cit.

45 OECD *Development Cooperation Report*, op. cit.

46 UNDP *Human Development Report 1994*, op. cit.

47 *Independent Review of International Aid*, op. cit. , p.118.

48 UNICEF *The State of the World's Children 1992*, New York p.35.

49 'The kindness of strangers' *The Economist* 7 May 1994, p.22.

50 For a review of the allocation of aid to social priority areas see Jespersen E *20/20: Mobilising Resources for Children in the 1990s*, UNICEF Staff Working Papers 12, 1994.

51 WHO *The International Drinking Water Supply and Sanitation Decade: End of Decade Review*, Geneva 1992.

52 UNICEF *The State of the World's Children 1992*, op. cit. p.35.

53 'The kindness of strangers' op. cit.

54 OECD *United Kingdom Development Cooperation Review* Series 1 1994, p.7.

55 *Independent Review of International Aid*, op. cit.

56 OECD *United Kingdom*, op. cit. p.24.

57 Jepma C *The Tying of Aid*, Development Centre, OECD, Paris, 1991.

58 'The kindness of strangers' op. cit.

59 National Audit Office *Pergau Hydro-electric Project* HMSO, London, 18 October 1993.

60 'Pergau fears of Trade Minister over-ruled by PM' *Financial Times* 15 April 1994.

61 Black I '"Very bad buy" that cost Hurd a High Court drubbing' *The Guardian* 11 November 1994.

62 ODA *Aid and Trade Provision Review* 1992.

63 See OECD *Development Cooperation 1993* Development Assistance Committee, Paris.

64 OECD *Development Cooperation 1994*, op. cit. p.28.

65 Aid conditionality is discussed in ODI *Political Liberalisation and Economic Reform in Developing Countries* Briefing Paper 1, 1994.

66 ODA *Dhaka Power Project Evaluation 550*, 1993.

67 ODA *Policy Information Marker System*, Statistics Department, ODA, September 1993.

68 World Bank *Poverty Reduction and the World Bank: Progress in Fiscal Year 1993*, Washington, pp.4-8.

69 ibid.

70 Griffin K and McKinley T *A New Framework for Development Cooperation*, background document for the UNDP Human Development Report 1994, UNDP 1994.

71 UNDP *Human Development Report 1994* op. cit. p.70.

72 Bretton Woods Commission *Bretton Woods: Looking to the Future*, Washington July 1994.

73 'Development initiatives', discussion paper for Christian Aid on IDA Replenishment, January 1995.

74 Helleiner G et al *Towards a New Bretton Woods: Challenges for the World Financial and Trading System* Commonwealth Secretariat 1983, pp.44-58.

75 'Fund seeking support for new issues of Special Drawing Rights' *Financial Times* 18 April 1994.

76 Oxfam *A Case for Reform: Fifty Years of the IMF and World Bank* Oxfam Policy Department 1995, pp.26-27.

77 Morse B and Berger T *Sardar Sarovar: Report of the Independent Review* Resources Futures International Inc, Ottawa 1992.

78 World Bank *Resettlement and Development: The Bankwide Review of Projects Involving Involuntary Resettlement 1986-93* Washington1994.

79 World Bank *Nepal Electricity Authority Arun III Hydroelectric Project Environmental Assessment*, Katmandu, 1993.

80 Oxfam, Letter to UK Executive Director of the World Bank, April 1992.

81 World Bank *Staff Appraisal Report, Brazil: Rondonia Natural Resource Management Project*, Washington, February 1992.

82 Oxfam *A Case for Reform*, op. cit.

83 'The World Bank, the environment, and development' *World Bank News*, May 1992.

84 Oxfam *A Case for Reform*, op. cit.

85 World Bank *The Inspection Panel Report on Request for Inspection, Nepal: Arun III Hydroelectric Project and Restructuring of the Arun III Access Road Project*, Washington, December 1994.

86 Duffield M 'Complex emergencies and the crisis of developmentalism', *IDS Bulletin* 25:3, 1994.1994

87 de Waal A *Famine the Kills: Darfur, Sudan 1984-5* Clarendon1989.

88 OECD *Development Cooperation Report*, op. cit.

89 Edwards M and Hulme D 'NGOs and development: performance and accountability in the new world order', a background paper for international workshop, University of Manchester, June 1994.

90 UN *International Documents Review*, 5:22, June 1994.

91 Biggs S and Neeme A 'NGOs negotiating room for manoeuvre: reflections concerning autonomy and accountability within the new policy agenda', background paper, School of Development Studies, East Anglia, June 1994, p.2.

92 Korten D 'Third-generation NGO strategies: a key to people-centred development' *World Development*, Supplementary Volume 15 *Development Alternatives: The Challenge for NGOs*, Pergamon, Oxford, 1987.

93 Hashemi S 'NGOs in Bangladesh: development alternative or alternative rhetoric', mimeo, 1990.

94 Atampugre N *Behind the Lines of Stone: The Social Impact of a Soil and Water Conservation Project in the Sahel*, Oxfam 1993.

95 ACORD *Development and the Environment*, RAPP Occasional Paper, 1991.

96 Ridell R and Robinson M *The Impact of NGO Poverty-alleviation Projects: Results of the Case Study Evaluations*, ODI Working Paper 68, 1993.

97 Chambers R 'All power deceives' *IDS Bulletin* 125:2, 1994, pp.14-26.

98 Edwards M and Hulme D 'NGOs and development' op. cit.

99 Butegwa F 'Promoting women's political participation in Africa', paper written for Oxfam UK/I's Women's Linking Project, International Conference, Thailand February 1994.

100 Melucci 'An end to social movements' *Social Science Information* 23:4-5, pp.819-35, 1984.

Index

Index

Index

Index

Index

The International Oxfam Group

The international Oxfams are autonomous, non-profit development agencies. They work to overcome poverty and social injustice through the empowerment of partner organ-isations and communities to achieve sustainable development and livelihoods, and to strengthen civil society in any part of the world, irrespective of nationality, race, political system, religion, or colour. The members of the group are Oxfam America, Oxfam Belgium, Oxfam Canada, Community Aid Abroad (in Australia), Oxfam New Zealand, Oxfam Hong Kong, NOVIB (in the Netherlands), Oxfam Quebec, and Oxfam United Kingdom and Ireland. The name Oxfam comes from the OXford Committee for FAMine relief, founded in Oxford, England in 1942. The Oxfam International Advocacy Office in Washington opened in January 1995.

Oxfam America
25 West Street
Boston MA 0211 1206
USA
Tel: 1 617 482 1211
Fax: 1 617 728 2594

Oxfam Belgium
39 rue de Conseil
1050 Brussels
Belgium
Tel: 32 2512 1487
Fax: 32 2514 2813

Oxfam Canada
Suite 300
294 Albert Street
Ottawa, Ontario K1P 6E6
Canada
Tel: 1 613 237 5236
Fax: 1 613 237 0524

Community Aid Abroad
156 George Street
Fitzroy
Victoria
Australia
Tel: 61 3 289 9444
Fax: 61 3 419 5318

Oxfam New Zealand
Room 101, La Gonda House
203 Karangahape Road
Auckland, New Zealand
Tel: 64 9 358 1480
Fax: 64 9 358 1481

Oxfam Hong Kong
Ground Floor 3B
June Garden
28 Tung Chau Street
Tai Kok Tsui
Kowloon, Hong Kong
Tel: 852 3 916305
Fax: 852 789 9545

Oxfam International Advocacy
 Office
1511 K Street NW
Suite 1044
Washington DC
2005 USA

Oxfam Quebec
23303 Notre Dame Ouest
Suite 200
Montreal
Quebec H3J IN4
Tel: 1514 937 1614
Fax: 1514 937 9452

NOVIB
Amaliastraat 7
2514 JC The Hague
The Netherlands
Tel: 3170 342 1758
Fax: 3170 361 4461

Oxfam UK/I
274 Banbury Road
Oxford
OX2 7DZ
England
Tel: 01 865 311311
Fax: 01865 312431